Rock N Roar
The Music of Scotland:
2014 And How We Got Here

To Paul

Andy Reilly

Thanks a lot, hope you enjoy!

To Paul

Thanks A Lot J
Hope You Enjoy!

ISBN:9781503043336

DEDICATION

A big thanks to Chris for images and artwork and a big thanks to Craig for the images. After that, I've had a lot of great support and assistance from so many people and I'd hate to single anyone else out for fear of missing out someone important or who has helped. All the support and assistance has been very much appreciated. The book is also for anyone who has put in time, money and/or effort in providing bands and artists the opportunity to play in so many venues.

If I never attended so many gigs, I may have achieved something with my life. Not that I'd have changed anything in this regard.

Rock N Roar

CONTENTS

Contents

1: The Concept 3

2: This Is New 6

3: Take Me Out 106

4: When The Music Starts To Play 123

5: Three Cheers For Our Side 135

6: Everybody Else 194

7: Every Picture Tells A Story 229

8: After The Fight 239

9: Pull The Wires From The Wall.......................................254

10: I Know Where The Summer Goes.................................269

11: Your Town...305

12: Some Andy Talking...313

Appendix A: Alternative Titles 442

FOR MORE INFORMATION AND A FREE EBOOK*

Visit Drone Publishing:
http://www.dronepublishing.com/2014/11/04/free-stuff/
*not this book – a different one

Franz Ferdinand – Glasgow Barrowlands – 2014 – Chris Reilly

Rock N Roar

1: The Concept

It was a year when the stars of track and field came to Glasgow, a year when Europe and America collided on the greens of Gleneagles and the year when Scottish people had the opportunity to shape their future. The Commonwealth Games, The Ryder Cup and the Independence Referendum ensured that 2014 would be a monumental year in the story of Scotland, but the year was about so much more than this.

It was a year when the passion and energy of the nation was rekindled. The Scottish football team regained its roar and people realised that it was okay to care about things again.

It wasn't an easy year, even leaving aside anyone personal opinion on the outcome of the Referendum. The number of food banks in use in the country rose dramatically, becoming more common and necessary than actual banks for many communities. The number of highs and lows meant that there were a number of times when you wanted to celebrate and there were times when you wanted to lay down and let the day pass over you.

Both of these situations meant that there was a call for music. No matter the occasion, be it sorrow or celebration, music has been at the heart of Scottish life, and the huge range of events taking place in 2014 meant that there was a need for a soundtrack.

My initial reason for starting the project was a way to get a handle on the Referendum vote. I've never been a person who has cared about the notion of nationalism or patriotism. The idea that I should like or favour one person over another just because of where they were born in relation to a made-up line has never been something that has held any interest for me. The Braveheart notion was never going to be a factor for me in the build-up to the vote and where would the fun be in basing your decision on a solely economic or political judgment?

Given the time I spent at University (and not all in the Union), I am pleased to say that I did give some economic thought to the process but I also started to think what was it about Scotland that made people feel proud to be Scottish? We can all rhyme off plenty of stereotypes and lazy accusations about people from Scotland and indeed the different areas of Scotland but was there anything in these elements that created something that people could hold on to or grasp for guidance when it came to making a decision that would impact on us for the rest of our lives?

The only element of Scottishness that I could say I legitimately held a strong interest in was the Scottish music scene. Were there elements to the Scottish bands that I particularly loved or was my liking for certain acts a matter of circumstance as opposed to any greater talent on the bands' behalf or musical preference on mine?

Very quickly, the structure of the book moved away from the political starting point into one which aimed to take a look at Scottish bands, Scottish music fans and the Scottish music industry. 2014, a monumental year in the history of the country, would be the starting point and it has to be said that the year has been filled with great Scottish bands and artists making music. However, to get to this point, it's clear that we've travelled a long way, with plenty of success stories and failures along the way.

As a nation, there's long been a desire to be sociable, to have fun and to be part of something. In the present day, being at a gig is very much a social thing, and the makeup of modern day gig-goers is vastly different from the fans that used to pack out venues like the Apollo. There has always been a demand for big gigs and special shows in Scotland but the continual demand for live music, at all levels, is greater now than it has been before.

The nature of the Scottish people has evolved as well. We still love a good time and a chance to get out and about with friends, but little by little, some of the hang-ups and conversational barriers are being broken down. This isn't always a good thing but much like a few decades ago saw a greater sense of freedom to sing in our natural language, recent years have welcomed a stronger wave of Scottish singer songwriters willing to open up about themselves and their viewpoint in life.

Of course, it's not just Scotland that has been evolving, the music industry has changed significantly, with it perhaps being unrecognisable in many ways to the industry that was in its pomp 30 or 40 years ago. New technology has changed the game and altered the rules. Many of the traditional artists are scrambling around desperately trying to stay relevant or in touch with what is going while waves of new acts use modern technology as comfortably as the older guard avoided it as best as they could.

There has also been an evolution in the money making models of the music industry, with artists now finding that their income is made in live shows and in spending time on the road. This is of benefit to the increasing number of people that are crying out for live music as entertainment, but it also provides a platform for acts to take control over their own events and develop their own audience. In 2014, a number of local acts, who you would class as up and coming (at best) were booking shows in 1,000+ venues and they were getting the numbers along to see them.

Social media ensures that bands can develop a fan base without venturing out of their studio, but when they do, they find that they are able to play venues that 10 or 20 years ago, a band of considerably greater stature and style would have struggled to fill.

Due to the nature of Scotland in 2014, there is a need to catalogue the events and create a record of what happened. There will be queues of people lining up to present a look back on the political and sporting elements of the year, and these elements have stories to be told as well. The music of Scotland in 2014 has its own story in its own right, and it is one that can be looked at in isolation, but it will be better understood by examining how we got here in the first place.

2: This Is New

2014 was the year when the people of Scotland were given a voice with respect to the future of the nation, and it was also a year when the spotlight of the world turned on the country for a number of occasions.

With this backdrop, it was always likely that 2014 was going to be a year when Scottish acts came to the fore and made the most of the occasion. This isn't to say the volume of notable acts and performers in the year was down to what else was happening in the country, for some acts it was just time the cycle came around again and for other acts, it was just their time.

Whatever the reason, there were more than enough Scottish acts and musical moments to capture the attention and imagination in 2014 and these were some of musicians, performers and moments that really stood out.

AC/DC

The news about Malcolm Young suffering from dementia cast a large shadow over AC/DC this year but the release of Rock Or Bust, the band's 16th studio album was a welcome way to lift some of the blues that surrounded the sad announcement.

Malcolm left some pretty big shoes for his nephew Stevie Young to fill but did you really expect the group to sound that much different? Malcolm was always the underpinning element of the group, letting the flashier elements take centre stage while he was keeping things under tight control in the background.

The album was trailered by single Play Ball and the title alone strikes you as being a typical 'DC track. Yeah it was used in America to promote their post-season baseball fixtures but a touch of innuendo is never too far away when it comes to the message that AC/DC is looking to get across. Even if you haven't heard the single but are familiar with the output of AC/DC over the years, you can probably have a good guess at creating the song yourself. Either way, it's a decent song and let's be honest, for most acts of their size, stature and pedigree still making albums, it's all about the accompanying tour or tours. There are rumours that Glastonbury has the band lined up for 2015 but surely the addition of the Hydro means that Scotland finally has an indoor arena that can give AC/DC the welcome they deserve. You don't want to always keep saying that "this could be the last tour" but the point is going to come someday, so they may as well bow out in some style!

Altered Sky

The band serves up pretty generic angst-rock for people that don't like to fit in with other music fans, but love being part of a gang of outsiders. This is always a popular genre of music, so there is no doubt that Altered Sky have a devoted fan base but it just feels as though the band has stalled in a year that was meant to be a big one for them.

There's been more talk of them associated with the Nae Danger energy drink as opposed to discussions about their music this year (there's also five notable brand recommendations to be found on the band's site), and ultimately, that's not something that everyone is comfortable with, with respect to bands. Then again, we accept sponsorship and corporate branding in every other walk of life, so why shouldn't an up-and-coming band go down this route?

The nature of how music is made and created is evolving all the time, and it may be that Altered Sky are just ahead of the curve in this regard. It's not as if there is any sign of the branding impacting on the songs the band have in their arsenal, it's just a case of decent synergy between a band and firms who share an audience. Whether that is acceptable to the majority of music fans and the traditional romanticised view of a band overcoming struggle and adversity remains to be seen.

That isn't really the problem with the group, it's more the fact that Altered Sky leave you thinking "is that it" or "shouldn't there be more on offer". The release of an EP in January 2014 should have been the catalyst for a year where the band propelled themselves to a higher level, it's not as though Scotland doesn't have an audience and pedigree for this style of rock music, but it just hasn't happened to a strong enough extent.

If you're really into this style of music, you'll love it, it's certainly catchy and will ensure you punch the air and bang your head at plenty of points but for anyone else, it's going to feel as though there is a bit too much style, and not enough substance, going on here.

The Amazing Snakeheads

And following on from AC/DC, further proof that Glasgow is a rock n roll city. Sure we've a love of country, a penchant for mods and by god, the clubs (or the dancing) are packed full every weekend but running through it all is that sense of old fashioned rock n roll. The desire to have a good time, even if to outsiders it looks like anything but a good time is taking place is fairly common. We're a party city with a lot of chaos going on. Most of us dip in and out, keeping things on the straight and narrow for most of the time, but there are plenty of folk that devote their life to it.

This is the starting point you take from The Amazing Snakeheads and the title of their debut album 'Amphetamine Ballads' leaves you in no doubt of the fast-paced and tension-filled fun that lies ahead. The continual references to vampires makes sense, this is an album made by people who see little of the daylight, coming to life at night and seeking solace in the dark bars and clubs of the city, sucking the life out of whatever comes their way, and at times themselves.

Violence, lost love, love that didn't bother turning up and general guttural shoutings are the order of the day with The Amazing Snakeheads, which is something that most of us can get on board with.

There was that sense of everyone buying into the image and identity of the band but before the summer had even kicked in, two thirds of the band's line-up had been changed, causing a bit of a change in how some people perceive the group. It makes no difference at all to the music but one of the things about a group like The Amazing Snakeheads is that they give you that feeling of being a gang, mates standing against everything the world throws at them.

When that identity changes to one that is more akin to a songwriter with hired hands, a little bit of the appeal gets torn away from the group. As said, it makes no difference to the music but sometimes falling in love with a band is about a lot more than just the sings.

The first time I saw the band, they were supporting Franz Ferdinand at the QMU and the spectre of Uncle John & Whitelock hung heavy over their entire set. This isn't really a bad thing, I quite liked the messy nature of that band but it also meant that they were never going to grab my attention in the way they would do if this was the first wave of seeing a band like this. For kids who are far too young to have been around 10 or so years ago, this band and their rollicking live show will push all the right buttons. This was probably shown by their Broadcast residency at the start of the year. Stumbling in one Saturday evening, the show just seemed too much of a schtick and while I'm fairly sure that the band buys into the performance and energy they give off in every show, it wasn't really working for me...although it was the end of a rather long day. It was working for the crowd down the front though which, not for the first time, led me to think that it was me that was missing something, not other people. I still haven't found it but the debut album is alright and definitely worth a few spins. The fact that they have managed to capture the sound and passion of the live shows on record is definitely a plus point with kudos to the band and the team at Green Door Studios deserving praise for that.

The moments when the brass kicks in are pretty good and sometimes the best moments are when there is a sparse quality to the song, perhaps just a simple bassline strolling along. This is probably because it comes after a period of aural assault, and when knowing that another one is along the way in the near future, a slight bit of respite is more than welcome. Memories is an excellent example of this style of song and truth be told, it's an album that has far more style, pace and moods than you would expect after having read about the group or caught a quick glimpse of them.

It'll be interesting to see what the future holds for The Amazing Snakeheads, if anything but if there is to be nothing else, at least 2014 will have been a bloody exciting year for all of the protagonists.

Bis

You wait 13 years for a proper Bis album and then you find yourself having to sell a kidney to keep up with the rate of releases! To be fair, 2014 marked the 20th anniversary of the groups formation, and while it wasn't a continual run, it was certainly an anniversary that was worth marking.

In May, the group released, Data Panik etcetera, a round-up of tracks from the lost summer of Data Panik and other songs recorded along the way. The attempt to start afresh under the Data Panik moniker was a bold one, with a harder and more new-wave style of sound that boded well for progression, but the group found it wasn't easy to move away from the Bis name. Some fans weren't up for allowing that to happen, and some detractors probably decided that they had already made their mind up about the band. The proper return of Bis was a welcome one and the new album was just the beginning of the celebrations.

Manda Rin's solo album was re-released in the summer but it was the November launch of a 42 track anthology and the December reissues of all three original Bis albums that brought the chance to properly reappraise the group. Even with this reissue, the early work still does little for me but from second album Social Dancing on, Bis were much more enjoyable and likable. There was a sense that the band was becoming more confident in themselves, which makes perfect sense because Bis were bloody young when they were shoved out into the limelight. At an age when the rest of us were drinking cider in the park and postponing thoughts of what we would do with our lives, Bis were bona fide pop stars.

With live shows coming in 2015, hopefully there will be a bit of consistency of appearances and releases from the band in the years to come.

Blood Indians

There's a fair few bloody cowboys in the Scottish music scene but there's only one set of Blood Indians. The group hails from Dundee, benefitting from the more than decent live music scene in the city and if you're a sucker for delightful female vocals over a darker musical backing, this is a band that should be on your list to check out.

The Blood Indians EP was released in the spring of 2104 and it offered a lot of promise. Middle track I Lie was the standout track, propelled by a striding bassline with the vocals coming to the fore from the half-way point before there is a bit of a wig-out near the finish. It packs an awful lot into the four minutes and you won't come away bemoaning the fact that it's just a 3 track EP because there is more than enough on show. It's a well put together three track collection that showcases a number of different styles, giving you a bit of confidence that the band will be able to pull together a strong album and put on live shows.

Broken Records

2014 was a good year for a comeback and Broken Records were another band that returned after four years away. The band had completely fallen off my radar and there was something low key about their comeback at the start of summer, which was a bit harsh on the group. There were spells from 2008 onwards when the band looked as though they were going to reach a strong level and their first two albums were excellent and well received by the media. There is often a lot of talk about the difficult second album but as many bands seem to hit a wall when it comes to working towards their third.

Broken Records, like many up and coming acts, find themselves on a cycle that sees the flow from first album into second album seem unbroken and there was probably a need for the group to take a decent break before coming back for another swing.

Clearly having a few members who can swap instruments provides the platform for a lazy Arcade Fire comparison but with songs like Winterless Son and So Long, So Late from their 2014 album Weights & Pulleys, there was a natural comparison to be made to the times when the

Canadians wrote and played with a bit of fire in their belly. You can also throw in a few comparisons to British Sea Power when they were at the peak of their powers. Basically, if you are looking for music with a touch of an anthemic feel but with none of that pompous arrogance that often comes along with bands that make big tunes that deserve to be played in front of a lot of people, Broken Records remain a very good shout. It was good to see the band back in 2014, it would have been nicer if they made a bit more noise about their comeback.

Campfires In Winter

The boys from Croy (and Cumbernauld) have been a bit quiet in 2014 but they made sure they saw the year out in fine style. With a number of festival appearances across the UK and the We'll Exist single bringing the band to a wider audience, the band made plans to cap the year off nicely with a festive show at Sloans in the build-up to Christmas.

They are far from the only act to have hit upon this style of event this year but while some bands are happy to draw a good year to a close, I think it's more about Campfires In Winter building a bridge from this year to the next, when hopefully their debut album will be with us before the end of the year. It's not as if the album is in the can and waiting to roll, so I may be jumping the gun on this but if their live show is anything to go by, the debut album should be one of the most enjoyable and eardrum threatening records of 2015. For now though, it's been a year of keeping in the public eye and ticking things over for Campfires In Winter.

Carnivores

Hailing from Paisley, three piece Carnivores throw an awful lot of things at you and whether this is deemed to be a good or a bad thing is entirely up to you. It's an attitude that I've noticed in a few of the up and coming Scottish acts that would be classed as rock bands, as opposed to rock n roll, indie rock or any other variant. The band's Let's Get Metaphysical album packs a wide range of styles and influences in, which is great but perhaps it does just spread itself too thinly.

Third track Crooked Teeth is excellent, the sort of poppy-punk song that you would easily put alongside the big hitters of the American market around 10 or so years ago. The thing is, it followed on from two songs that were much heavier and it comes before Apathy In The UK (good title, a true reflection of the modern day while tipping the hat to previous days), which has that short and stabbing riff style with shouty vocals. The song also spends far too much time discussing the actions of Lenny Henry, which is either madness or genius. It's a thin line between those two results and I haven't worked out where I think the band falls on the matter!

For me, the melodies of certain tracks will be enough for me to come back and listen to Carnivores time and time but I'll pick and choose the songs that suit me, and I think this should be the approach for most people. Watching Fireworks is really enjoyable but then the next track on the album, Scottish Football, is far too angry, overbearing and aggressive for my liking (just like the topic of the title!) but there'll be plenty of folk who hold the exact opposite opinion.

The musical feel of Rage Against The Machine (and no doubt plenty of other bands that I haven't paid any attention to) comes to the fore time and time again and there are certainly worse bands to be compared with. When it comes to musical diversity, it can be a hard one to call. If your songs sound the same, you'll get criticism as a one trick pony and being very limited in your output. If you have a catalogue of songs in various styles and sounds, you reduce the likelihood of getting across to people. It's not as if the album comes across as a compilation record, it is still a cohesive unit but for me, I'd have a really enjoyable EP or mini-album from the record. The thing is though, so will plenty of other people with a completely different track listing, so in that regard, the band are likely to make a connection with folk at some point.

Chris Devotion & The Expectations

There hasn't been too many acts mining the sort of sound that of US A&R bands of the 1980s of late, but if you feel as though this is something that you have been missing out on, Chris Devotion & The Expectations may be just what you are looking for. It's pretty much all upbeat and high energy from the group on their debut album Break Out and even the moments where there is a slower pace or a quieter sound, it just feels as though the band is taking a quick breather before launching into another clap along and sing-along moment.

There are tons of backing vocals, plenty of handclap sections and no doubt a few cheap tricks along the way. It's an album that wears its heart on its sleeve and that isn't a bad thing. There are some styles and genres that are being milked too often but in turning back the clock, Chris Devotion & The Expectations are managing to serve up something quite fresh and exciting, purely for the fact that not many other people are doing the same thing. You may think that if other people aren't doing it, should you be, but thankfully the band has ignored that line of thought and set about creating something that they love. Knowing drummer Graham, this is clearly the sort of music that gets the thumb up from the band, so if you want to see a band enjoying what they do as opposed to finding one that takes decisions because it is the right thing for their career, this is a band to check out.

If there is ever a Scottish movie that has a final scene playing out over a pool party or a beach setting, this is the sort of music that should be sound tracking it.

Chvrches

It was a year when Chvrches focused on touring and promoting as opposed to offering a great deal of new material but there was something to enjoy near the end of the year with an absolutely bizarre project put forward by the BBC.

In recent years, one of the best film soundtracks has been the Drive soundtrack, helping to create an atmospheric and edgy mood in the film featuring Carey Mulligan and Ryan Gosling. It's a film soundtrack that can be placed alongside classics such as Midnight Express soundtrack and it will be placed alongside future high quality soundtracks. All of which begs the question why did BBC3 and Zane Lowe rescore the soundtrack? Pointless stuff. As a slight aside, the day that the reworked Drive was first shown on BBC3, Chvrches announced that their debut album had gone Gold in the UK, which was the far more pertinent and celebratory element for the band.

Still, it allowed the band to record and release Get Away. It's an atmospheric track, probably a bit restrained in places, but it's a soundtrack song as opposed to a major single so it is understandable that this will be the case. The band also provided a song Dead Air for the latest Hunger Games soundtrack. That is exactly the sort of fan base you want to get in with, they're the sort of people who will buy everything from folk that they love. Again, the song doesn't offer up any surprises with respect to sound or style and like Get Away, it has a slightly restrained feel that you think makes it the ideal candidate to fit into the story line.

I have absolutely no idea what the Hunger Games malarkey is all about but from reading comments under a video clip, a lot of the fans seemed to suggest that the Chvrches track would be far too upbeat and optimistic for the tone of the film (and presumably, the book). It's far from being the brightest or most optimistic Chvrches song you've ever heard so I'm not convinced the film it is from is going to be the feel good family film of the holidays. Still, they'll no doubt be following the second film dark, third film gloriously upbeat with some wee bears thrown in for marketing purposes approach of Empire Strikes Back into Return of the Jedi.

Another reason to like Chvrches, if you feel as you need a reason other than the music, is the way they actively try to promote ticket sales/purchases between fans through twitter. The hashtag #leaveoutthetout has become synonymous with the band. It's just a small thing, and plenty of artists will retweet messages of fans looking to sell tickets but the simple step of advocating and supporting this sort of behaviour can make a big difference. Lauren, with the TYCI Collective and her writing, has been at the forefront of serious debate and the promotion of women in the music industry but the group deserves great praise for the simple act of working hard to allow fans to buy and sell tickets with other fans.

The band also found time to run their own record label, Goodbye Records, releasing material by artists by Soak and Mansionair. When you add in three shows at T in the Park, three shows at the Barrowlands in 2014 and of course, three members of the band, meaning 3 is the magic number for Chvrches. For a band formed in 2011, the third year for the group was pretty monumental and it remains to be seen whether they can push on for another big year in 2015 or whether they are going to need to take a breather or two before they come back swinging again.

Deathcats

Surfs Up Punks! Deathcats are an immensely likeable band for a number of reasons. They make great videos, their on-stage chat is very funny and they also make pretty frenetic and exciting music. It's always tricky (and slightly lazy) to describe a band by referencing other bands but if you start off with The Ramones, throw in a touch of surf pop (say by The Tyde) and then mix it with a lot of Buckfast, you'll be starting to head in the direction of the Deathcats. Okay, we're probably talking about a concoction that is predominantly Buckie but their 2014 album All Hail Deathcats was as good a call to arms as any you would have heard from a Scottish act in 2014. The Amazing Snakeheads may have had the swagger to go with their rock n roll, but Deathcats had the sunny disposition to go alongside some top tunes that meant you very quickly get on their side when you hear them.

They've also got a song named after everyone's favourite Cockney kid-on hardman Danny Dyer, so if you love EastEnders or ridiculous acting, you have an excellent starting point with Deathcats.

Ella The Bird

Just to be clear from the start, I'm not using some sexist and outdated term to describe a girl called Ella. Ella The Bird is the stage-name, which Siobhan Wilson adopted in 2014, a girl who seemed to have had headlines and columns written about her on an almost weekly basis in the year gone by.

A virtually non-stop run of gigs on her own, as a support act or at the numerous festivals around the country propelled Ella The Bird in front of so many people and while Dear God may have represented scant pickings with respect to recorded output, it was a great tune, more than strong enough to nestle its way into the back of your mind. On first listen, you take away that Siobhan is a talented singer with a good range but after a few listens, the shifting pace of the track starts pushing and pulling you around, taking you on a journey. It's just one song, so can you imagine what her album is going to be like if she continues in this vein of form?

Ella The Bird is the latest (at the time of going to press) in a very long of talented female singer-songwriters and again, put her in front of people and she will make a connection.

Calvin Harris

Two number one singles, a high profile romance ending abruptly and then being dissected in the gossip pages for months and an album packed with some major names from the world of music, Calvin Harris is a proper pop star. Gwen Stefani, Ellie Goulding and Haim were all roped in to work with Harris and let's face it, there's a pretty good chance that every one of these songs will be released as a single during 2015. The boy loves gaining as much exposure from his songs as he can but let's face it, the stats around Calvin Harris don't lie. He puts the work in and if we are to believe the rich lists (we really shouldn't believe anything we read in the media), he's making more in a year than Scotland could hope to rope in from oil.

The November release date of the album is a perfect time for the big end of year Christmas sales but it will also provide him with the platform to tour extensively throughout 2015 and while he would be a stick on for a show or two at the Hydro, you have to wonder if Harris would actually be more suited, and suitable, to the DJ night of the Summer Sessions of Bellahouston Park, if it returns for 2015. You'd also like to think that there is a T in the Park headline slot with his name on it already.

It seems silly to say that the artist who obtained two number one singles in 2014 had a quiet year but you can bet that 2015 is going to be even more eventful for the lad from Dumfries.

Hector Bizerk

One of the biggest issues about Scottish rap and hip-hop acts is that it's been an area which has often been used for comedy and parody, with Johnny Beattie perhaps creating the lowest point for the genre, and maybe even the country, with The Glasgow Rap. This means that any Scottish rap or hip-hop act has to work pretty hard and be extremely good to transcend the sneering or dismissive attitude that will come their way.

The biggest compliment you can give to Hector Bizerk is that they transcend all sort of parody or tomfoolery. This is a proper act with something to say and the stories are excellent, giving you the story of modern Scotland. Just because it is being served up in a different matter from what you may be used to doesn't make it any less valid, in fact, if it provides a platform for people who would otherwise feel stunted in their ability to communicate about their surroundings, it is even more vital. There are a few Scottish acts making waves in this musical genre at the moment, and it's all down to the fact that they are making good music with a social outlook. We've all probably got a different idea of what the best style of rap and hip hop is but for me, it's still about Public Enemy and the Beastie Boys, so the fact that there are people detailing what life in Scotland is like has to be seen as a good thing. Doing this, while maintaining a sense of humour isn't easy but it is definitely something that Hector Bizerk achieves.

It's not just as though the appeal of the band is down to the vocals, as much of the praise praised on the band is down to the music with Audrey Tait well regarded within the Scottish music community for her drumming skills.

The Fish That Never Swam EP, released in September

2014 is a great way to dip your toe into what the band offers. The title track, and last song of the release, is excellent, prowling along with menace and intent, drawing on the stories associated with the Glasgow coat of arms. There is a bit of variety across the four tracks and while second track The Bigger Picture has too much 80s horn (in sound, not a notion of sexiness relating to someone like Sam Fox) for my liking, it's a good wee release and if you are looking to recapture the sound of summer 2014, this is the band that appeared at more festivals than the sense of dread that appears the morning after a shambolic and drunken night before.

Henry and Fleetwood

Given the small(ish) nature of the Scottish music scene, it is perfectly understandable why there is so many collaborations and joint projects between musicians from different bands. Some of these partnerships are obvious, whereas some come seemingly out of nowhere.

This is definitely the case with Henry and Fleetwood but regardless of how it came about, we should be thankful for its emergence. The duo consists of Martin John Henry, from De Rosa, and Gillian Fleetwood, from The State Broadcasters and The Duplets. They are currently working on an album that will hopefully be released in 2015 but they introduced themselves with Forestry, the first song from a forthcoming EP, titled On The Forest Floor. So far, so much in touch with nature and while fans of either of these artists will be keen to have a listen, there is plenty on offer for music fans in general.

The track starts off sparsely, the male vocals carrying the song but before too long, the instrumentation starts to build and if you ever wondered about whether a harp could play a role outside the traditional folk sphere, be prepared to have your conceptions challenged. There is a sense of foreboding that progresses through the building harp runs, blending well with minimal guitar notes. The two artists also trade vocals, crossing and blending together, eventually culminating in a finish that is frantic without ever feeling as though the track runs away from itself.

While you should never take too much from just one track, the quality of the song, and the history of both artists, suggests that there is more to look out for from these two.

Holy Mountain

At the end of the third song of the Holy Mountain set at the Last Big Weekend at Richmond Park, I turned to my brother and said; "That's bad news", to which he replied, "what is?" and I said; "The band. It's Bad News" and we both laughed at the comparison between Holy Mountain and the fictitious rock group which emanated from The Comic Strip troupe. The over the top riffs, the eagerness to get the taps aff and a pulverising approach to music means that this is a band that isn't really about compromise. They do have a better edge to them though that means that they are alright to like. I caught them twice at big shows over the summer and on both occasions, they came across really well. There won't be too many bands who in the space of a month play after Sidney Devine and then play just before Swervedriver but Holy Mountain did and they delivered exactly what you would expect from them on both of these occasions.

2014 saw the band release Ancient Astronauts, their full length debut album, and it more than lived up to the expectations of anyone who had caught the band over the past couple of years. Their label, perhaps not the most unbiased source but definitely a label to trust when it comes to music, called the record the "rock album of the year" back in April and they may have been right. The band has covered War Pigs by Black Sabbath, it is not as if they shy away from their influences, but they've created a cohesive and strong record that represents their live performances. If you think that rock has become a dirty word in recent times, you'll find that Holy Mountain agree with you and they absolutely love that fact!

Honeyblood

It was all looking too easy for Honeyblood. There was a wave of momentum carrying the girls all the way from Glasgow to

SXSW to acclaim and praise from the critics to sold out shows all across the country & Europe. Throw in a debut album that fizzes from start to finish and there was going to be a strong argument for making Honeyblood the Scottish band of 2014.

The debut album is excellent; it's fuzzy, warm, choppy, melodic and at times, biting. When females make music, there is an almost inevitable rush to draw comparisons with other female-focused bands, and of course, all of the notable comparisons have long been made about Honeyblood. That's not to say that these comparisons aren't true, they are spot on at times, but that's not the only thing that is going on.

The latter half of the album has a few moments tucked away that sound like early poppy Blur, around the time they were realising that modern life was rubbish but hadn't quite started hanging around parks. There is that poppy, punky and spiky sound coming across in songs like Fortune Cookie and All Dragged Up but of course, it is the more immediate tracks like Killer Bangs and Super Rat that strike you right in the face. I never really took to Super Rat when it was played live, I thought it came across as quite childish but on the album it's transformed, and is a clear single. The production work on the record is of a high standard and there's a good bit of swearing on the last track, which is always welcome. For the album alone, 2014 was a triumphant year but things never run smoothly, do they?

This is because it all went wrong on the tour supporting the album, with 50% of the group being replaced. Statistically, this was a smaller percentage than the percentage The Amazing Snakeheads had to replace, so numerically it wasn't that bad, but when you're a two-piece, losing one member of the group is going to have an impact.

With Shona leaving the band in the middle of their September tour, it poses questions about what happens next for the group. Barring two cancelled shows, the tour carried on as normal with a replacement drummer called up at short notice. While it's clear that it was Stina who conjured up the songs, there was more than enough chat from Stina and

Shona to suggest that this was a proper band, with Stina explaining that Killer Bangs was written about the need to get Shona back in the band after she took a break relating to her career post-studies. 2015 is going to pose a good few challenges for Stina but no matter what happens, she'll always have 2014 to fall back on.

The latter part of the album tour, and the NME tour, was carried out with Cat Myers on drums. This means that Cat joins a select group of musicians who have been in two bands that I really like (Cat was one of the many drummers who barely kept the drum stool of Saint Judes Infirmary warm) and she joins such lauded names such as Paul McCartney, Peter Hook, Bernard Sumner and Stephen Morris.

The band played King Tuts as part of the NME Tour and there was a notable difference in the sound, Cat's playing style being ferocious throughout the set, adding volume and tempo to the gig. On some songs it worked really well whereas on others it possibly detracted from the melodious and more subtle moments.

Whether it's under the same name or not, Stina is still going to be going strong in the next couple of years, and hopefully Shona will get involved with another band or at least set herself on a career path that keeps her happy. A bit of a shame how that all ended up but they're not the first or last band to fail to keep it all together when it looks as though things were really going places.

RM Hubbert

It's been quite a few years for RM Hubbert and you wouldn't have blamed him for taking a year off after such a run. 2014 hasn't been the busiest year he has experienced in the past few years but he managed to stay in the spotlight for a great part of the year. He kicked off the year in great style, supporting Mogwai at the Royal Concert Hall, and he would later support the group across Europe and the UK in October. He was once again in the running for the SAY Awards and while Young Fathers took the award, Hubby was highly commended for his 2013 record Breaks & Bone. The year also saw the release of a collection of B-sides and rarities from his previous three albums, which was probably as good a way to draw a line under that period of his life.

There was also the small matter of El Hombre Trajeado reforming and playing for the East End Social, so you can hardly write off 2014 as being a quiet year for the performer.

King Creosote

With around 40 or so albums released in one format of another, there are probably few topics that Kenny Anderson, or King Creosote as he is much better known, hasn't tackled but for 2014, he was at the helm of an ambitious project entitled From Scotland With Love.

A documentary film consisting of archive footage was being compiled to coincide with the Commonwealth Games and rather than having a standard narrative, it was decided that there would be a musical narrative, which is where Creosote came in. The footage is brilliant for people of all ages and the music really adds to the footage, strengthening the images and stories that were unfolding onscreen. As a piece of soundtrack material it hit the spot from beginning to end.

It's an album that stands alone as a fine album but when used in conjunction with the film, it's a stirring and moving piece that will no doubt be used for many years to come as an example of Scottish history, and of the great work that was carried out to mark one of the most eventful years in Scottish history.

LAW

If you judge an artist by the company that they keep, it is easy to see why there has been so much talk about LAW in 2014. Working closely with Young Fathers, one of the top Scottish acts of the year was always going to ensure that some of the spotlight fell on Lauren Holt. However, if your are looking to judge an artist, the music should form part of the process and this is an area where LAW has more than enough to speak for herself.

Or sing for herself, because the vocals on the two EPs released in 2014 are what really stands out. In modern times, this is the sort of vocal and music combination that catapulted Beth Gibbons and Portishead to great acclaim but it is clear that the singing influences on LAW go back a lot further. There is a whole lot of old school soul going on here, even when clashing against a backing which at times touches on modern industrial sounds.

One of the best things about the tracks released by LAW so far is that repeated listens bring out something new or something else to admire. On one day you'll state that Lilo is your favourite track, a song that really showcases the diversity and breadth of talent on show here but then on other days, the laid-back swagger of Haters & Gangsters draws you in before taking over. Sometimes when you see a name being written about in a variety of different places you will be a bit wary about the push and promotion but with LAW, you can at least take comfort in the fact that her EPs indicate she has the talent to back up all of the praise that has been offered to of late.

Annie Lennox

Amongst all of the chart success that Annie Lennox has achieved over the years, a great deal of the praise she has received has been due to her work in supporting charities and people who need help the most. Back in 2011, Lennox was awarded an OBE specifically for "tireless charity campaigns and championing of humanitarian causes." You then have to wonder why, if she really cares about humanity and removing pain from people's lives, she released an album of jazz standards in 2014?

Still, if Rod can get away with stealing the American Songbook to give his career a new lease of life, there's probably nothing wrong with Annie venturing off in a different tangent. Given that 2014 is her 60th year on the planet, she's more than earned the right to do what she pleases musically. And of course, no matter how "jazzy" the album is, it's going to be preferable to Dave Stewart doing the same thing isn't it?

Le Thug

When you get near the end of the year and you try to compile your Best Of lists, there are always some tracks or albums that were released early on in the year that get forgotten about. Unless you are the sort of cool kid that compiled everything you listen to on a spreadsheet or database, there's a chance that you could overlook something that you really shouldn't.

For the life of me I couldn't place when Le Thug last had a release out but EP2. Art Software dates back to February of 2014, so it is a great example of such an occurrence. There may only be three tracks on the EP but it's the quality of the three tracks that matter. It'll help to have a love of My Bloody Valentine and some of the washy early 90s sound but there are more than enough electro hooks to keep you moving or at least nodding your head along with the music. The vocals are excellent, chiming perfectly with the music but coming across as another layer of the overall sound as opposed to being something that sits in front of or over the music. It'd be nice to get much more music from the band but at least they seemed to be playing a lot more shows in the Autumn so they may be starting to be more proactive when it comes to playing. Hopefully it won't be too long until we get another EP or maybe even an album.

Loki

Some artists understood the fact that the eyes of the world were going to be on Scotland in 2014 and when it comes to relevancy and exposure, this was the ideal time for them to make their mark. One such artist was Loki, yet another respected name in the Scottish hip hop scene, who compiled a concept album, based upon the idea of a future Scotland after a No vote. If King Creosote made the album of the year for Scotland looking back, Loki made the one looking forward in his worst case scenario.

With a title of G.I.M.P. - Government Issue Music Protest, there's no doubt that this is the work of a man that has something to say and it's a mightily ambitious project, combining thoughts of current day politics with a sci-fi look into the future. It's not a topic that is going to appeal to everyone but again, it could be the medium to get the message through to some people and make them feel as though they have a voice that is speaking on their behalf.

Like myself, Loki grew up in Pollok, and he has mentioned many times the difficulty that the area experienced in previous decades. I was pretty fortunate to have a great upbringing in that part of the city but from school and my mates who I played football with on the streets and any spare grass, I knew that wasn't the case for everyone. Loki himself is the first to admit that he has fought his own demons over the years but with his music, and a series of programmes he created for the BBC where he attempted to examine anti-social behaviour and social deprivation, he is a talented individual with a desire to shine a light and offer support to those who maybe don't receive the help they need from the rest of society.

Whatever you think of the independence Referendum and whether you got the outcome you wanted or not, one of the most important things about the year is that there does seem to have been an awakening in many parts of Scotland that there is a need to do for more others. Some will say that it is the Socialist streak that runs through the nations, while other will wish to avoid that idealism and merely put it down to the fact that it is in our nature to look out for others when they need it most. Either way, it's an album that plenty of folk will love for its music and its ambition but you can bet that there will be many people wishing Loki all the best for the way he has worked hard on behalf of others.

Model Aeroplanes

Model Aeroplanes released two singles in 2014 that were so smiley and poppy that you can feel your teeth starting to rot due to the upbeat nature of it all. Innocent Love and Electricity both clock in around the jukebox friendly two and a half minute mark, and both of the songs were light, breezy and melodic. It's absolutely no surprise that with some peppy tunes and youth on their side that the band developed quite a following in a short space of time.

The band found themselves on the bill at the BBC Radio 1 Big Weekend Gig in Glasgow and they have the sort of sound that could easily lend itself to the mainstream airplay that the channel needs to pursue. The band certainly have a different sheen to their music and image that some of the other 2014 vintage of Dundee bands displayed and while they don't quite have the same instant in your face commercial nature of The View, you wouldn't be surprised if they followed along that path.

Aidan Moffat

2014 was quite the year for Aidan, from the Tom Weir photoshoot promoting his Where You Are Meant To Be tour where he delivered ceilidh fun while exploring the Scottish language to the "you never seen it coming" release of Vagrants_09_14. Heck, he also managed to release a kids book, The Lavender Blue Dress, and yes, it's a proper kids book, not an ironic one or one of these kids books that are really for adults. There are plenty of strings to Aidan's bow, which is just as well because you really wouldn't think that the foul mouthed singer of Morning Song, the opening track of Vagrants, should be allowed anywhere near kids.

The World Around Us, the second song on the album, harks back to the Arab Strap days, kicking off with a standard run down of a day in the life of Aidan before it jets off into a discussion on the beauty of the world around us. It's a well delivered take on how to get more from life, and how some people don't, and it's got a blinding chorus. This track stands up very well amongst the best music of Aidan's career but it's a really good album with 7 original tracks and 3 covers. With the songs coming from a few sources and across a number of years, it could have been a ragtag collection but it sits together rather well. Also, if you pondered how Aidan would sound covering Cher you have the chance here and thankfully there is no need for autotune! Aidan still serves up some excellent YouTube playlists late at night on Twitter so if you're up late and in the mood for some music to push you through the morning, make sure you follow Aiden. The big man loves Taylor Swift and by 5am, you will too.

Mogwai

Was 2014 the year that Mogwai finally went over the top? 2013 was a pretty big year with respect to exposure for the group, with their soundtrack to the TV show, Les Revenants, putting them into millions of homes and the ears of many new listeners. An outdoor gig with their Zidane film soundtrack was another highlight for the group but they really stepped it up this year.

Kickstarting the year with a Celtic Connections performance at the Royal Concert Hall and their 8th album Rave Tapes ensured that there has been Mogwai from the word go in 2014. The band may have settled on a style for their albums but they make this sort of music better than the vast majority of people around the world today. It gave the band a Top 10 hit and ensured that their shows around the world in 2014 would feature a few new favourites around the classics that the group have cultivated over their close to twenty years existence. The band also marked the 15th anniversary of their second release, Come On Die Young (CODY), with a 4 LP or 2CD issue featuring demos, rarities, hard to find tracks and live versions.

You would think that this would have been more than enough to keep fans excited but in an attempt to make sure that the year is forever associated with the group, the band bookended 2014 with the release of their Music Industry 3. Fitness Industry 1. EP in December. The lead track Teenage Exorcists was an excellent song, hinting at an appreciation of New Order, while perhaps being closer to what people would consider to be a conventional song than they have managed to create in many years. It's an excellent song and even though it looked as though Remurdered would easily be my Mogwai shout for track of the year, this late contender may just have sneaked in at the death.

With Edinburgh and Aberdeen shows joining Richmond Park in Glasgow as chances to have seen the band in Scotland, the group were also notable in their backing of the Yes vote in the Scottish referendum. The group wasn't to get the outcome that they desired but it certainly wasn't through the lack of effort or trying. With 2015 seeing the band celebrate 20 years in the business, there will hopefully be a lot more focus placed on the group, giving them the reward that their efforts and music deserve.

Paolo Nutini

If you are going to leave your audience waiting for five years, you better come back with something strong and hope that your audience hasn't found anyone new to love. Perhaps Paolo got a bit lucky in that he wasn't really usurped by any new pretender to his throne but it seems as though his new album hit the spot for the fans that had been waiting patiently for new music from the Paisley kid.

He's not an artist I have a lot of interest in, he's been involved with too much cod-reggae for my liking and any act that slips in the word "funk" while implying they are swearing is always going to raise my suspicions a bit but there isn't really anything to get upset about with what Paolo does. He has seen a rush of people who would normally sneer at this style of music or artist giving him their backing and it's certainly been the inspiration of a number of conversations which have started along the lines of "So the wife bought the album..." or "The girlfriend has been playing this quite a bit and it's actually quite..." With that in mind, Caustic Love is well on course to be one of the biggest selling UK albums of the year and it debuted at number one on release, being the fastest selling of the year at that point. It was very quickly classed as a Platinum album and with a big UK tour in October and the inevitable Christmas promotional push, there is no doubt that the album would have found its way into many more homes towards the end of the year. This pattern will no doubt continue in 2015 and if Paolo and his management have any sense (which of course they will), they should look to milk the 2015 festival circuit as hard as they can!

Two sold out shows at The Hydro hardly puts him into Still Game territory but that's around 28,000 ticket sales for an artist that had been absent for five years, so you have to say that there is still a great deal of love for Paolo, which is fair enough. The fact that Nutini postponed both of these gigs from their initial October dates, due to tonsillitis, was a blow to many fans, especially with the late nature of the call-off for the first of the two gigs. In one sense though, moving gigs that were initially set for a Monday and Tuesday night to a Friday and Saturday (albeit in January) may allow more of his fans to have a more enjoyable night at the Hydro. While a lot of people would have been annoyed or inconvenienced by the gig cancellations, it at least gives his fans with tickets something to look forward to in early January.

His pro-cannabis comments this year may have sparked some controversy but on the whole, he's an inoffensive artist with a great voice and songs that people love, so what's not to like? Iron Sky has been one of his most talked about songs of the year, and it's a great showcase for his singing style and it's alright, but I've been seen the track described as a psych rock style of song. Anyone who thinks that this is psych rock really needs to grab a hold of The 13th Floor Elevators or The Seeds and then we can talk, but on its own merits, it's alright and so is Paolo. I suppose I'll talk about acts like Mogwai or Young Fathers as being the Scottish musicians that made the biggest impact on the year but when it comes to shifting units and bums on seats, 2014 had Nutini stamped all over it.

Over The Wall

And while there were plenty of new bands demanding attention in 2014, there were some bands quietly sneaking out. At least Over The Wall managed to put on a couple of farewell shows to bring the group to some form of proper conclusion. One of the band's songs was featured on Skins but with respect to impact, their song Thurso would have been loved and sung, hummed and whistled by thousands of Scots in the past few years. As the theme tune to Burnistoun, it was the perfect setting for one of the most enjoyable Scottish comedy shows of the past.....well, of all time to be honest, there's been a fair few bad comedy shows from this fair nation! The problem was that most people probably never bothered about who was behind the theme or even pondered the fact that if it was a band or an artist responsible for it.

The Treacherous album stands as the groups only long player but they can take some comfort in the fact that their music reached a level of awareness that many bands can only dream of, even if fewer people knew their name!

Owl John

This is exactly what you want from a solo album. The sound of the Owl John record, from Scott Hutchinson from Frightened Rabbit, will be welcoming enough for fans of the group, but different ensure that it will draw new people and unsure folk in. I quite like the folky sound of Frightened Rabbit without saying they were anywhere near my favourite Scottish act. This album adds something a bit different to the shape and sound, and is probably all the more refreshing for it. With a Frightened Rabbits record, this diverse style of sounds would probably have been criticised a lot more vocally, especially with the band now being on a major label and having notable commercial success.

It was a bit ironic that after having finally opened up the songwriting efforts of the group to be a more collaborative affair that Hutchinson immediately returned to writing by himself for this project. It's an interesting stop-gap and it will be really interesting to see if the sound of this record travels with Hutchison as he makes his way back to the band. It'll also be interesting to see how long fans have to wait before the next Frightened Rabbits is released.

Paws

Maybe Fatcat Records really like teacakes and Irn Bru (which would go some way to explaining the label name), but they have never been slow in recognising good Scottish talent. A look at their roster indicates that they have backed The Twilight Sad, Frightened Rabbit, We Were Promised Jackpots, Honeyblood and of course, Paws.

The group released their second album in Youth

Culture Forever and its good enough to sweep you away. You could argue that the production isn't at its best but this works in its favour, giving it a greater sense of urgency and a fuzzier background for the big melodies and hooks to soar above. It's a messy (in a good sense, not sloppy) record that will have you punching the air at various points, which is exactly what you want from a summer record.

The band were also responsible for one of the busiest and most hectic Scottish shows of the year when they and their US pals We Are Scientists hot footed it from T in the Park to head to Bloc in Glasgow. Fair play, the burgers in there are of a far higher standard than what you will find in Balado, and after a feed, the two acts decided that they may as well play in the venue too!

They've spent a hell of a lot of time in America this year, and it's good to see an act taking the time to put in the grinding hours that you need to do to even make a dent on the other side of the Atlantic. Sometimes you get lucky and everything falls into place but on most occasions, American success is about playing in dives, shaking hands and wondering if it was all worthwhile. It's good to see a Scottish act sticking at it and not just chucking it when home becomes a distant memory.

The Phantom Band

It's not as if I ever moved away from The Phantom Band but for whatever reason, I never really took to the second album, certainly not as much as I did Checkmate Savage. The band's debut album remains an excellent album and perhaps it just raised the bar a bit too high for me. I'm glad to say that third album, Strange Friend, found The Phantom Band back on track for me although I think a few people are saying that they much prefer the second album to this one. You can't please all the people all the time...

The band played a set in the Art School at the start of June and given that I had just returned from Primavera, I wasn't really up for a gig but if I was going to go one, I wanted it to be a proper show with volume and bludgeoning power. I got exactly what I wanted so I was alright Jack but I can see why there were complaints from the people I was with about a lack of subtlety and a drop in the nuances that they normally expect from the group. It worked for me, and a couple of months later, outside in the pouring rain in Glasgow Green, the band provided another strong set that did the job for me again.

Songs like The Wind That Cried The World, Doom Patrol, Sweatbox and Women of Ghent stand up with anything the band has served up yet, which isn't bad going for a third album. Perhaps they were invigorated by the time apart, and maybe Rick's solo success provided a catalyst for the band to push on, but I think the third album showcased an energy and vitality that had been missing from The Phantom Band for a while. Hopefully the band can push on from here and settle into a pattern where they release a series of solid albums, solidifying their presence in the Scottish music scene, moving them from cult artists to established favourites.

Prides

Pop music innit? The media may have jumped on the inclusion of Prides at the closing ceremony of the Commonwealth Games as though it was some monumental triumph for the hard-working indie community of Glasgow, but it was a triumph for Island Records, part of Universal Music Group, who just happen to be the largest music corporation in the modern. Not that you should hold a label against a band, there's been more than enough brilliant releases on Island and Universal to shut up even the harshest of music critics but it was hardly a rags to riches of an unknown band plucked from obscurity against all odds.

When it comes to songs like I Should Know You Better, if you hadn't heard it before and someone told you it was a One Direction song, you wouldn't blink an eye or have a reason to disbelieve what you had been told. That's fine, there's clearly a big market for that sort of stuff and the Prides lads should be positioning themselves for it, but it's not going to be for me and I wouldn't thank you for coming across it at a gig. This point was made when I found Prides sandwiched in between Kasule and Public Service Broadcasting at Freshers Week at Strathclyde University in September 2014. The opening act were excellent, combining a post-rock sound with homages to Coatbridge's finest and the headline acts blend of banjos and public service information clips made for an excellent night. The middle band provided the chance to grab a pint and get in touch with the old alma mater...which sadly never turned out to be as much fun as it looked when Rodney Dangerfield did it in the 80s comedy classic Back To School. "Hey, you're alright..."

Remember Remember

Given everything that was taking place in Glasgow in the middle of summer, releasing an album in the heart of it all may not have been the brightest idea if you were looking to get the strongest level of exposure for the release. Then again, given that Remember Remember were one of the bands who would play at the Kelvingrove Bandstand for free during the course of the Commonwealth Games, perhaps it was the perfect time to capitalise on the heightened level of attention that the band would receive for this.

Whatever you think of the marketing plan behind the album, there's no getting away from the fact that Forgetting the Past, the band's third album, more than speaks for itself. I'd be the first to admit the elongated intro to opening track Blabbermouth doesn't really grab my attention but beyond this, it's an excellent album from a band that has evolved considerably in the past few years. Okay, the fact that the band was initially just Graeme Ronald means that the addition of other musicians would be an evolution of sorts but this is a bigger, brighter and stronger album on offer here. It certainly wasn't the sort of album I thought would come from the act that provided the support slot to one of The Royal We's (another should have been bigger Glasgow act featuring Graeme) at Stereo many years ago. Tracks like La Mayo have plenty of heart alongside their sparse electronic and multi-instrumental soul while Why You Got A Blue Face? builds into a monster that deserves to be played at full volume on a very regular basis.

There may only be 8 songs on the release but with only one track clocking in at less than 4 minutes and three songs lasting more than 8 minutes, there is the chance for the tracks to expand and explore. This may be one of the albums that slips down the cracks, understandable given the high volume and quality of music this year, but it really is worth checking out.

Simple Minds

When a band has a singer who grabs so much of the attention and focus, it is inevitable that you will be drawn to their input on a new album. Big Music was Simple Minds 16th album of a lengthy career and frontman Jim Kerr was the aspect that really stood out on the album for the first few listens. It has to be said though, not for the right reasons.

The vocals are hideous. Not because they are bad vocals, but they are just completely devoid of life or emotion. They instantly bring to mind the jaded and listless mutterings of Mark Knopfler from Dire Straits or Dave Gilmour from Pink Floyd when both of these bands were at their dullest. Simple Minds may have claimed to have gone back to their roots and revisited the music that they wrote before they made their way to the stadiums but the feel and excitement of the songs fell way short of their early days.

The thing is, you can look at notes, chords and lyrics on a page and do your best to recapture it, but music isn't just about the structure, style or tablature. No offence to Jim but the life he currently leads in Sicily isn't going to fire him up in the same manner that his early life in Tollcross would. Quite simply, the Villa Angela hotel he runs isn't the Bellgrove Hotel in the East End of Glasgow, and there's no passion or drive to be found in his vocals. Say what you want about the new U2 album (and who hasn't?) but Paul Hewson still manages to instil a bit of passion and energy into his delivery, something Jim fails at.

Musically there are some nice touches and flourishes, with Simple Minds clearly taking a lead from some of the bands they have inspired over the years. The synths and electro-fills are decent enough but being honest, they are being done better by many other bands these days. A neat link to the present day can be found in lead single Honest Town was co-written with Iain Cook from Chvrches and there is supposedly more material to come from this collaboration. Another indicator that modern bands have tapped into early Simple Minds can be found on the intro to Sweatbox on the latest Phantom Band album as this bears more than a passing resemblance to the Minds classic I Travel.

Much like U2, Simple Minds will find that this is a record that pleases their hardcore fans, and there have already been a few "best since the early 80s" comments in reviews. They'll make a few sales in various formats and they'll set up a big tour or two but it's an album that is only relevant to a well-defined audience. The idea that the album represents a return to form will only indicate how far the band has slumped in recent times. However, Simple Minds have shown that they are willing to return to their roots and embrace the music they made before they hit the money trail and if the shows in support of the album are truly representative of their back catalogue, there will be likely be some great nights in store for long term fans of the band.

Skinny Dipper

The duo has been back in trend in music of late, and while the raw sound created by two musicians bucking against each other can be quite thrilling, there is always a lot to be said for going larger and lusher. Skinny Dipper isn't an act that lets everyone in the room clatter on just because they're there; there is order and structure in this 8 piece with debut EP Masks showcasing a measured yet pleasingly melancholic sound. There are plenty of times when the vocals and strings soar, but I wouldn't go so far as to say it's an uplifting record. It's a strange one, it's neither upbeat nor downbeat but there's an honesty that tugs away at you and it's quite an emotional set of songs on the EP. They also come across well in the live arena, with the 8 members somehow squeezing themselves on to the stage in the Bowlers Bar during a showcase for their record label Olive Grove.

Slam

If there is one thing the more mature clubber will tell you, it sometimes takes a bit longer to get started. Once you are up and running, it is like turning back the clock and there is no stopping you, but you certainly can't fire onto the dancefloor at the start of the night in the way that you used so many years ago.

In many ways, this is replicated in the new Slam album, Reverse Proceed. The album starts well, there is a strong ambient vibe and it is all well created but it takes around 20 minutes for it to spark to life. Up to this point, you know its Slam, there are enough reminders and focal points to keep you on track with that but it certainly isn't the Slam that we all know and love. Then again, if you are a firm believer that the build and the anticipation is as much of the fun as the release itself, the first quarter of the album will appeal to you.

In fact, it's not really until the 25th minute mark (the album flowing seamlessly from start to end) and the beginning of Ghosts of Detroit that you really feel the album is shaking to life in a sustained manner.

The second last track on the album, Rotary is excellent and like most of the latter half of the album, it's a song that you want to hear in a club, as opposed to on the stereo at home. This can make it difficult to properly judge the merits of an album like this because while you instantly know how good it is, it won't be until it is being pumped out of a proper soundystem and you are in the right frame of mind that it'll really come to the fore.

Then again, if you are aware of Slam and you know what they are capable of producing when they DJ, you will know exactly the spirit and emotions these songs are going to inspire when played in the proper environment.

The Slam lads are still as busy as ever and Reverse Proceed indicates that they still have the touch for making records alongside their live performances.

So Many Animal Calls

Another great example of the good work being carried out by the Bloc+ label, So Many Animal Calls released the Burden EP in 2014 while also getting their hands dirty around the country. The band have been ploughing away for a couple of years now but they still manage to sound quite fresh and youthfully optimistic. That's always good for a band, the moment you start to lose that sense of wonder you find that things that start to slip away from. Lead track from Burden, From The Sick Bed, despite its title is a romp musically, racing away to big finish, and displaying plenty of sparkle and enough drum rolls to ensure your mind doesn't start to wander off before the track comes to a conclusion.

The rest of the EP may fall into the trap of all being a bit similar, but that's perfectly acceptable for an EP. You'd start to lose interest with an album of that ilk but on Burden, So Many Animal Calls do enough to draw attention to themselves and get out before they start to bore you.

The Son(s)

By and large on first listen The Things I Love Are Not At Home by The Son(s) is a relaxed and laid-back folky piece that glides by effortlessly. It doesn't have too much that stands up and begs to be noticed but if you are looking for a pleasant album that will potter away pleasantly in the background without being too distracting, it comes across as being what you need.

There is one moment that stands out though, and maybe not for the best. Halfway through The Numbers Have You Wrong, the song suddenly flips into a late 70s style Fleetwood Mac blissed out meander. It's quite a worry and quite a massive twist compared to what had gone before this point. Crikey, it's not so far away from something that you could imagine Clapton doodling while being out of his nut on ching and whatever else he was pumping into his bloodstream at that point in his career. For some, that'll be a compliment but for some of us, it's a moment that has the potential to turn your bones to glass.

After that, the album returns to type and the last song

even manages to sound like something Gruff Rhys would serve up in his more melancholic moments. And more importantly than that, it's the key that unlocks the album. Listening to the record again with that last song in your mind, you get a better sense of what the album is trying to achieve or where it fits in. It's a record that needs a bit of familiarity to make sense of and enjoy but it is an album that once you get it, you'll return to it a good few times.

Stanley Odd

Although Son I Voted Yes ensured that Stanley Odd would receive a considerable amount of attention in the build-up to the Independence Referendum, it was by no means an opportunistic track hoping to cash in on the focus of the nation. In the first half of the year the group released the Chase Yirsel EP which was also packed with plenty of political references and concerns about the state of the nation and the UK.

The most notable thing about the emerging rap and hip hop scene in Scotland was the fact that these bands and artists had a lot to say about the world around them. As we were all reminded by Dan Le Sac and Scroobius Pip, "guns, bitches and bling were never part of the four elements and never will be", and our acts reflect this. If you are into the bands for the music, you'll have plenty to enjoy but if you want to hear something relevant, you'll be equally delighted to take some time to delve into the lyrics of the group.

I'm certainly not going to sit and pontificate whether this is the true voice of the kids of Scotland (we'll leave that to the Guardian or a Newsnight Review special) but there is definitely something happening with this genre in Scotland that hasn't really been there before, and it's definitely something that deserves attention and praise. The band also released A Thing Brand New, their third full-length album. Of course, while it seems as though there is a new wave of acts of this style coming through, Stanley Odd have been around since 2010 – sometimes it just takes some of us a little bit longer to catch up with what is taking place. The band has probably played in some places they may never have thought they would this year (the Usher Hall for one but the group also played at a festival in Malawi), but if they continue in this vein, 2015 could be even bigger for them.

Suspire

Some bands have to work harder to grab your attention. The fact that Suspire seem so proud of wearing the "synth-pop" badge on their sleeve makes them for the watching. Any band that seems so in thrall to the 80s needs to work that bit harder to prove that they are relevant in the modern era, and not just some throwback or nostalgia act. That's clearly a bit harsh, there are some guitar bands that are the laziest revivalists you would ever be able to find and in the right hands, the synth can be as exciting and as refreshing as any instrument. Maybe it's the pop element, synth music is fine, pop music is fine but for some reason, stick the two of them together and you have something that is considerably smaller than the sum of its individual parts.

Single On A Clear Day still has that slightly oh so clever feel that rings of the 80s but it also has a niggling groove that turns out to be quite infectious. Album track Yes (an admittedly loaded title for a song released in September 2014) is a stomper and the things that you think may actually weigh the band down actually conspire to lift the band to a higher level. There really isn't too many acts making this sort of music at the moment, and because the music feels unique and is of a decent standard, Suspire are worth checking out. It's not as though you want to labour the point about them having a slightly retro feel but this is something that is likely to bring more people to the band than a review that tries to be as clever or as arty as possible. If you go by the fact that bands make music for people, it's important to point the right people in the right direction, and anyone that loves 80s sounding upbeat pop will find plenty to like about Suspire.

The Twilight Sad

Even before the release of Nobody Wants To Here & Nobody Wants To Leave, 2014 was a pretty monumental year in the life of The Twilight Sad. The reissue of the group's debut record and related tour was a good marker for the band and a strong reminder of why so many people fell in love with them in the first place. Add in a few notable festival performances and the band would have experienced a year that most Scottish acts would have loved to have achieved.

Of course, the release of the group's fourth album at the end of October took the year to a whole new level for all associated with group.

I know that the image around The Twilight Sad is one of an intense band that makes miserable music, but this clearly isn't all that the band has to offer. The title track is an example of the fact that the band is often up to more than one thing at a time. There is a melancholic feel to the track but the layers of sound give it a busy nature, creating a sense of urgency. If the track is offering sadness, it isn't just lying down and letting the sadness engulf and envelope itself, it's on its feet, looking to move forward and make sense of things. The second half of the song is much more uplifting, the tempo continuing to drive on, and this isn't the only song on that album that has this feel.

It may be simple to dwell on the more downbeat nature of some of the songs or parts, and the band probably point as many people in this direction as the critics, but there is optimism and hope on the record. Yes, it's the hope that is probably the worst bit of life but sometimes music plays a part in the improvement or rehabilitation in life as opposed to being there for the celebratory moments.

Some of the best moments come when James vocals dip down, sitting more in the mix, as opposed to being the focal point. Drown So I Can Watch is a perfect example of this, the singers vocal's bringing a sense of hope and restrained positivity when they are lower in the mix and the track almost seems jaunty and upbeat considering some of the tracks around it.

The critics have been vocal in their support for the new record as the reviews for the album has been universally positive with a number of 10/10s from reputable outlets. It's a certainty to rank highly in the end of year polls and if the band doesn't win over more fans with this record, you have to wonder if they ever will.

To their credit, The Twilight Sad are not a band who have ever looked to chase fame, money or main stage adulation, but it would be nice for them if they made more money and were liked by more people than what they are now. The band just fell short in reaching the Top 40 albums (reaching number 51 after first week sales), but the fact that there was even talk of the group reaching the Top 40 was a triumph alone. You also get the feeling that the album will continue to make steady sales for a good while.

With the group already announced as being on the bill for SXSW 2015 and plenty of shows, tours and festival appearances lined up, next year may be the chance to get the audience that they, and many other, believe that they deserve.

We Were Promised Jetpacks

With 2013 being the 10th anniversary of the band forming and 2014 seeing the group release their third album, Unravelling, things have been surprisingly a bit downbeat in the WWPJ camp of late. Given the passing of time and the fact that one of the band members, Michael Palmer's, has been dealing with Hodgkin's Lymphoma, this actually shouldn't be surprising but a lot of the band's interviews and social media comments have made reference to make or breaks and wondering what comes next. The title of the album is hardly going to give people confidence about their mental state either, and after a couple of listens, the record seems flat.

The album was only released in October of 2014, so it's not as if there has been a lot of opportunity to get to know the songs too well or even hear them played in the live arena, but the music has, in places, brought the feeling if ennui that the band has spoken about to life. It's not the full album; I Keep It Composed is an excellent song, bristling with a menace and energy that sparks the album to life after a slow start. There are songs like Night Terror, which at times moves like trying to walk through porridge but which still manages to offer some neat guitar lines and a loping bass line which helps to perk up your interest. Moral Compass also has verses which bring to mind Arab Strap, which is fantastic because if anyone is using Arab Strap as their moral compass, they could be in for a questionable life!

It's quite an involved album that can drag you into it, which may not be a bad thing if you have the time to give it repeated listens. Hanging out with lads from school ten years after you are no longer legally obliged to can be quite a draining process but there will hopefully be a bit more life (and vitality) left in We Were Promised Jetpacks.

Wozniak

Wozniak are just one of the many acts that have taken to Kickstarter and they managed to raise more than enough funds to create their Pikes Peak EP in June of 2014. They may have only been only looking for £1,000 (only!) which clearly pales when compared with the ridiculous sums of money known artists like Neil Young can conjure up on Kickstarter for their whims of fancy, but in many ways, a relatively unknown act raising a grand is a much bigger accomplishment. With 62 backers, the band managed to raise £1,117 and if any other act is looking for guidelines on how to get the best return for their project, it seems as though the offer of a limited edition T-shirt alongside a copy of the EP was the biggest success with respect to parting people from their cash.

Generating funding in this way is a great way for bands to record and release music, but it has to up the ante when it comes to a release as well. You'd have to hope that the group had their music in place before looking to record it but even with that in mind, there is an almost untold number of elements and issues that can befall a band in a studio. The fact that Wozniak managed to exit the studio with their Pikes Peak EP and being relatively unscathed for the process is a big win for the group and for the nature of this funding.

The songs are pretty decent as well, which is clearly half the battle, if not more. Paper Hat and Kreuzberg, found in the middle of their EP, could run and run for much longer than they already do without you feeling that they were overstaying their welcome. Maybe it's the shit weather and our lack of interest in talking about a lot of stuff but as a nation, we have this whole post-rock and feedback malarkey down to a fine art in some places. Wozniak have definitely played a role in creating this situation and outcome. For following through with their Kickstarter project and having a really good release to show for it at the end the band should be commended, but even if the release was created in a more conventional manner, it would still be well worth seeking out.

The Vaselines

Just the mere 25 years from the release of their debut album, The Vaselines got around to releasing their 3rd album with V For Vaselines. That is clearly a bit lazy but when you think that they split up at the release of their debut record, they've done quite well to make it beyond the first record and a return of two albums in four years is certainly a lot more palatable than 3 in 25.

The cover artwork for the release may be slightly off-putting. The Raveonettes struggled to pull this look off around half a decade ago and to be fair; they were a lot younger and not Scottish. You shouldn't judge an album by its cover, or even by the naff level of chat that the duo manages to contrive together on stage. It's a light-hearted poppy romp through the ages, touching on a number of styles and movements. It's not going to be an album that anyone bar devoted fans will hold to their hearts for too long but it certainly isn't an album that anyone can find anything to dislike about. And as the lyrics on Crazy Lady say "so what if it has all been said before", it's an enjoyable record that could maybe do with a bit more oomph at times but there are more than enough fun moments to make it worth a listen to.

The Vigo Thieves

Believe sounds like that utterly tragic Kings of Leon song about drinking the water and family. They rightly got panned for that nonsense and just because The Vigo Thieves are an up and coming Scottish band doesn't mean that they should be exempt from criticism. The song sounds as though it's been written solely for Sky and the ad breaks around football matches. If that is indeed the case, fair play to the band, because writing a song to order isn't an easy to thing to do and if this is the case, they have absolutely nailed it.

In one sense, it's good that new bands don't feel as though they have to be tied to the indie bandwagon, making scratchy records and ensuring everyone knows how real they are about their art. There is nothing wrong with aiming for the stars and looking to be as popular as possible. It's just that it can come across as being a bit soulless and far too polished. With Believe being tied into the national team's qualification campaign for Euro 2016, there was obviously a need to write something big that can be enjoyed the masses in the stands and pubs. However, not since the mid-60s, when The Kop was known to batter out the early hits of The Beatles and the best version of Anyone Who Had A Heart or the late 70s when Sailing was a popular anthem on the terraces, has this been something worth celebrating.

It's not just Believe, This Love and Heartbeats are also both highly polished songs that are firmly aiming for the middle of the road. With sold out King Tuts and Arches show, and their own show at the ABC at the end of the year looking like being a big hit, there is clearly an audience for The Vigo Thieves, and there is a market in between boy bands and indie bands. So far, it all just sounds a bit samey from the group and while the building blocks for a long and prosperous career are there, they haven't yet released anything that makes me want to them give a proper go. Mind you, I've probably still got a mental block with the SFA tie-up because let's be honest, if there is one group of people with a horrendous taste in music, it is the Tartan Army!

Vukovi

The group probably feel as though they've wasted enough time so it's no surprise that their live shows and September 2014 single So Long Gone don't waste any time in getting up to speed and getting you on your feet. Vukovi seem an all-energy act, barely pausing at time to catch breath or letting that bass strings stop reverberating.

They're the sort of rock band that carries such a pulsating rhythm that they pack the dance floor. Thankfully not in some horrific rock/dance crossover (surely we've seen the end of that sort of nonsense) but in a continually moving, almost paranoid fear of not being able to stop. With that in mind, and the fact that they have been stop-starty, for various reasons, Vukovi look to be another band that has their eyes on a busy 2015. So Long Gone and a couple of live shows near the end of the year was a good way of easing themselves back into action, and reintroducing themselves to the music scene but the band will know that next year is when they really need to step it up.

The Xcerts

It's a simple formula, pop music with big hooks. The band's third album, There Is Only You, was released in November 2014 and it's sometimes hard to know where the band fits in.

They're too chirpy and knowingly commercial to appeal to the indie kids while the guitars and accent may move them out of reach of the more traditional pop music buyers.

When you think that the band formed at school, it is easy to see why they started off with a poppy outlook, but they haven't lost this, or moved away from it, in the past 13 years! Yeah, the band has been going for as long as the time that the core members weren't in a band. Just getting beyond your mid 20s and knowing that you have spent half of your life in one band must be quite a feeling. Still, The Xcerts released two albums in quick succession in 2009 and 2010 but it's been four years between the second and third album.

It's not as though the landscape has changed too much and the band did spend a considerable part of this four year period touring, supporting and promoting. However, you do wonder if there is still going to a fanbase for the group, or whether their core crowd will have moved on to similar acts during their time away.

The new album sounded big and catchy when

listening to it but five minutes after I turned the music off and focused on something else, I'd struggle to relay anything of what I had just heard. I'm sure after repeated listens you'd be able to scream all of the words and riffs back to the band at a show but unless you really invest that time into the album, it's a bit like candy floss – nice and pleasant at first but you wonder if it was worth it later on?

The Xcerts will be another band that need to work hard in 2015 to ensure they stick around...but no matter what happens, they've already had a fair old innings.

James Yorkston

A fine man from Fife. He's never going to be the type of artist that bothers the charts (he could though, he has more than enough stylish folky moments to have fitted into any of the Nu-Folk movements / revivals / hipster pickups that have popped up over the past decade or so) but James Yorkston just keeps on rolling. 12 years on from his debut Moving Up Country, Yorkston continues to move up with his 2014 album The Cellardyke Recording and Wassailing Society being another excellent and consistent release from the man. The news that Alexis Taylor from Hot Chip was behind the production desk may have raised a few eyebrow and concerns about whether James was finally going to go electro in the hope of bringing in new fans and funds. There was no need to worry and with a handful of willing recruits and familiar faces alongside him, Yorkston has shown that he has plenty of life left in him. There was also a Saturday night showing at the Kelvingrove Bandstand, bringing a blend of the old and the new to an open air gig in Glasgow that ran through the seasons quicker than a guitar handover!

With a book that is an interesting to read as his music is as enjoyable to listen to, James Yorkston is clearly a man that has plenty of talent and is a Scottish treasure that should be looked on with pride. He also seems to have a decent, if dry, sense of humour, so you can always expect to get some good chat from him when he is playing.

Young Fathers

The group was easily one of the most noted bands of 2014 with award shows falling over themselves to shower praise on Young Fathers. High profile award shows are not always right but in this respect, they certainly weren't wrong. The winning of the Scottish Album of the Year award for Tape Two was initially the biggest factor in bringing Young Fathers to people this year but for a band looking to making their mark, their debut album proper will always be of interest. Dead certainly lived up to hope and expectations.

One of the best things about Dead is that while there are plenty of very good songs on the album, it really works as collective piece. At just over 30 minutes, it isn't asking you to undertake a major commitment to listen to the album in one go but it is an album that really works well as a continuous piece. If you listen to music on the commute or while dragging yourself through a workout or run, it is an excellent accompaniment. (Mind you, given my fitness levels, a couple of Ramones songs would probably be too long for any workout I undertake!)

The fact that Dead won the Mercury Prize completing a cross-border double was a fantastic achievement and one that was fully deserved. They weren't the bookies favourites but the late October award of the Mercury prize saw them clinch a total of £40,000 across their two main award show triumphs. However, the real prize was gaining a bigger platform to reach out to lot more fans. One of the things that came to the fore in the immediate aftermath of the act's Mercury triumph was the fact that they had sold fewer than 3,000 albums before they won the award. This may have been some newspaper and media outlets attempts to "put the band back in their box" after their success, but it had a different impact for many readers.

Obviously sales are no longer the be all and end all for acts these days (which is just as well) but when you consider the praise that has been offered to Young Fathers this year, it really does drive home how people are moving away from buying albums. The morning after their Mercury triumph, Young Fathers had a total of 8,217 followers on Spotify with their most popular track (I Heard, the opening track from the Tape Two EP) having received close to 600,000 plays. The most popular song from Dead was Get Up, which had received over 460,000 plays. Given that this was the track that the band played live at the award show, this would likely become the focal point for many new followers of the band, so it would be understandable if the listening figures for this track rocketed before the end of the year. (For a bit of context, the most popular Spotify track for fellow Mercury nominees Royal Blood was Out Of The Black, with over 3.5m plays).

Given that the average fee for each play of a song on Spotify is worth $0.007 (USD) to an artist, most up and coming bands aren't going to make their living from Spotify. However, it can be seen as one income stream with a bag of the fag packet calculation for I Heard suggesting that the song would have brought in around $4,200. Based on the exchange rate at the start of November, Spotify should have been handing over more than £2,600 for that one song. It is easy to see why established artists like Taylor Swift and Thom Yorke can decide to withdraw their music from streaming sites like Spotify and create a situation where they will receive more sales, but for up and coming artists looking to gain exposure, Spotify will play a role in helping them to develop.

If you look on Soundcloud, the most listened to track from Dead is Low, with over 209,000 listens while there are a number of other songs with over 100,000 listens. Soundcloud is still coming to terms with monetization and over time, this is likely to be another streaming service that could provide income for groups. It may be that when YouTube fully jumps into the streaming market, the other streaming options will diminish but given the fact that many independent labels have criticized the terms offered by YouTube, it may be that there is a need for alternative streaming options, which may provide more prominence to up and coming artists.

With the album also available to buy on Bandcamp, it is probably not an exaggeration to say that the traditional methods of judging commercial success are not entirely relevant when it comes to evaluating the awareness of popularity of Young Fathers and groups like them.

Hopefully the success in award shows will bring about more awareness of the group, and increased sales, but it may well be that live performances and a continual increase in streaming figures will be of greater long term benefit to Young Fathers than traditional album sales. The career trajectory of the group promises to be an interesting one that is worth looking out for.

The fact that there are some really interesting Scottish hip-hop acts at the moment is a boost for the act because it helps to have a bit of a scene alongside them and around them but there is no doubt that Young Fathers have achieved their success through their own work and talent. One of the things that I really like about the act is that they are comfortable with dropping the quantity but increasing the quality, and I think that is something that many acts could benefit from. Young Fathers are very much one of the poster acts of alternative music in 2014 but there is no reason to think why the band shouldn't be around to achieve a lot more success. November 2014 was spent in Berlin recording a new album with the band promising it would be available in the first few months of 2015. 2014 was an almighty year for the group but it may be just the beginning. It would have been easy for the group to have spent November milking the post-Mercury spotlight for all that it was worth but the fact that they committed to recording a new album for quick release was testimony to the work ethic and positive attitude that the group had shown throughout the year.

There were also acts like Casual Sex, Tuff Love or Atom Tree who did enough to register for 2014 but you get the impression that there will be a lot more in store from these acts in 2015. I promise to try and minimize the amount of times I say that I like Casual Sex, but they are a band with clever songs and a very enjoyable live show so I'm sure that I won't be the only person professing their fondness of Casual Sex in 2015.

While some bands and artists have grabbed the attention during 2014, a number of musical events also deserve to be considered in their own right.

The In-store Show
Paper Aeroplanes – Friday 21st of February

In-store shows are usually tied up with a single or an album launch, primarily aimed at getting a release as high into the charts as possible. With the diminishing importance of physical releases and indeed the charts, there has been a dip in these sorts of events, but they can still provide a good way for bands to whip up publicity and mobilise their fanbase. Of course, that is the way they are used by big acts or boybands, for some bands, it can be all part and parcel of inching further ahead.

Being located in Glasgow city centre, it was quite simple to head along to Love Music on Dundas Street so seeing a lunchtime tweet that there would be a show at 4pm from Paper Aeroplanes was enough to make a plan. The band was currently high-tailing it down from Inverness, en route to a show in the Glad Café on the South-Side. To their credit, their management's credit or the store's credit, a mini in-store set was lined up.

They were a band that I had heard the name of and could hear what I thought they sounded like so with a quick Spotify check, I was fully clued up and actually quite looking forward it. A quick check on Twitter indicated the set had been put back a bit, the band were genuinely hot-footing from the Highlands and it turned out I arrived in store just before the band did. I don't think they even stopped for a drink before Richard Llewellyn and Sarah Howells set up and started playing at the front of the store.

There was a full live band touring but two acoustic guitars and vocals are all you really need to hear the songs in full flight. Sarah is quite the renowned trance vocalist, providing the melodies and delivery for songs many people have heard far too many times to mention but haven't clicked that it is the same singer in all of them. She's enjoyable and catchy for these trance tunes but I'm not going to lie, I'd much rather her hear sing in her group as opposed to the vocals for trance. That's all just a bit too uplifting and sportswear in social settings for me!

The psychology of the in-store show when you aren't a big group must be a challenge. If you just enjoy playing music and are keen to get your music in front of as many people as possible, you can see why it would be a great thing to do. However, when the number of people in the store who were browsing (which wasn't high) outnumbers the people watching the group (including the employees), you have to wonder what the impact on the act is.

If there was one, they weren't letting it show and it was as enjoyable and as intimate as you want it to be in a brightly lit room as you stare out on to a grey and wet Dundas Street as people scurry in and out of Queen Street station. One of the most interesting elements of the show was the polite and muted applause that greeted the end of every song. As Sarah pointed out, there was probably an embarrassment factor for the crowd as well, with no one in the audience wanting to be the person that sets off on a rapturous round of applause while no one else appreciated what was on offer. After that elephant in the room was mentioned, things lightened up a bit and the next song closer was greeted much more enthusiastically.

I'd definitely be up for more of these types of shows taking place, especially at the end of the working week on a Friday. Perhaps 4pm isn't the best of times but with a drive from up north and then soundchecks and dinner to be negotiated before their own show, it was probably the only time that the Paper Aeroplanes could squeeze in a show. I'm glad that they did.

Record Store Day

The atmosphere at Mono and Monorail was absolutely electric, no doubt fuelled by the sunshine that was present over the Easter weekend. Chocolate eggs and the resurrection of Jesus are big factors for a lot of people to make the most of the Easter break but sunshine, vinyl and alcohol are always going to be huge reasons for any

Glaswegian leaving the house. In fact, all it takes is one of those options to be present and you'll have interested punters so when you bring the three of them together, the people will be out in their droves. While there was clearly a lot of fun and revelry taking place, as it was in Mono, there was still an air of respectability about the sunshine celebrations. Around the rest of the city, taps aff records were being set by peely-wally men and women looking to roast their skin a stunning shade of pink but at Mono, shades and denim were still very much in style. It would take more than a heatwave to make this crowd lose sight of the importance of dressing fashionably.

I had been at a lunchtime football match on Record Store Day and decided to pop in after the game but before heading home. Before I had even made my way into the venue, Adele Bethel (formerly of Sons & Daughters and who had DJ'd at the event earlier in the day) and Graeme from Remember Remember were outside amongst the throng of folk enjoying sunny weather and a very positive atmosphere and attitude. Making my way to the bar, other familiar faces such as Graham the drummer from Bis and Chris Devotion & The Expectations or Ian from Kain and El Rancho Relaxo were milling around.

The Glasgow music scene in Glasgow is a genuine one, there are clearly lots of people in and around the industry that have a huge love for what they do and the music that other people create. Days like this should be a celebration and it was great to see Mono and Monorail packed out. Monorail is a tremendous shop and Mono, while not entirely perfect, has a lot of great things going for it and some of my favourite ever gigs have taken place in the venue. They stock a wide range of Williams Bros. beers and at this point, Helen Marnie, of Ladytron and solo fame, was serving up an eclectic and enjoyable set.

It's exactly the sort of event that people love and hopefully stores like Monorail, Love Music and all the other independent record stores made a lot of money on Record Store Day. The fact that Mono and Monorail had loads of bands and DJs on, in addition to their food and drink options, made them a natural choice. Love Music does very well to squeeze bands in but at times, it makes it all a little bit uncomfortable. The company also tried to offset the disadvantage of not having a bar on the premises by welcoming Heverlee along to their premises to dish out beer from a mobile bar. There's no doubt that record stores need to make as much of an occasion out of Record Store Day as they possibly can, but in reality, they should be pushing as hard throughout the year.

There was a convenience factor in choosing Mono for me, it was on my route home but even if I was heading out of the house, located in between Love Music and Mono, Monorail would have been the place of choice. This was likely down to the more prominent alcohol element on offer and the fact that there would be more space at Mono but also due to the fact that the King Street venue had a better line-up of acts and artists. The fact that Love Music tries to do in-store shows on a regular basis is a great thing and getting Paper Aeroplanes in the shop earlier in the year was a great coup for the store. It's just that, for me, a lot of the acts performing in store on RSD held no interest and would actually make me go out of my way to avoid them. There is clearly an audience for bands like Colonel Mustard and the Dijon 5, their self-promotion has been great and they seem to be developing a following, but their cheery and quirky nature just leaves me cold. Maybe that says a lot more about me and my idea of having fun but knowing that they were on the bill at Love Music meant that I would choose to avoid the place in case of being caught up in such a tight space with the band and their fan-base.

While I'm a fan of the idea of RSD and the benefit it can bring to record stores, I must admit, I'm not entirely supportive of what it has become. All of my viewpoints should be considered with the knowledge that I don't buy vinyl these days and I haven't in a long time. It would take something extremely special or rare for a band or artist that I really love for me to even consider buying vinyl. That's not to rule it out completely, part of the fun of being a big music fan is the irrationality that goes along with it but I don't get excited about limited edition 7" singles or bonus releases of live shows on vinyl.

Some of the problems I have with RSD include:

- It's a forced limited run, pushing prices up and creating hype
- This creates a situation where eBay sales are rife
- A great deal of RSD products are overpriced
- Many smaller labels, and genuine vinyl supporters, find themselves out of the market as the bigger firms book the vinyl pressing activities to coincide with this time
- It takes advantage of some fanbases

I'm not going to get too upset about the influx of pop acts (One Direction being the major one in 2014) jumping in on the act, RSD isn't about a genre or about music buyers who are somehow "better" or more worthy than others. It's about shifting units for stores and if this comes from selling limited edition 7" or 12" singles to fans who would otherwise avoid these stores, surely that is good for all concerned? It may well be that it'll help people to discover new types of music and that should never be discouraged.

It's clearly been tough for record stores in recent years and with downloads being more readily available and people liking the convenience of buying music from their home and in a digital format. The solution isn't really to have one big day where a store makes a massive percentage of their takings for the entire year (although it does help), it should be about providing a service and product options that people want to buy.

Over the years, I've had some great chats in record stores in and around Glasgow about acts I love or new bands I was only discovering. I still recall chatting to David Barbarossa in Fopp about ARE Weapons and their wonderful Suicide style track, Street Gangs. There was a summer I was temping in Paisley and a great deal of my time and money was spent in The Record Factory on Causeyside Street. If you ever wanted to have a chat about Radioactive Man, that was one of the best places to do so outside of the Rotters Golf Club. There was even the Sunday afternoon session in Mono where the pumping of Follakzoid's II album over the PA led three of us to buy the album within a matter of days. Record stores still have the potential to introduce you to new acts and impact on your life. Anyone that knows me personally will have been bored senseless with my praise of Follakzoid, getting to the stage where I was actively cheering Chile goals at the World Cup because the band hails from there.

The Beta Band scene from the High Fidelity film may be a bit fake but it was a brilliant scene and it captured the essence of what record stores can do to people. Even if it is just about creating a platform for taste-makers to play us all like puppets and part us from our cash, the way I and a lot of my friends have taken to Follakzoid since that day in Mono proves that we need to keep record stores alive.

This is something that gives indie record stores an edge and they would be advised to focus on this. You tend to find that the folk that work in these stores are amongst the most passionate and knowledgeable music fans you will find. They certainly don't do the job for the money; working in a music store is clearly a labour of love for many people. Rather than waiting for a once a year event, where the staff are too busy to really discuss music, independent record stores should look into hosting talks, discussion nights or special events as much as they can. The advent of social networking makes it easier for these events to be publicised and brought to the attention of willing customers. You'll find that most bands and DJs would be more than happy to help record stores make more of an impact on a regular basis. Of course it's hard and it's not as though this is an idea that will be totally new to record store owners and staff but seeing the enthusiasm for Record Store Day should remind them that there is a love and warmth for record stores and it would be great if they could do more to reward buyers and encourage them in on a more regular basis.

It also needs to be remembered that Record Store Day represents a big investment for many record stores. It may be a case of speculating to accumulating but it can be a gamble. At 10am on Sunday the 20th of April, the day after Record Store Day (Or RSD+1 as the store's twitter feed referred to it), Love Music stated that they still had around 700 LPs and 300 singles. Not everyone can make it along on RSD, and while all of the highly prized records are likely to have been sold, there was still plenty left for punters and collectors to come along and buy. It's good that the store was promoting the fact that they still had material worth buying relating to the big day but looking at it in another way, the store had 1,000 pieces of vinyl, all brought in over the previous week and adding to the stock already in place, still for sale after the big selling day had passed. That isn't a good thing for a business and it possibly indicates another factor in why record stores are becoming ever more manic and pressing in their promotion.

Most of us know how the record business works. The labels and distributors will push downwards on the stores as heavily as they can. As well as charging high prices for certain releases, it wouldn't be uncommon for stores to find that they have to take stock of unfashionable releases in order to get the big names in. Getting stock of the big releases is essential for any record store to have success on RSD and this means that they can be rolled into taking stock that they are unlikely to get rid of. For something that was initially started to provide support and assistance to record stores, it may well be that Record Stores Day actually causes a longer-term headache and problem for stores.

You'd think that RSD would be more than enough music related fun for a weekend but those of us without loved ones or whose family members were far too busy to want to spend time with you on Easter Sunday*, there was another way to get your musical kicks. On another glorious warm and sunny day in Glasgow, and by now with many residents of the city suffering from acute sunburn, dehydration and exhaustion, I headed off to the reserved area of Hyndland and the Hyndland Bookshop for the Glasgow launch of Simply Thrilled: The Preposterous Story of Postcard Records. A neat coincidence meant that the event was taking place 35 years to the day since the first Orange Juice gig, making it a perfect time to launch the book. The author, Simon Goddard, put this down to coincidence, with the driving forces behind the launch of the book being RSD and the general anniversary of Postcard Records. It was a short and sweet launch, hindered by the layout of the store. Much in the same way that you admire Love Music for putting on live bands when they clearly have very little space to do so, the same was true for the Hyndland Bookshop. It was a good event but clearly the store looks to use most available space to sell books, making for a slightly cramped way to spend an hour.

It was a worthwhile hour, there was some insight into the story of the label and the characters involved although it did seem as though the threat of legal action prevented many of the best stories of the era from being told. In saying that, there were plenty of accusations of the main protagonists in the story suffering from varying degrees of mental instability. Not to imply that you had to be mad to want to start a record label from a flat in Glasgow but it no doubt played a role in the charm of Postcard Records.

I had better add that given that I wanted to go to the Postcard Records book event and then watch some football, it was entirely my decision not to see my parents on Easter Sunday, not theirs! It saved them having to buy me an egg and let them do their own thing; it was a decision that suited all parties!

Stag & Dagger

Well, there's another Stag & Dagger over and done with. The scheduling of the event left a lot to be desired and some of the venues were a bit uncomfortable at times but on the whole, the music more than made up for any shortcomings of the day. It wasn't possible to see all of the bands that I wanted to see but the ones that I did catch were great. Sadly this meant missing out on acts like Ezra Furman, Casual Sex, Tennis, Courtney Barnett and Lanterns on the Lake but there were still plenty of great acts on the bill to check out.

Arriving just in time to see Honeyblood play acoustically in Coda Hairdressers made me realise that it had been an awful long time since I had headed to a hairdressers with any real intent! Quirky venue choices can add something to events like this but this was not a good call. The venue was rammed to capacity and there was a great deal of humidity in the air. If the conditions were like that when people had their haircut there would have been an awful lot of frizz to contend with. At least the flyers with the stage times came in handy with Glasgow girls fanning themselves like Southern belles. Anyone looking to stave off dehydration in such pressing conditions would have found themselves paying £3.50 for a can of pale ale or cider. Mind you, the pale ale did pack a punch with a 6.9% percentage. The set was short and sweet with a slant on tracks that weren't going to be included in the band's set later on that evening.

Syd Arthur played a prog-sounding set in Broadcast and while prog is a genre that is often more miss than hit, it was a good set and a good introduction to the band. Next up in Broadcast were Honeyblood. Their live show certainly indicated that there is going to be a lot to enjoy on the record and their thrashy and melodious mix was very well received.

Broadcast is a venue that gets a lot of complaints and at times it can be difficult to get a clear sight-line but the sound is always good and I've seen some tremendous gigs in there. The two sets I caught at Stag & Dagger lived up to the reputation the venue is offering.

From here it was over to ABC (via a quick stop for a bite to eat) and Royal Blood. Another duo, again with blood in their name, and another high-energy and high volume set. Royal Blood were excellent, easily the set of the night for me and I'll look forward to catching the band again. It was a pretty relentless set with the crowd in ABC2 going pretty wild.

The same couldn't be said for upstairs in ABC1 where Buster Bluth was playing to a crowd that didn't seem to have much interest in what he had to offer. (Okay, it was Albert Hammond Jnr.) Throughout the set, the audience started to drift away and while there were songs of decent quality, the show didn't really connect at any point. Perhaps it was just too big a stage for the artist by himself without his day-job band members.

After this it was back down to ABC2 where The Fat

White Family rounded off our event. This was another loud and chaotic set, shaking off the ennui that hung around the AHJ set. The smaller venue came to life and singer Lias Saoudi wasted no time in delivering his best Iggy Pop impersonations. The band came across as much spikier and chaotic playing live than they do on record and with Saoudi launching himself into the audience, there was a typical rock n roll conclusion to what had been a rock n roll day.

The SAY Awards

You could maybe say that in Scotland there is not enough being done to support young mothers (while of course there will always be some folk that think too much is being done), but it is rare to hear about the plight of young fathers being discussed. This is why it was a brave and exciting move by the Scottish Album of the Year awards to pinpoint Young Fathers for recognition! Before this joke gets me in trouble, it was of course the Scottish act Young Fathers who came out on top of a highly competitive field in the 2014 SAY Awards.

There is an argument that musicians and artists shouldn't be subjected to award shows, because the notion of one artist or album being deemed as being better than another doesn't sit easily with a lot of people. Clearly music is subjective and personal taste has such a strong role to play in whether people like a record. You have the charts to act as a barometer of public opinion, and quite frankly, if that is a measure of what is best, you'd be as well banning music. In this regard, if an award show can put some focus on artists that may not sell in volume but have created a strong piece of music, there is no real harm in doing it. Some award shows exist to sate the desire of record companies and sponsors to have some time in the spotlight and to have a right good night out but there are award ceremonies that can bring acts to people's attention and ensure that good quality music is showcased. For the full effect of the promotional benefit to the acts involved to be realised, there needs to be a winner of the award and the justification for having these events starts to take shape.

Not all award shows and ceremonies are the same, and as the SAY Awards is still pretty much still in its infancy, it is still finding its way and creating an identity. Not all award shows are good, not even ones that seem to focus on new bands, with a particular highlight being Popcop's retelling of the 2011 Scottish New Music Awards. (Typing "Popcop award show" into Google brings up the page as the number one result.) In some ways, I wish I had been present at that event because who doesn't love observing a car crash now and then but it's probably best I didn't get the opportunity to heckle Sandi Thom as she may have been a punk rocker with the remains of a pint in her hair (not that I'd have actually thrown a pint, I'm too tight and too fond of alcohol to get up to those sort of shenanigans).

You sometimes get the feeling that awards shows, not necessarily the SAY Awards which has only been around for a couple of years, but certainly the Mercury Award, believe that there is some joy to be found in deliberately choosing a leftfield winner. There is an argument that these award shows aren't really for big bands, as they don't need much more exposure. It was only right that the public vote ensured that Biffy Clyro earned a place on the shortlist but would the exposure have earned the band any more sales or shoved them in front of any new fans? It's unlikely. However, should an award show of this nature be just about shining a light on emerging talent and ensuring that everyone gets a fair crack of the whip? Deep down there is part of you that just wants to throw the award at the best album made by an act in the past year, and of course, this takes us back to the start of the argument of how can you really determine what the "best" album is.

With all that going on, and bearing in mind that the winner receives £20,000 (with the rest of the shortlist receiving a grand each), I'm more than happy for the winner to be somebody left of centre that deserves some form of financial recognition for their work, that they may not have received up to this point. You could easily make arguments for Biffy Clyro, Chvrches and Mogwai to have won the award, and they would all have welcomed the cash, but giving the recognition and money to an emerging artist is never a bad decision. You also knew that Steve Mason was never going to win the award, even with an enjoyable album, because that would completely shatter the image of Steve as being the unlucky artist perpetually just missing out on wider acclaim that he deserves.

The diversity of artists in the shortlist was notable, showcasing what a strong period it had been for Scottish acts. There were a few up and coming acts making their name, and a handful of mature artists still showing that they had a magic touch about them. There were a couple of electronic acts, some cool indie kids and even a touch of Scottish hip hop.

With Young Fathers and Hector Bizerk making the shortlist of 10 for the SAY Awards, there was a representation of Scottish hip hop that hasn't been since DC Thompson decided that Oor Wullie needed to update his image for the youth of today and styled him in a backwards cap and a stolen Ford logo hanging over his dungarees. Add in the emergence of Stanley Odd (who weren't in the running with an eligible album for this award), and you have to say that this is a genre that is very much in trend in the country at the time, and for that reason alone, it was fair enough that Young Fathers was the winner.

While there was inevitable discussion over who should have won, there was also some chat about whether Young Father should have been eligible for the award. Their album was actually an EP, and although it had 9 songs on it, it came in at around 23 minutes. You used to get CD singles with a longer running time in the mid-90s, so should this release have been counted as an album?

The definition of an album, as defined in the format and eligibility guidelines, states an album "must contain 6 or more tracks and/or be over 30 minutes in length." Tape Two fails on the 30 minutes in length section but the crucial "and/or" element, with the other criteria being met with the fact that there are 9 tracks on the release, means that the release meets the criteria outlined for the event. Rules are rules so Tape Two had every reason to be included on the list and its quality meant that it had a fair chance of winning, which it ultimately did.

Young Fathers are not a band that overstays their welcome on their releases. Tape One has 8 songs and clocks in at around 20 minutes, Tape Two has 9 songs and lasts for around 23 minutes while the relatively speaking prog-rock classic Dead has 11 songs and lasts for half an hour. The thing is though, is this a bad thing? Surely it is better to have fewer tracks and a shorter running time if it cuts out filler material. When was the last time you really heard an album that was "all killer, no filler"?

This is one area where the advent of digital music may have an impact. With acts being able to write, record and release whenever they want, there may not be the need to spend too long on records, if a band has a track or songs that they are proud of, they can get them out online there and then. The media is always telling us that no one is buying albums any more these days, so why bother with them? There are more than enough albums that have been released in the past couple of years that will have double the length of time of the Young Fathers releases without being half as good.

It may not fit with our concept of an album, and it's going to be the end of those BBC4 documentaries about the making of classic records, but if that's the worst of it, we'll probably all survive. You aren't going to get 60 to 90 minutes of artists talking about their struggles of recording four songs and then releasing it in a digital format the following week but that's fine. If album mythology goes the same way as many of the other great aspects of music such as taping the charts from the radio and moaning about how Top of the Pops isn't as good as it used to be, then so be it, we'll still have the music.

It's not as though bands are making much, if any, money from their records these days and the more digital releases they have, the more excuses they have for launch nights and tours. There can be a tendency to think that things need to be done in a certain manner because this is the way that they have always been done, but that really isn't the case anymore.

It may be that the SAY Awards in 2014 made a really bold move, one that can be seen to be challenging the concept of what an album is these days. Or it may just be that more people on the panel liked the Young Fathers release than there were people that liked any other record. There is probably a tendency to overthink these things and no matter what album was selected, there is no way that everyone would have been pleased.

One thing that is certain is that if the Say Awards returns in 2015, the winner is likely to cause a great deal of controversy and debate, because there has been a great collection of albums by Scottish albums released in the past year, including Young Fathers "debut" album, Dead (which went on to win the Mercury Music Prize). I look forward to the controversy and debate surrounding the 2015 SAY Awards.

The shortlist for the 2014 SAY Awards was:
Biffy Clyro – Opposites
Boards of Canada – Tomorrow's Harvest
Chvrches – The Bones Of What You Believe
Edwyn Collins – Understated
Hector Bizerk – Nobody Seen Nothing
Mogwai – Les Revenants
RM Hubbert – Breaks & Bone
Steve Mason – Monkey Minds in The Devil's Time
The Pastels – Slow Summits
Young Fathers – Tape Two

East End Social

1994 may not be a year that everyone looks back on fondly in British music, but there were plenty of good moments that have had a lasting impact and legacy. In 2014, the 20-year anniversary look-backs have been coming thick and fast, and at times, for some of the most spurious reasons. However, there is one 20th anniversary that has not been trumpeted from the rooftops and as you would expect from the people at Chemikal Underground, they have hardly been rushing to draw any attention to themselves. In fact, they have been working hard in making sure that 2014 is a year that creates its own legacy and lasting memories as opposed to taking a walk down their own memory lane.

The East End Social was created by Chemikal Underground in an attempt to create a musical programme that added a cultural edge to the sporting nature of Glasgow's summer but there has also been work to provide a social impact on the east end of the city.

Before we delve into the work of the East End Social, let's take a brief look at Chemikal Underground and why they deserve their own special place in Scottish music history. The label was set up in 1994 by The Delgados to release their debut single Monica Webster/Brand New Car. Given the talent, importance and popularity of The Delgados, if the label was only of note for releasing this single, it would have earned its place its Scottish folklore but the label has championed a considerable roster of Scottish talent.

Acts like Aerogramme, Arab Strap, Bis, De Rosa, Holy Mountain, Mogwai, Mother & The Addicts, The Phantom Band, The Radar Brothers, RM Hubbert, Sluts of Trust, Suckle, The Unwinding Hours, Yatsura and Zoey Van Goey are just some of the artists that have found a home with Chemikal Underground over the years.

Postcard Records may be the Glasgow record label that has the romance and majesty around it but the variety and quality of work released on the Chemikal Underground label means that this is a label that is revered around the world. There will be some people that love everything that the label has released but given the diversity on offer, it is more likely that everyone familiar with the label will have their own preferences. There wasn't any act that you would refer to as being a bad band on the label but whether you preferred swooping pop choruses, intense instrumental passages or some of the sleaziest and outrageous rock n roll you could ever hope to find, Chemikal Underground wouldn't let you down.

The past twenty years has seen the label do more than enough to please the music loving community but for 2014, in line with the Commonwealth Games hitting the city, they decided to do something that would bring benefit to the local community. Cost and convenience may have been factors that drew the label to Bridgeton and the east end of Glasgow but having found a home, the label has decided to give something back and add a bit to the festivities and celebrations.

It is important to remember that not everyone in the local community was as convinced about the positive impact or the legacy that the Games will leave on the east end of the city. BBC Scotland are never slow at missing a trick when it comes to showing the darker side of life and much like shows like The Scheme or the one about Sauchiehall Street, the corporation was able to show the grimier side of life in the east end. If you go digging and scratching anywhere in Scotland, you'll find conflict and perhaps scenarios that are far from an ideal world. The issue with the way the BBC Scotland reports these problems is they dress it up for viewing consumption and do nothing to present a more optimistic side or a solution to any of the problems. There will be more people in the east end of Glasgow who are unaware of Chemikal Underground as those that are familiar with the label but the fact that the label has made a conscious effort to positively impact on the community speaks volumes for the people involved with the label. It's not as if arts can provide solutions that will help with poverty or the poor health of people in an area, but it can have a positive impact on a community. Making people feel as though they belong, that there are opportunities for them and just giving people something to focus on and enjoy has to be of benefit to the community.

As you would expect, there have been some brilliant gigs lined up by the East End Social and there has been a widespread of venues feeling the benefit of the live shows. You would expect the Barrowlands to feature extensively as a venue for any collection of Glasgow show, but the diversity of venues and locations in the East End Social programme has been innovative and inventive.

Local learning centres, Rutherglen Town Hall,

Dennistoun New Parish Church, The Bowlers Bar and Platform in Easterhouse are just some of the venues that have sat alongside the Barrowland Ballroom. The collective has also thought outside of the box with major events taking place along Duke Street, in Alexandra Park and the grand finale of the East End Social summer work, the two gigs taking place in Richmond Park.

While it is the gigs that will get the most attention in the East End Social programme, the organisation deserves a lot of praise for the range of activities they have put on for people. A range of tea dances provided something for people that like their music of a classier vintage while the King Ayisoba gig shone a focus on the music and rhythms of Africa. In fact, many people were saying that the tea dances at the Barrowlands, allowing many people and couples to return to their former haunt, were a major highlight. These are things we can sometimes take for granted in life, but having the chance to connect to a place that was central to your life 50 or 60 years ago is something that people will cherish. I've clearly been to the Barrowlands on plenty of occasions and had some excellent times but you can guarantee that some of the former dancers returning to the venue of their childhood would have experience emotions that very few modern gigs could even contemplate competing with.

While gigs and music can help bring a bit of happiness and sunshine into people's lives for a short spell, music can play a stronger role in the lives of some people. The programme included a talk at the Apple Store on Buchanan Street highlighting the work that is being carried out by the Playlist for Life initiative. This is an innovative initiative that aims to use music to help treat dementia and a number of sessions and workgroups are being offered in Bridgeton.

Hopefully, everyone reading this won't need me to tell the power of music and how it can affect people emotionally. We all have songs that evoke memories of certain moments or times. You'll have heard people talk of a song that instantly reminds them of a holiday or couples that have a song that they recognise as their tune. With music having the power to trigger thoughts and memories, you can see why it is being used to provide support to people who are suffering from or watching their loved ones suffer from dementia.

It's not as though Scottish people have to look too far in their family tree to find conditions that have plagued their family or which frighten them considerably but dementia and other mental ailments are something that concern me greatly. Knowing that there is great work being carried out in this field in Scotland (the organisation is based in Dunfermline) is pleasing and the fact that the East End Social have taken steps to be involved and provide support in this field is brilliant news. Loads of people will have enjoyed excellent nights out and great days with the gigs and events but if the work carried out by Playlist for Life and East End Social can help loved ones to connect or to bring some joy to someone's life, that's a real positive thing to take from this year and the work of the programme.

With work along these lines, it would almost be easy to overlook the fact that there were some brilliant gigs and sets along the way. The Glasgow Mixtape event was a fantastic day, one that the rain couldn't ruin, and that is discussed all by itself later on. Uncovering The Bowlers Bar was a treat, with a chance to see some great acts closeup while paying a very small fee at the bar is always a thrill. The Olive Grove Records day was an excellent affair and then The New Mendicants were brilliant a week or so later. I was away in Barcelona for Primavera when the Duke Street Expo took place, but all the reports of that day said it was an excellent event that was well-received. The line-up looked fantastic with acts like King Creosote, Admiral Fallow and Rick Redbeard appearing amongst many others. With a combination of free events and paid for ticketed events, there was a chance to appeal to hardcore fans and casual music fans alike and it seemed to bring a great buzz to the area. I was born in Duke Street hospital and while I'm not really a person that has much attachment to places, I'm always happy to see something good happen in that part of the city.

The footage of the All Day Reggae event in Alexandra Park looked fantastic and for many people, the East End

Social left the best to the end with The Last Big Weekend. I had already seen Mogwai twice in 2014 by this point, but you can't really get too much of the 'Gwai and the rest of the line-up was outstanding. In Honeyblood, Holy Mountain and Swervedriver, the first three acts of the day, the Saturday line-up had more exciting talent on offer than some festivals offer up over the course of the day. The length of queues for the food and drink attempted to put a slight dampener on the day, but the mood of the crowd remained excellent and the music continued to be of a great standard. Headliners Mogwai delivered another excellent set and if this was to be the last weekend of the East End Social, at least it went out in style.

The great thing about the line-up of events was that other people can reel off a completely different list of acts that they caught and still think that they had a wonderful time. The positive comments that people made about the El Hombre Trajeado show in Platform in Easterhouse, about the Remember Remember show in Dennistoun New Parish Church and about the Nectarine No.9 set in Rutherglen Town Hall suggested that all of these events will live long in the memory of those that managed to get a ticket.

The summer of 2014 was obviously a special one in Glasgow but if the city was only able to offer up sport to the locals and guests, it would have been a missed opportunity to showcase what Glasgow does best. The free gigs at the Kelvingrove bandstand were an excellent treat but in connecting the East End to the rest of the city and creating a platform for so many brilliant artists and performers, the East End Social went above and beyond. I know the people involved with the event didn't carry out their work to receive praise or acknowledgment, but they were instrumental in making sure Glasgow was buzzing over the summer of 2014. I'd be delighted to hear if there are plans for future East End Social events or if there is any way to carry on the great work that has been carried out.

The Glasgow Mixtape

The second and final Saturday of the Commonwealth

Games may have been a day where many of the athletes were going for gold, and plenty of fans were hurrying to a major venue, but there was still a lot to enjoy at Glasgow Green. The Green was a key hub of The Games, serving up plenty of chances to congregate en masse to watch the sports, and to see a range of entertainment. There had been a few musical events on the Green over the course of the games that caught my eye, some I made it along to, others that life got in the way of, but there was no way that I was missing out on The Glasgow Mixtape, curated by East End Social, with Vic Galloway and Nicola Meighan taking care of the MC duties for the two stages. It has to be said though, Nicola won a watch with the split of the duties, she managed to get the outdoor jobs in the decent weather and then indoors when the weather took a nasty turn. As Nicola suggested on twitter, maybe Vic was being the chivalrous gent or maybe Nicola was just quite jammy, which is never really something you want to admit on social media.

Anyways, it is hard to ignore the fact that the rain was a big factor of the day but as usual, you have to get on with things. I'm not sure if it is an old Scottish saying but the notion of there being "no such as bad weather, just bad clothing" is as true for music festivals as it is for any other outdoor pursuit. However, at times you do question your sanity when the rain is chucking it down and you're more than happy to watch a band play. Mind you, for many people looking at the bill, it wasn't the massive puddles that presented the biggest threat to enjoying yourself, it was the tiny bubbles.

Sydney Devine eh, old steak n kidney. A perfect example of The Scottish Cringe, a man who never let his own lack of talent hold him back from developing a career. I'm not sure where Devine stands on the critical scale these days, is he now an artist whose back catalogue will be re-appraised with a few hidden classics being pushed as a sign of his perpetual "alrightness" or was it just something for the grans and granddads? If nothing else, we should celebrate the fact that Sydney is one of the very few 70s and 80s TV presenters that can be wheeled out in the modern day. Sure, Sydney was responsible for making a few criminal records but at least he doesn't have one, like many of his peers at the time.

Mind you, when he started to talk about his recording sessions in South Africa, you wanted to reel him back in quickly before there was a need for a conversation about the darker elements of the Commonwealth and why all of these countries have the link that facilitated their involvement with the Games. Hopefully there is no Live At Sun City album in Sydney's back catalogue!

Okay, Sydney was never going to be for me, but due to the nature of the licensing of the event, I was ensconced within the drinking playpen with a pint, well within earshot of Sydney's set. He came bounding on, serving up a range of classic country songs and then 50s and 60s hits. The start of the set was littered with good songs; I just didn't care for the delivery of them. Mind you, in pubs across Glasgow on a weekly basis, revellers love hearing songs they know being mangled by poor quality singers engaging in the ancient Japanese torture method called karaoke. For plenty of folk, it's not the singer that matters, it's the song. And as long as the song is familiar to a song they know and love, they'll enjoy the set. For that reason alone, Sydney's set would have been the highlight of the day for many folk, but there was a notable dip when he turned his focus to songs more readily associated with him, as opposed to standards of his genre or era.

Next up on the Living Room stage were Holy Mountain, a natural fit alongside Sydney's pleasant and polite crooning...You wonder how many people looked at the bill and thought "Holy Mountain, maybe a bit religious but they're probably a nice group, let's hang around for them".

It's unlikely that Sydney will cover tracks called Bolting Bastard or Swifty Fuckwits, but that was all part of the charm of the day's line-up. Holy Mountain wasted no time in turning up the volume and delivering powerful riff upon riff. The vocals weren't as prominent in the mix as they could have been but this didn't impact on the power of the set, or indeed, my enjoyment of it, which is clearly the most important aspect to take into consideration when setting sound levels!!

The worst of the weather was yet to come, it was merely dull and overcast at this point, but the pulverising nature of Holy Mountain may have been the calling card for the more troubling weather which was to follow. While the band is much better suited to playing indoors in a small and sweaty venue, they took to the outside with aplomb, even indulging in a bit of taps aff tomfoolery. This wasn't required but the band was working up a sweat and by the end of the set, there wasn't a head within 200 yards that hadn't been nodding or bopping along with the music. Sure, there were a few parents exposing their kids to loud songs while posing for pictures with their devils horns in the air, but there wasn't anything novelty about the set, it was a genuine loud and heavy musical assault and I'd like to think there'll be a few folk checking out the band's output after this set. There are probably still large chunks of the set still rolling about in the attendees head and hearing canal.

Errors were up next and again, this is a band that is probably far better suited to an interior venue but similar to Holy Mountain, they put on a great show. It was slow to begin with but by the end of the 30 minute set, the space in front of the stage was being treated like any decent dancefloor. There was a good flow to the performance, it built and built, which isn't always the easiest thing to do when you don't have a clue what the audience is like. At least with support slots, you can have a good guess at who'll be hanging around but Errors were playing to weans, grandparents and all ages in between. Okay, in some parts of Scotland, the gap between wean and grandparent barely touches 30 years but there was a good spread of ages in front of Errors.

If Holy Mountain got the people rocking and Errors ensured the kids were dancing, Malcolm Middleton was sent around to bring everyone down! Not really though, Malcolm may come across as a right miserable so and so, especially in his lyrics, but it was a set peppered with many upbeat elements. Some of the greatest pop moments deliver a downbeat or depressing outlook with an upbeat and happy tune, which is something that Malcolm is able to deliver in spades. Ably assisted by the highly talented and hardworking Jenny Reeve, the rain and rising wind was the perfect accompaniment to a man who has made a career from not looking on the bright side of life. Perhaps Fuck It I Love You isn't the best song to play to a field with many kids in it, and following it up with We're All Going To Die, with its cheery chorus of "you're going to die alone" didn't help matters but of course, you need to dig deeper than the surface with Malcolm and his music.

If anywhere in the world is going to get a touch of black humour and the perpetual battle of balancing hope and despair, it is Scotland in the summer and you could argue that Malcolm Middleton's show was the perfect mid-afternoon Scottish festival set.

There is a time and place for everything though and before stepping into the Playhouse, there was a need to leave your cynicism and dour nature outside. Edwyn Collins was due on next with an acoustic set and if you're going to stand and moan about a bit of rain, thinking about the way that Edwyn has battled in the past few years soon starts to put your grievances and grumbles into place.

I don't think there is any need to sugar coat it, seeing Edwyn climb up the stairs at the side of the stage was a bit uncomfortable and if I was to make a comparison, it would be to the time Brian Wilson shuffled on stage at the Armadillo many years ago when yet another Brain's Back tour swept the world. Of course, Brian turned out to be on great form that night, ably assisted by a great bunch of musicians, and Edwyn managed to do the same, albeit backed up by just one guitarist.

James Walbourne provided the musical accompaniment on acoustic guitar, but you could tell there was a friendship and camaraderie between the two. He may not be that young man anymore but Edwyn is still able to deliver the sound of Young Scotland, and this was a set spanning the ages. The songs served up ranged from the first Orange Juice single Falling and Laughing, all the way through to recent solo work, including set opener Losing Sleep.

There were plenty of classics on show with Blue Boy, Rip It Up, A Girl Like You and Low Expectations. The latter was a particular highlight, Edwyn still able to deliver great melodies and style in his performance. There were plenty of magical moments throughout the set and Edwyn was never slow in showcasing the talent of his guitarist, who was encouraged to let rip with solos and mini workouts throughout the set. The fact that Edwyn's set marked the changing of set-times from 30 minutes to 45 minutes for the day was a pleasant surprise for me, and there wasn't a moment wasted. With Glasgow in the spotlight and the musical side of the city being placed to the fore once more, it's only right that Edwyn gets his share of the spotlight. There's always been a touch of hope and despair about the music, and indeed life, of Edwyn Collins but as the rain battered the mini venue, it wasn't just the rain and wind that made you pleased to be inside.

Another strong reason for spending time indoors came from the music that was being played in between sets. Before Edwyn came to the stage, Stephen Pastel was manning the decks, delivering tunes for the adults to dance to and for the kids to sit on the floor and look bored to. Youth, its wasted on the young, let me tell you that. After Edwyn, Helen Marnie was taking over the DJ duties, and while I would have preferred Helen to play a solo set drawn from her debut album, with a few Ladytron classics thrown in for good measure, you knew that her DJ set was going to up the tempo and bring the electro back to proceedings. The rolling of applause from the end of Edwyn's set hadn't subsided by the time Helen took to the decks and talk about making an entrance.

If you're not yet acquainted with the teaches of Peaches, feel free to check it out, but you may wish to avoid blaring it out in front of the kids! Having heard Helen Marnie DJ before, I knew it going to be a good set; I just didn't expect her to go for it in such a big way direct from the start. Some of the parents may have been peeved at the nature of the track kicking off her set, but it was an invigorating step on from the acoustic nature of Edwyn's set.

In fact, if I have one regret from the day, it was not sticking with Helen's set for its entirety. This was down to the fact that The Bluebells set was awful, and this had nothing to do with the PA that cut out a few times near the end of the set. This isn't a criticism of the PA system or set-up; it had performed excellently throughout the rest of the event, in extremely trying conditions. Actually, perhaps the PA was doing everyone a favour by dampening the effect of the group. The band seemed keen to be the architects of their own downfall when they sabotaged the one song that the vast majority of umbrella wielding crowd had gathered to hear. The accordion addition to hit single Young At Heart added an element of twee when no additional twee was needed, and if you are the sort of person that believes in karma, the resulting sound problems may have been an act of swift retribution. Commandeering soul classic I'll Take You There, slipping in a mention Glasgow Green, for the finale provided another familiar moment for the crowd to cheer and sing along with but again, the sound system spluttered as the set tailed off. Sydney Devine's set was better than this one, so at least in that respect, The Bluebells were doing their bit for the aged.

The rain wasn't for giving up which meant that the time spent waiting for The Phantom Band was a bit damp and miserable. There was no opportunity to Race Bolt and no opportunity to slide down Ford's big chute, both coming a cropper to the weather conditions, but the bands kept on playing, testimony to the set-up and a lot of hard work. The Bluebells set had its sound problems and one of the screens at the side of the living room stage had to be lowered due to wind but when you think about the day, you have to say that the management of the day was above and beyond what you would expect. There was an entry management system in place for the Playhouse arena, understandable given the rain, but for Edwyn's set, it still seemed as though there was plenty of space and if you were so inclined, you could have found space at the front, even if you entered after the set began.

With song titles like The Wind That Cried, The Howling

and Sweatbox referencing the summer rain, The Phantom Band found themselves playing in apt conditions, with the band making continual references to the conditions. You get the feeling that they appreciated being dry and protected from the rain while the crowd were being battered from all angles. The worst that the band had to endure was a missing "The" from their name on the big screen behind them. This was pointed out by Rick and before the end of the set, this issue had been rectified. When you consider that the East End Social is the brainchild of the band's record label, you would like to think that they would know the name of the group. You dread to think how any passing krautrocker would have felt upon seeing the name of the group and then rushing down to the front of the stage only to find it wasn't the band initiated by Jaki Liebezeit. Then again, if you're the sort of fan that appreciates the work and music of Jaki, you should get the Phantom Band.

A 45 minute set was perhaps the limit of what you wanted on a day like this, but it forced the band into delivering a compact set. Sure I would have loved to have heard Women of Ghent but it was a well-paced set, drawing on the band's output, as opposed to just the latest album. Thankfully the sound held firm and the group were in good form. The group hasn't really gotten into touring gear with their new album yet, the full bloodied tour not scheduled until September and October, but you wouldn't have thought there was any rustiness. Okay, rustiness comes after weather like that as opposed to before and during, but if this the sound of The Phantom Band machine when they are limbering up for a full-on live assault, there is clearly a lot more to come from the band. Before you knew it, the 45 minutes were up and the band was making their way off stage to finally get soaked like the audience.

While there were still acts to come, I always felt The Phantom Band would be my cut off point. It would have been good to have seen some of Bis but there was an overlap and then there was the chance of getting turned back from the Playhouse Stage. The Amphetameanies, Admiral Fallow and Lloyd Cole were all still to come but after having been on site for over 7 hours, the conclusion of The Phantom Band set was all that I needed to hear to get out of the park, back into the city and experience some warmth and comfort.

It would have been easy for the Glasgow Green organisers to go for an all-out pop event that would appeal across the board so it was great to see them put their faith and trust in the East End Social, who served up exactly what the Glasgow Mix Tape set out to do. You were never going to get close to all of the Glasgow bands you wanted to hear on one bill but for an event across two stages that reached out to a wide audience, there was something for everyone.

Like Dylan In The Movies

I really wanted to love the Stuart Murdoch film God Help The Girl and I was more than happy to chuck money at the Kickstarter project for the film. This granted me access to the Glasgow premiere, the Q&A after it, the party after that and some badges and a big poster. More importantly, it was a bit of putting your money where your mouth is. There has often been a cinematic style quality to the music of Murdoch and his band, and who better than him to bring Glasgow to life on the big screen?

It wasn't a bad film, and perhaps my hopes that it would be a great film slightly worked against it, but on the whole, I was left a bit underwhelmed by the film. The main issue for me was that I didn't really get or like the three lead characters. As a mid-30s Glasgow man, I probably shouldn't be having an immediate kinship with young twenty-something's living in the city but even with the age gap in mind, I never warmed to the lead characters. The cameos from the Wake The President guys was enjoyable and Cora Bissett brings a touch of quality to the vast majority of things she touches, but it just never connected with me.

It was clearly a project that Stuart held close to his heart, and obviously the trials that Eve endured were inspired by some of the own issues that Stuart had experienced in his own life. If it connects with people who have been fighting their own battles, the film will have been of great benefit, but this isn't to say that there wasn't anything to enjoy the film.

The songs were as bright and poppy as you would expect and of course, you spent most of the scenes trying to work out the location and then letting your mind run riot with your own memories of these locations. Even if the film was just an opportunity for Stuart Murdoch to write a love letter to Glasgow, it was worth putting together.

There is an argument for at least one film set in Glasgow to be released each year. The city gets an awful rap and it can be easy to start taking the sniping and cheap digs to heart. The best part about God Help The Girl, and that includes the soundtrack, is the fact that you get some sort of insight to the Belle & Sebastian world, the other side of Glasgow that doesn't get the attention it deserves.

In 2013, Not Another Happy Ending, a weak-ish rom-com featuring Karen Gillan (and music from TeenCanteen, Twin Atlantic, The Proclaimers and Emile Sande) filled the quota for films that showcased Glasgow in its majestic beauty and in 2014, God Help The Girl more than met the requirements. Hopefully there will be a film for 2015 that provides the sights and sounds of the city with a storyline and characters that have you rooting for them to win.

Moving on from a film with a bunch of characters that I couldn't find anything to love about to a film with a character who has more than earned the love and respect of myself and countless people around the world.

Edwyn Collins has never been to everyone's taste but with Orange Juice and in his second flush of fame in the 90s, he has been a purveyor of high quality pop music. Pop music with a twist, not always cut out for the masses, but on occasions there was an alignment which meant that his take on music sat well with what the mainstream wanted to hear.

Following on from the Glasgow Mixtape day, it's obvious I'm a fan of Edwyn Collins, so this was always going to be a character I was rooting for. Seeing him play at that event reinforced how fragile he looked after his ordeal, but the set also indicated that he was more than capable of putting on a great show. It certainly hasn't been easy for Edwyn to get to this level, and it certainly wasn't easy for his loved ones either.

The film isn't just Edwyn's story; it is as much about his wife and manager Grace Maxwell, and the ordeal she has been through in the past decade.

It isn't an easy film to watch at times, but given the nature of the story, it shouldn't be an easy piece to watch. A more conventional documentary may have been more palatable while still making all of the key points, but the slightly unsettling and cutting in and out is far more effective in pinpointing the confusion and loss that Edwyn and Grace have endured.

It is also a film that looks stunning and as you would expect, the music is as theatrical and as fitting as you could hope for. It's a movie that will mainly be viewed by the converted, by the people who know what Edwyn has endured and where he is today. These people will love it, but it's a movie that deserves a much wider audience, much like the man himself.

A Night At The Karaoke

With Frank Zappa once saying that "Most rock journalism is people who can't write, interviewing people who can't talk, for people who can't read", you wonder what he would have made of karaoke? He probably would have liked it because he was a twisted man but for me, karaoke is a form of torture, perhaps best summed up as "karaoke nights are hosted by people who can't sing, allowing people who really can't sing to perform for people that don't like music."

However, there is no doubt that karaoke is hugely popular with a lot of people putting a great deal of time and effort into these events, with even more people enjoying karaoke events as part of their social calendar. Many bars are delighted to bring in an event for a few hours that ensures punters turn up and spend some cash, so you can see that it is a win:win situation for so many people.

If we take the line that singer songwriter nights are good because they allow people the chance to perform while providing an audience with the musical entertainment they are looking for, it would be wrong to view karaoke in any other light. They both provide a platform for performers, they both help bars to bring in an income and they both provide an excuse for people to come out and socialise with others while enjoying music.

With that in mind, there is a need to think about the karaoke aspect of the music scene in the country at the moment. With X-Factor and similar shows, the dream of being famous for a few minutes is bigger and brighter than ever but even without appearing on the TV show, anyone can have their 3 minutes and 15 seconds in the spotlight by singing at an event like this.

I happen to stay in a flat that is located a couple of floors above a Glasgow bar that is well known for its karaoke events. It's a major reason why I leave the house on a Friday and Saturday night. However, on Friday the 12th of September, I decided to stay in and actually open the windows of my living room, allowing the karaoke performances to trample into my home.

For the evening, I sat bewitched and bewildered by a non-stop flow of people lining themselves up for a small spot of stardom. Given that I couldn't see the performers, it would be like The Voice, judging each performance on the singer and the song as opposed to looks or dancing. Now that I've tried this once, I'm more than willing to welcome Kylie over to my flat one Saturday night if she fancies trying this experiment and then comparing it to her TV show. Given that her time on the show saw Kylie spending her Saturday nights in the company of three questionable judges, spending time in the company of just one moaning musical critic would surely be a step in the right direction for her.

So with the explanations out of the way, onto A Night A The Karaoke.

Friday the 12th of September 2014.

At 8.30pm, and with no fanfare at all, the karaoke event was off and running.

American Pie

"The day the music died." It would be hard to find a lyric that was more fitting for a karaoke session.

It cut out early but it was just a chance for the host to warm her vocals up before giving a brief welcome to the punters that had turned up at this stage.

Mustang Sally

A song with plenty of opportunities to shout and sing in a gravelly voice to indicate that you have soul. The song also provides a bit of interaction for the audience with the backing vocal of "Ride Sally, ride" being jumped on by the attendees that had arrived sharp for the evening's proceedings. The song also provides an opportunity to serve up passive aggressive remarks to any women called Sally.

I Get That Sweetest Feeling

Best known version by Jackie Wilson, this version by Jocky Wilson. (Apologies to Dexys and TOTP for the blatant theft of this gag.)

New Shoes

Paolo is clearly a big favourite in Glasgow and the chorus of this song was well received, with the singer belting it out over the backing of a number of woops and yelps. It was a very different story for the verses though, which were mumbled with the conviction of a child explaining the absence of their homework due to the hungry nature of their dog...when the child doesn't even have a pet.

Everybody's Changing

Keane. Fucking Keane.

Daydream Believer

The original is a classic, an example of song writing brilliance, superb studio skills and then presented to the world by one of the best pop bands ever. Never mind The Monkees, this was grunted out with all the passion of a constipated monkey, easily winning the race to be the most tuneless track of the opening half hour, an accolade which was hopefully acknowledged by the singer buying a round of shots for the entire bar.

I Touch Myself

Good to see the watershed was in play with the baying crowd having to wait until 9pm had passed before they were allowed to join in with a song about frigging themselves off. It's at times like this that not being in the bar and avoiding the no doubt erotic cabaret that was unfolding on the stage was a blessing to be thankful for.

Walking In Memphis

A bizarrely popular song that seems to be a staple of karaoke events and tuneless singers. Maybe it's the reference to Elvis, the King of the Karaoke, taking other people's songs and belting them out with the confidence/arrogance that they belong to him that makes it a hit at these nights. Mind you, with Colonel Tom Parker pulling some tricks and threatening artists, Elvis actually did co-own some of the songs. Not a bad trick when he wrote as much of those classic hits as you or I did. This version leaned heavily on the Cher version, which means it had plenty of warbly bits that are supposed to indicate talent but perhaps suggests that the singer was experiencing the shakes after being without a Blue WKD for more than 2 minutes.

Bad Bad Leroy Brown

If you ever thought that Bad Bad Leroy Brown would be a killer song for whatever X Factor winner rolls off the assembly line, you'd have been in luck. However, you can't imagine "the baddest man in the whole damn town" would be too impressed with having his praises sung over a rinky dink piano fill and swing-style beat. Maybe it was only after he heard this version that Leroy became "became badder than a junkyard dog", because it made me feel like punching someone and it wasn't even about me.

Everybody Hurts

Just to cheer everyone up, up next was REMs all-time classic pop track that never failed to put a smile on your face, Shiny Happy...no wait, no, that would be something you could tolerate hearing on a Friday night. What the audience were subjected to was a no doubt well-meaning but awful sounding version of the band's biggest track. Everybody hurts? Yes, yes they did.

Perfect

"It's got to be perfect." It wasn't but by this point, it was easily the best delivered song so far, the singer instilling the track with a relaxed vibe while actually taking the edge off of some of Eddi's shriller moments. It may have taken close to an hour but there were go, a song that wasn't terrible...perhaps it's time to settle in for the evening and see how this pans out.

Brown Eyed Girl

This is easily a contender for the song I dislike most in the world. It may have been sung brilliantly, I don't know, I took the opportunity to take a comfort break and stick the kettle on (no, it didn't fit). I actually quite like Them but I can't say I've ever taken to any of Van's solo stuff, which obviously leads to comments like "oh you must listen to Astral Weeks, its brilliant." "Nah, it's not", is my standard response. If I stare through a person when saying that it's usually enough to end the conversation but you know what music fans are like, sometimes no is never enough, even when it's all just a matter of opinion. If I had a pound for every time I was I was dragged into a conversation about Van Morrison against my will, I'd have £8...which would actually make me richer than what I am this moment.

That's Life

Given the current suspicion surrounding the BBC in the run up to the referendum and their general historical activities, singing the theme tune to the popular Esther Rantzen TV was a bold move, but the end of song reference to sausages, sang in the style of a talking dog, was a neat touch, bringing the house down with rapturous applause. Back outside my head and in the pub, it was of course the Rat Pack standard That's Life that was being crooned. Again to be fair, this wasn't bad at all and a big step in the right direction after Garbage Van.

Let Me Go

This is a regular favourite in the karaoke bar, belted out by the male compere. Supposedly it's by Gary Barlow. I've absolutely no idea what the original is meant to sound like, probably quite muffled with the sound of Barlow choking on his tax-free millions, but that version is still going to sound better than this. It takes nerve to get up and sing in front of people, so fair play to people that sing at karaoke on a regular basis, but to do it regularly without any singing talent is a feat of such bravery or stupidity that it is hard to comprehend at times. Occasionally breaking off from singing to shout for a bit isn't a mark of talent or soul, it's probably an indicator that you are not all there.

The Wonder Of You

Oh Elvis, there are many things about you and your mystique that make me wonder, not only about you, but about the people that hold you in such high regard. A bit slow paced for the middle of a Friday night out but the performance seemed to be well received.

Rotterdam

A right good sing-along chorus on this one and it did seem to elicit plenty of interaction from the barflies and dwellers. They were never particularly cool or a band you would stick posters on your wall but when it came to decent pop songs, The Beautiful South knew what they were doing. Funnily enough earlier today I found out that most of the original band, apart from Paul Heaton and Jacqui Abbott who are working together, are touring as The South. Clearly there were other components of the group who played their role but you wonder how big an audience there would be to see the rest of the band. It'd be akin to going to see Oasis with neither Noel or Liam on stage.

With Or Without You

A mere few days after U2 and Apple combined to jam the group's new album into people's computers and listening device, here was a step back in time to when people really liked U2. Stadium rock at its best and even if the singer was at his best, a pub wouldn't have been the right setting but at nearly 90 minutes into the evening, the crowd were clearly well refreshed by this point, carrying the backing vocals into the night sky quicker than you can say, "How do I delete this off my iPhone?"

Blanket On The Ground

Now you're talking...a country classic that the Glasgow masses will lap up. Of course it's naff but when you hear the handclaps running throughout the song, you know you're on to a winner with the audience. Probably sung as well as, if not better than, the original, which could be a compliment to the current singer or an insult to the original version. My conscience is clear either way.

Valerie

Whether you refer to The Zutons version or the Amy Winehouse fronted Mark Ronson cover, Valerie is a song that just puts a smile on your face. It is lively, got a great sentiment and the music is brilliant. The fact that this cack-handed and ham-throated version can't totally diminish the joy of the song shows you what a brilliant track it is.

Creep

Kudos to the girl belting this one out as if her life depended on it. Not sure if this is going to be the crowd favourite of the evening, but it would definitely make an excellent TV reality show track, especially with a dedication to Simon Cowell or that creepy looking old Irish guy that is still hanging about the X Factor – Louis, that's him. From Blanket On The Ground To Creep with just one song in between, that's probably a strong point of karaoke, it can touch on a wide variety of music in the course of a short period of time.

I Want That Man

Well, I hope you aren't relying on your vocal skills to win him over. Like using a mallet to open a tin of Campbell's soup, this version absolutely slaughters Debbie Harry's version (and yes, Debbie was calling herself Deborah by this point in her career, but we'll stick with Debbie if that is alright).

Sex On Fire

It seems like a long time ago now but Kings of Leon were really exciting and interesting at one point. I can still remember the drive to T in the Park in the week that the band launched their debut album, blaring it out in the car and looking forward to their early afternoon outdoors slot. It's like a different band now and this song was probably the tipping point, bringing them a new audience and waking the band up to the fact that they could earn a lot more money by being blander.

This wasn't a good version, even compared to X-Factor versions.

That's Amore

When the moon fills the sky....a terrace anthem in Glasgow but here, halfway through the song, the addition of loud backing vocals by what I can only assume was Alvin & The Chipmunks brought the song down to comedy level. Was this used in one of the remake Chipmunk films? If not, it was a bizarre addition which certainly brought a chuckle to me, which was probably not the intention.

Slow Hand

On the day that Nigel Farage came to Glasgow, you could only assume that Slow Hand was played as a tribute to all right wing racists, with Farage no doubt sharing a good few political views with Eric Clapton. Turns out that it wasn't that Slow Hand that was being sung about, it was the Pointer Sisters song, and hopefully there was no reference or tribute to Farage to be found with this track.

Mr Brightside

With this song, the verses are too fast if you are not a clear and confident singer. The choruses were fine and were sung by the audience as much as the designated vocalist but it made for a really uneven song. Glasgow quite likes The Killers don't they? I suppose they are pretty big all across these isles, having played at Wembley..although there have been plenty of bad performances at Wembley of late...and that's just the bands, never mind the English football team! (Play to the crowd, chuck in a dig at the rival every so often and the people love it.) They deserve a kicking for that human or dancer line though...and probably another one for opening up the conundrum of whether you can only be a soldier if you've got soul and then all the other hilarious comparisons that followed. Yes, you have ham but you're not a hamster, aren't you hilarious?

Great Balls Of Fire

Jerry Lee Lewis, another one that belongs in the "for the watching" pile alongside a great number of recording artists, some of whom seem to have escaped without their reputation being tarnished. The only mercy about this song was that it was extremely short.

Words

The Bee Gees, wrote some brilliant songs and they wrote some really bad ones. Up to the disco stuff, including Nights On Broadway and the theme tune to Grease (sung by Frankie

Valli) was pretty good and the stuff after this was pretty bad. This should indicate that Words was decent but this version leaned on to the saccharine Irish cover version (I genuinely couldn't tell you if it was Boyzone or Westlife that sang it, and there's no way I'm having that on my internet search history). The crowd, having put up with more than two hours of music by this point, were getting a bit chatty, drowning out a lot of the singing. Which was nice.

My Way

"I did it my way". No you didn't, you did it the exact same way as everybody else. This song has to go down as the most ironic song of all time, served up by people whose only chance of showing that they have a streak of individuality is to sing a song that indicates they have less originality than A Stars on 45 lp. (How to explain that to the kids, they don't even know what records are let alone the concept of the Stars on 45 collections.)

Does Your Mother Know That Your Out

Aye, she's at the bar getting the cider and sambucca in. Getting close to two and a half hours in and this is the first airing of Abba, that's not too bad for a karaoke evening. And it's the Abba song I dislike least (or like most if you are going to be fussy), so there is a lot in its favour. It's a bad cover version though, from the shiny and shimmering pop of Sweden's finest to the grunted bellowings of a middle aged Glaswegian, this is how not to win a Eurovision.

Basket Case

What in the name of the wee man is this nonsense? Did Busted or McFly ever cover this Green Day song or this is a special karaoke version with a pop sheen to it? "Sometimes I give myself the creeps", oh it's not just you pal, it's not just you.

Try A Little Tenderness

In the right hands, Try A Little Tenderness is a classic song, moving from touching love song to a right good stomper. In the hands of Otis Redding backed up by Booker T & The MGs, it's an excellent song that will last the ages. In the hands of someone who first heard the song when that sweaty Irish lad in The Commitments farted it out, it's anything but tender. Or enjoyable.

Let Me Entertain You

Oh do fuck off. Easily the worst song and worst sung song of the night. So bad it would make you pine for the glory days of the original version, sung by that daft laddie with a ridiculous ego and who missed the heyday of Sunday Night At The Palladium by at least two decades.

The fact that no one seems prepared to step in and stop this atrocity makes it worse, everyone in the bar is as culpable as the "singer" for allowing this to happen. If this was a boxing match, it'd at least be funny because the singer would be getting battered.

I Saw Her Standing There

Aye, and I heard her singing there too unfortunately. The song ultimately gets a pass though for the ludicrously loud and over the top woos. The sort of woos that Little Richard couldn't match, even if he caught himself in his zipper when not paying attention in the toilet.

All These Things I Have Done

The one about the ham and the hamsters. At least the singer seems to understand the nonsensical nature of the song and dispenses with bothering to singing, deciding to bark at the audience as though he had been tied up outside while his owner went in for a quick pint or 7. Awful singing but no doubt the sort of performance that people would have cheered and had a right laugh about.

California Dreamin'

The Mamas and The Papas. Whatever you made of their personalities, they were an amazing vocal talent, creating some of the most intricate and melodically pleasing performances you could ever hope to hear. This is an excellent song and it greatly benefits from not being overplayed like some songs of the era. All subtlety and nuances of the original have been chucked out with this version though, currently in the back of a taxi crying and vowing to never drink again.

Summer Lovin'

Wella, Wella, Wella, ...That's the only good bit of this song. "Tell me more, tell me more", no seriously, everything else was rotten although at least it did allow for a duet, the first one of the evening. There should be more duets at karaoke; it helps to share the blame.

Angels

Oh sod this, we've already had one song by this clown this evening...another comfort break beckons.

Nobody's Perfect

Turns out its by Jessie J. It's an absolute dirge. We're into the final half an hour of the evening and we appear to be limping towards last orders.

Keeping Me Up All Night

Oh right, this is the one when the small cheeky one from Take That tried to imitate the small cheeky one from The Monkees. He failed. This really is a smug song, quite grating too. Now if they had attempted to rip off Randy Scouse Git, that would at least have been interesting. Maybe people have moved on to get the last train or bus before the witching hour, but there has been a notable dip in the energy of the last few songs. That's the demon drink for you; it takes the edge off of your karaoke nights.

Come Fly With Me

"If you could use some exotic booze" – I've got some Tia Maria and a few bottles of that Desperado lager, nae limes though. This is a rabble though; the sound quality had actually been alright for the most of the evening so the garbled mess is all down to the singer as opposed to the sound system with this one.

Dignity

It is now a free for all, like the final song of a night at a major charity event, with loads of folk belting this one out. The mic is being grabbed and pulled like the last Tesco turkey before Christmas but it probably adds a bit of charm to the version. It may lack dignity, but the "gaun yersel hen" notion is coming through loud and proud. An interesting track on the last Friday before the referendum vote, karaoke is not often the place for political insight, but who knows, maybe there is a strong Scottish feeling growing in the bar. Or maybe it was the chance to bellow "set them up again, set them up again, set them up again" at the barmaid before the bell was rung for last orders.

Things Can Only Get Better

Well, they couldn't get much worse. Perhaps mindful of coming out strongly in favour of a Yes vote, the karaoke supergroup now hogging the stage turn to the New Labour classic to ensure that the Yes and the No folk all get a song they can enjoy. It's the sort of fair-mindedness that Glasgow excels at.

Proud Mary

She'll not be feeling too proud when that hangover kicks in. Hmmm, it's the Tina version isn't it? What's wrong with the Creedence version – in fact, every song should be a Creedence version, even if the CCR were nowhere near the original track. Nothing against the Tina version, but when you think about the fact that even though it has a massive change of pace and tempo, it contains no surprise or excitement at all. Still, regardless of the version, there have been tons of worse songs than this one tonight and there's a lot of throats straining to get these lyrics out. There was a need for a bit of energy and up-tempo action needed, and this song certainly delivered.

It was the last song of the evening and while people didn't have to go home, they had to get the hell out of the pub and away from my flat.

Bloc+ Music

In September 2014, there was an album made available for free and shoved in the face of consumers so hard that there was an inevitable backlash against the release. While you may think that getting something for nothing is a good thing, in an industry when many artists are struggling to earn any income, this seemed like an extravagant move made by a major corporation and musicians that really should know better. For everyone that loved the idea and execution of the release, there were just as many people that disliked the idealism or triumphalism that seemed to be present at the time. Yes, it is fair to say that the Bloc+ Music compilation album caused a lot of controversy when it was placed online for free to the general public!

No wait, it was the U2 and iTunes collaboration that caused all the controversy and the Bloc release was actually well received by the people that came across it. It wasn't being shoved in the faces of people, certainly not in the manner that the establishment's Dirty Burger was being shovelled down the throats of hungry patrons, and it showed that free music can be appreciated, but it has to be offered in the right way.

Without being bogged down in the U2 argument, or even giving people the platform to question whether Bono is a big old walloper or not, it is fair to say that many people in and around the music business disliked the idea of a mammoth machine like U2 giving music away freely when so many artists were struggling. Was it fuelled by fears that the album sales would actually be quite low or have U2 accepted that they make their money on the road, and not in record stores or from downloads? The circumstances around this release provide a really interesting topic, one upon which Thom Yorke provided more fuel for the fire by releasing his album via the appropriate gate-keepers on a pay scheme on BitTorrent, and it is a topic that will no doubt be discussed at length for a long time to come.

Some people just don't like U2 and if they handed out a free fiver with every release there would be a grumble about the fact that you could risk a paper cut sticking the money in your wallet, but for some labels and acts, giving music away for free is the most effective way of developing an audience...in the hope of making money in the long run.

The Bloc release provided safety in numbers and if every individual fan of a group got the album and gave it a listen, there was a hope that people would fall for other bands too. As a label, it works perfectly well as a showcase, highlighting the strength of talent that they work with, and for the venue, anything which provides some insight into bands that will likely be playing in the venue soon is never a bad thing. For the punter, they get music for free, so all in all, it is a winning situation for everyone, as long as the music was good?

Was it?

Yes, but of course, with an album of this nature, it is

unlikely that you will like all songs and bands on the release. If you do, tremendous, you have won a watch with the release but in reality, there will be some acts that aren't for you but as long as you can pick up some new artists who you hadn't heard but you like the sound of, this sort of sampler is more than worthwhile.

The sampler gets off to a great start with Vanishing Tanks by Adam Stafford and then takes things even higher with Deathcats. Not to hark back to U2 too often, but fans of the band at their peak (pomp?) would find a couple of things to like about Adam. Don't take that as insult but Vanishing Tanks is a lofty song that has the feeling of a classic track that would find itself easily at home in arenas and outdoor gigs as much as it would in Bloc itself. The percussion adds a more indie and unique feel, steering it away from the overly commercial but even after just one listen, you'll find yourself singing or humming to some of the melodies and even a few of the guitar riffs. If you find yourself wanting to sing along to a guitar riff, you've found a track you're going to come back to on a regular basis!

Deathcats do what they do, proving themselves to be worthy purveyors of uplifting guitar pock and rock and indicating that the label understands the point of a label. It is a chance to introduce people to an act and what they offer. There's no sense in choosing that arty track that is pulled out after 40 minutes of a set, there is a need to showcase a band doing what they love which is certainly something that comes across with Solid.

And "solid" is a great word for the release. From the purposeful march of Basehead by Cutty's Gym (with some excellent basslines and then some highly fuzzed-up guitars) to the frantic power of Not A Cop by Vasa, it's not a release with a consistent musical theme, but there is a good level of consistency of quality.

There are a fair few high quality instrumental passages on the release, with Aches by Verse Metrics appealing to anyone who has ever causally nodded along to a Mogwai track in the past 10 years. The fact that they add some passionate yet understated vocals into the mix only adds to the hint of menace that is contained in the track. Trich by Philadelphia is another great instrumental and by this time, you have to doff your cap to the folk that have selected the music to include on the release. Clearly you need to praise all of the musicians and artists involved for making the music in the first place but pulling together a release of a high standard certainly isn't easy, so you need to give the label its due, and also make sure that you come back to check out what else they have to offer.

Also, the release ends with a song called Generic Clapton, by The Gastric Band, which is an excellent title and a pun so divisive that I'm quite annoyed it had never occurred to me at any point until seeing it on the release.

The second release in the series came out in mid-October, and it had a very different tack from the opening release. This was a punkier, rockier and a lot more angry release, so if you didn't think the bands or genre of the first record was too appealing, the second release offered something greatly different.

It showcases the diversity of the label that they can create full releases around particular genres and a strong point of the release is that on first listen, it comes across as a solid and cohesive album. I think this is down to the fact that the biggest moments are of a similar nature but it's a record that opens up a lot more on first release. I was all for labelling it a straightforward collection of that angry and angsty punk that has been around for the past 10 years or so, but it's a lot more evolved than that, a lot more.

With Felix Champion and So Many Animal Calls getting the release off to a strong start, these songs have genuine punch the air choruses that would do well in decent sized venues across Glasgow and beyond, and while the success of Biffy or Twin Atlantic may be too big to emulate, these acts should be able to pick up a proportion of that fanbase.

Some Hate It Hot by Bianca isn't as punchy or in your face as the opening two tracks, which means it may pass you by on first listen but give the release a couple of listens and it starts to unfold beautifully in front of you. It has an understated use of melody, which is always a good thing, and quite refreshing considering the songs it comes after. Algernon Doll, with Justine, builds back towards the nature of the opening two songs, bridging back into a heavier style of music for the next couple of songs.

It's not really something I'd spend a lot of time listening to, the vocals of bands like Stonethrower or Bright Side do nothing for me, leaving me to think the singer just needs a good coughing session and he'll be as right as rain, but clearly there are plenty of fans and followers for this style of music. A lot of the music was pretty decent though (the guitar licks from Bright Side are very well suited to the song) and Without A Whimper by Get It Together features some really sprightly fills and runs in the second half, with an American 80s rock vibe perhaps standing out against some of the heavier moments on the release.

The Sinking Feeling are slightly reminiscent of Idlewild when they got angry, A Sudden Burst of Colour served up an instrumental that wouldn't have been of place on the previous release and Min Diesel sees this release, like the first one, ending on a bit of a pun. Which I always approve of, so that's great news, but it's actually a very likeable song, having a bit of relaxed Pavement style guitar lines taking you to an end of a release is never a bad thing.

In early November 2014, with deadlines for this book being dismissed like a request for another pint after last orders, the third part of the Bloc Ensemble was released. You don't need too long (not even the full running order of its 13 minutes and 17 seconds) to recognize the brilliance of Gustav Björnstrand by The Cosmic Dead, a hypnotic psychedelic wonder that by virtue of its length and power becomes the focal point of the record. It isn't the only great moment on the release though, far from it, and The Cherry Wave offer up Melt which will also ensure your hearing is impaired for a number of days (in a good way). 2014 has been a decent year for shoegaze lovers and anyone that is venturing back or uncovering this style of music for the first time will find a lot to like about this track, and this band.

The Shithawks take it back even further, capturing a bit of the Suicide sound before venturing off into a punkier/garage rock style. It's pretty chaotic but that is where its charm lies.

The third release, on initial listen, is more varied than the previous two, but there is a thread of outsider noisy rock tying it all together.

When you take on board the diversity of the releases, without any diminishing of the overall quality, you really need to doff your cap to Bloc+ and their work this year. As a compliment, I'd compare the releases to the monthly CDs that Mojo used to give away as an introduction to different musical genres. Back in 2003, the magazine gave away Instant Garage and then Roots Of Hip Hop, following it up with Raw Soul and Blues Power the following year. These were carefully curated free CDs that gave you a fantastic introduction to the origins of certain musical genres, and the Bloc+ releases come across as being as definitive and painstakingly put together. Maybe the label has just got really lucky, but you get the feeling that there is a hell of a lot of work and effort gone into the releases and I can only hope that they keep on coming.

Tenement Trail 2014

It takes a lot of hard work and effort to put together and promote one night with a couple of bands so you have to be mad to arrange an all-day event across 5 venues and more than 30 acts. Then again, when you have enjoyed the sort of run that TenementTV has in 2014, you probably think that you can turn your hand to anything.

The latest Tenement Trail was a resounding success and the fact that the reviews that are tumbling forward of the event is showcasing so many different acts indicates the strength in depth of the line-up. Some people will have been unhappy about some of the clashes over the course of the day, which is unavoidable for any music event of this nature, but it's far better to focus on the qualities and positive elements of the event, of which there were many.

Vladimir

It wasn't even 4pm and Vladimir set up a dark and

atmospheric set that was almost a set of two halfs. The first half of the set featured a number of slow builds but the cover of Born Slippy was the turning point with the second half of the set being faster and, if possible, louder. I'd caught Vladimir in the same venue back in the Spring and the band seemed a lot more confident and on form at this point. The early start didn't spook them and the venue was far busier for this show than their previous Broadcast performance, which probably pushed them to a higher level.

Deathcats

With songs about poppers and feelings of tiredness from being up about silly o'clock to Skype your girlfriend in New Zealand, Deathcats certainly have a rather unique feel about them. Musically, they were excellent, delivering the sort of deliberate that would be horrific in the wrong hands but comes across as fresh and daring here. As the band stated themselves, it was an early stage time, but there was a big crowd and it was a set that would have graced any evening down in Sleazys.

You'll also find that the Deathcats deliver quite enjoyable chat from the stage so if you are looking for a chaotic and enjoyable evening out, looking out for this name of the gig listings will provide you with plenty to look forward to. When you have the guitarist jumping into the crowd before 5pm, you know that you're watching a band that doesn't bother with conforming to the standard rules and expectations.

Blood Indians

Three bands in and two of them were hailing from Dundee, the East Coast was threatening to take over the West. As you would expect, a lot of the same faces from the Vladimir gig, on and off stage, were present in Flat 0/1 for the show and with the greyness of the day rolling in through the window, the Blood Indians set was good, although perhaps a little bit subdued.

The band were hampered with a sound that didn't quite seem cut out for them, although the last song of the set was treated to a lush production which managed to work quite well. Even from a set that didn't seem to have the best sound on offer, it was fairly obvious that Blood Indians have got a number of good songs in their arsenal, which means that they'll be worth returning to at a later date.

Whether that is in Flat 0/1 remains to be seen though! In fairness to the venue, they had Joker IPA on tap, which is always a welcome sight but upon asking for a cider for one of our party, seeing a pint being poured from a 3 litre bottle of Frosty Jacks was a bit unsettling! I think it's been at least half my lifetime since I had gotten that close to a Frosty Jack and even at that it was never explored without the addition of some blackcurrant. Still, it wasn't for me, I had my Joker so I was alright (Frosty) Jack, so I simple passed over to the pint tumbler to the cider drinker and let chaos commence. I believe the recipient got their revenge on me later on in the same venue when they bought me a sambucca. I also ordered a round of Mad Dog but that was just for fun.

TeenCanteen

After what had been a pretty raucous afternoon and early evening so far, it was good to take things a little bit easier with TeenCanteen in Broadcast. The girls have been quietly developing a positive buzz in recent times and their short set suggested that they have a lot in their favour.

Honey remains as fresh and as exciting (while still feeling like a song you have known for years) as it did on first listen and the set closer, Sirens, could quite possibly have been the strongest song of the set, which was promising since it was billed as a new track.

There is probably something to be said for some of the songs having stronger lyrics but then again, with the melodies and harmonies offering a sweet girl-group vibe, it may be that the lyrics blend in perfectly well with the overall mood and feel of the songs. That will be something for individuals to make their mind up on but if you're looking for a band that will offer you plenty of reasons to smile and be carried away with their music, TeenCanteen are an excellent choice.

Tijuana Bibles

Switching to the ABC2, while the Buzzcocks were limbering up upstairs in the main venue, certainly took the event to a higher level. From the minute the Tijuana Bibles walked on stage, there was a notable step-up with respect to stage presence and professionalism. Not to say that the previous bands were poor, but they were all acts that felt like they were on the way up and still looking to make their mark. The Tijuana Bibles walked on stage as if they were ready to play in a stadium.

I personally would have liked a few more choruses and a bit more substance from the group but with others in our circle proclaiming them to be the act of the day (by a good distance), they clearly did something right. A well-populated ABC2 agreed with that opinion and there is no doubt that Tijuana Bibles have the swagger and power to reach out to a much larger audience so you'll likely hear a lot more from them.

Vukovi

With Hella Good by No Doubt blaring out over the PA before the band took to the stage, you probably had an inkling of what was about to occur. Vukovi delivered an all-out assault with plenty of energy and excitement and if there was one complaint about the set, it was the fact that it flew by too quickly. Not saying that this style of music was completely my thing, but I'd have liked to have heard a good bit more of it to make up my mind about it all.

After having seen a lot of straightforward rock and roll bands during the day, it was good to see someone mixing it up a bit and the energy shown on stage was a big side-step from some of the bands had been on earlier. Not in any better or worse way, just different. It wasn't all rock and roll though because in between lead singer's Janine Shilstone breathless performance, she did ask for permission before clambering up on amps at the side of the stage. Sometimes rock n roll is missing a bit of politeness so that was good to see in amongst the madness of the rest of the gig.

Vukovi aren't a band that have had to seek out their

troubles but it looks as though they're on a bit of a roll now and they've definitely got the sort of sound and style that could take them over the top with a big audience. The thing is, if the music goes over the top, the band members will likely be right behind them, jumping in for a bit of a crowd surf!

After all that energy, we took a brief detour via Palomino on Bath Street to say hi to some birthday revellers. They had Williams Bros. on draught and they had the Beach Boys and Teenage Fanclub on the stereo, I was fairly happy about that! There wasn't much time to linger though and it was back into the flat...

Campfires In Winter

At this point of the evening, you are looking for something to shake you up a little bit to keep you going through to the end of the evening and Campfires in Winter certainly delivered. They may look like quiet and unassuming lads but by god they can make a racket. Recent single We Exist was casually placed into the early run of the set but the whole set was strong and my ears are still ringing from their show.

The contrast between themselves and Vukovi couldn't have been starker but both were great in their own way. The Campfires lads showed that you don't need to bounce around to create a level of energy and the intensity was slightly at odds with the laidback and cosy surroundings that Flat 0/1 suggests. With a touch of red lighting there was a suitable tint applied and as we raced to the end of Saturday, the best set, on a day of excellent sets, was put together. If you haven't checked them out, you should get on board with their post-rocking ways.

Atom Tree

The night was going to roll on for a few hours more in Flat 0/1 with Atom Tree technically being the start of after-party before the DJs got a hold of things. The venue was starting to get quite crammed and a delay to the start time meant that I never really caught much of Atom Tree as we were moving on to meet up with other folk. The two songs I did catch sounded good, and from what I heard of them beforehand meant that I'm sure the set would have carried on in the same vein but sadly that will have to wait until another time.

And the same can be said for the Tenement Trail but from the feedback on the day and on social media since then, there is certainly going to be the demand for another one. That was 7 full sets I caught over the day and enjoyed every one of them. Everyone has their own approach for these sort of events and while some folk prefer to jump in and out seeing as many snippets of acts as possible, I prefer full sets and just having to accept the fact that you miss some brilliant bands. I even missed out on one of the venues, not making it to Tuts, meaning that my bingo card wasn't complete...but not to worry, there's always the Tenement Trail 2015 to give it another go.

The Big Names Come To Town

Given that there were plenty of eyes on Scotland in 2014, it was understandable that some big names and brands wanted a piece of the action. Radio 1 and MTV are no longer the taste-makers with respect to breaking new bands that they were a decade or two ago but they clearly still want to appeal to as many people as possible. MTV has the sponsors and advertisers to keep satisfied and Radio 1, well, who knows why they're still scampering around but they are.

Radio 1 was the first off the mark with respect to making their way up north and they decided to bring their Big Weekend with them. The event would be staged over 3 days, the first night being a dance music orientated evening in George Square while the Saturday and Sunday would feature artists playing across three stages in Glasgow Green.

Events like this which are mainly free (apart from a small booking fee) will always see demand outstripping supply and there is no ideal way to meet the needs of the public. From Facebook, there did seem to be a strong local audience, and there are steps taken to ensure that a sizable proportion of local fans get their hands on the tickets. You may not like all of the acts on the bill but having the chance to see artists such as Coldplay, Katy Perry, Calvin Harris, Paolo Nutini and Pharrell Williams after only paying a booking fee is a positive thing for most music fans. These are all artists that charge a premium price for their shows so the fact that there was an opportunity (for those who were lucky in the ballot) to see them for very little is definitely a good thing.

It wasn't really an event that appealed to me but then again, Radio 1 isn't for me. Acts like the 1975, The Vamps, and Bastille hold absolutely no interest to me but they are clearly commercial acts that have a big audience and hopefully some people will have seen them perform and then develop a taste for seeing live bands. If events like Radio 1 Big Weekend act as a gateway to other live music events, the whole industry can be a winner, even if it is primarily set up for listening figures, red button content and shifting units for the major labels.

There were positive and negative elements to the event. Up and coming local bands like Honeyblood, Algernon Doll and Model Aeroplanes all had the chance to play in front of a new audience and hopefully pick up some experience and exposure. Chvrches continued their attempts to get in front of as many people as possible and the appearance of acts like Paolo and Calvin showed again that Scotland is capable of making music that a great number of people want to hear.

It is not as if it was all good news though. The fact that the second stage was titled the "In New Music We Trust" stage and yet featured Example and Kasabian as headliners would make you question how much trust the station puts in new music but that is a gripe for another day. Still though, with 60,000 weekend tickets being snapped up in next to no time, it was a weekend that many people will remember for many years to come.

That event was the second time the Radio 1 Big Weekend (or whatever variant of it was organised) has been held in Scotland while in November, the MTV European Music Awards returned to Scotland for a second time. Back in 2003, the event was held in Leith while The Hydro was the setting for the 2014 event. This event was further justification for the building of the Hydro, giving Glasgow a venue that could hold this sort of event with ease.

Perhaps mindful of fitting in with the city, the event was hosted by a bold woman that is more than happy to speak her mind, who loves to swear and who is proud of her curves and appearance. They could have picked any number of females out of the nightclub queues on a Saturday night in the city to fit this role but MTV decided to play it safe and bring in a professional for the job. This meant that Nicki Minaj was the host for the Hydro event.

As you would expect, there were a host of big names on the bill with acts like Minaj, U2, Coldplay, Royal Blood performing and appearances by acts like Ozzy Osbourne and Taylor Swift. Perhaps the organisers thought they were listing a Scottish act to perform in Ed Sheeran but of course, Ed's hair colour is just a ruse to try and obtain him more sales north of the border. With that in mind, it was left to Calvin Harris to fly the flag for Scotland. Harris was lined up to perform at the event and was also nominated in the Best Electronic and Best UK/Ireland act. You may also think that a band with the name of 5 Seconds of Summer hail from Scotland but I'm reliably informed that the boy band actually hails from Australia. 5 seconds? They get around 5 months of summer down there, that name is just rubbing it in!

One strange thing to have arisen in the build-up to the event was the MTV Music Week, which was being billed as a specially programmed series of gigs and clubs in the run-up to the MTV Awards. It was actually MTV jumping in and re-branding a number of gigs that had been arranged to take place in Glasgow. It's pretty obvious that no matter week you arrive in Glasgow, you will likely find a range of gigs on offer. This particular week saw MTV Europe claiming gigs by Chvrches at the Barrowlands (although only the first of 2 nights), La Roux at ABC, 2 Bears at King Tuts, Circa Waves at Oran Mor, a Colours Special and then Trevor Nelson at the ABC as part of their own line-up.

They did however line up a special gig, which more than

made up for the shameless piggy-backing they did with the other shows. Putting Biffy Clyro on the same bill as Slash in the Glasgow Academy is a night that will greatly appeal to fans of the acts, rockers and folk that enjoy a good night out. It was also good to see that Biffy were able to allocate a portion of tickets for their existing fanbase but much like Biffy's Barrowlands shows, demand greatly outstripped the supply of tickets.

Those We Have Lost

Robert Young

When someone is universally known for being rock n roll, their passing will always come as a bit of a shock. Robert 'Throb' Young may have been absent from Primal Scream since 2006 but the news of his death in September was a blow for music lovers around the world. At 49 years old, Throb was of no age and the fact that it appears he was starting to take an interest in making music again only makes the loss even harsher to take.

For music fans, Throb made a massive impact. He had a fantastic look and he could play guitar with the best of them. Then there were the interviews and editorial pieces, all giving the impression that this was a guy that could out party the rest of the band, no slouches in that department. Primal Scream were a good time band, a party group and Throb seemed the ring-leader in that regard.

Of course, the hushed talk about his departure of the band and the demons he was battling at the time makes you look back on the days with a slightly different tinge but his death was a shock. Social media is not always the best place to be, especially after someone famous or in the public eye passes away, but after the initial shock about Throb's death, social media allowed for the sharing of so many great stories. As I said, Throb had a big impact on music fans with his larger than life persona but it was great to see that he had as much, if not a bigger, impact on so many people around him. These weren't the standard platitudes served up after someone passes away; these were tales of people talking about a genuine warmth and friendship over decades.

A nickname like Throb may have all been part of the mythology of Robert Young and indeed Primal Scream, but although his passing was sad, it was touching to read so many personal and uplifting tributes to the guitarist.

While Throb was the biggest casualty of the year in Scottish music (at least to the point of printing), he wasn't the only loss.

Jack Bruce

The passing of Jack Bruce on the 25th of October was a low point of the year. Bruce was an immensely talented bassist and whether he was making music that would be found at the top of the charts or was created for a more specialist audience, the Bishopbriggs born bassist was regularly found performing at a high level.

Bruce suffered a period of ill health back in 2003 when he was diagnosed with liver cancer and after undergoing a liver transplant in the same year, he was close to death as his body rejected the organ. Thankfully he recovered, appearing in 2004 to perform Sunshine Of Your Love at a Rock Legends gig in Germany before Cream reunited for London and New York shows in 2005.

Before 2010, Bruce had been commemorated by the Royal Scottish Academy Of Music And Drama and Glasgow Caledonian University. These were timely acknowledgments for the tremendous body of work created by Bruce and it is likely that many more tributes will be made to him in the years to come. With over 50 years in the music industry, Jack Bruce created a legacy that will live on for generations but with the riff of Sunshine Of Your Love Alone, he is assured of a place in music history.

George Donaldson

He may not be a name that everyone knows but the loss of George Donaldson in March 2014 was one that was felt with a heavy heart by many people. Best known in Glasgow under title of "Big George" (admittedly he wasn't the only Big George performing in the town), George was a big hit in bars such as Jinty McGinty's and the Tollbooth regularly playing in these intimate bars when his schedule allowed.

This is because George had a whole other career as part of the massive Celtic Thunder group, a huge production performing Celtic tinged folk and poppy classics to a massive fanbase around the world. There probably aren't too many people that had The Tollbooth and The White House on their performance CV but George did, performing for President Obama at a St Patrick Day's celebration. The fact that he was as comfortable performing to such prestigious company and in arenas in stage productions that rivalled the biggest musicals as he was armed with just his guitar, his wit and his talent in some low key Glasgow bars indicated that George was an immensely talented man. I was fortunate enough to know George and his family well, George's mother was my God-Mother, and you couldn't hope to meet a nicer family.

When you add in the tragic news about Malcolm Young, there has been a fair bit of sadness to go hand in hand with a lot of joy and celebration in the Scottish music scene of 2014.

3: Take Me Out

There is a real passion for live music and socialising in Scotland, but it would be wrong to say that this was just a modern phenomenon. In fact, there are some historians who would argue that the social activities of some of the people of today are tamer than previous generations. There has long been a desire for Scottish people to head out for an evening and find a way of escaping from their daily routine, with live bands and music being part of the tapestry of entertainment that has helped to shape Scottish life.

The era of the Music Hall in Britain started in the mid-1800s when the competition level between bars reached a point that there was a need to draw in punters and then retain them. It was no longer enough just to offer alcohol; pubs that were thriving were now serving up food and entertainment. Singers and comedians may have been the prominent acts on stage, but there was scope for all manner of variety acts and performers, making stars in many local areas. These stars developed their own audience, their name guaranteeing more people coming through the door, with an increasing number of venues offering the performances in a separate room, where a fee was required to gain entry to the event. The phenomenon of music hall may have started off in London, but it was welcomed all across the country with Scotland taking to this style of performance in a big way.

Of all the Scottish towns and cities that took to Music Hall, Glasgow took to it the most, and this is said to be down to the fact that the city had a dense population. Now, this can be taken as an insult or a statement of fact, but getting away from the drudgery of working life was a big factor in why this form of entertainment took off in a serious manner in the city.

Although the Barrowlands is regarded as one of the best loved venues in the country and is known all over the world, there is an argument that it isn't even the most important venue in the local area. There will be plenty of historians who will point to the Britannia Music Hall (or the Panopticon or the Britannia Panopticon, depending on what you want to call it) in the Trongate as being the Glasgow venue that should be hailed above all others.

The hall was built in 1857 and it claims to be the oldest surviving music hall in the entire world. The venue was a place where Glaswegians would attend to escape the monotony and humdrum of their everyday life, but the venue is well known for being the venue where Stan Laurel made his debut performance on stage. This took place in 1906 on an amateur night. Given the audience's preference for relieving themselves where they stood as opposed to climbing down the stairs to find a toilet, perhaps the venue can claim to be the place where Stan said "this is a not very nice mess you've got me into"! It was also in 1906 that the hall was bought over and the name of the venue was changed to the Panopticon.

There were big changes brought in with the change of owner. A freak show was installed, akin to people paying good money to see Future Islands after their career defining performance on the David Letterman show, a waxwork section was introduced and there was a rooftop carnival put in place. That is exactly what Glasgow needs, more rooftop exhibitions. There was also the introduction of an indoor zoo, a feature that is kept alive today all across the city centre in a wide range of bars, pubs and nightclubs.

The Panopticon can also claim to be one of the first ever Glasgow buildings to have electricity and it was also one of the first ever cinemas in Scotland. The venue stopped being used as an entertainment venue in 1938 when a tailoring firm took over and converted the building into a warehouse. In the present day, the building is being looked after by a Trust who have restored the spirit, if not thankfully all of the elements, of the original music hall.

While the Music Hall era was a short-lived, but very popular one in Glasgow, the fact that the venue also served as a cinema was important. This is because Glasgow, and indeed the whole of Scotland, threw themselves into cinema and the escapism that goes with it. Many of the music hall acts wowed audiences by providing songs and entertainment packed full of local references but with the advent of motion pictures, there was a whole new world opening up and

Scottish folk jumped on...after a while.

The first show of cinematography in Scotland is said to have taken place at the Empire Palace Theatre in Edinburgh (where the Festival Theatre now sits) in 1896. It seems as though the initial run was not a success but after the Great War, Scotland fell in love with the cinemas with new buildings, including some of the grandest venues you could ever hope to see, springing up across the country. There were cinemas being built in virtually every small community and at one point, Edinburgh alone had more than 40 cinemas. In Glasgow, there was a similar level of excitement with people of all ages flocking to the cinema.

Eventually, the golden age of cinema would diminish, usurped by TV, but there was an era when going to the cinema was as common a part of life as brushing your teeth or changing your socks. Again, feel free to add in your own joke about how regularly these acts did or didn't happen across the country. While there is still a high demand for cinema in Scotland, one of the biggest legacies of this era can be found in the stunning venues that were created to meet the demand for movie lovers. Sadly, many of these buildings are now demolished, consigned to the history books, old photographs and memory banks of those who knew that you could see a film by handing over a jam jar or two. Thankfully though, there are still many examples of great Art-Deco constructions and a number of these venues (perhaps via a slight detour as a bingo hall) are now the gig venues of the modern day.

Live bands and dances were also a popular activity for many people during and after the golden era of cinema. The dance events were the perfect opportunity to meet a new beau or partner and after you had swept them off their feet/been swept off of your feet, the cinema would be the next step in cementing the relationship. This flow was at the heart of life for many Scottish people, which is why so there are so many strong memories of these events and of the buildings that housed them. Many of the buildings looked fantastic, but it was the events and situations that transpired within the buildings that meant the most to people. There was an awful lot of love stories created and ended in these places and when it comes to mapping the story of a person's life, these are the elements that carry the most weight.

Of course, when it comes to entertainment and the aspect that many Scottish people fell in love with, there is an obvious activity that springs to mind.

The topic of how football fans have shaped and been shaped by the Scottish psyche is the subject for another book (by another author), and it would be wrong to dwell on the topic too much here. Football has an almighty ability to derail virtually every other topic in Scotland so the football chat will be kept to a minimum. What can't be denied though is that the Scottish people have a massive passion for football and this ties in with the enthusiasm and intensity they have shown in going to gigs, the movies, dancehalls and any other activity that comes to the fore as a diversion from everyday life. This is a country that bought into roller skating in a big way; we'll jump on anything if it provides some respite from everyday life!

The attendance of 149,415 for a Scotland versus England match at Hampden in 1937 is recorded as being the second largest football attendance ever (beaten out by a reported crowd of over 180,000 in Brazil for a game against Paraguay). The Hampden match, therefore, holds the European record for attendance figures and the huge passion held for the game in Scotland is shown by the fact that the Scottish Cup final held at Hampden a week later (between Celtic and Aberdeen) attracted a crowd of 146,433, which is the biggest attendance for a club match in Europe. In the space of two Saturdays, close to 300,000 people descended upon the south side of Glasgow to watch football.

The record attendance of a UEFA football match belongs to Glasgow, with the 1970 European Cup Semi-final second leg between Celtic and Leeds United attracting a crowd of 136,505. The record attendance of Ibrox stands at 118,567 which is the British record for a league match. These attendance records are very unlikely to be broken which means that the enthusiasm that Scotland holds for watching football will never be beaten. Another huge night came when both Celtic and Rangers were playing in European semi-finals on the same night in the same city. More than 155,000 people packed the terraces at the two grounds even though both games were being shown live on terrestrial television.

Outside of Glasgow, the attendances may not have been as big but that doesn't mean that the passion and enthusiasm for football weren't the same. All across the country, folk would escape from the pressure of work and family life by making their way to a football stadium. There was not the same opportunity to see live games on TV back then as there is today and folk flocked to games in huge numbers.

When it comes to football crowds, a lot of people will be po-faced and debate whether people are going along for the football or for other reasons. Such is life in Scotland, but it would be a fair assessment to say that not everyone went along just for the football. However, this is down to the fact that attending football match for many folks was, and indeed still is, a social thing providing something to do with your friends. A football match, much like a concert, provides a reason for people to get out of the house or be around their friends. There is an opportunity to be at the heart of something, hopefully something which will provide an opportunity to say "I was there" in later conversations. Okay, not everyone who attends these events remembers everything about them but these events have their own appeal that goes way beyond what is actually unfolding in front of the audience.

So, given the way that Scottish people love social activities and being part of something, there should be no surprise at the way that the people of Scotland fell for music, and live performances, in such a big way.

Live music has always been popular but in the past two decades, there has been an increase in the demand for and provision of live events. You may not admire the music or the legacy of the Britpop era but a number of the acts were hugely instrumental in creating a buzz and energy about going to concerts again. There was a sense of excitement from their music and the way that this movement grew alongside the unfortunate element of lad culture meant that going to gigs became more of a social and communal thing.

That element, combined with other factors, including the huge popularity of T in the Park, has helped to create the situation where gigs are a great night out. Of course, as with many other social activities, the price of gigs for established acts or in certain venues has increased drastically. This has had an impact in two different ways.

In one way, it has forced the gig into being more of a special event. This means that there are more people willing to make more of an occasion of these gigs, commonly adding a meal in beforehand and perhaps even making a night out of it afterwards, whereas they wouldn't have previously. With Noel Gallagher playing at the Hydro in March 2015 with standing tickets on sale for £60, it's a very long way from the time punters saw Oasis play twice at the Barrowlands in December of 1994 for less than a tenner. Of course, Noel, his management team and the promoters know that there will always be idiots and mugs who will hit the buy button before they properly think about the price (hello!)

The other outcome is where smaller bands are selling more tickets and pushing themselves up to a higher level with respect to venues and audience sizes. In the latter few months of 2014, both The Vigo Thieves and The La Fontaines were lined up to play the ABC in Glasgow. The main hall in the venue has a capacity of around 1,360 people, so you have to say fair play to both of these bands for being placed in a venue where they can be considered as a viable act. Neither of these acts offer anything positive for me, especially The La Fontaines, but it's clear that they have developed a local-ish audience that can be expanded upon. Whether it is a night to drag out all of the friends, extended family and associates or it is a great excuse for fans to drag their mates along to a gig, it's clear that local bands and emerging bands are playing at much larger stages than what they would have been in the past.

When looking at the history of the great venues in Scotland, it is not just the performers and the crowd engagement that standout, there are other elements too, and this ties into a slightly darker element of Scottish life. The

Britannia Music Hall is famous in the entertainment history of Glasgow, but it is also a venue known for being a place where people would urinate where they stood, so in that respect, it is not dissimilar from many of the major outdoor festivals or music events that have taken place in Scotland over the years! Anyone who attended the Oasis gig at Loch Lomond back in 1996 will quickly agree that the decision to hold a gig in a setting with plenty of trees wasn't the best decision. This was just before (and perhaps a factor in) the introduction of urinal troughs for men at these major music events. That made a massive difference and everyone benefited.

It is easy to say that the average Scottish male has his faults, particularly when alcohol is involved. The inability to control your bladder affects some men in the same fashion that other men find that they are unable to control their temper or their tongue. It would be wrong to say this about all men and it would be wrong to say that it was only men who were affected by this sort of behaviour.

Even the Scottish females have a chequered history with this sort of behaviour at Scottish gigs over the years. From the girls who struggled to contain themselves when faced with The Beatles and other fresh-faced pop acts of the day to the modern day women, enjoying a group day out seeing acts like Take That or Bon Jovi at Hampden, Murrayfield and other large venues and arenas, trouble can come from both genders. Anyone that seriously believes that raucous, drunken and sometimes questionable behaviour is the sole premise of Scottish men has never been close to any of these major events.

Of course, the vast, vast majority of people attending these major events are well behaved and pretty much keep themselves to themselves but all it takes is one or two small groups and you can feel as though the event is over-run with folk you don't want to socialise with. It isn't the mild-mannered folk chatting normally that you remember from these events, it is the girl who was taking a pee behind a van only for the van to move or the guy who had such a heavy weekend it made Easy Lionel look like someone nervously starting their first day of work. This means if we see things we don't like; there can be a tendency to overstate their impact.

In Scotland, we've got a tendency to enjoy life and ourselves. This means we go to big events, we like to socialise and drink (and enjoy other recreational activities), with all of the additional elements playing a role in our overall sense of fun and enjoyment. It is not as though this is just about Scottish music fans, this is a problem that the country is trying to come to terms with.

It may not make easy reading, but the statistics outlined on the SHAAP, the Scottish Health Action on Alcohol Problem; site should make for some sobering reading. For all of the people who have been accused of homicide in Scotland over the last 10 years, alcohol has been a contributing factor in half of these cases. There are estimations that 65,000 children in the country live with a parent who has a problem with alcohol. This means that our problems are being passed down from generation to generation with many youngsters resigning themselves to suffering from the same fate that has marred the life of their parents. Estimations suggest that 25% of the children who have been placed on the register for Child Protection are there because of issues with alcohol or drug misuse. It is also believed that around 33% of all divorces cite a partner's excessive levels of drinking as a contributory factor.

One of the best things about the political debate in Scotland in 2014 was that there has been a greater level of maturity in discussion about the debate and what needs to be done to take Scotland forward, regardless of the outcome. There needs to be a focus on the alcohol problem in the country.

For many people, the debate and discussion about the Independence Referendum came down to numbers. People were mainly looking for the bottom line and one of the most regular questions was "How much will it all cost us?" Given that it was only possible to make projections on the costs after a Yes or No vote, it was possible and beneficial for the opposing side to shoot down the costs, leaving people none the wiser. However, there are some costs that can be stated with a strong level of certainty, and that is how much alcohol misuse costs Scotland.

•   Over £800m every year is cost in reduced productivity and output, including lost working days and absenteeism related to alcoholism.

•   The cost to NHS services in treating people with alcohol related issues is over £400m per year

•   Alcohol misuse drains £170m from social work services every year

•   There is also said to be a cost of around £385 for the emergency services and criminal justice

These figures alone should be enough to stop people in their tracks, but one of the biggest issues about alcohol misuse is that it impacts on people, in a way, where no cost can be realistically placed. This doesn't mean that there is no cost, often the opposite, but it makes it a lot harder to state how bad this is.

And yet, I know all of these figures, I know of the health issues and I know how unproductive I can be the day after a good few drinks. As a freelance writer, if you're not working, you are not making money so you really need to make sure that you are on the ball as often as you can. Even with all that knowledge though, if I was at a gig or back in the pub after being at the match, I'd feel my right hand was missing something if there wasn't a pint in it. It's not as though I am alone in this, put some people in a social situation and their mind will instantly think of alcohol as if Pavlov's dog was trained to enjoy a good swally at the ringing of a bell.

There is no doubt that a couple of drinks can relax people, it can help them to express themselves more confidently, it can put people in a better mood and it can generally improve the atmosphere if you are socialising. The people who would hum and haw, if you're lucky, through the first hour of a gathering or event are transformed into the life and soul of an event thanks to a couple of drinks. You can see why people think this will be a good mood to be in if you are going to an event.

If you're paying a lot of money for an evening, you want to

be as receptive to the show as possible, and if a couple of drinks means you will be relaxed and in the mood for an evening of music and entertainment, then what's the harm? The harm comes in the overstepping of the line, when the impact and the influence of alcohol stop being a positive influence and start to become a bad influence. For some people, this never comes, they know their limits and they always stay on the right side of enjoying a drink without ruining a night-out. For other people, the level changes. The nature of alcohol and the way it reacts in the body mean that you don't necessarily react to the same level of alcohol, in the same way, every time you take it. There are other factors involved with the impact that alcohol has on you, which means that a level that has been perfectly fine 7 or 8 times may be too much for you on the 9th time. There are also people who don't care about their limit and actively go beyond this point because they believe that this is the best condition to enjoy a gig.

The fact that everyone is different and that different responses occur means that there will never be agreement on what is right and wrong about alcohol use and misuse. There will also be people who will oppose any movement to temper alcohol misuse on a personal rights and freedom angle, as opposed to actively wanting to ensure people can drink as much as they want. There is definitely need for a change though, and there will need to be a change to Scotland's attitude to alcohol.

Amidst all of the other comments, promises and remarks that Alex Salmond made in 2014, the line that made reference to Scotland being "a nation of drunks" was one that caught a great deal of attention. As with any sound bite, taking the line at face value and with no context makes it sound really bad and gave people opposed to Salmond something new to rail against. It even brought a negative response from many people who would normally be supportive of the First Minister.

The worrying thing is how to properly and effectively broach the issue of Scotland's alcohol problem. Sure many of us like to take a wee drink now and again, some of us like to take a big drink on a far more regular basis and no matter what decision is taken on alcohol pricing, availability and promotion, some people will feel rightly aggrieved that their civil liberties are being impinged upon.

I'd much prefer a First Minister facing up to the fact that there is a growing alcohol problem in Scotland rather than denying it or blaming it on other factors. While I'm not entirely supportive of The Alcohol (Minimum Pricing) (Scotland) Act 2012, I do appreciate that something has to be done to change matters. However, there are also plenty of occasions where I feel as though the Scottish Government has shied away from their supposed tough stance on alcohol. One example is the Offensive Behaviour of Football Fans Act. Blaming football fans is an easy target, a way to rush through needless powers that will provide the Police Force with more overtime and a general raising of the fear and blame culture in society. The Tory Government in the UK in the 1980s knew that they could attack football fans while their class-colleagues in the media would support them and shamefully, the Scottish Government has acted in a similar fashion in recent years.

Scotland, while being a fantastic country, has its problems and there is a need to strike hard at sectarianism, violence and domestic violence that runs throughout the country. Alcohol goes hand in hand with all of these aspects and there is definitely a need to focus on the individual element and the multiplier effect that alcohol can have on the element. Solely attempting to remove the alcohol problem in Scotland won't impact on the underlying elements that cause many people to blow their top. It is also fair to say that focusing on the problems while pushing alcohol to one side isn't going to help in the long run either.

It is clear though that the Scottish Government has decided that alcohol is a major factor in some crimes and not relevant in others, which is a bit of a concern for the long-term resolution of these problems.

The role of alcohol in creating great atmospheres and the sort of reaction that bands love is well known, but often left unsaid. People are happy to criticise the influence of alcohol on football fans when there is a bad outcome, but it is rarely mentioned when football fans create an atmosphere that brings the game to life or is admired around the world. The Hampden Roar wasn't only inspired by good football and attacking play, we are talking about the Scottish national team here! An element of the Hampden Roar and the stunning Glasgow crowds that are respected across Europe for the backing of their team is down to the fact that a proportion of the crowd has been influenced by alcohol. Most are at an okay level, some are inebriated and it should also be remembered that the ones that haven't been drinking find it easier to join in with the atmosphere because most people around them are singing and engaging with their fellow fans. You don't need to be drunk or enjoy alcohol to sing at games (my dad hasn't drank alcohol since the 60s and he can still be found backing his team vocally at games) but you'll find it a lot easier to do so if those around you are singing and getting involved. In Scotland, all form of social engagement and interaction is easier when it is lubricated by alcohol.

In the world of football, fans drinking and the impact of this action is deemed to be a negative thing while, in the music world, the exact same thing is deemed to be a positive thing. In music, there isn't the same competitive element; there is no common enemy to spark your anger and darker emotions. There is also the fact that on most occasions, the size of the crowd is generally small enough that major disturbances or disobedience don't really have any larger impact. At the end of the day though, the impact and influence of alcohol is pretty much the same regardless of what activity that is being enjoyed.

Figures released on the 13th of July 2013 indicated that a total of 91 arrests were made at the 2013 T in the Park, a rise from the 30 arrests that occurred at the 2012 festival. It only took just over 30 arrests at a football match to rush in new laws, but there was no rush to unleash the Offensive Behaviour of Festival Patrons Act and sadly, there was no movement to arrest Mumford & Sons or The Killers for the obvious role they played in inciting the crowd to break the law (at the very least, these acts should get done for their crimes against humanity). When trouble happens at football stadiums, there is a rush in the media to condemn it and there is always some numpty saying that these games should be played behind closed doors. When it happens at T, there is an overall attitude of "it's just high jinks and people enjoying themselves" while The Killers are welcomed back to Glasgow in the summer of 2014 for their own headline show.

Talk of The Killers and their headline slot at the Summer Sounds series of gigs taking place at Bellahouston Park in Glasgow 2014 brings to mind the controversy that arose over the shows that took place in 2013. In this case, there was annoyance from local residents, jumped on by local media, but the media reporting subsided as quickly as it had risen. The Kings of Leon event on a Thursday night passed by without too much fuss, trouble or even excitement but the Saturday show by Avicii and the Tuesday evening set featuring Eminem caused controversy in the local media.

"Fury as DJ Avicii gig in Bellahouston Park descends into drink and drug-fuelled bedlam" was one headline and the opening line of the article was just as sensational, running; **"An open-air gig headlined by Swedish DJ Avicii turned into an orgy of drink and drug-fuelled violence."** There were 29 arrests at the Avicii gig and 34 arrests at the Eminem gig, worryingly with 2 of these arrests being for serious sexual assault.

The biggest issue for local residents though came with the amount of litter, vomit and urine that ended up on the streets and gardens that led the way to and from the park.

I was in the local area on the Saturday evening for the Avicii gig (my parents stay close to Bellahouston Park) and while I felt the crowd was young and clearly drunk, years of festivals and big shows had clearly numbed me to the excess of what was going on...or I was a just lot more comfortable or blasé with what was taking place. While no one is happy to see their parents living close to such an event, my parents were probably quite lucky that they stayed close to the main entrance to the park, which meant that there was a heavy steward and police presence. It seemed as though the residents that experienced the biggest problems were the ones that stayed on side-streets or far enough from the entrance and exit for stewards to no longer be provided, but still on the way for people looking for transport or heading back into the city centre.

It was clear that there were plenty of underage kids drinking, which means the arrest rates could have been through the roof if the police were following the letter of the law, but the biggest issue came down to the fact that this was all happening in the one place.

The weekends before and after the Avicii gigs would have likely seen the same people drink the same amount of alcohol and/or consume a similar amount of drugs as they did at Bellahouston Park. It's just the fact that everyone was doing it in the one place that made it seem like such a big deal, an argument you can also make for football matches – but it is likely that it is the people who are impacted on that makes it the big story.

When you compare the media reaction to the Bellahouston Park gigs to T in the Park, it seems as though the location is the big difference. Given the size of T compared to the Summer Sessions, the level of carnage at TITP would have been much greater but as it was carried out away from local residents and usually quiet streets, there wasn't the same uproar. The Summer Sessions provided the media with an angle, local residents having their peaceful life being disrupted whereas at T, everyone who was there knew what they were in store for. With the big football games being shown around the world and having an impact on life away from the stadium, it is again the people who are being impacted on that makes it the story as opposed to the number of arrests or the people who actively pay to enjoy themselves at the game.

The rights and wrongs of football crowds in Glasgow are a different story entirely but when you have football fans being victimised for a certain type of behaviour while similar behaviour at different times gets praised or rewarded, you can understand why people feel aggrieved. And when people feel aggrieved and they drink, a new cycle gets underway.

The fact that getting drunk at a festival or a big event is held up as being a badge of honour in some quarters is best summed up by an on-stage quote from professional clown Robbie Williams (or Robbie Wilson as he should forever be referred to after a famous Gallagher Brothers putdown), who said; *"We used to have the record for the number of girls fainting. Now we have the record for the most middle-aged boozed-up women. I, Robbie Williams, am proud of you."*

I should also make it clear that it's not just artists I seem to dislike who have an audience that doesn't know where to draw the line with alcohol. There probably haven't been too many Low or Wilco shows around the world interrupted by rowdy fans but in Glasgow, both of these acts have been slightly derailed by an over boisterous crowd. The Low gig featured a full-on fight between some of the attendees, which is certainly not something that you would have predicted before the event.

The different attitudes to drink at certain occasions and indeed the varying attitudes to alcohol itself lies at the heart of what makes Scotland what it is and the nature of Scottish people. We've always been known for providing audiences that are up for a great performance and we have crowds that are known and revered all over the world. If we took away some of the negative element of the alcohol and its impact, we may lose a piece of what makes us special. This is a terrible thing to say, and you don't need to have alcohol to have a good time, but it's going to take generations of cultural retraining and development to remove that from the Scottish psyche and personality. The fact that our major music festival is basically named after the best-selling lager in the country is something that we all take for granted or don't even notice these days!

Music and social events are important for our psyche and well-being though. Music helps to bring people together, giving them a reason to spend time with each other. Music can be a fantastic release from the working week and the stress of everyday life. The role of alcohol in shaping a crowd's willingness to enjoy a gig needs to be noted but part of the gig going experience comes from letting out the anger and frustration that you can feel in life. Whether it is the enjoyment you take from watching talented performers play or you are in the middle of a heaving crowd, singing every note and putting as much of yourself into the set as the band is, music is a crucial component in staying sane and being happy in life. For some people, it is this element, as opposed to the alcohol, that provides the Scottish crowd with the fire that is known and admired all over the world.

There is also the fact that with our weather being so miserable, we need to have activities that can be carried out indoors. Whether this comes in the form of bands and artists playing and rehearsing indoors or actually going to see a gig, knowing that there are ways and places to meet your pals that also provide shelter from the wind and the rain is a great comfort.

The weather is one of the most enduring topics of conversation in Scotland, with the changeable nature of the weather being the biggest issue that many people. It would be fair to say that the Scottish climate is far from being the worst in the world, it's fairly moderate in the grand scheme of things, but it seems to get a lot of people down. The wind, the rain, the low temperatures and the lack of sun are all elements that seem to make life hard for people and they are all evident in everyday Scottish life.

Another thing that is apparent in Scotland is that for a small country, there are a lot of differences in the standard climate in different regions. The winds coming in from the Atlantic means that the western side of the country can be rather damp, with the western element of the Highlands recognised as being amongst the windiest and wettest placed in Europe. On the other hand, Edinburgh, Fife, Aberdeen, Angus and other locations on the eastern side of the country have a pretty decent standard of rainfall. You may not think that many areas of Scotland have a level of annual rainfall that compares strongly to Barcelona, Rome and even New York, but that is the case on the East Coast. It's bloody freezing though which is why you don't get too many comparisons between the capital of Scotland and the capital of Catalonia.

So we have alcohol, we have a need to escape from the miserable weather and the need to escape from our miserable lives, are there are any other reasons why people fall so deeply in love with music? Take your pick.

Music can be a way to meet new friends and partners and relationships and marriages all over the world are created thanks to a live show or a certain song. Given that the first dance is one of the most important traditions of a wedding day, there is no getting away from the fact that music is at the heart of the most emotional and important aspects of people's lives. With this in mind, it is perhaps surprising that more people don't go to gigs on a regular basis.

There is also the fact that music can help us to get a point across that we couldn't find the words to say ourselves. Whether it is the music or more commonly the lyrics, music has enabled people in Scotland to sum up their emotions in a more eloquent way than they could themselves. Music can mean everything at times and when such an emotional pull exists, there is always going to be a demand to experience it and enjoy it as much as you possibly can.

Of course, there are times when you can't find a song to effectively express what you are trying to say, but when that happens, you might want to think about creating your own songs.

4: When The Music Starts To Play

Whenever there is talk of a Scottish psyche or trait running through the nation, it only takes a few minutes for it to be debunked. If you canvassed 5 Scottish people, you'd likely get 6 different opinions or personalities, at least, shining through.

However, it is clear that literature believes that there is a duality running through Scottish people, with perhaps the most notable example being the Strange Case of Jekyll and Hyde by Scottish author Robert Louis Stephenson. That may be an example that is a bit too extreme to consider as being true to life but then again, if you ever met someone during the day then late at night after a trawl around Sauchiehall Street or The Grassmarket, you'd understand the life-changing power of the strange elixir that is served up to Scottish people.

The thing is though; the nature of this duality that is attributed to Scottish people is, like many stereotypes, borne from a true place. At times Scottish people can be frugal with their money yet equally, the friendly nature and generosity of the people are very well known. We're a hard working nation with a history of farming and industrial work yet we are also a nation that is well known for letting its hair down and being able to party with the best of them. We're also able to be reserved and polite one minute and then the most gallus and over-confident people of all time. We've a history of painful defeats yet seem to be able to venture into every new battle or fight with an unshakeable belief that this is the time when it will all go to plan. All of these elements mean that it is impossible to say that there is a single trait or characteristic running through the Scottish people but there is a flexibility of emotions and characteristics on offer.

In many ways, it is easy to see why the singer songwriter night is a major part of Scottish life. The benefits it brings to the pubs is clearly a major reason for the promotion of these nights but if there wasn't a steady stream of musicians and artists prepared to put themselves in front of an audience, there would be no night on offer.

It is one thing forming a band and honing your craft but it is an entirely different matter when you put yourself up in front of an audience all by yourself. In a band, there are other people to blame, other people to bounce ideas off and there is safety in numbers. When it's just you and an acoustic guitar, you're pretty exposed and it takes a fair bit of courage to get involved with this style of event.

One of the things about these artists, often arriving on stage with nothing more than an acoustic guitar and a viewpoint on life, is the fact that everyone can get involved and join in. There is no real barrier to picking up a guitar and telling the world something. This doesn't mean that everyone should, not everyone has a desire to share what they have to say and not everyone can sing (I am blessed with the inability to carry a tune, even in a reliable bucket).

It would be virtually impossible to run through all the great solo songwriters in Scotland and you can guarantee that if I named 50, there would be a queue of folk lining up with a 51st name that I missed but should have had at the top of the list. You learn that many people become really passionate about their backing of songwriters, and it's not just about a family member or someone that plays in their local bar, it's because people make genuine connections.

When it comes to focusing on songwriters that appeal to you, it's not enough to say that there is a link between Scottish people and we'll automatically connect to each other. There are strong arguments to be said for the fact that people in the Highlands have little in common with people living in the central belt, and if a Northern writer was to write from the heart with a local aspect and viewpoint, they may struggle to find an audience in Glasgow or Edinburgh. The artist shouldn't be downbeat over this; you only have to look at the diversity in Glasgow artists to know that you won't find agreement in the city.

Postcard Records and Orange Juice may have been trumpeting the sound of Young Scotland across Britain but you can bet that a few streets away from West Princes Street, the home of the label, there would be more than enough people moaning about that racket and how that doesn't speak for them. There are different viewpoints and it's hearing an act or artist that provides you with a song that speaks to you or perhaps opens your eyes that is the more important element when it comes to finding a songwriter you love. Of course, the more connections you have, including location, dialect and outlook, the more likely it will be that you make a connection with an artist, but sometimes, things just click.

I think we can all pick out artists that we like and artists that we don't like and it sometimes isn't about the quality of their work. I adore the music of James Yorkston, I have done for a great number of years and I'll never tire of praising him to other people. In conversation with people about artists of this nature, you can guarantee that before too long, the name of Alasdair Roberts will crop up. It is clear that Alasdair is very highly regarded and there are people who are much bigger fans of him than I will ever be of James Yorkston. And yet, I have never really taken to the music of Alasdair and wouldn't really thank you for taking me to a show where he was playing. It's not that his music is bad, far from it (although I do find his vocal style to be an acquired taste), but I do find his particular style of storytelling to be a style that slightly jars with me. This came to the fore one night back in 2006 when Alasdair was supporting the Silver Jews at the Bongo Club in Edinburgh, almost encouraging me to take up smoking so I had a legitimate excuse to stand outside the venue when he was playing!

When it is just you and your guitar on stage, there is less to mask the message or tone that is being delivered. Much in the same way that many people will likely not take to my written style or recurring ability to lapse into bad quality jokes, the songwriting style of an artist is always going to be divisive. There are clearly some musical acts that I slate and actively dislike and Alasdair Roberts isn't one of them, he's just a songwriter that doesn't really appeal to me, and I don't think there is anything wrong with saying that. Okay, if you launch a foul mouth tirade at a songwriter that you don't like, you're the person in the wrong, not them, but on the whole, there's enough space for everyone to find the acts that they like and politely move away from the acts that just don't do it for them. (Seriously though Alasdair, if someone does point this passage out to you, get in touch, and I'll give you a free copy so you can burn it!)

There are also tons of Scottish songwriters that you just never get the chance to hear or properly listen to. Names like Beerjacket and Withered Hand are well known in the music scene and have a strong audience that has been built up over the years. However, I'd say that I've watched solo artists like Evan Crichton or Siobhan Wilson play more often because of the circles I move in and the times that you are going to gigs. These are all acts that have moved through the stages of bedroom writing and then to and beyond the singer songwriter nights. For some people, these events are a stepping stone, for others, they are the peak of their ambitions.

The nature of the music played by most singer-songwriters may often be considered as folky and a bit lightweight but there is certainly nothing slight about the courage and ambition shown by people who create their own material and play it in front of people that they don't know. A typical singer songwriter audience is there to have a good night and will be on the side of the artists but equally, they aren't going to tolerate unprofessional performances or extremely poor showings. Nerves can often mean that a person doesn't play or sing as strongly in a venue as they do at home, but it is possible to tell when an artist isn't taking things seriously. Unless you have a masochistic streak running through you, there must be more enjoyable ways to spend an evening.

Sometimes the need to make music comes from something as simple as voicing things that get bottled up inside of you and the need to let them out in order to stay on top of things. No matter the reason people have for making music, they should be commended and it is not as if someone getting into music with the hope of finding fame and fortune should be taken more or less seriously than people who take up an instrument or start songwriting in order to find an outlet for troubles they face in life.

As stated, there are many traits and characteristics associated with Scottish people but a hesitancy to declare our feelings and emotions has long been a main one. Given that there was also football to watch, there was no real need for a Scottish man to bother their friends, family or loved ones with what they were actually feeling or thinking. Best to leave that sort of talk to other nations, there were more important things to be going on with.

Of course, that isn't a healthy way to be and bottling things up or completely overlooking or disregarding them is a bad thing. There has been gradual improvement in the need to open up and be forthright about things (the things that matter, you usually didn't struggle to find a Scottish opinion on things that don't really matter in the grand scheme of things) and when you consider the poor health record of the country, this has to be seen as a positive step. The phrase "the sick man of Europe" is one that has been laid at the doorstep of Scotland for far too long and far too many people have suffered in silence or found that they left it too late to receive treatment that could have made a difference. It's not as though this problem is solely a Scottish problem or a Scottish male problem but this is a group of people who have had issues in this area.

This is why the number of startlingly open Scottish singer-songwriters in recent years has been a positive aspect. More and more performers and artists have been wearing their heart on their plaid sleeves, which perhaps indicates a shift in the emotional thinking of the nation. Just as impressively, there has been a wave of really impressive songwriters from Scotland in recent times. The number of bands and solo artists performing music that is deemed to be more genuine, honest or even intelligent than a lot of what is being played today has been impressive and perhaps even startling. Of course, all it takes is one or two acts to fit this mould and others will realise that it is possible to create music in this nature and the Scottish folk scene is one that has quite a following all around the world.

The notion of songwriting and performance as a way to

stay happy and safe, or at least minimise the risk of putting yourself in harm was brought to the fore by RM Hubbert when we was announced as the winner at the SAY awards in 2013. RM Hubbert, or Hubby as he is commonly known, has been in and around the Scottish music scene for over 20 years. With a history that stretches back to the early days of Alex Kapranos (Huntley at the time) and which includes the post rock majesty of El Hombre Trajeado, Hubbert has achieved a career that many would be jealous od. This doesn't automatically bring happiness though and in an interview with STV at the award show he was asked how he was dealing with depression, he replied; "I haven't overcome it, I deal with it. This is how I deal with it. I have chronic depression, it comes and goes. I feel better when I talk about it, and I find it easier to talk about it when I'm onstage with a guitar in my lap."

With this in mind, performances and recording can be seen as being a cathartic experience for Hubbert and his openness to talk about his condition, and some of the situations which he believe led him to feel this way, has hopefully helped himself and many others. Music is often the backdrop to so many good moments in life but it is also there for the moments that are tough. I'm sure we can all name albums that got us through some difficult or trying times (Ladies And Gentleman We Are Floating In Space by Spiritualized or The Great Destroyer by Low would be up there for me) and there is no doubt that music can help people to feel better about themselves. Being able to put a song on and feel some sort of kinship or realisation that maybe everything isn't that bad has to be a great thing. If RM Hubbert can feel a bit better about life by making music and playing gigs, hopefully the fact that he is helping other people to make progress in their life will help as well.

It's important to realise that it is not just men that can sometimes bottle up their emotions and need to find ways to let off steam in a meaningful manner. Depression and mental health issues can hit men and women, people of all ages and backgrounds.

A couple of years ago, while flicking through the TV

channels after a night in the pub, I stumbled across BBC Alba and Rapal, their main music show. On the screen was a striking young artist with big hair, a big voice and on the basis of this one song, a big talent. A further song later on in the same show indicated that Anna Sweeney knew how to write a decent song or two. With social media being what it is, the following day I located her on Twitter with the hope of finding out more about her music and live performances.

At first, Anna was posting demos and talking positively about her music but after a while, although it may have been sooner with the busy and ever updating nature of Twitter making it difficult to truly follow a person's timeline, the music chat seemed to dry up. Not long after, Anna was admitted to hospital suffering from an eating disorder and depression. In an attempt to focus on her health, she turned her back on her music career and with that; I felt it was best for me to unfollow her on social media while wishing her all the best in her battle.

In July 2013, Anna gave a lengthy interview with the Popcop site, and she also cited the importance of music in helping her through her troubles. At the time, Anna was only playing and making music for herself, but thankfully, in the summer of 2014, Anna returned to the music scene, littering Soundcloud with a series of demos and playing sets in Stereo and King Tuts over the summer months. She also started at Glasgow University in the autumn, hopefully indicating that she had made good progress from the issues that grounded her when she was initially tipped to make a mark on the music scene. At the time of the first wave of interest in her musical output, Jim Galletly made a remark along the lines of if you placed Anna on Later With Jools Holland you would have an overnight star and it's easy to see why he came to that conclusion. The bright and breezy nature of her songs could quickly catapult her to the level of Amy McDonald or Nina Nesbitt without much fuss or effort.

The stories of Hubby and Anna may be at the more extreme end, but finding a creative outlet can help people to come to terms with the issues that they face in life. You may never hold ambitions of being a star but finding a way to get some things off your chest or help you to put things into perspective has to be seen as something to have in life.

When it comes to things that we don't really like to talk about in Scotland, the list would be as long as Great Western Road, Prince Street and Union Street (Aberdeen version) combined. Our own well-being and mental health in general is something that we try to avoid discussing and this is an ingrained attitude that has been part and parcel of Scottish life for more years than any of us would recall. Then again, it is not as if talking openly about sex is high on the agenda for a great deal of the population and it is not as if we are all that comfortable dealing with success either.

Obviously Rod Stewart has enough confidence in himself to enquire if you think he's sexy and AC/DC sculpted a career from songs that were dripping with sexual content. Sometimes it was wrapped up in innuendo while at other times it was in your face, but you were never far away from it with the 'DC.

Both of these acts are hugely successful and as has been pointed out before, you could argue that the vast majority of pop songs are overtly about love and sex, but it is also recognizable that both of these acts honed their songwriting skills away from Scotland.

Another act who broke away from Scotland before adding a sexy sheen to her performance was Sheena Easton and you could argue that the double whammy of sex and success made it a lot harder for her to maintain her success in Scotland and the rest of the UK. It's not as if we are totally against success as a nation, but if you turn your back on Scotland, even in people's perception, you will face a backlash. Heading off to America to create a career which would see her work with Kenny Rodgers, Don Johnson and Prince meant that some people would be more than willing to take Sheena down a peg or two if the chance arose, but her songs didn't help. It's easy to feel a kinship with a Bellshill lassie that sings about the morning train but when she starts banging on about her Sugar Walls, public opinion is going to work against her.

Of course, there will always be acts that buck the trend,

with Arab Strap being an act that never shied away from sharing their carnal activities. Heck, their name alone indicated that they were more than experienced when it came to matters of the bedroom, the kitchen, the hallway and even round the back of Falkirk High train station if the opportunity arose.

The thing with Arab Strap, and this was the case for everything that they did, was that there was a sense of realism about their lyrics and stories. You would like to thank there would be some sense of sensationalism or exaggeration for the sake of creativity, but it is never as if they sought to exaggerate to put themselves in a better light. At times there was a grimness about Arab Strap but when it came to finding an act that speaks their own language and sings in their own tongue, Arab Strap were in a league of their own.

Of course, you can probably throw the change of accent at Sheena as well. She wasn't alone in toning down, or throwing away, her natural accent to make it in pop music but she was very notable.

The fact that Scottish accents were masked or hidden, especially with respect to the charts, shone through when The Proclaimers made their breakthrough. The language, tone, accent and the place names mentioned in their lyrics made people sit up and take notice. It may have been the desire to walk 500 miles that brought them worldwide acclaim but with Letter From America, the group made their mark in a way which introduced many parts of Scotland to the world.

When you think of the ease and comfort with which contemporary Scottish bands sing with their natural voice and with which they sing about their immediate surroundings, there has been an evolution from the 1980s. Many of the current bands may not naturally lost The Proclaimers as an inspiration, but their influence has definitely had a far reaching impact. There is a greater tendency for Scottish people to pick up a guitar and be more comfortable with who they are than there was in the past, even if we have a folk history that should be acknowledged and praised.

It's not as if there has been a time at any point in the last 50 or so years when there hasn't been people picking up instruments and showing a desire to make music, and in acts like Bert Jansch and John Martyn, there have been Scottish or Scottish-associated acts that have inspired countless people to pick up a guitar. With Neil Young covering Bert Jansch's Needle Of Death (admittedly a song he had already heavily borrowed from for Ambulance Blues) on the Jack White produced A Letter Home album, released in 2014 after Bert's death, new fans are finding Bert's work all the time. Similarly, the work of John Martyn is being uncovered by new acts and artists all the time.

Jansch would regularly play in an Edinburgh club that would also provide an early home for Robin Williamson and Clive Palmer, who after the inclusion of Mike Herron, would become the Incredible String Band (ISB). Palmer would also run a short-lived late night folk club in Glasgow that would create a legacy that would outlive its own lifetime and sadly even the lifetime of many of the artists that there.

The address of 134 Sauchiehall Street may not mean too much when it is said like that but this is the address of the Savoy Centre and it was on the fourth floor of this building that the ISB would develop their set that would be the platform for their debut album, and their only album as the original trio. They weren't the only notable acts to play here though with Bert Jansch also coming through to play and artists like Matt McGinn, Davy Graham and Alex Campbell also took to the stage. With Billy Connolly and Ian McGeachy (later to change his name to John Martyn) in attendance, and the night MC'd by Hamish Imlach, the world of folk music can point to the Savoy Centre as having been a major influence in its development. Nowadays, the only reasons to visit The Savoy Centre is if you want a set of keys cut during the daytime or your face cut during the night time.

Now of course there will be Savoy regulars and employees who will say that is very harsh and of course, that is true. The Savoy Nightclub, like many of the establishments in Glasgow, is no longer the beacon for violence that it once was and it is all about what people feel comfortable with. I'm not one to say that Sauchiehall Street is as violent or as scary as the BBC documentary or some people would suggest, but when walking the length of the street late on a weekend evening, the only section where I am especially keen to get my head down and keep walking is the bit that features the Savoy and Victorias. Okay, this is mainly due to the fact that the music policy is rubbish but for people of a certain age, there is no doubt that the Savoy and Victorias carry a certain stigma.

You also wouldn't fancy the chances of the folk crew of 1966 if they were pitted against a standard Savoy crowd from the 70s, 80s or 90s!

So there has been a long history of nights being run to encourage songwriters and there appears to be no signs of this demand slowing or stopping. Some people will cite the rise of reality TV shows, and the inevitable backlash against it, as being part of the current fuel for the desire that people have shown but technology has to be a large part of the reason.

Given the emergence of YouTube and the quality of downloadable or stream-able video content, it has never been easier or more convenient to learn how to play guitar from the comfort of their own home. Books and/or tutors have played a massive role in helping songwriting talent develop over the years but with a huge array of video clips and tutorials available online, if you have access to the internet, you can watch and practice from your bed, couch or anywhere else you are comfortable.

Technology has also helped a shift away from guitars, whether it is through more electronic instruments or apps, but there is always going to be a level of instrument and picking up a guitar and writing songs. Apps like Garageband can make the recording process easier and websites like Soundcloud or Bandcamp provides budding artists with a good platform for showcasing their music to a wider audience but there is always going to be a need to get out in front of the public if you are keen to experience the full flush of adrenaline and buzz that music can give you. For the bedroom artists with their acoustic guitars, singer songwriter nights will represent the logical step forward.

5: Three Cheers For Our Side

The history of Scottish music can be dated all the way back to the Iron Age with evidence of stringed instruments in the country dating back to this time. It is likely, although unconfirmed that the instrument was created and played by Ronnie Browne of the Corries, in an attempt to spark the local community into life. Even then, the working day was punctured with rallying cries of "come on" as Browne skived off of doing proper work.

Music has long been at the heart of Scottish life, passing on tales and stories for how people should live their lives. At times, music has been at the heart of religious life in Scotland and at others, because music may give the impression that people were actually enjoying themselves, has been banished. In more recent times, there have been more than enough Scottish acts and artists that make music which no one can enjoy, so perhaps these tracks would have been more suitable to those previous times.

When attempting to consider the impact of Scottish music and artists on general pop culture, there is a need to have a barometer of pop culture, with the introduction of the UK singles charts in the early 1950s being as good a place to start as any. The first charts were hardly the most all-reaching, the NME phoning up a number of stores to see what was selling and then creating the rundown from their findings, but before too long, and through a number of different lists coming to the fore, there was some semblance of recognition for the songs that were being bought up and down the United Kingdom.

It took a while for a Scottish artist to make an impression on the chart, but the impact that they made is still being felt today. Let's face it, it all began with Lonnie. Okay, Lonnie Donegan took the Blues from America and wrapped it up in the skiffle style but he would provide a blueprint for many artists and even entire genres of music that would follow. The Beatles, The Stones, Led Zeppelin, Jack White and oh so many more, your boy Lonnie beat you to it with his cover of the track, previously most commonly associated with Leadbelly to this point, Rock Island Line. Skiffle music was basic, but it was cheap and easily accessible, allowing people the chance to play along with items that they could find in their kitchen. You wonder how many Scottish mums lost their rag when coming to find their kitchen, and so many of their important household items had been used to transform the kitchen or lobby into a makeshift gig venue. He may have provided a template for rock n roll in the UK, but you can bet that Lonnie Donegan was responsible for quite a few kids getting a belt around the lughole!

There is also a lot to be said for the fact that skiffle music had a different sound and lyrical feel to the more contemporary songs that were being played on the radio, or indeed in the dance halls of Scotland. This wasn't music for wooing, it was music for living, with skiffle drawing on the same country and blues tales of people gone wrong, love gone wrong and life being generally a bit grim. Some of the songs dwelled on these matters while others looked for a bit of escape. Clearly the lyrics were a lot tamer to what would follow in future decades but skiffle was central in bringing a grittier style of music to the masses and through Lonnie, Scotland was at the heart of it all.

Of course, the traditional Scottish sound was still going to be the main draw for many people when it came to music. The only Scottish artist that could get close to the popularity of Donegan was Jimmy Shand, the accordion player who took up residency on the wireless. With Blue Bell Polka, released in the mid-fifties, coming in at the opposite end of the Scottish music spectrum to where Donegan was operating, there was a field day for people looking to draw comparisons between the different styles. Jimmy Shand would always have an audience, but it would become clear that his appeal would fade with respect to a wider audience. For spells, the love and admiration for Scottish music would diminish from mainstream audiences while the influence of American artists and styles would continue to rise.

Mind you, there would always be room for a Scottish novelty track to crack the charts. Whether it was an opportunity for ex-pat Scots in England and Wales to reconnect with their homeland or to present Southerners with an opportunity to laugh at the curious Scots and their even more curious ways, Scottish music would never be too far away from making a splash. In 1958, the nation rocked around the clock to 'Hoots Mon', a big band track featuring the lyrics of "There's a moose loose aboot this hoose" showcasing what life in Scotland was like on a daily basis, at least if your idea of Scottish life was based on The Broons. Over the years, this sense of Scottish style and music would be touched upon in a variety of tracks, including the sad and touching lament of Andy Stewart to his pal Donald, who appeared to have left the house without putting on his slacks. This track, a good few decades later, also propelled Stuart Anderson into the spotlight as another Scottish artist being forced to turn tricks for the braying masses down south. As long as the kid enjoyed himself and earned some cash, good for him, but in the grand scheme of things, there can't be a lot of joy when you are labelled as the third best known Scottish schoolboy after Oor Wullie and Jimmy Krankie. Andy Stewart's version, featuring an Elvis impersonation which was about as interesting as the time Elvis waved from a plane in Prestwick, did a lot of damage to the traditional Scottish music scene, at least for mainstream followers.

On the whole though, the 1950s wasn't a great era for Scottish artists making it into the charts or making a splash when it came to pop music and bands. This was an era when music was starting to flood in from the United States and that provided all of the excitement that people were looking for. In dance halls up and down the country, musicians were learning these songs and unfurling them in front of an expectant audience, so the magic of live music was present, it just wasn't an era when there would be a great deal of originality or creativity from Scottish artists.

The 1950s, and the introduction of many different American styles of music would go on to have an influence on the Scottish artists that would emerge. Skiffle would die out, but Lonnie Donegan hung on in there, continuing to bother the charts into the 1960s. The longer lasting influence of skiffle would come in the form of the American music it would introduce to Scottish music lovers, most notably country music. You could argue that the Wild West nature of many Scottish towns and cities lends itself perfectly to country music but even to this day, there is a tremendous love and admiration of country music in Scotland.

Like all musical genres, you get good country music and bad country music. Your opinion on what constitutes good and bad will depend on your viewpoint, but there has been an enduring respect for this style of music and it is easy to see why. Strip away the outfits and the personas and country music offers up talks of wine, women, redemption, heartache and friendship, all of the things that life revolves around in Scotland. With the right melody, it doesn't matter if the lyrics are singing about Texas or Tunnocks, people will connect to it and while it may embarrass or annoy some people, country music is definitely a major factor in the story of Scottish music and the music that Scottish people love.

One artist who helped to bring country style to Scottish fans was Angus Murdo McKenzie from Springburn, who went by the more popular name of Karl Denver. Denver had seen the world, he had been in the merchant navy and more tellingly for his country style, he had spent some time in Nashville Tennessee, before being deported as an illegal immigrant. His time in America gave Denver his name and a love of country music.

Denver took up residency in the UK charts, having more than 10 hits in a three-year period between 1961 and 1964. Songs such as Mexicali Rose, Marcheta and the global smash hit Wimoweh, showcased his yodelling skills and brought acclaim to the artist. Wimoweh was a truly worldwide phenomenon, sung by a Scottish artist with an American style but the song itself was an adaptation of a folksong from Africa and it managed to reach the number one spot in Australia. The song would be covered in many guises and styles over the years bit it also provided Denver with one final appearance in the spotlight thanks to the Happy Mondays.

Denver guested on Lazyitis, a 1989 single from the band

and featured with the band in the video and on a number of live shows with the group. This tie-in with the band also led to Factory Records, the Happy Mondays label at the time, releasing a new version of Wimoweh and another track called Indambingi. These two periods were over 25 years apart, but Denver had enough momentum on the back of his revival to release a country album in 93 but he sadly passed away in 1998 while was recording a follow-up album.

Another young Glaswegian talent that was being inspired by the wave of records from the United States was Alex Harvey, who was yet to earn the sensational moniker at this point! This was the era when Scottish audiences were crying out for artists to bring the sound of the US to them in the various clubs and it is believed that it was a version of Shout, performed by Harvey and his band, that inspired Lulu and her Luvers to record the song, which would become a smash hit and a defining song for the lassie from Dennistoun. In that regard, you may want to reappraise your opinion on the career of Alex Harvey but if it wasn't him that brought the idea to the fore, it would likely have been someone else, Lulu would have happened by hook or by crook.

Lulu eh? There's a name that has many people recoiling in horror at times, perhaps only being beaten by Sheena Easton when it comes to being considered as the most unpopular Scottish artist. Maybe its jealousy, maybe it's that ever-changing accent but for some reason, Lulu is far from the top of the list when it comes to Scottish pop acts. With a number one US single with To Sir, With Love and Top 10 UK singles in the 60s, 70s, 80s, 90s and 00s, there is a strong argument to be made for Lulu as being one of the leading Scottish acts over the years. The thing is though; there are also reasons why she should be overlooked quickly, with the collaboration work with Take That and Ronan Keating being highly prominent.

No matter what she has managed over the years, nothing has really come close to Shout, remaining her signature tune 50 years on. Lulu was wheeled out for opening of the Commonwealth Games in Glasgow, not in the main Opening Ceremony, she was annexed off in Glasgow Green and there she was, belting out that old classic to an audience that only wanted to hear that song. With a TV career that was arguably more important than her singing career and an all-important Eurovision triumph, it's not been a bad 50 years in the business for Lulu.

We were now venturing into the era of The Beatles and The Stones, forcing bands into incorporating their own original material alongside the covers they were serving up to their fans. Again, the Scottish music scene didn't contribute too much in the grand scheme of chart success but the Stones manager, Andrew Loog Oldham, was partly behind a Scottish act called The Poets. Their track Now We're Thru was a standard pop ballad of the time but the band was forced into dressing like Robert Burns and conforming to a stereotype that did them no favours in the long run.

A number of artists gathered a good local following from playing their own version of the Stax and Tamla Motown sound, but there was a feeling that the Scots never really got involved with the swinging sixties, although a troubadour who originally hailed from Maryhill was right at the heart of it all.

Donovan Leitch gets a pretty unfair rep at times, being labelled as a Dylan clone and being ridiculed for some of the more whimsical elements of his output. Sure, Mellow Yellow sounds slightly ludicrous and Catch The Wind gives more than enough ammunition to those slating him for being a Dylan follower but that would be to miss the point. One of the problems that Donovan had was in being inspired by so many of the same artists that inspired Bob and of course, timing. Sometimes, if you're not first, you're nowhere. Over the years there have been countless artists that have tugged on the hem of Dylan and made decent careers for themselves, it just was a shame that Donovan was working in a similar field at the exact same time as one of the most inspiring musical artists of all time.

His hippy nature may be slightly laughable but when Donovan turned a bit psychedelic and weird, he considerably upped his game. With songs like Season of The Witch, Sunshine Superman and Hurdy Gurdy Man, Leitch was a main mover in the psychedelic stakes, shown by his friendship with The Beatles at this time. Leitch influenced the sound and shape of The White Album while he and the fab four were in India. Although it was not used in the single version, George Harrison contributed a chorus to Hurdy Gurdy Man, which Donovan has used in his live performances for a number of decades. With 7 Top 10 singles between 1965 and 1968, Donovan was no stranger to commercial success, and he even managed a number one US single.

For me though, his best moment came in the second half of Atlantis. The first half set the scene, Donovan intoning about the story of Atlantis but the latter is absolutely magical and you would be happy to hear it roll on for much longer. Donovan was definitely at his best when he let loose and even though this was an acoustic moment, more closely related to his early hits, it showcased his great voice and ear for melody.

The fact that a kid from the North of Glasgow went on to be the biggest selling pop star in America (at least for one week) was proof that the citizens of the country could achieve anything if they set their mind to it. Another Glaswegian star of the late 60s and 70s hailed from Bishopbriggs. To be fair to Jack Bruce, he moved around a fair deal in his youth and it is reported that he attended 14 different schools as a child. This would have brought him into contact with the weird and wonderful of Glasgow life, but you have to wonder if that was any sort of preparation for dealing with Eric Clapton and Ginger Baker in Cream. Yes, the band were aptly named, featuring three highly skilled musicians at the top of their profession, the cream of the crop as it were, but Baker and Clapton were highly difficult people to get along with. Bruce had worked on and off with Baker and Clapton for a number of years, and the stories of friction and fights between the different parties led many people to be surprised at the thought of them forming a band. There was even bigger surprise at the fact that the group managed to hold it together for two years and four albums. Bruce is regarded as one of most versatile and accomplished bass players of his time, even if he commonly refers to himself as being an okay jazz musician.

With respect to the charts, Marmalade, or Dean Ford & The Gaylords as they were known when they were developing a local fanbase in Scotland, would have the biggest impact. The band caused a scene in a number of support slots at the Marquee Club on nights when Pink Floyd and The Action were the headline acts. These slots were so popular the band was offered the chance to be the resident act at the Marquee in the summer of 1967. The band also toured with a number of major acts such as Traffic, Joe Cocker, The Who and Gene Pitney.

Chart success was to follow with Lovin' Things, which hit number 6 but followup single Wait For Me Mary-Anne only reached number 30, a cause for concern. Of course, everything was to change in the January of 1969 when the group made their way to number 1 with a cover version of The Beatles Ob-La-Di, Ob-la-Da. This was the first time a Scottish artist made it to number one and to celebrate this feat, the group were invited to perform on the show while wearing kilts. No one asks English number one artists to perform on Top Of The Pops wearing Morris dancing outfits and Tom Jones wasn't asked to wear something stupid that signified he was Welsh. Mind you, as Tom may have put it, this viewpoint of the Scottish people was not unusual, and to be fair, Marmalade were probably too busy enjoying the moment to be overly concerned about what they were wearing on the show. The Beatles cover would eventually sell over 1 million copies around the world before the summer of 69 *(perhaps the very fact that Bryan Adams was celebrating)* and has shifted more than 3 million copies around the world in total. Yes, many fans were keen to get a slice of good old fashioned pop from The Beatles without having to put up with "all that other nonsense from The White Album" but no matter the reason, there was a Scottish band at the top of the pile.

The history of Marmalade also taps into the story of Benny Gallagher and Graham Lyle. Gallagher had co-written a song with Andrew Galt, called Mr Heartbreak's Here

Instead, which would be released by Dean Ford & The Gaylords, who, of course, would evolve into Marmalade. Gallagher first paired up with Graham Lyle in the late 1950s and in 1966 and the two moved to London, probably being the only two Scottish people who felt that moving to London in that year was a sensible idea. The duo worked by day and write at night, eventually catching a break with a deal with Apple Records, writing some songs for Mary Hopkin. Those were the days that the pairing had been waiting for since moving to the English capital, although they would soon have the opportunity to be stars in their own right.

They first tasted success as part of McGuinness Flint, but it was as a duo that they would achieve worldwide success with songs like Breakaway and Heart On My Sleeve, not bad going for two lads from Largs. They would also continue to be viewed as strong songwriters, contributing pieces for artists like Art Garfunkel and Tina Turner.

In the 1970s, rock was coming to the fore and Scottish musicians were not going to miss out. Brian Connolly, hailing from Blantyre, was the most prominent element of the band Sweet, who would go on to be a massive name in the 70s, moving from rock into glam with ease. When the band was at the top of their power, Connolly was wearing the sort of outfits that you would be very brave to wear in Blantyre at the best of times, but this was a beguiling time when glam rock swept up a great deal of Britain under its spell.

Staying true to the ideals of rock were Nazareth, hailing from Dunfermline. After moving to London near the start of the 70s, the band was a consistent and likable force throughout the decade. They may never have bothered the top end of the charts too often but in Hair of The Dog, album and song, the band were well known throughout the mid-1970s. In the US, a version of the album featured a cover of Love Hurts, written by Felice and Boudleaux Bryant, but covered by The Everly Brothers, Roy Orbison, and tying into that country sound once again, Gram Parsons and Emmylou Harris. The track went into the top ten of the US single charts and it remains one of the best known versions of this popular songs.

These acts showed that Scottish artists could combine commercial success with credibility, but it is probably fair to say that the real commercial success of Scotland in the 1970s had very little to do with credibility. Middle of the Road were massive, sitting at the heart of the bubblegum pop wave that captured so much of the UK hit parade at the time. The group shifted more than 5 million units in the 1970s, a worrying trend.

Another worrying trend, and one that is not quite the modern phenomenon that many people think, is the fact that the group first came to public prominence on Opportunity Knocks, when they were known as Los Caracas. They joined Neil Reid and Lena Zavaroni as Scottish artists who would obtain their breakthrough with appearances on "talent TV shows." Decades later, artists like Sheena Easton, Michelle McManus, David Sneddon, Leon Jackson, Tommy Reilly, Darius Danesh and Susan Boyle would also make a breakthrough thanks to these shows. Sheena Easton's story is one that will be looked at a bit later, but it would be fair to say that Scottish artists that broke through thanks to reality TV shows achieved different levels of fame and acceptance.

The story of Lena Zavaroni is a shocking one, the danger of placing young children into the spotlight without providing them with the proper backing and guidance to steer them through danger. At the age of ten, the young singer found herself in the record books as being the youngest person to have a top ten album in the UK. However, within three years, Lena was suffering from anorexia nervosa and within a further two years, she had been diagnosed with clinical depression. The pressure that was placed on the youngster must have been huge, and she never fully recovered from this period in her life, passing away from pneumonia at the age of 35.

Lena's story was tragic but in the long run, it seems as though Reid was survived unscathed, no mean feat when you are written up in the record books as the youngest person to have a number one album in the UK. Susan Boyle's story is also a controversial one, but you get the feeling she has achieved some semblance of peace with her success and her fame. Similarly, Michelle McManus must be absolutely howling with laughter to herself at the fact that she has managed to make such a long-running career out of appearing on the show. These shows can provide people with an opportunity to change their lives. It isn't always for the better and it can be extremely difficult putting yourself in front of the spotlight, hoping for acceptance and praise from snooty judges who are in the business of being catty to gain viewers and the viewing public themselves.

So, the mid 70s was a mixture of rock, glam and naff pop, which provides you with the perfect platform for the tartan teen sensations from Edinburgh would become one of the biggest acts in the world. The story of the Bay City Rollers would fill a couple of books and you would get a completely different story from every member of the band and the community around them. Yet again, tartan was deemed to be the main selling point of the Scottish group and in homes all around the country, teenage girls were getting into trouble for appropriating curtains, shawls and rugs to associate themselves with the group. Britain fell in 1974 and 75, with a twenty-week TV show and Bye Bye Baby staying in the top slot for 6 weeks. In 1976, America, Canada and Australia were also to fall under the reign of tartan terrors. Things move swiftly in the teen market and by 1977, the group was falling part. They would stumble on, and then eventually blunder their way through countless reunions and heartaches but for a period in the 70s, tartan was at the forefront of the UK music scene. 1975 even saw Alex Harvey, with the Sensational Alex Harvey Band, achieve success with a cover of Delilah. It had taken an awful long time for Harvey to get the accolade that many believed was deserved, but he got there in the end. With Gerry Rafferty (partly with Stealers Wheel and then in his own right as a solo artist) and the Average White Band also puncturing the upper reaches of the charts, there was a lot to be said for Scottish music achieving singles success.

If you thought that Bay City Rollers were the worst offenders in being over-hyped tartan terrors in the 1970s, you clearly don't know about (or have blanked out) Ally's Army and the expedition to Argentina with the expectation of returning with some gold. Scotland was in the grip of World Cup fever, probably best shown by the fact that more than 30,000 people turned up at Hampden to watch grown men stand and wave from a bus as it made its way around the track.

Not only were the Scottish national team planning an assault on South America, there was to be an attack on the UK music charts as well. Andy Cameron took Ally's Army all the way to number 6 and to Top of The Pops. This provided Andy with the chance to parade around in the Scottish kit while wearing a tartan scarf in front of the entire nation. If anyone missed the introduction by Tony Blackburn, they may have thought that one of the girls from Pans People had let themselves go. It was a football chant for the terraces placed on record, but its exuberant nature, and absolute arrogance, captured the mood of the pre-World Cup nation perfectly. Anyone that could tear themselves away from the lead single found another novelty track on the B-side, this time featuring Andy moaning about how his attempts to be a punk rocker were foiled by his mammy. It was a piece of nonsense, but it was a bit of fun, and it probably captured the sneering attitude that many of the older generation had about the punk movement. Still, within a few weeks, Scotland were back at home, Ally McLeod had been declared a joke figure (a harsh treatment of a man who had a better tactical mind than his bluster and soundbites would indicate) and even punk rockers could claim to have had a longer shelf-life than Scottish World Cup hopes.

There was also an official Scottish World Cup song this year, a far better song that reached higher in the charts (number 4), but for some reason, the novelty nature of the Andy Cameron record sees that as being the one that gets mention, although this was possibly because that song was actually sung by a Scottish person. This book will switch sides on the "is Rod Stewart a Scottish person" argument time and time again, but purely for fun. If Rod declares himself to be a Scot then of course we are having him. Ole

Ola (Mulher Brasileira) kicked off a Samba beat and had a considerable amount of swing to it, while still capturing that distinctive Rod Stewart swagger. There have been a lot of bad football songs over the years, but this isn't one of them and the remembrance of the quality of the track has been blighted with the abject showing by the team. Football songs that tend to shoehorn the names of the playing squad into the lyrics are inevitably rubbish, but this came as close to pulling it off as you could hope for. The expectations of World Cup success were found throughout the song, the match commentary from the goal that clinched World Cup qualification was present, but if there was one note of possible doubt in the song, it was found in the line of "I only wish that we had Danny McGrain", reference to the fact that the national team would be missing one of their truly world class players due to injury. It's not to say that the absence of McGrain was the reason why Scotland performed so badly at the World Cup, but if he was fit, the team would have been greatly enhanced. Amazingly enough, this wasn't the only time the brilliance of Danny McGrain was marked on record. In 1996, Glasgow band Big Wednesday released a song called Sliding In Like McGrain, with the defender's legendary tackling prowess being just one of the factors that the band members recalled from their childhood.

While he was not part of the squad that helped to record material for the '78 tournament, McGrain was part of the 1974 and 1982 squads that also unleashed songs on the charts. The 1974 World Cup in West Germany was the first time the national team had qualified in years and the first time in the era of the official World Cup song. The imaginatively titled, yet slightly dull, Scotland, Scotland came with the much more imaginative Easy Easy, featuring lines like "yabba dabba doo, we support the boys in blue" and a musical backing that may well have been half-inched from the Bay City Rollers. Scotland reached number 20 but arguably performed better at the World Cup, coming home undefeated and missing out on the next round by goal difference. There were a lot of ifs and buts after that campaign like if only the team had gone for goals against

Zaire or what if Billy Bremner's close range stab at goal against Brazil had inched the other side of the post?

In 1982, McGrain was back in the charts alongside the rest of the squad, BA Robertson and John Gordon Sinclair, with We Had A Dream, a track that blends typical Scottish humour with the typical banality of football songs. It's a song that appears to be fondly remembered to this day and it reached number 5. It was to be the last big hurrah for the official tournament tracks. Big Trip To Mexico in 1986 was written by Tony Hiller, the man famous (or infamous) for creating Brotherhood of Man. He was also the man behind a number of football songs, including the 1986 England song, We've Got The Whole World At Our Feet. That they did, but when a stocky little Argentinean had the whole ball on his fist, they found that they were soon to be heading home. Of course, whenever the first Maradona goal in that game is mentioned, there is a legal requirement to mention the wonderful second strike, when it seemed like half of the English team were weaved and twisted around.

The 1990 song, Say it With Pride, couldn't have been more late 80s, early 90s if it tried. Alongside the squad members adding occasional vocals and their presence for the promotional material, the track featured Donnie Munro, Fish and James Grant and guitar riffs and licks that were so symbolic of the era they deserve to be placed in a time capsule. The track failed to reach the top 40.

In 1996, for the European Championships taking place in England, Rod was back on board. Since 1978, Rod had achieved a couple of hits but clearly he was looking to get some publicity for himself and put himself back in the spotlight!! No of course not, Rod Stewart, at this point, as he was in the 70s and as he remains today, is an absolute superstar, loved all around the world, apart from certain places in Glasgow, especially when he comes on stage with some green and white garb around him!

Over 100 million records sold around the world, six number one albums in a row in the UK, over 60 UK hit singles with more than 30 hitting the top 10. With more than 15 top ten singles in the US and having had the privilege of playing to untold millions around the world; Rod Stewart is easily one of the biggest recording artists of all time. For a guy that fell into music because he thought it would give him some laughs, some beers and some blondes, the lad has done alright for himself!

So, the 1996 song, Purple Heather was taken from his latest album of the time, reworking the folk classic Wild Mountain Thyme. It's a great song, it was a good version and because the event was taking place in England, it probably had the right notion of Scottish pride flowing through it; it just really wasn't a football song. Two years later, for the France '98 World Cup, Del Amitri released a song that was so bad, Scotland have not been allowed to qualify for a major tournament in case they released anything of its nature again. It's a harsh ruling, but it's probably a fair ruling.

So those slight football detours have taken us away from the 70s, but let's return there and to banish the thoughts of failure in the Argentines, it is probably best to consider a big Scottish triumph of the era.

There is an argument to be made for the Royal Scots Dragoon Guards having the biggest Scottish success story of the 1970s with Amazing Grace rocketing to the top of the hit parade and being a huge smash around the world. The bagpipes would feature on another smash hit later on in the 70s with Paul McCartney paying homage to Mull of Kintyre, where he had owned property since the mid-60s. The track is clearly inferior to the Frank Sidebottom cover, but the song was to become the first UK single to sell over 2 million copies. It was also a Christmas number one for Wings, the band The Beatles could have been. For so long, bagpipes had been the sole preserve of the build up to Scottish Cup final day and yet here they were in the 1970s infiltrating every element of modern life. These songs showcased that the bagpipes could be utilised on massive hits, but it was a song first released in 1975 that showed bagpipes could be used with devastating effect in a great song.

Quite simply, It's A Long Way To The Top If You Wanna Rock 'N Roll is an astounding track and its one that is actually improved by the appearance of bagpipes, as opposed to being hindered.

It is safe to say that Australia will put up a fight in claiming the 'DC but it's usually safe to ignore any argument put forward by an Australian and The Young brothers remain proud of their Cranhill origins. In 1963, William and Margaret Young emigrated from Cranhill to Sydney, Australia taking three sons George, Malcolm and Angus and daughter Margaret. Their older son Alex stayed behind in the UK to further his dreams of being a musician but it was his male siblings who headed down under that would make the biggest splash on the music scene. George was a member of The Easybeats, a fairly popular and commercial beat-combo but it was the success of Angus and Malcolm that would overshadow everything else.

The Youngs were joined by another Scot in the band as original vocalist Bon Scott was born in Forfar and grew up in Kirremuir. In this regard, you can see why the boys used the bagpipes in their music but there is a whole lotta more (and a whole lotta Rosie) to the music of AC/DC than merely relying on their Scottish roots. You could spend days dissecting the AC/DC sound, their phenomenal live shows and whether it is right for Angus to still be wearing that school uniform but in the interest of brevity, a quick look at their biggest moments indicates why this is a band that is held in the highest regard.

Back In Black is a phenomenal record, made all the more remarkable given the speed it was recorded with during the turmoil surrounding the passing of Bon Scott. New vocalist Brian Johnson quickly slipped into place and the band made a record that not only stood as a tribute to their departed singer, it became the album to own for anyone who liked their music on the heavier side.

The thing about this album is that it is the only heavy album that many people own. Glasgow is a city that embraces all music cultures and there is a great deal of crossovers between music lovers but even a good portion of the twee indie kids in the city have this album. They may not be completely au-fait with the 'DC back catalogue but when it comes to Back In Black, they know the score.

Some of the key highlights of the band's career include:

- Over 200 million album sales
- Just under 50 million album sales for 'Back In Black' alone
- Inducted into the Rock N' Roll Hall of Fame
- Having streets in Madrid and Melbourne named after them

...not bad for a couple of kids from Cranhill and their mates. The fact that the 'DC returned in 2014 was very welcome news for music fans around the globe, but the joy was restrained with the announcement of Malcolm leaving the band due to his diminishing health. It may have been Angus that grabbed the attention and headlines but Malcolm created rhythm guitar lines that you could set your watch by, and his impact on the band, and countless bands to follow, is in some ways unmeasurable. It's not always a good thing to be able to sum up your feelings about a band in one easy sentence or soundbite but in their own words, "For Those About To Rock, We Salute You", you can get to the heart of AC/DC in no time at all.

While it is easy to see musical decades as being distinct, there is clearly a lot of bleed and influence between different decades and many of the acts that would go on to wow music fans in the 1980s would get their break or at least take their initial steps in the 1970s.

The vocal talents of Aberdeen born Annie Lennox first came to prominence with The Tourists in 1979, with the group releasing three singles in this year. With Blind Among The Flowers stalling at 52 and The Loneliest Man In The World peaking at 32, there was no indication of the band achieving great success but this was to change with a cover of the Dusty Springfield classic, I Only Want To Be With You. This reached number 4 in the UK charts. The band would roll on into 1980 but by 1981, Lennox and Dave Stewart were working as the Eurythmics. By 1983, with the Sweet Dreams (Are Made Of This) single and album, the group were on their way to being major stars. A number one single, in There Must Be An Angel (Playing With My Heart) was to follow in 1985. In the 90s, Annie Lennox would achieve even greater solo success than what she achieved with the band, positioning herself as one of the leading artists of the era.

Edinburgh act The Rezillos ensured that there was a Scottish marker for the punk revolution that took place in the late 70s with I Can't Stand My Baby being released in 1977. With New Rose by The Damned being recognised as the first UK punk single being released in October 1976, the fact that there was a Scottish punk act on the scene in the summer of '77 was good going. The band would achieve success with Top Of The Pops peaking at number 18 in 1978. You also had The Skids with the Saints Are Coming featuring on an EP released in 1978 and Into The Valley being released in February of 1979. The punk movement wasn't massive in Scotland and even some of the bands that were influenced by the fiery nature and simplicity of the music were at pains to point out that they weren't actually a punk band. This may have been partly down to the general public feeling towards punks and it may have been related to the fact that a number of towns and cities placed a ban on punk acts playing. It would be fair to say that the punk movement was a good breeding ground for many musicians in Scotland, with the output of Zoom Records being a case in point.

The label was started by Bruce Findlay, a record store owner and the organiser of the Edinburgh Pop Festival, which debuted in 1973. This saw acts like Can, Procul Harum, The Incredible String Band, The Chieftains and John Martyn take to the stage in the Empire Theatre, over a three week period. The label released material by The Valves, PVC2 (who had Midge Ure in their ranks), Zones and Simple Minds. The label was also close to signing The Skids but they eventually recommended the act sign for the Dunfermline label, No Bad Records, which was started by another record store owner, Sandy Muir.

Punk was good but with respect to Scottish acts and artists, the Post-Punk era would prove to be a lot more fruitful. While the music of the best punk bands still stands up today, you get the impression that it was the energy and the action taking of the punk that had the biggest effect, certainly in Scotland. Realising that there was no longer a need to head to London in order to achieve success, there was a huge spur for independent acts and labels to develop in their own right. It wasn't easy and there was a lack of infrastructure that could have helped many more acts to emerge from Scotland in the 1980s, but on the whole, it was an era where an impact could be made.

With respect to Post-Punk, the success of Dumbarton lad David Byrne, in Talking Heads, was a notable landmark but it was the act of Scottish record labels pushing on local acts that had the biggest impact. This was also an era when a notable East versus West divide would come into play.

In the East corner, imbibing on salt and sauce was Fast Product, a label that would release music from acts that would go on to be massive names. In the West corner, although not quite the west end, was Postcard Records, the true home of the sound of Young Scotland.

Edinburgh took an early lead and while Fast Product didn't focus on local talent (although punk/post-punk/slightly touching on New Romantic act The Scars released a single on the label), you cannot argue with the talent that the label worked with. Fast Product sprung forth in 1977 and the band released the debut singles of The Human League and The Gang of Four. The label was also to provide a home to two Joy Division tracks and on their final single, the label introduced The Dead Kennedys to the UK with the release of California Uber Alles. Bob Last, the brains behind Fast Product, would also be responsible for Pop Aural, who had the Fire Engines on their label.

The role of Fast Product as an inspiring label should not be overlooked, but it is hard to see beyond Postcard Records as the major success story of Scotland at this time. The releases on Postcard may only date from February 1980 to August 1981, with only four different acts being featured, but the influence of Postcard Records has resonated for years. The label was initially set-up by Alan Horne to provide a place where Orange Juice and Josef K could release material. These two acts were joined by The Go-Betweens and Aztec Camera. With Orange Juice signing to Polydor in 1981, the label faded away but if it burned quickly, it also burned brightly. These four acts and similar acts of the time, such as

The Fire Engines, have influenced bands ever since. Notable musical movements of the 80s included the C81 and C86 periods, where the style of Postcard Records acts could be heard across a number of tracks. It is also fair to say that anyone who has ever tapped a toe in the general direction of Franz Ferdinand's music owes a debt of gratitude to this era

A top ten single finally beckoned for Orange Juice in 1983 with Rip It Up peaking at number 8. A chaotic (drunken) Top of the Pops performance may have halted the likelihood of further commercial success for the group and it provided a quick insight into the band. There was no doubt that Orange Juice were keen to be a big selling pop act with many fans, but they weren't prepared to play the game in the way that they needed to. Whether you want to tie this into the Scottish trait of so often shooting themselves in the foot or the fact that Edwyn and company were contrary buggers, you wouldn't be far wrong!

Other Scottish acts were able to play the game more successfully; in fact, the hit parade overrun by Scottish acts. Simple Minds and Big Country, from Glasgow and Fife respectively, managed to play the game so well that they became international stars. Simple Minds would become stadium artists, selling millions of albums and even cracking America with Don't You Forget About Me while Big Country unleashed a Scottish sound of the 80s, fusing the notion of bagpipe music with guitars. Both acts evolved and developed from punk and post-punk but in the mid-80s, they were massive commercial rock stars. Both bands would find that reaching the top of the charts and all of the other pressures heaped upon you wasn't all it was cracked up to be but when it comes to finding bands that introduced a touch of Scotland all over the world, these two bands would be at the top of any list.

Another artist that made it through the punk-phase and would then reap rewards in the post-punk and early 90s synth pop scene was Midge Ure. For punk musicians, being told to shut up would be one of the lightest bits of abuse you would receive from your audience but if you were to say "Shaddup You Face" to Midge Ure, there's every chance that he would break down and cry. Midge, as part of Ultravox, had crafted one of the best pop singles of the early 1980s and once again, the Great British record buying public proved that they were an untrustworthy and to be honest, unsavoury bunch.

Sometimes when a novelty song triumphs, it's a source of joy, such as the case when Mr Blobby beat Take That to a Christmas Number One but for Midge, it was another case of him being the nearly man. Let's not forget that this is the man with co-writing and production credits on one of the biggest hits of all time, Do They Know Its Christmas?, and yet the majority of people don't know this. Midge was a great musician and music man, but he didn't have the knack for publicity like Bob had. Midge and Bob did a hell of a lot of good with the Band Aid and Live Aid projects, but Bob certainly did a lot better for himself out of this period.

You get the feeling that Midge doesn't mind that too much though, with charity being the real winner. However, there were other moments when Midge may have been standing on the brink of being the major story, only to find it moved away from him. He claims to have turned down the role of singer in The Sex Pistols. Midge could, and probably should, be a lot more famous than he is, especially when you think of all the things that he has been around, including Visage, Thin Lizzy and a band with former Pistol Glen Matlock. He then brought Ultravox back to life Billy Currie, who he worked alongside in Visage, and it was this group that would lose out to a poxy novelty tune that would rack up over ten number one spots around the world.

Still, he finally reached the number one spot in the singles chart in 1985 with If I Was, a song that was nowhere near as good as many of the songs he had created at this point in his career. Then again, as Midge had already learned, the best songs don't always make it to the top of the hit parade.

The 80s was a boon period with Aztec Camera, Altered Images, The Associates, The Bluebells, The Blue Nile, Cocteau Twins, Lloyd Cole & The Commotions, Deacon Blue, Barbara Dickson, Fairground Attraction, Fish (with Marillion), Hue & Cry, Hipsway, Jesus & Mary Chain, Love &

Money, The Proclaimers, Jimmy Somerville (with Bronski Beat and The Communards), Texas and Wet Wet Wet all making inroads into the charts or connecting with an audience around the UK.

While most of the critical acclaim regarding Aztec Camera surrounded their early work (with a 30th anniversary tour of debut album High Land, Hard Rain being extremely well received), it was the band's third album, Love, that would be their biggest commercial smash. The album reached the Top 10 and in Somewhere In My heart, the group bagged a top three slot. The song regularly features in recollections of the 80s and the entire album featured a focused attempt at achieving success in the American market. This wouldn't be achieved, and some long-standing fans weren't too keen on the new direction, but for music fans of this era, this is the Aztec Camera period that is most fondly remembered.

Of course, when it comes to fond memories of the 80s, Clare Grogan of Altered Images will be high on the lost for many folk. It takes a bit of nerve and gall to write a song called Happy Birthday, although if you are going to choose a title and idea for a song, why not choose the song that has been sung the most times ever! The Altered Images track was very early 80s, capturing the new wave pop sound, and it was a huge smash, reaching number 2. The song was released in 1981, the same year that Grogan was brought to a wider audience thanks to her role in Gregory's Girl and the band also reached number 7 this year with I Could Be Happy. The Happy Birthday album would only reach 26 but 1982's Pinky Blue reached number 12 with the band's final record, Bite, reaching number 16 in 1983. This album was the poorest selling of the group's three albums and they split before the end of the year. In 2002, Grogan revived the Altered Images name and is still performing with an all new line-up.

The band also featured Johnny McElhone, who upon the break-up of the band, would go on to have moderate chart success with Hipsway before starting Texas. The fact that he was in 3 major acts with varying degrees of success is an interesting note and no doubt sees McElhone being an answer in a number of pub quizzes across the country.

McElhone wasn't the only performer of the era to appear in a number of successful acts and you could argue that Lawrence Donegan achieved even greater diversity in his career. Donegan was the bassist for The Bluebells, whose Young At Heart was a popular hit in 1981, and then a number one single in the early 90s after a car commercial revived the song. The bassist moved on to Lloyd Cole And The Commotions, a band formed when Cole was studying at the University of Glasgow, and then when they split up, he was employed as an assistant in the House of Commons to the Labour politician, Brian Wilson. Donegan would then eventually become a golf correspondent and author, ensuring that he had at least 3 separate careers that most people would be highly envious of.

The diversity in success, critical and commercial, of these acts was one of the most fascinating elements of the rise in Scottish music acts of the 1980s. It is not as if the Associates, hailing from Dundee, achieved sustained success but for fans of the group, their admiration and respect for the vocals of Billy MacKenzie is still as strong today as it was at any point. There is an element of tragedy in the life (and death) of MacKenzie but to focus on that would be to miss the point and to overlook the talent and majesty of his vocals.

Similarly, you would never say that The Blue Nile were the biggest band to emerge from Scotland but with respect to quality and music that genuinely touched the people that love it, they have to rank as one of the most important acts the country has ever produced. The Blue Nile created songs that sang so eloquently of Glasgow and their surroundings that people couldn't fail to be swept up in what they delivered. Walk Across The Rooftops received rave reviews and introduced the band to the world. Follow-up album Hats may only have reached number 12 in the UK album charts but with respect to being loved, and setting a blueprint for many artists to follow, this was a band that were placed on a pedestal. Even in the spring of 2014, Guy Garvey from the band Elbow, appearing at the Scottish Hydro, highlighted his love and admiration for The Blue Nile.

You would also never argue that the Cocteau Twins were a

highly commercial act but they are another band that deeply touched a great number of fans and followers. The band regularly topped the UK indie singles and album charts while the Victorialand album reached number 10 and the Heaven or Las Vegas album, released in 1990, peaked at number 7. Four of the groups albums were classed as having attained Silver status by the BPI, but sales figures can't do justice to the majesty of Liz Frazer's vocals, an instrument in their own right. The range and diversity of her vocals created their own language, utilising sounds as opposed to words to inject emotion into the tracks. The complexity of the vocals delivered by Fraser placed her under huge pressure at times, with the singer commonly referred to as being a recluse and an artist that suffered from perfectionism. The thing is, with such a vocal talent, it is easy to see why you would be keen to make the most of what you had been given in life. Elizabeth Fraser remains one of the most unique singers and stands as one of the finest achievements Grangemouth has given to the world.

There's always been scope for bands to become big without having number one singles or a list of songs that are known all across the country. Many Scottish acts fit neatly into this category but there have been Scottish acts that sit at the opposite end of the spectrum, which is where you will find a couple of acts from Edinburgh, notably Fish and The Proclaimers.

One of the things that Scottish artists have to be wary of is acting like a dick in the eyes of their audience. Some artists get a lot more leeway than others but there is no doubt that in Scotland, if someone is acting out of line, it won't take long until they are pulled up for it. From Sheena Easton to Glasvegas, there is no shortage of artists that had all the potential to go to the top but managed to throw it all away by pissing off their fans.

However, one artist that managed to act like a dick and still be loved by a lot of people was Derek William Dick, better known as Fish. In the 80s, Fish was just one of the many Scots artists regularly peppering the Top 40 as the lead vocalist in Marillion. Fish was in the band for 9 years, helping them to achieve their biggest level of commercial success. The thing about Marillion now is that while they aren't a band that has any relevancy to the charts, they are a major act with their fan base who are more than content to do their own thing. The current wave of the group has been one of the notable leaders of turning to a ready-made audience to pay for new albums, cutting out the need for labels and middle men.

That wasn't the case back in the mid-80s when the instantly recognisable unique vocal delivery of Fish was booming out of radios and TVs across the land. The band started off with a prog-rock sound, drawing comparisons with early Genesis and Rush. The lyrics of Fish stood at odds with his appearance, making them quite a strange band in sound and looks. It was on the group's third album that they turned to a more commercial sound, albeit still retaining their prog rock roots. The album virtually contained two continuous pieces of music, one on each side. In this regard, you have to give the band credit for maintaining close to the image that they had developed over the years, while providing something much more palatable to a wider audience.

Kayleigh was the song that brought the group to a wider audience, reaching number 2 in the charts. As opposed to being a song about one girl, it transpired the track was dedicated to a range of girls, all of whom Fish had done wrong over the years. Stories of lost love always chime well with listeners and buyers and you can guarantee there were plenty of people crying themselves to sleep while listening to this song and substituting Kayleigh for whatever ex-partner was in their mind. The song was prevented from hitting the top spot by a version of You'll Never Walk Alone, which had been released in the wake of the Bradford City stadium fire.

The follow-up, Lavender, reached number 5, hanging around for a good while in the upper reaches. Oddly enough for a prog act, the song had to be extended for its release as a single, extending the minor section on the album into one that was more suitable for radio play.

The album both of these tracks came from, Misplaced

Childhood, secured a number one spot in the summer of 1985 and spent an impressive 41 weeks on the charts. The record was voted the album of 1985 by the readers of Sounds Magazine.

Marillion were not to be first, or the last, act to find that life in the spotlight wasn't all it was cracked up to be. Their next album, Clutching At Straws, was another hit, peaking at number 2, their second highest ranking in the album chart, but perhaps most tellingly, it only remained on the charts for 15 weeks, the shortest spell of any Marillion album to this point. The group was at breaking point and the lyrics focusing on drinking, life on the road and excessive behaviour were hardly a subtle reference to the mind-set of Fish, or the group. Within the year, Fish had quit the band and neither he, nor the group, were to achieve success of this nature again. To be honest, they were probably all quite happy about that in the long run.

Another East Coast act that had to deal with fame and acclaim was the Proclaimers. The Leith duo sold more records than any Scottish act of the era, apart from Simple Minds, and did so in a charming and engaging manner that ensured that there was a wave of emotion sweeping them along to chart success around the world. Letter From America and I'm Gonna Be (500 Miles) may have been the rip-roaring tracks, belted out with their natural tongue that pushed the act to great heights, but there is so much more to The Proclaimers than their massive anthems. Touching laments to their family, friends and locations sit neatly alongside political numbers and rousing tracks that appeal to people of all ages. In fact, it is easy to forget or overlook the strongly political message contained within Letter From America. Having such a catchy hook and refrain can work wonders for selling records but it can sometimes detract from informing people about the decline of life in Scotland. Over the years, general opinion about the band has focused on the bigger and poppier moments and the act has developed into one that is an ideal choice for any festival or major tour. This may diminish some of the stronger elements of their back catalogue but when it comes to giving the punters what they want, The Proclaimers remain an act to rely on.

You could argue that the rest of the major Scottish acts in the 80s flitted in somewhere between the critically acclaimed Blue Nile/Cocteau Twins position and the commercially popular Fish/Proclaimers area. One act that could never seriously boast of major success with respect to radioplay or rundowns, but who were regarded as a proper act with big concert and album sales were Runrig.

There are plenty of Scottish things that people travel far and wide to see. The rolling hills and the stunning lochs are essential in drawing in tourists but you'll also find that deep fried Mars bars are an essential element of every Scottish guide book these days. This isn't something to be proud of, but when it brings in people with folding money to spend, you can see why there is a tailoring to the market. It's not all bad though and one of the most attractive things we can offer as a country is the tradititonal Scottish wedding. Sure, the hip flask adds a certain panache to these all-day events, and the modern addition of bacon rolls in the evening session are very much welcome, but the success of Scottish weddings lies in other aspects. The kilts and tartan are a vital component of the day and if you are looking for something that tops off the perfect day, ensuring great memories are taken away, it's the final celebration at the end of the night.

These days, it's probably not a legally recognised Scottish wedding unless Loch Lomond by Runrig results in the bride and groom being engulfed by family, friends and well-wishers. Runrig are another band that are massive, known over the world and instantly considered to be a Scottish act. Loch Lomond was the band's debut single (found on their second album, and released close to the 10th anniversary of the band forming), just about scraping into the top 100. It would eventually crack the Top 10, after a Hampden Remix, selling strongly for charity.

It wasn't until the group signed with Chrysalis that they started to make serious in-roads with respect to a more widespread level of acclaim. The act would never be one that was cut out for singles success but their albums performed well, while providing the platform for their live shows to be in demand. 1989's Searchlight album reached number 11, The Big Wheel struck number 4 and in 1993 Amazing Things peaked at number 2 in the album rundown. It was an album hailed as a classic and a collective piece, as opposed to something for singles to be harvested from.

The band managed one more album with their most well-known component, singer Donnie Munro, Mara, which was also to be their last album with Chrysalis Records. That was in 1995 but as of 2014, the band is still active, having clocked up more than 40 years of service.

For all those years, there is probably no greater compliment to pay Runrig than the fact that their music has been central to so many people's happiest day. The band shouldn't get too carried away though because with their song usually featuring as the last song of the night at weddings, it has probably sound tracked more fights than Eye of The Tiger!

Deacon Blue are another band who are still touring and wowing audiences, bringing their tales of life in Scotland and their social views to a wider audience. In the latter half of the 80s, US soul music provided the platform for major success. Acts like Texas and Wet Wet Wet, while being rightly derided for being a bit naff in the 90s, but in the late 80s, the lads from Clydebank ruled the roost.

The group's debut album, Popped In Souled Out, eventually sold over two million copies and the band achieved a sustained period of commercial success in the UK, Europe and in the American market. In 1989, the band played a free concert on Glasgow Green, attracting over 40,000 people on a wet September day. This was a fantastic achievement but even at the time, there were complaints about the new songs, with the Glasgow Herald review noting that a notable number of fans started to drift away before an hour of the set had been played. Such is the nature of free concerts, you will get people turning up to see what the fuss is about and to be part of the occasion but equally, if they haven't invested money in the set or emotionally in the band, there is nothing to keep them hanging around if they don't feel the set was great. The set wasn't the greatest advertisement for their upcoming album and upon looking back; the act's debut album was their creative highpoint. Greater success followed in the mid-1990s thanks to the cover of Love Is All Around, taken from Four Weddings And A Funeral. The band achieved single success with original material as well at this point, but there was a feeling that the single and ticket sales owed as much to the personal fan base of lead singer Pellow as it did to any affection for the material that was being released by the group.

Texas also bounced back in the latter half of the 90s, becoming more commercially successful than they were during the first flush of fame. At this point, the band's promotional activity centred less on the group, and more on pushing lead singer Sharleen Spiteri directly into the spotlight at all times. It worked, with White On Blonde becoming their biggest selling album. The album reached the number one spot, even eclipsing debut record Southside, which managed to debut at number 3 in the charts. The band's second and third records, Mothers Heaven and Ricks Road, were not well received and many felt that the band's days were numbered or at the very least, there was a need for their fourth album to be a massive success. It was and by 2013, Texas can claim to have sold more than 35 million albums around the world.

While there was a market for stylish and over-produced music from Scotland in the 80s, there was always room for the chaotic. The Jesus & Mary Chain, from East Kilbride, would smash and struggle their way through a number of early gigs which were more about the event and the aggro as opposed to the noise and confusion that was emanating from the stage. Over time though, the JAMC would get it together, helped by Glaswegian Alan McGee at Creation Records. The early focus on the group may have been about the aggro and the chaos but in debut album Psychocandy, the Jesus & Mary Chain delivered an album that still sounds as fresh and brilliant today as it did back then. The record attempted to blend the Velvet Underground and the melodious pop of Phil Spector, succeeding in a strong way. It wasn't only an album that proved there was much more to the band that chaos, it set a new blueprint for countless bands, indicating that you could mix feedback with harmonies in a meaningful and beautiful way.

Away from the stomping pop hits, the shiny soul and the chaotic feedback, there were still routes for Scottish artists to break through. Mike Scott hailed from Edinburgh and his take on Celtic folk music, alongside the Waterboys, saw The Whole Of The Moon become an international anthem, with the band showing that they had a lot more about them than just the one hit.

The 80s were a phenomenal time for Scottish artists but as with any party, there would be a hangover to come in the 1990s. It's not impossible to have fun with a hangover, there were still a number of success stories to talk about for Scottish artists but there was certainly nothing like the triumphalism that Scottish acts felt in the 80s. With record labels culling many artists and a change in the popular genres, it was an uncertain time for many acts and artists.

Of course, if the major labels were no longer interested in taking the best that Scotland had to offer, there was always an opportunity to fall back on the indie label blueprints outlined at the end of the 70s and 80s. A casual look at the upper echelons of the charts may have seen fewer Scottish artists than the previous decade, but there was still a lot going on.

Firstly, 1990 showcased Glasgow as The European City of Culture. To many within the city, and most around the rest of Scotland, this seemed like an ironic title but Glasgow was changing, not always but predominantly for the better.

One of the most exciting components of the year was the Big Day 1990, billed as offering "free music from the heart of Glasgow." The event was spread across four different locations, Glasgow Green, the People's Palace (separate from the Glasgow Green stage), George Square and Custom House Quay.

The split was intended to run as follows, with George Square featuring local Glasgow bands and Celtic acts. Custom House Quay would be used to throw folk, jazz and acoustic together and the People's Palace setting would feature world music. This left the main Glasgow Green venue, Flesher's Haugh, as the stage where the main acts would appear.

Over time, this event has been boiled down to Sheena Easton being pelted with beer and glowsticks and Deacon Blue having a political rant but it was a lot more than that. Artists lined up for the big event included Adamski (riding high in the charts at the time and confusion over his set may well have played a role in the bottling of Ms Easton), The Associates, Aswad, Average White Band, Big Country, Billy Bragg, The Chimes, Deacon Blue, Sheena Easton, The Fat Lady Sings, The 4 of Us, Goodbye Mr MacKenzie (was there ever a band that looked more thrown together than this lot? Everyone had their own individual style, looking like the least cohesive band you had ever seen), Nanci Griffith, His Latest Flame, Hothouse Flowers, Hue and Cry, Les Negresses Vertes, Love and Money, Kevin McDermott, Maria McKee, John Martyn, Natalie Merchant, Paco Pena, Eddi Reader, The River Detectives, The Silencers, Martin Stephenson, Michael Stipe, Texas and Wet Wet Wet. It wasn't just an event for Glasgow, music lovers and big event hunters flocked in from all over Scotland, with crowd estimates coming in at around anything between 100,000 to 250,000 people. The event was also shown on Channel 4, ensuring the event was viewed across the entire UK. Like many events of this nature, the music was often secondary to the day out and social element with many people's memories now based upon what they read or seen on TV as opposed to what they experienced themselves. Not that this is any different from any other major event, but the strong Scottish presence on the bill highlighted the impact that Scottish music had on the world.

There is also the argument that the event showcased the Scottish mentality, particularly how returning "hero" Sheena Easton was treated. It is not entirely true to say that the Scottish psyche is one that hates it when local people become a success, if anything, the Scottish psyche is tied a bit too closely too backing local artists. However, when a successful artist appears to forget all about her roots, and then strolls on stage with that accent, it was always likely that it was going to end in tears. The media were quick to point out that Sheena Easton had been stand-offish and not very helpful in the run-up to the event, almost as if they were trying to justify the actions of the crowd.

Within two years, Easton would obtain US citizenship and she vowed after the Glasgow Green debacle to never perform in Scotland again. This period may have been the final highlight in her career but Easton has continued to make music and tour, while it is believed that she has made numerous intelligent financial investments in the United States. The Glasgow (and Scottish) audience may hold little time for artists that turn their back on their country, but there is no denying that Easton achieved some major success in the 80s.

She was the third UK female solo performer to break into the US Top 100 and she managed to appear twice in the same UK top 10, with Modern Girl and 9 to 5 (Morning Train). With over 20 million album sales around the world and being able to boast of being placed on the 5 main Billboard charts at the same time, Easton can look back on her career with much happiness and pride. For the record, she was placed on the Pop and the Adult Contemporary chart with 9 to 5 (Morning Train), on the country chart with We've Got Tonight, alongside Kenny Rogers, on the dance chart with Telefone and on the R&B chart with Sugar Walls. Add in a James Bond song and working with Prince, Sheena Easton can afford to laugh off her Glasgow Green appearance.

To further emphasise the popularity of the city as a music venue, the following weekend, Glasgow Green would play host to the Stone Roses, in another concert that has gone down in the history books.

Del Amitri were a breakthrough band in 1990, although the group had been toiling away since the early 1980s. There were spells when it looked as though the band would achieve success, a deal with Chrysalis Records, praise from the Melody Maker and a tour with The Smiths all suggested the band was bound for greater things, but it never materialised in the mid-80s. The miserable anthem Nothing Ever Happens, released at the tail end of '89, start of 90, struck a chord with listeners and the band were to become a staple act of the charts and radio for most of the 90s. Hitting number 2 and 3 in the UK album listings, while having single success in America and playing to large audiences, ensured the band was a major entity for most of the 90s, even if they were always a step apart from what was deemed to be the commercial sound of the time. While some bands give you the impression that they were delighted to be playing the fame game, there was always more of a world-weariness about Del Amitri. The ever evolving line-up may have helped to keep things fresh and spark new ideas, but it limited the sense that this was a gang and it meant than when the battle became tough, there was never going to be a collective spirit to keep the band going. The band is another act that have managed to benefit from the demand for reunion shows of late, although, for many people, they remain the act that sang the football song about getting on that bloody plane. It was a bold move to go with such a downbeat tone, although imploring hope, about France 98 but sadly, for band and country, it wasn't one that paid off.

The changing nature of the music scene in the 90s led to a few Scottish bands being ushered in while most of the 80s old guard were being ushered out. Grunge was in, Nirvana was where it was at and Kurt Cobain had a lot of positive things to say about a few Scottish acts.

The Vaselines were given tremendous exposure, not just through the patronage and praise of Cobain, but for the fact that the band incorporated Molly's Lips and Son of a Gun into their set and recorded output. These two songs featured on the Incesticide compilation album and versions have surfaced on some of the Nirvana reissues over the years. The Vaseline's reworking of Jesus Don't Want Me A Sunbeam was issued on the MTV Unplugged In New York album, with Cobain name checking The Vaselines before playing the track. Of course, in true Scottish style, The Vaselines had long split up by this point although they did briefly reform in 1990 to support Nirvana in Edinburgh. Regardless of not being able to fully capitalise on the acknowledgement from one of the biggest acts in the world at the time, the royalties would have done Eugene or Frances no harm at all. The Vaselines are another act who have managed to patch up their differences with the groups third album, V for Vaselines, released in September 2014.

This friendship between Nirvana and The Vaselines also led to Teenage Fanclub becoming friends and touring buddies of the band. There is no doubt that this connection put Teenage Fanclub in front of a lot of more people at the time, but it would be wrong to say that the Fanclub's success was down to this. In fact, with Spin Magazine ranking Bandwagonesque as their number 1 album of 1991 (with Nevermind listed at number 3), some of the most committed Fanclub fans could argue that it was the patronage from the Bellshill boys that made the difference to Kurt and company!

Follow-up album 13 didn't quite hit the spot but after that, Teenage Fanclub hit a run of form that has easily placed them as one of the greatest Scottish groups of all time. They've never been a band that has been in step with the times, sometimes landing fortuitously in the middle of a scene, sometimes standing so far apart from a scene that it is hard to picture how they would make their way back in.

Ironically enough, this could be argued as the backdrop to the release of Grand Prix, an album the group acknowledged as being their most American in style. Releasing this style of album at the start of the summer of 95, one of the Britpop summers may have been career suicide, but it turned out to be a masterstroke. Being on Creation Records at the time, one of the most important labels at this point, helped but in reality, the quality of the songs on Grand Prix would have made the record a success at virtually any point in the sphere of popular music. Tracks like About You, Sparkys Dream, Mellow Doubt, Don't Look Back, Neil Jung and Discolite still sound as brilliant today as they did back then. The great thing is, there will be people reading this who will rhyme off the other half of the album as being the highlights of the record. It was a tremendous slice of melodious guitar pop and The Fannies were to repeat their success on follow-up records Songs From Northern Britain and Howdy.

There may be more time between Teenage Fanclub albums these days and there may not be as many magical moments on the new releases as there used to be, but Teenage Fanclub still manage to deliver something magical special on every release. At the point of writing, the group's most recent record was Shadows, with classics such as Baby Lee (written by Norman Blake, Jo Mango and Ziggy Campbell) and When I Still Have Thee sounding as magical as anything in the band's back catalogue. Teenage Fanclub was one of the acts announced to play a set at the reopened Kelvingrove Bandstand, with the gig selling out in next to no time.

Meanwhile, if grunge was delivering the platform for swathes of youngsters to find an outlet for their disenchantment with modern life, other youngsters were looking to dance away their anger and frustration. Primal Scream, with the help of an abundance of producers and pills, finally hit upon the right formula for over the top success. Loaded would change the future of the group, creating a platform for Screamadelica to fuse together pop, rock, dub and dance in a cohesive collection. When you think how many different artists and producers were involved in making the collection, it may well be one of the few examples of too many cooks improving the broth! The clamour for tickets for the Screamadelica reunion shows highlighted the massive impact that this album had on many people. For some, it was a good album to have alongside the rest of their collection but for many people, it was a gateway record, opening up a world of dance away from the traditional sounds of guitar music.

Being worn out and a shift in drugs to something harder would see Primal Scream switch to deep Rolling Stones territory on their next album. This delivered commercial success with Rocks and Jailbird, but there were more than enough people feeling upset about the about-face delivered by the band. Getting back on track after the Give Out But Don't Give Up era was going to be difficult and many people believed it to be beyond Primal Scream but in Vanishing

Point and XTRMNTR, the band delivered two stunning records. A lot of it has to do with age, and while I love Screamadelica, I was too young to get the full benefit but XTRMNTR was at the perfect time for me. It was an album perfectly of its time and it was a ferocious album, continuing the process outlined on Vanishing Point. Again, a long list of collaborators helped to deliver more than the collective sum of individual parts on an individual Primal Scream record, and this is an album that deserves to be ranked alongside the best music that Scotland has ever produced.

Okay, there is an argument that Primal Scream by this point were less Scottish than the C U Jimmy character created by Russ Abbot (there's a topical reference for you) but with the Gillespie, Throb and Innes unit at the fore, flanked by a team of excellent additions, it's definitely an album that can be claimed as Scottish.

Another band from the late 80s and early 90s that showed Scotland knew how to rock out was Gun. Gun were a band who will forever be remembered for their cover of Word Up by Cameo but while this may have given the group their biggest hit single and a raft of new fans, it probably alienated some of their original following who had stuck with the band for a number of years. Gun were quite often seen as being the next big thing, receiving plenty of positive press and touring as the support act to big names such as The Rolling Stones, Bon Jovi and Def Leppard. This may not be the coolest of names of late 80s / early 90s acts but when it comes to getting your music in front of as many people as possible, there were not many better support slots to find at the time. Word Up was released in July 1984 and reached number 8 in the UK charts, the band's biggest hit.

Another Scottish artist achieving chart success in 1994 was Edwyn Collins. It may have taken a few releases and an appearance on a couple of soundtracks but the song eventually made it to the upper reaches of the hit parade and Edwyn was in high demand once again. This was the era of Britpop though and even though the name suggested that it was something the entire nation could enjoy, there was definitely a London vibe to it. If you weren't from London, you had to make sure that you partied in the right places in London to be pushed by the media.

Scottish acts like The Supernaturals and Whiteout were lumped in with this era while acts like 18 Wheeler found themselves considered part of the process due to their inclusion on Creation Records.

If there is something that runs through the Scottish music scene like grease from a pie and a sense of "we're making it up as we go along", it is the ability to steal defeat from the jaws of victory, or even defeat from the nose of a draw. The list of Scottish bands that may have made it bigger than they did will be longer than the queue to chuck eggs at politicians when that is finally legalised and shown live by Sky but one band that could have achieved a lot more was 18 Wheeler.

18 Wheeler are remembered for a couple of things, neither of which are about their music. Firstly, it was their gig at King Tuts that Oasis cadged onto the line-up, allowing them to play in front of Alan McGee. This changed the shape of British music in the 90s, and it ensured that companies such as Adidas, Ben Sherman and Fred Perry did rather well for themselves from the mid-90s onwards. It also ensured that charity shops and second hand record shops had more than enough copies of Be Here Now or Standing on the Shoulder of Giants to cater for any emergency.

The second thing that 18 Wheeler received publicity for was that Tony Blair got their name wrong when introducing them at a party conference. He couldn't get a number and a word in the correct order and yet he had the power to take the country to war. It really makes you think doesn't it....of course, that is Philanthropist of the Year Tony Blair we are talking about now...

Anyways, if you knew they two things about 18 Wheeler then you probably know a lot more than most people but this would be a shame. The band were hit with an early setback in 1994 when David Keenan quit to set up the Telstar Ponies but with Steve Haddow recruited, the band released their debut Twin Action that year. A year later, Formanka followed, with the band being derided or overlooked for the influences that they wore so obviously on their sleeve. In a bold move for a west of Scotland group at this time, 18 Wheeler had decided to listen to the sunshine melodies of the West Coast of America and of course, Big Star, using these styles as the blueprints for their early career.

Sure they were shambolic and an example of the madness that encapsulated Creation Records at time but in Year Zero, released in 1997, they made an album that was a whole lot better than most of the music that was being churned out at the time.

If anything, the album was a bit ahead of its time, ironic given its title and the blend of rock and dance would likely have been better received a few years down the line. Still, music success is often all about the timing and while 18 Wheeler had the tunes, they never had a lot of luck. The sound of their first two albums saw the act tread a familiar path for Glasgow indie acts and this was safe yet unexciting territory, but album number three was a brilliant side-step, maintain the melodies but supercharging the musical backing. While Year Zero never brought the band any more success or acclaim, it was a bold move that the band should have been commended for taking.

Creation dumped them during the recording of their 4th album, which never seen the light of day, and the band have been consigned to a mere footnote in the annals of music history. Probably the reason I remember them most was for a stunning show in the Cathouse after the release of Year Zero. It was a short set, not even spanning the whole album, but it was tight, exciting and the drinks were priced stupidly low. That and they were supported by a band that had a flute player in it, a band dubbed *"the fluture of music"* before they have even finished their second song *(as I said, the drink was very cheap)*.

So there you go, 18 Wheeler, they came, they did some stuff and they went away again. They are not alone for having that as their epitaph in the world of Scottish music but I'm really glad they made Year Zero.

Creation was also the home to Hurricane #1, the new act from Ride's Andy Bell, featuring singer Alex Lowe, hailing from Blairgowrie. Their debut track Step Into My World was highly impressive, but this was by far the best track the group had. Bell then spiralled from there into Gay Dad before landing the role of bass player in the revamped Oasis line-up. There was also The Gyres, a Blantyre band that talked the talk and played with many of the leading lights in the Britpop era. Sadly, a BBC Scotland documentary, and their own graffiti around Glasgow is the thing that sticks in people's minds of the time.

In the same era, Bis were making a name for themselves, featuring a much talked appearance on Top of the Pops, as the show attempted to inject new life into a show that was starting to flag. Too much focus was placed on the "first unsigned act", something which wasn't really true and a matter of semantics, and not enough was made about how the band's performance was something that stood out from everything else that was on the show. One of the conversations you will hear most about Top of the Pops from the 60s, 70s and 80s was of parents questioning the rubbish their kids were enjoying and saying that the music from their time was so much better. The 90s on TOTP didn't feature too many acts that would have gotten under the skin of parents but Bis definitely achieved with their performance of Kandy Pop.

The early hype probably didn't help Bis because they were a band that evolved, and in my opinion, greatly improved over time. A quick listen to them at T in the Park in '96 indicated that they weren't for me at the time, but the Eurodisco era of the group remains a strong period that I really liked. In an ideal world, we'd have a lot more records from the Dirty Hospital offshoot but there is no doubt that Bis are a band that have a large and dedicated fanbase and again showed that you didn't have to be part of the scene to break through. Bis would release some material through Chemikal Underground, another success story of the Scottish music scene.

Chemikal Underground was formed in 1994, primarily to release The Delgado's material, but a look at the acts that have appeared on the label indicates how influential they have been. Postcard Records may get most of the praise for being early innovators but for being a label that has stuck around and made a massive difference to bands and people's lives, Chemikal Underground deserves a massive deal of respect.

The fact that the label has chosen to focus on giving back to their own community, see the East End Social section, as opposed to resting on their laurels is a great example of why they are so important in the Scottish music scene. That section covers the label and The Delgados in more detail, but with respect to Scottish music from 1994 onwards, Chemikal Underground was at the heart of it all. They may not have always delivered chart success but if you look at year-end lists and albums that people have taken to their hearts, there will be a lot of acts from this label.

A brief selection of Chemikal Underground artists lists names such as Aerogramme, Aidan Moffat, Arab Strap, Bis, De Rosa, The Delgados, Holy Mountain, Malcolm Middleton, Mogwai, Mother and the Addicts, The Phantom Band, The Radar Brothers, RM Hubbert and the Sluts of Trust. As Teenage Fanclub may have put it, "ain't that enough?"

Mogwai and Arab Strap would make their mark on the UK scene in both the 90s and 00s, but there would be other acts that would reach greater success in the charts. Travis were one of the biggest bands of the post-Britpop era, which probably indicates the comedown that people were experiencing at this point. The band was able to tap into the mainstream conscious and for a spell, they were huge, and a massive draw for festivals.

My favourite Travis anecdote, which will remain unattributed to save the person abuse from Travis fans, and to slightly annoy the person as well, dates back to the early days of the group, perhaps even when they were performing under the Glass Onion moniker. The group were on stage in King Tuts when there had been an over-enthusiastic use of the smoke machine, leading front man Fran Healy to quip (as the tabloids newspapers would say), "Someone has set this place on fire".

To which a response of "Well, it wasn't fucking you guys" was shouted back. It was the sort of audience participation that had English comedians fearing for their lives when their tour approached the music halls of Glasgow and it is good to see that bands were subject to the same attitude.

In all fairness, Travis weren't awful but musically, one of the worst things that the band achieved was becoming big. The first album, while being far from polished or clever, was alright. It was bright, spunky, energetic and all the things that debut albums should be. The sense of spirit and adventure was in the right place, and tracks like All I Wanna Do Is Rock and Happy would come in handy for when the group made it big. Mind you, no one really mentions The Glitter Band influence on Tied To The 90s these days.

The second album showed progression, it showed maturity and it showed someone gave Fran the big book of Oasis chords with the Wonderwall page earmarked for him. The group had four hit singles in 1999, taking advantage of a dry spell for the big guitar bands of the time with Travis filling the gap neatly and becoming quite popular in a short space of time.

The singles, and some of the album tracks, were all nice enough in their own way and you can see why they went huge. For festivals and big shows, it was exactly what people were crying out for and with lines like "Why does it always rain on me?" their place on the festival circuit was assured.

The only thing is, that was about it for Travis. Some of the following singles had a Byrds influence, some tried to re-capture their previous success but with every new release fewer and fewer people seemed to care about the albums. To this day, they'll still be a draw for festival crowds but there was something painful about watching the group make small talk with the idiots from Sunday Brunch, and Travis have a bunch of guys who aren't bad in the media. Still, if the festival crowds are happy, then the band's so happy and they'll make a living through touring and royalties for as long as they want.

An act that never that bothered the singles charts at the time (or now being totally honest) but who managed to give the music establishment a bloody nose at the end of the 90s was Belle & Sebastian. Although the group was on their third album at this point, they had been nominated for the Best British newcomers at the Brit Awards. This was a public vote, with the backing of Radio One, and many people believed that the popularity of Steps would see them win the award. Despite this, the Glasgow band triumphed, hilariously annoying Steps, Five and Pete Waterman, who was suitably raging at the lack of award for his manufactured drivel. It didn't take too long to break about a story about the vote being rigged with students from two universities in Glasgow voting en masse. There was likely to be some form of coercion into getting behind the local band and getting it up the mainstream, but there was definitely a groundswell of support for the group in their home town, with Isobel Campbell studying at Glasgow University.

In many ways, this was an early warning for the music industry, and other industries, of the power of the internet and the ability to whip people up into a frenzy that will see them take action. While Steps had a fan base, there was no real grass root element to it and with the bands' younger fan base not having access to the internet as much (it certainly wasn't as widespread as it is today), it was not as easy for a fan base to come together. Sometimes a fan base will mobilise itself for good as it did in this matter and sometimes it can mobilise itself for negative reasons. An example of this came when Manchester City were inviting suggestions for the naming of a new stand. Paying respect to a former player is always popular with supporters and not too many eyebrows at the club would have been raised at the strong level of support for Colin Bell. Some City fans would have genuinely voted in favour of recognition being bestowed upon Colin but in reality, the wider football community had stepped forward with much glee and hilarity about the thought of one of the stands at the stadium being named the Bell End.

In that case, much like the case with Belle and Sebastian versus Pete Waterman, The Bell End was to lose out. For some people, Belle and Sebastian have lost some of the sparkle and magic that made their initial records so delightful but there is a great deal to be said for the fact that the band has evolved and become an entirely different creature. This is partly due to the simple process of growing older and with there being so many members of the group; different people have been afforded the opportunity to showcase their talents and strengths. Stuart Murdoch remains the focal point of the group but the band is now a fantastic live act and they have provided a number of stunning songs and albums over the years.

A switch to Rough Trade, and with Stuart Murdoch coming more to the fore again as opposed to the collaborative approach that has focused on the band's previous two long playing releases, saw the band hit their stride once again with the Dear Catastrophe Waitress album. For me, the band would hit their peak with Your Covers Blown (released in 2004 on the Books ep) and then the 2006 record, The Life Pursuit. The Write About Love album still had its moments, with I Didn't See It Coming and I Want The World To Stop being excellent tracks, and there is a lot to be said for the band now being recognised as amongst the elder statesmen (and women) of the Scottish music scene. The importance and popularity of the act was signalled by the fact that they were selected to play a set at the Kelvingrove Bandstand to celebrate the opening ceremony of the Commonwealth Games.

In addition to the success of the band over the years, there is also the fact that Isobel Campbell made her escape from the group and provided us with a modern day Nancy and Lee with her musical partnership with Mark Lanegan. Like Nancy and Lee, they seem an odd pairing but of course, that is one of the reasons why it works so well. Another more important reason of why it worked so well was the music. The songs were excellent and as long as you give Lanegan the opportunity to sing, he is always going to shine.

And one person that managed to shine for a brief but very bright spell was Finley Quaye. Finley was born in Edinburgh and in 1997, he lit up the charts with Sunday Shining and Even After All. Debut album Maverick A Strike went Gold within 3 weeks and at the 1998 Brit Awards, Finley won the Best British Male award. The nominees who had to stay seated while Finley celebrated included Gary Barlow, Elton

John, Paul Weller and Robbie Williams. The 1998 Brit Awards may be more remembered for Chumbawamba nominating John Prescott for the Ice Bucket Challenge, but it was probably as good as things got for Finley. The Spiritualized single from 2000's Vanguard album was probably the last big musical moment from Finley, and sadly it seems as though he hadn't had to seek his troubles in recent years. Finley was declared bankrupt in 2012 and in 2014, stories started to circulate in the media about Finley being homeless and needing a place to live. Clearly, musical fame and adulation is no guarantee of anything in the long term and with hindsight, Finley (like all of us) would probably have made different decisions at certain times. While you wouldn't expect him to get back into the charts, you obviously hope that he gets a helping hand to get him back to a reasonable level of living.

If Finley Quaye is an example of an artist that had it and then lost, one act that falls under the "one that got away" category would be Geneva. The band, hailing from Aberdeen, were being pushed in all the right places in 1997 and with the final days of Britpop falling all around the UK, there was definitely a need for something different, something less in your face and perhaps more beautiful. The vocals of Andrew Montgomery remain sparkling and crystal clear to this day and the band had anthemic songs that grabbed you by the heart.

Perhaps they were just a bit too clever and intelligent, Travis were far more direct at tugging at the heartstrings, and this is why it was them that went over the top instead of Geneva. A performance at the Glasgow Garage in January 1997, as part of the annual NME Tour, should have been the catalyst for success (especially since the band appeared alongside Symposium, Tiger and Three Colours Red).

Other NME Tours between 1996 and 2000 featured acts like The Bluetones, The Cardigans, Stereophonics, Asian Dub Foundation, UNKLE, Idlewild and Coldplay, amongst others. When you think of the some of the success and acclaim that some of these acts achieved, it perhaps rankles that Geneva didn't achieve more.

Record label wrangles and perhaps even stupid things like the band having a name and image that was slightly similar to Gene may not have helped and eventually the group disbanded after two albums in 2000.

Idlewild was an Edinburgh act that achieved success and they made more of their NME Tour appearance than Geneva did. There was something more universal about the appeal of Idlewild and if you were cold, cynical and of a marketing viewpoint, you could see that the Edinburgh band were positioned in between Geneva and Travis. Over the years, especially from 2000's 100 Broken Windows release, the band had a more polished sound, which brought them to a wider audience and earned more radio play. Prior to the release of this album, the group gained some much needed exposure when they supported US band Garbage at a gig to commemorate the opening of the Scottish Parliament. Many people might have felt that a band called Garbage was the ideal name to commemorate the opening of Parliament, even if the new building wasn't finished in time, but they were an apt choice. The Delgados were also on the bill, but the set brought about a strange bookending of the 1990s for live music in Scotland.

Way back in 1990, Glasgow was to place to be with the City of Culture focus and music fans flocking to the Big Day out on the 3rd of July. Here, on the 1st of July 1999, Edinburgh was the city music fans were interested in and at the heart of it all was Shirley Manson.

Edinburgh-born Shirley was one of the many different components that made up the Goodbye Mr MacKenzie slot in Glasgow and here she was, performing as lead vocalist for a massive US band. For many people, Garbage were brought to their attention through the inclusion of Butch Vig, legendary producer and the man behind Nirvana's Nevermind amongst others. At this gig though, it was all about the homecoming performance of Shirley and the set went down well. Maybe this indicated that Edinburgh gig-goers were better behaved and less jealous than their counterparts or perhaps it indicated that Shirley Manson knew how to conduct herself. I was never really a fan of their music, but I won't hear many bad words said about Shirley Manson!

The new millennium may have promised a lot of new excitement and drama, but there really wasn't too much change to notice. Travis and Idlewild remained the Scottish acts that were selling a lot of units and they were briefly joined by Colin McIntyre, under his Mull Historical Society moniker, who unleashed a selection of unbelievably catchy tunes.

Despite Primal Scream's attempts to meld the dance floor and the live arena, there hadn't really been many DJ success stories from Scotland in the charts. This certainly wasn't an indicator of the quality of club nights and DJs operating in Scotland, it was an indicator that was taking place in Scotland didn't chime with what the singles market was. If you are taking commercial success as a barometer or starting point for the great music created in Scotland, there is always an element that is going to be overlooked. No matter what sort of dance music you liked, venues like the Sub Club and the Arches in Glasgow, Club 69 in Paisley and The Calton Studios (or Studio 24) in Edinburgh have played host to some of the most innovative, exciting and thrilling dance nights across the country. Scotland has managed to pull together a number of major dance events and for many people, the reason to head to T in the Park every year is to spend a few days in the Slam Tent. There is no denying that dance music is massive in Scotland, but it never really moved beyond the market it was playing to on a weekly or monthly basis.

This isn't to say that the music of Mylo is on the level of the legendary club nights and events that have sound tracked the lives of so many Scottish music lovers since the 90s, but it certainly tapped into something. His Destroy Rock & Roll album took off massively, shoving a lot of people onto the dance floor when they wouldn't have expected to do so. In the words of the song, he came down from the Isle of Skye and he may have been awfy shy given his lack of hitting the publicity trail but in 2004 and 2005, the music of Mylo was massive. It was a release treated like a band release, with Mylo touring traditional venues. A King Tuts gig in

September 2004 was a massive success and Mylo performed in the Slam Tent in 2004 and 2005. Another hilarious element from Mylo's gig at King Tuts in September 2004 was the fact that the band called Your Codename Is: Milo played at King Tuts in October 2004 and I know of people who turned up that night expecting it to be the DJ!

The role of the DJ was to play an ever increasing role in the short-lived career of one Scottish act. Some bands achieve commercial success through years of hard work while some have exceptional talent. There are also some bands that have great connections or they achieve a big break through fortune and luck. There are also some bands that achieve a smash hit through being fly wee bastards. Take Speedway for example.

The band jumped on the mashup bandwagon that was popular in 2003. One of the tracks that was getting a lot of attention online and on some radio stations had been the blend of Genie In A Bottle by Christina Aguilera and Hard To Explain by The Strokes, which was pulled together by The Freelance Hellraiser. There was no progress made in obtaining a commercial release for the mashup with record labels not wanting to co-operate so Speedway stepped in with a cover version of the Aguilera track that chucked in as much of The Strokes sound as possible. It reached number ten and ensured the band got a lot of publicity and exposure. It was exactly the sort of track that the tabloid media in Scotland loves and the band was afforded a good deal of publicity at the time.

The thing is, you have to wonder whether this was the right approach to take to launch a band onto a wider audience. There is nothing wrong with kicking in the door to the party but if you are going to do it, you better make sure you have one hell of a party piece lined up. Speedway had nothing.

The groups second single hit number 12 but after this, their album, Save Yourself, bombed and their next single limped into the low 30s. Before too long, Speedway had split up, propelling Jackson into a career path which seemed to jump from bandwagon to car crash, although she at least seems to have settled on a particular style now with her group The Chaplins, but how long that will last before she veers off onto something else, who knows?

One of the escapees from Speedway managed to find his way into The Feeling, and while the quality of music may not have improved too much, at least there was a bit more commercial success and the illicit thrill of being in Sophie Ellis Bexter's backing band for Dan Sells to enjoy.

Of course, returning to the success of Mylo, if you are looking at Scottish acts of 2004, the name on your lips would have been Franz Ferdinand. A perfectly timed January release of Take Me Out saw the band reach number 3 in the singles charts and you couldn't escape their songs on the radio or the music video stations for the rest of the year. In many ways, Franz Ferdinand became the archetypal Art School band and if you are going to do that, what better city to do it in than Glasgow?

They were playing on the Main Stage at T in the Park summer and before the end of the year they had scooped the Mercury Music Prize. For those on the outside, it may have seemed like a classic overnight success story but the work and effort that the band, with Glasgow stalwarts Alex Kapranos and Paul Thompson in particular, had put in over the years was evident. This may have been a debut album, but the songs were honed to a level of pop perfection, intelligence and commercial success running through it. There may have been very little new about Franz Ferdinand, but it was a fresh and interesting package that saw the band being taken to the hearts of indie kids and mainstream fans across the country and beyond.

As you would expect from a band that had been working at their overnight success for a number of years, their follow-up album wasn't long in coming. You Could Have It So Much Better, released in October of 2005, didn't deviate too far from the debut album's theme and style but it featured an expansion and widening of the palate. Anyone fearing that they would become too big to write catchy pop hits were more than sated with Do You Wanna, but fans looking for progression were more than satisfied with tracks like

Outsiders. It would take four years for the band's next release, a bold album and one that is probably underrated by many people. Tonight: Franz Ferdinand suffers as much with the passing of time between releases as much as anything because in tracks like Ulysses, No You Girls and What She Came For, the sense of commercial sensibilities were still very much alive. Even if commercial success never followed for the album, the appearance of tracks on commercials and TV spots helped to keep money rolling in. Clearly tracks like Lucid Dreams grabbed the attention in reviews and many people may have shied away from the record for fear of it being an experimental mess. It wasn't but then again, if you view the band as an art school group, can you ever be surprised at their desire to change things up a little bit.

It would be a further four years until the next album, Right Thoughts, Right Words, Right Actions with this record being viewed as a favourable return to form. There were clearly a few moments that harked back to the earlier work of the group, and more than a few moments that drew attention to the Ray Davies school of song writing but on the whole, it was another consistent Franz Ferdinand album, that fans of the band should be more than happy with. If by this stage, you don't like Franz or you have moved on from what you perceived as their sound, fair enough, this isn't an album to get too excited over but it was definitely a record that deserves to be placed alongside their early work.

It would be wrong to claim Snow Patrol as a Scottish story but clearly Dundee and Glasgow had a large part to play in the evolution and development of the band. The group made two fantastic albums that didn't really do much for them even though they were gigging like mad around Glasgow and Scotland. Seemingly at a low end, after being dropped by their label, the band struck upon a new sound and went massively mainstream. The group then continued to mine this sound and formula they uncovered and there was an argument to be said for Snow Patrol being one of the biggest bands in Britain at the time. Even if the music was no longer as innovative or as exciting as it was when they first started out, and fair play to them for finding a career path that brought so much success, one thing that was always pleasing about the group was the fact that they could, well mainly Gary Lightbody, be seen at plenty of gigs featuring up and coming bands. Making money shouldn't be seen as a crime and you can bet that Snow Patrol managed to take many of their long-standing fans with them when they crossed over into the mainstream. There is sometimes a snobbish reaction to bands breaking free from their early indie bubble into a wide-stream audience, but for acts like Snow Patrol, and Lightbody in particular who comes across as a decent bloke, you can't really begrudge them...even if things did get a little bit dull after a while.

Lightbody was also the driving force behind The Reindeer Section, an indie supergroup that released two albums. Containing members of Arab Strap, Belle & Sebastian, Astrid, Teenage Fanclub, Idelwild, Mogwai, The Vaselines, Mull Historical Society, Snow Patrol and many more, this was a collective that would have packed out Nice N Sleazys by itself, and it probably did on many occasions over the years.

At this point, and depending on your age, you are starting to think that the bands you mention as breaking through can be seen as current artists and acts. There have been a broad range of artists from Scotland making it to the big time in recent years and for people worrying about there being too much of a Glasgow focus, there has been a good spread of acts from around the country.

The View were massive for a spell with many people loving the fact that they had the same jeans on four days, but of course, this marked the band out as being a bit posh in their native Dundee, where the wearing of jeans on consecutive days was never an issue of counting, just occasionally sniffing !

The View, or to give them their current title, "The View? Are they still going?" conquered the UK music scene for the briefest of moments and all without changing their trousers. For a band closing in on their 10th year together and who have released four albums and a compilation record, it seems a bit off to boil down the career of The View to Same Jeans, but even when looking through the list of singles they released, it becomes quite difficult to recall anything about the tracks. This is a bit of a shame because while non-Dundonian viewers needed subtitles to comprehend them, they definitely had a way with melodies. They had the tunes and they were scally lads, sometimes causing a bit of trouble for themselves along the way. The cheekiest scamps from Dundee that existed outside of the world of DC Thomson burst on to the music scene with all of the pep and energy of The Monkees on cocaine, which was probably an accurate description given the lead singer's drug bust.

The band reached number 15 with debut single Wasted Little DJs, repeated this feat with follow up single Superstar Tradesman and then smashed the top ten, reaching number 3 with Same Jeans. Since then, the band has only made it back into the top 40 once, with double A-Side The Don/Skag Trendy in April 2007. The band's debut album, Hats Off To The Buskers, debuted in the number one spot but there have been declining fortunes for the band ever since. The View have got the potential to be a festival and touring act for as long as they want to be while producing material for their fanbase when they want to. The View is exactly the sort of band that should be looking to make the most of the modern music industry by engaging with their fans directly and then hoping to reconnect with as many lapsed or new punters from the summer circuit. There's never any shortage of Scottish music events with drunken punters wanting a band with one or two songs they can sing along with their pals, and The View are exactly the sort of band for that style of event.

The emergence of The View sparked a mini scene in Dundee at the time, most notably with The Law, but it would be wrong to think that this was the only impact that Dundonians have had on the charts.

For Scotland's fourth largest city, you have to say that a roll call that includes Average White Band, The Associates, The Law, Ricky Ross from Deacon Blue, Danny Wilson and the View is not bad going. We've already mentioned that Snow Patrol owes a nod to Dundee, with the group being formed while the original members were at university in the city. The lead singer of Placebo, Brian Molko, grew up in the city, and KT Tunstall, while being associated with Fife, went to the High School of Dundee. Even in 2014, Dundee bands are making a name for themselves with Vladimir appearing on the T Break stage at T in the Park and the city hosting a number of innovative gig and club nights.

Talk of KT Tunstall turns the attention to Fife, another area which has achieved widespread success in recent years. Fence Records is another label that deserves a great deal of exposure and attention. The label dates back to 1997 when it was formed by Kenny Anderson, better known by his performing name of King Creosote. Over the years, with the label sadly calling it a day in 2013 (mainly due to differences between Anderson and the Pictish Trail), Fence released music by James Yorkston, U.N.P.O.C., Kid Canaveral, Randolph's Leap, Withered Hand, eagleowl, FOUND and many more. Fife can also boast of The Beta Band, a wonderful act but probably another band that can be classed as one of the acts that got away.

With the release of their initial three EPs, later bundled together as The Three EPs, The Beta Band raised the bar and there were massive expectations on the band's debut album proper. Sadly, the band failed to live up to this, for a number of reasons, and even the band was quick to dismiss the record. All of the momentum and goodwill that had been built up to this point had evaporated and the band was back at square one, in fact, they were probably restarting a few spots behind square one.

The band released To You Alone as a single indicating that they hadn't entirely lost the plot and in 2001, their second album was released to much more approving acclaim. The title Hot Shots II may have been a bit too tongue in cheek for some but the songs, including Squares, Human Being, Gone and Broke ensured that this was a much better album than their debut release. Heroes To Zeroes would follow in 2004, similar in sound to the second album, but the band was to split not too long after. Leaving behind tracks like Inner Meet Me, Dr Baker and She's The One ensures that The Beta

Band will always receive praise but there is a general feeling that the band never lived up to their potential. Steve Mason has been prolific in recent years, recording under the title of King Biscuit Time, Black Affair and his own name, always receiving a great deal of critical praise for his work, even if commercial success didn't follow. The rest of the group formed the Aliens, an act best known for the infuriatingly upbeat The Happy Song.

Spinning off from the form of KT Tunstall in another direction, there has been a steady procession of solo female artists breaking through into the mainstream from Scotland. Up next after KT was Sandi, and wasn't she an enigma wrapped in a puzzle wrapped in a terrible marketing campaign? She wished she was a punk rocker with flowers in her hair. I wished she was anything apart from a recording artist.

The whole Sandi Thom rise to fame was as puzzling as it was rapid as it was puzzling. Yes, puzzling crops up twice because it was initially puzzling how this artist shot out of nowhere to suddenly become massive and it was also puzzling why anyone was admitting that they liked the song, which was rotten.

Yes, there was meant to be a juxtaposition of the hippies and the punk styles, showcasing the fact that good old Sandi just wanted to play it all and bring people together. However, maybe it's just not in the Scottish psyche to see others experience overnight success in such a notable fashion. That and the song was rubbish.

Given that Sandi was a noted supporter of the SNP, her absence from any promotional material or soundbites in the lead-up to the Referendum indicated her fall from grace. Mind you, Sandi and the SNP were embroiled in their own version of the expenses scandal over the reported large sums of money that was spent on hiring Ms Thom to play a show, to travel around and for her party to have breakfast. The breakfast bill came to over £500; it's probably fair to say that they never popped into Wetherspoons to get their day started.

Still, by the end of 2013, Sandi Thom had released five

studio albums and a compilation album. Wow.

Just as the Sandi Thom bandwagon was starting to fall apart, there was a new up and coming female artist to take note of, and this time, there was no convoluted backstory or hype machine cranking up the attention. There was no massive lead single but in the end, this helped Amy Macdonald to develop more naturally and organically. Tales of how she developed a passion to play guitar after watching Travis play at T in the Park and how she wrote a song for Pete Doherty may have been neat rock n roll tales, but they were a lot more likable and believable than what was being served up by Sandi Thom's marketing team.

The slow build and more palatable attitude put Amy in a good position and eventually her debut album would go on to sell more than 3 million copies. With a million sales of her second album and rumoured sales of no more than 500,000 albums on her third release, it would be fair to say that Macdonald has lost her way a bit. She would draw a crowd to festivals and her own individual tours across the country would still sell well but she's an artist you would more commonly associate with the gossip pages of the Scottish tabloids as opposed to her actual music. She has done herself no harm by becoming the lead singer of choice for the Tartan Army at Hampden for Scottish international games (although Nina Nesbitt may swoop in to steal that crown from her) but you wonder where Amy goes next with respect to sales.

In one regard, and this is something that is true for a great number of artists, does it really matter about album sales anymore? The money is in the touring schedule and festival circuit for artists these days and this is an area where Amy Macdonald should be more than capable of maintaining interest.

While the emergence and development of the internet provided artists like Sandi Thom with immediate exposure but then exposed their limitations, it may be the thing that provides the most solid platform for artists like Macdonald. She may not have the fanbase of the first album, but Amy still has more than enough fans to reach out to and engage with online. This should ensure that there is a demand for new material and if she gets around to writing a hit or hits again, she'll be well placed to push out to a wider audience. Given her love of expensive cars, she'll want to keep working (she also only turned 27 in 2014 so she plenty of years left ahead of her), it just depends if Amy Macdonald still has the energy and motivation to keep on writing and playing if she can see her audience diminish in front of her.

The difference in tales of KT, Sandi and Amy, would maybe have put some Scottish girls off of making the big time but they kept on coming. In fact, if you thought that the girls mentioned above managed to cross over to the big time, you hadn't seen anything yet!

As Bono so eloquently put it, "Sande Bloody Sande." Who can forget the glorious summer of 2012 when London hosted the Emile Sande Games and decided to mark the occasion by getting some sports people to run about for a couple of weeks?

Emile topped and tailed the games, appearing at both the opening and closing ceremonies. Such was her omnipotent force that year you'd have sworn she attended the opening and closing of every door in the country.

You have to say her management team and label did a marvellous job for her in 2012. If there were a chance for Emile to promote herself, she was all over it and didn't this show in the record sales? In an era when people don't buy records, they bought Emile Sande's record. Some people probably bought it twice, once for the home and another copy for the car or shop.

There was a great deal of fortunate timing for Sande in 2012. Adele was pretty much lying low and the involvement of Dangermouse meant that Norah Jones was finally making an album that was great, interesting and worth listening to.

I don't think it's an insult to say that Emile Sande's album was neither great nor interesting. I very much doubt Emile will lose sleep over that opinion, not with her awards, kudos, praise and cash to help her sleep soundly.

It's also not to say it's a bad album, it's just a bit meh with a couple of big catchy moments that stuck in people's minds.

A couple of big catchy moments that seemed to soundtrack so many of the biggest events of the summer of 2012, a summer that a lot of people have fond memories of. She put the graft in, she got her reward and Scotland had another success story to cling on to. A few number one singles and over 2 million album sales in the UK alone is an outstanding achievement in anyone's book so fair play to Emile on that.

Way to raise the bar for the follow- up album though Emile, no pressure with that one...

Even after the year of the Sande, Nina Nesbitt was the next to stand up and give it a go. The small girl with a big guitar and a big voice made a good impact, garnering a lot of praise, a lot of publicity and enough sales to ensure that the record label maintained an interest in her. Again, it will be interesting to see where Nina goes next.

That's not to say that the solo artist success stories from Scotland were all down to the girls. It would be great to talk about artists like RM Hubbert, Withered Hand and Beerjacket as making an impact on the charts but this wasn't the case. All good and interesting artists in their own right but the only new solo Scottish male that got the charts all hot and bothered in recent times has been Paolo Nutini.

Paolo got his break standing in for David Sneddon, and that probably did everyone a favour. Nutini had a top ten single with his debut release, Last Request, but hasn't achieved this feat since. Mind you, with a number 3 album, two number 1 albums and more than 5 million sales from his three records, he won't be too worried about that. Taking the number of album sales over three records, it is not as if there is much of a difference between sales figures of Nutini and Amy Macdonald but there are some notable differences between the two acts, which means that there is still cause for optimism in Paolo's camp.

Firstly, the promotional activity for his latest album Caustic Love, his first album in 5 years, is still very much ongoing. With a Saturday night appearance at T in the Park being covered by BBC3, a number of UK festivals in July and August, a North American tour and then a UK tour, which initially featured 2 nights at the Hydro before they were postponed due to the artist suffering from severe tonsilitis, there'll be a lot more sales to consider for Caustic Love before the year is out. There is a sense of momentum with Nutini that Macdonald doesn't have, and maybe she needs to take some time out of the limelight to create a better buzz from her next return.

There is also the fact that Nutini will always sell a considerable number of albums to women of all ages while Macdonald's fanbase is a bit more fragmented. She was certainly well liked by Radio 2, with her hits being a staple of the station, but artists can very quickly find themselves marginalised when new acts offer something fresh. Whether Amy is able to continue to sell records in a large way is up for debate whereas for Paolo, if the lad does nothing daft he can expect to have a career akin to Rod Stewart's stretching out in front of him.

With respect to rocking acts, the Fratellis burned very brightly for a short spell, having a massive impact and then probably struggling to come to terms with it all. It looks as though the band is back to have another crack at the music game but it's unlikely they'll come close to matching the buzz and excitement of their debut album. Not to worry though, in sports stadiums and arenas around the world, Chelsea Dagger will be the sound of joy to some fans while it acts as a stabbing movement to the heart of others. Biffy Clyro have also become rather massive, appearing at 10 T in the Parks and having the pleasure of writing the song that was sung by an X Factor winner, Many of Horror, even if the Matt Cardle version was retitled When We Collide.

That may have been a strange move, and one the band tried to later distance themselves from but when you think that the single had clocked up more than 1 million sales as of the summer of 2012, it wasn't a bad decision from the group. They managed to get their own version into the Christmas week Top 10, never a bad week to chart highly, and there was very little backlash over the band's decision. All in all, it was a smart move by the band.

For an act like Biffy Clyro, chart success is never the best judge of their merit or talents, although it should be noted that the highest the band has ever reached with a single is number 5, achieved with Mountains. Initially released as a non-album single, there was considerable interest in the track and when the BBC Scotland chose the track as their theme for T in the Park coverage, it was permanently lodged in the ears of many music fans. The band finally achieved a number one album with Opposites, after reaching 2 and 3 with Puzzle and Only Revolutions. Known for their live set as much as their releases, Biffy Clyro are clear proof that chart success is far from the be all or end all for an act.

The last look at Scottish success with respect to the charts, at least up until 2014, has a dance element to it. Calvin Harris has become a monster with respect to sales and recognition. Any artist clocking up five number 1 UK singles as the lead artist (the fifth coming in September 2014 with Blame) with another two as a featured artist, has to be doing something right. Add in two number one selling albums and a place in the record books for having the most top ten singles from one album, nine, and it's obvious that Harris, hailing from Dumfries, has had the golden touch in recent years. So much so that according to Forbes, an American business magazine, Harris was the highest grossing DJ of 2013, with the magazine suggesting he earned $46m. Converting that to £ sterling, Calvin Harris probably earned over £25m for a year's work.

That isn't a sum of money that Chvrches can compete with but when it comes to a band working hard to develop their audience, this is an act that knows the path to success. They aren't at Emily Sande level but a clear indicator of their willingness to work came with the fact that the band played three times at T in the Park 2014. The band played their own set, they stepped in to play a set on the BBC Introducing stage and then when London Grammar pulled out, they stepped in once again. At the end of it all, Iain from the band took to twitter and said; "3 IN THE PARK! Sleep now, yes?"

They're an act that has received a great deal of press and praise with media coverage at the mountain of festival performances they have delivered ensuring the band is well known. You can bank on the band clocking up continual sales from their debut release for many years to come and even though the band will probably be deserving of a good rest at the end of the 2014 festival cycle, hopes will be high for the next release from the group.

It's been over 60 years since Lonnie Donegan led the first Scottish invasion on the UK charts and while it's not been a continual presence, there is no getting away from the fact that so many of the most popular and interesting artists over the years have hailed from Scotland. The importance of the Top 40 is diminishing and it is no longer important for an artist's career and progression. With the internet providing music fans with the chance to hear new material at will, there is no longer the need to huddle around a radio on a Sunday for the biggest hits of the week or to check out Top of the Pops for the popular songs of the era. The record industry will ensure that the charts always remain in place but there is an increasing opportunity for bands to achieve a strong level of success without placing any focus or attention on hitting the upper reaches.

Over the years, many Scottish acts felt that the distance between themselves and London was a drawback in their career, and halted them from achieving bigger success with respect to sales or industry recognition. Whereas bands would previously tour to promote their singles and albums, the opposite is more likely to be the case today. With many artists giving singles and even albums away for nothing online, the focus for the financial aspect of their career falls on playing live shows, tours and selling merchandise.

The importance of a great song and great music will always remain in place and the diminishing of the UK Top 40 will have no impact on that. What is in place now is a more level playing field that is more level, away from the Top 40 listing that could be rigged by the biggest labels with the best connections and sizable budgets. This is something that is likely to help Scottish acts, who would often be marginalised due to their location and distance from where the main labels are found.

6: Everybody Else

There is surely a book to be written about the Scottish bands that didn't stick around for too long or get the acclaim that their music deserved. However even if these acts didn't find the fame and fortune that could and should have been theirs, they still managed to leave a massive dent in the hearts and ears of people that followed them. Until that book is written, this is hopefully a step in the right direction of acknowledging some tremendous Scottish acts.

Aerogramme

It would be a great shame if the legacy of Aerogramme was solely linked with Chvrches (and apologies for bringing that up already but let's get it over and done with), because Aerogramme were an excellent band in their own right. Bearded before beards were cool, Aerogramme were hugely powerful and a perfect band on Chemikal Underground, being one of the big reasons why Glasgow is cited as a regional home of post-rock.

The band ploughed on with a devoted following in Scotland and enough fans dotted around the world to keep them going but sadly probably not enough to make it all worthwhile. Add in the passing of time, some health concerns and the general level of shit you have to deal with in juggling the life of a musician and some semblance of normality and Aerogramme sadly decided to call it a day in 2007. At least they went out with a bang at the Connect Festival, heading off into the sunset on their own terms.

It's also probably not too cool to highlight a cover they did when the band had so many top class songs of their own, but their cover version of The Flaming Lips Lightning Strikes The Postman is an excellent version of the chaotic original. It's noisy, its brash and yet at times the vocal melodies manage to create the sense of Big Star, so if you are looking for an easy way to get into the band, feel free to start here and then delve further.

Alan Trajan

He's not a name that many will be familiar with, but an obscure late 60s album that gets dug up from time to time by fans of the obscure and the devoted, Trajan has been likened to the wave of British rockers who had soul (but weren't soldiers). Most commonly bracketed alongside Joe Cocker and Stevie Winwood for their work at the time, the Firm Roots album was released in 1969.

Trajan would remain in the business, adding organ and backup for a number of acts before heading down to that London. He would fill some time playing in bars and jazz clubs, but sadly passed away at the start of the new century, years of hard living and drinking taking their toll on him. If you're ever faced with a musical bore from the 60s who promises you *he* (it is statistically likely to be a he isn't it?) has all the classics and all the underground hits, test their knowledge by slipping Alan Trajan into the conversation.

Arab Strap

When it comes to creating music, one of the most common pieces of advice budding songwriters receive is to write about what they know. Many acts see this as the perfect opportunity to write about their surroundings and Arab Strap left you in no doubt that Falkirk was a pretty grim place to be.

Never have the glorious pursuits of drinking and shagging sounded so downbeat but there was something infinitely charming about the sound of Arab Strap. Even as their sound evolved, becoming more polished with every passing release, the lyrics were honest, revealing and at times, a celebration. Sure the living could seem a bit shit at times but life didn't have to be shit, with Arab Strap painting a picture of life in Scotland that so many people emphasised with.

There's something immensely likeable and enjoyable about Arab Strap. They may not be the sort of band you want playing when your mum or dad walk into a room, but for singing in a proper voice and telling genuine tales of life, Arab Strap did it better than most.

The Beatstalkers

The Beatstalkers, the biggest Scottish pop group of their time, the Caledonian equivalent of The Beatles and so on and so forth. You get the impression that the story of The Beatstalkers is one that grows the further we move from the band's heyday, which never amounted to actually releasing an album.

The story of the band's free show in Glasgow Green being stopped due to too many people, with the band having to escape through the City Chambers, is a fantastic rock n roll story and certainly evocative of the time. This was an era when there was a sense of excitement in the air surrounding popular beat combos and The Beatstalkers were in the right place at the right time.

Perhaps the fact that a limited number of Scottish record stores were eligible for the charts limited the band's impact, and it may have been that their rough R&B was far better suited to the stage than in albums being played in homes across the country. Either way, The Beatstalkers have a legacy that far outstrips their recorded output, and they also put tartan on rock stages long before Slade and The Rollers.

BMX Bandits

You can go through most of this list and say that the band is typically Scottish or indicative of their hometown but this is very much the case with the BMX Bandits. A rolling and almost ever changing line-up has seen Duglas T. Stewart remain at the heart of the band and has seen him be positioned as one of the Godfathers of Glasgow indie. There's a very good chance if you're in a small venue watching a twee or quirky indie act in Glasgow, Duglas will be there, watching and thoroughly enjoying himself. Sometimes he'll be dragged on stage to sing; sometimes he'll be left in peace, but he's always there...if not personally, then at least in spirit.

One thing that probably works against the BMX Bandits is the fact that they have an almost omnipresent vibe to them. Sometimes acts need to split up, go missing or even pass away before they are properly recognised. We'll always have Serious Drugs and the one about Kylie having a crush on us, but you get the feeling that the BMX Bandits may just keep on rolling, outliving us all and all of the other new indie acts in the country.

Boards of Canada

Some Scottish acts pride themselves on waving their saltire as proudly as they can but other acts give you the impression that they exist with their own bubble. Boards of Canada, two Edinburgh brothers, have created a body of work that could have hailed from anywhere in the world. However, just because there doesn't appear to be any roots in their work doesn't mean that there isn't anything to warm to in the band's output.

If anything, the sense of warmth and comfort that shines forth from the track, often capturing a cinematic feel, is the biggest thing you take from the group. One of the things that always struck me about Boards of Canada is the fact that there isn't really a musical genre that properly captures the music that they make. The band is billed as an electronic duo, but they are as far removed from the cold and bouncy nature that springs to mind when you think of many electronic acts. They've also been billed as an ambient band, but again, there is often more spark and energy in their music than what you would normally associate with that style of act. This means that taking an amalgamation of these styles and genres would give you a better idea of what BoC serves up as opposed to looking for one defining style or sound.

With no live performances for over 10 years, Boards of Canada may not have had the chance to engage an audience in the way that other acts have managed to, but that takes nothing away from the high quality of songs on their major releases.

Camera Obscura

If you're ever looking for inspiration for sticking to your guns and following through with what you believe in, Camera Obscura will provide exactly what you are looking for. The band hasn't changed their sound or made any sweeping changes to their songs or performances over the year but little by little; they have been expanding and increasing their fanbase, so much so that they are now considered to be a band capable of drawing a big crowd to their own shows and to festival events.

Championed by Belle & Sebastian and John Peel right from the start, there was always been a strong level of support for the group, but they've never been a band I have ever taken to. One of the things about Scottish bands is that it can sometimes be difficult to judge what sort of mood they are in or what their stance is. At times, Camera Obscura strike me as one of the most aloof bands you will ever come across and then on other occasions, I reason that they are probably the sort of people that just like to keep themselves to themselves. That's never a bad thing and you'd probably wish that some bands would be a lot more like that.

The only issue with this is that I never seem to have developed any real emotion or investment in the band. Of course Lloyd I'm Ready To Be Heartbroken was a phenomenal pop song but even from that album, I didn't really get any other form of connection, or any interest in why I would should bother if this girl was being heartbroken or not. And that's not me, I generally have a reasonable level of interest in the activity and emotion of others but with Camera Obscura, and this includes having seen them live on various occasions, I've never really once felt that they were willing to open up and be a band that you'd give your heart to. Plenty of people clearly feel different about the band, and they're a good wee group, they just leave me a bit cold.

Chvrches

And moving on neatly from a warm band that leaves you cold, Chvrches can lazily be described as a cold band that leaves you feeling rather warm. Let's stick with the lazy description for now but of course, that is far from being the full story. It almost seemed as though Chvrches arrived fully formed, but the band just did their early growing up behind closed doors, only venturing out when they had plenty to offer. When you think of the backdrop of the individuals and the connections they would already hold in the Glasgow and Scottish music scene, this made sense. As soon as word got out about the act and their line-up, people were interested in what they had to offer.

The fact that Chvrches came out firing from the start, and in such a strong manner, meant that it wasn't too long for the hype machine to start getting worked. There has been an awful lot of people talking about the group, but I think in a good manner and I think their debut album, the Bones Of What You Believe, is one you'll return to time and time again. I've said at various points that I'm still not as convinced by their live-set up as much as the album, but there are probably two big reasons for that. Firstly, band's need time to develop their live show and the speed of progress behind Chvrches has probably limited this. I also find it harder for electronic acts to come across as strongly as they would like in the live arena. I love Ladytron, but I probably witnessed as many gigs where they failed to hit the spot, many times due to the sound, as gigs where I felt they were outstanding. For me, it seems harder for predominantly electronic acts to create a live show that works in the traditional gig setting but as the reaction of crowds around the country, Europe and America indicates, plenty of people love what Chvrches serve up and I'm sure it'll only get better.

During the 2014 festival circuit, the band started to make the right noises about their second album, and while there will be an element of pressure on the group to build on the success of the debut record, I'm pretty much looking forward to it.

Cosmic Rough Riders

Rubbish name, slightly better tunes. You definitely got a few rough riders hailing from Castlemilk, but I wouldn't like to vouch for their cosmic nature. The band recorded and released two albums by themselves before Alan McGee signed the band on a one-album deal to Poptones. This release, Enjoy The Melodic Sunshine, pulled material from the band's two initial releases, alongside a couple of new songs. It brought the band to a much wider audience, seeing them become a popular act for a lot of people and in the year-end polls, but the limited nature of Poptone's size, budget and distribution capabilities left the band hanging around in the middle ground. The band cracked the Top 40 twice and eventually sold over 100,000 copies of the album, but it was to be their one major tilt at the top.

When the lead singer quits to go solo, it can be difficult for a band to carry on and while the CRR stuck at it, and do so to this day, their brand of warm and melodic guitar pop is unlikely to help them scale the heights again.

Delgados

John Peel was a big fan of The Delgados but he was far from being the only person who loved the group. The group deserves a great deal of praise for their Chemikal Underground label but at times you feel as though the label, and all of the brilliant acts on it, overshadowed some of the stunning work that the Delgados produced in just over a decade.

There was always something real about the band's music. It would come with glorious melodies and moments that would soar but there was almost a resigned feeling to their lyrics, a feeling that life usually won when you were battling against it. Like all great pop bands, there was a dark and menacing edge to the Delgados songs and whether they were making the music as big as it could be or utilising sparseness, they were always engaging and thrilling. They seemed to be one of the bands that loads of folk you knew loved or spoke highly of but never seemed to make it beyond the critics and the serious music fan. You can see why they probably decided it was best to call it a day when they did but their musical legacy alone will see them remembered fondly for many years to come.

Django Django

It's another debatable one with respect to being a Scottish act but let's find some way to fit Django Django in. The group may have been officially established in London but the members of the group met in Edinburgh while they were studying at the College of Art so that is surely good enough to claim them as one of our own.

The band's debut album is one that owes a lot to the drums and if you don't find the record to be an infectious little number that makes you want to dance, you may have something wrong with your ears. Not all of the sounds work, there's a fair few kitchen sinks being thrown at the album but collectively, it's an energetic and shuffling collection that definitely benefits from repeated listens.

The Django's were also responsible for me hastily rewriting my best ofs for 2013 when they played a stunning set in Sleazys for The Hot Club on the 30th of December. It was such a good night, I was more than happy to make the next night a more relaxed and laid back affair, a whole lot of dancing and late night boozing of Sleazy's finest wares combining to create a night that wasn't going to be bettered the next evening! 2014 was a quiet year for Django Django but hopefully they'll rectify that in 2015.

Endor

One of the things about the Scottish indie scene is that you can sometimes get a band that is absolutely lovely but you find that opinion around them varies between falling in love with them and having no knowledge of them at all, with no point in between. Being loved by one person is a better state of affairs than being liked by 5 but when it comes to earning money to keep being in a band, you need to develop the likes and let the loves take care of themselves.

There have been plenty of acts that can be placed under this banner but it is a very fair description of Endor. Their Endor album, released in 2010, is so warm and welcoming from opening track All Your More Buoyant Thoughts that you think everyone who hears the band will chuck stupid amounts of cash at them to ensure they keep on making music of this nature. Lush guitars, poppy backing vocals and breezy brass made this an upbeat treat but for some reason, it wasn't enough to take them to a higher level or to make the hassle and effort that being in a band entails worthwhile.

It's not as if this fate has only befallen Endor, there must be a ton of local acts that will think what might have been, especially when you think about the quality of many bands that did manage to make it through. If you need cheering up, have a listen to Endor. If you need to feel sad, listen to them and then contemplate that they never made it.

Errors

Are you dancing? If Errors are asking then the answer is always yes. A great signing on Rock Action Records and hopefully there will be some form of synchronisation of releases between Chvrches and Errors to allow this band the chance to have a chance to develop their fanbase. Errors don't have the commercial pop edge that their more mainstream counterparts have, but they deliver catchy and melodic electronica that gets you on your feet. Come Down With Me is also the sort of pun-based album title that we should have more of, and the quality of the album lives up to the quality of the title.

Frightened Rabbit

Sometimes all it takes is one festival performance for you to change your mind about a band. It wasn't that I had anything against Frightened Rabbit; it's just that with so many bands to listen to, you can't check out everyone. What I had read about the group wasn't really exciting me or driving me to check them out and the brief snippets that I did hear did absolutely nothing for me. That all changed at Rockness 2009 though when with no other credible acts on at the same time, and the threat of rain looming, their tented performance beckoned.

And it was hell of a good. Whoever was with and behind the band at the festival did a great job, handing out saltire flags which saw the crowd whipped up to an excited state, but the set delivered exactly what you wanted for a mid-afternoon slot. It was loud, chaotic and there was a lot of power and passion in the vocals of Scott Hutchison. The band's name will either draw you in or make you run away but the music was something else and it wasn't a surprise to learn that Atlantic Records whisked the group away from

FatCat Records. A Top 10 album followed, and while some of this was down to the increased promotion and support from a bigger label, there had clearly been a building to this stage over the years. There is also the fact that the two best received albums of the band's time has come when Scott went through breakups, which will surprise very few people who have ever taken an interest in the creative process. It is often a lot easier, and a lot more interesting, to create art when you have something to rail, rally or bounce against.

It's not the sort of thing that you would wish on an individual, but you can see why fans of the band will be hoping that Scott only finds happiness and love away from his main periods of song-writing.

Future Pilot AKA

Alongside helping plenty of other bands to make music, Sushil K. Dade ventured out by himself for a number of albums under the Future Pilot AKA moniker. He got plenty of assistance from his friends in creating music that touched on a lot of influences. It was probably far too widespread of a musical style to make people sit up and pay attention, but anything that I heard from Future Pilot AKA, I quite liked, even if I was never rushing back to hear a song or an album again and again. Sushil was last seen musically with the Burns Unit, the supergroup project focusing on the work of The Bard, and there is nothing to indicate that there is anything more in the pipeline from the artist. When you go to an artist's webpage and read the latest news story telling you to visit MySpace for the latest news, you know that things have been a little bit quiet for a while.

Also, according to his Wiki entry *(I know, I know)*, perhaps a more apt name would have been Future Driving Instructor AKA. Still, Sushil was a prominent player at a busy time for Scottish music and he has left his mark on the scene.

Glasvegas

A band with a look and image that was enough to make Alan McGee lose his top and see them bundled off on tour with Carl Barat and the sub-standard act he was peddling after The Libertines imploded and Pete had robbed him of his self-worth. Glasvegas remain a brilliant example of style over substance, a feat the band is still pulling off after three albums. This is an achievement that deserves a fair bit of praise and every time it looks as though Glasvegas may chuck in the towel, or have the towel grabbed from them, they seem to bounce back for another round.

They're certainly brawlers looking to remain in the industry for as long as they can, you can't take that away from them...

Kain / Raising Kain

For a rock n roll city, Glasgow probably hadn't developed as many rock n roll bands as it should have done, at least rock n roll in the traditional sense. However, Kain (later renamed as Raising Kain) certainly gave it a right good go. They had some decent tunes of the genre, they had the swagger, they had the fanbase and they knew how to cause a scene.

Kain were a great live proposition and managed to turn in a number of great support slots in the city. It's probably a bit annoying (for them) though that my favourite Kain story relates to an interview, as opposed to any of their shows. The band had received a decent spread in the NME and a few days after the publication, I bumped into one of the band members and in making idle chitchat, mentioned it was a good interview and a great bit of exposure for the band. He didn't look too enthused (that's what rock stars are meant to do when given praise from a nobody) but he then provided the real reason for his lack of enthusiasm for interview. In amongst the music chat, there was a reference to cocaine use, and the band member's mum didn't take too kindly to this sort of talk regarding her boy! It just goes to show, no matter how rock n roll you want to be in life, you should always bear in mind what your mammy will think about it.

Class A drug use and music media coverage wasn't enough to propel the group to a wider audience and eventually, the band spluttered to a halt. Ian, the lead singer of the band, went on to become the main man at El Rancho, pulling together club nights and a record label that is a little bit country but still a whole lot of rock n roll.

Life Without Buildings

While it is easy to start off a summary of Life Without Buildings by stating they were an art school/scene band, which is true, it doesn't really take into account the fact that they don't really sound anything like any of the other bands you would class as a Glasgow art school band. The combination of Sue Tompkins vocals and the slightly post-punk instrumentation can lead to The Slits references being made, but again, that doesn't really give an indication of what the band sounded like.

Tompkins vocals, at times stuttering and repeating, at times short and clipped, acted more like another instrument adding to the music mix as opposed to being the conduit for lyrics and tales. There was an almost youthful spirit to the band, no doubt driven on by the unique vocals, but the songs still sound really inventive and really well produced to this day. The Leanover is infectious, nipping away at you like a wee yappy dog but the album contains a number of different styles and sounds, while still maintaining a cohesive sound and style. Sadly, the band's debut album was also their only studio album, with a live album being released long after their demise. There has been a resurgence in awareness of the band in 2014, largely down to the reissue of the debut album, but this is an album and band that are likely to be brought up in conversation for many years to come.

Mogwai

It's always the quiet ones to look out for. Well, in Mogwai's case, it is the quiet, quiet, earth-shatteringly loud, quiet ones that you need to look out for. Emerging in a manner that left you pondering if they were an Alan Partridge or The Day Today skit on a stereotypical central belt Scotland act, Mogwai quickly confounded the music industry. Over the years, the band has proven themselves to be one of the most intelligent and progressively creative acts in Scotland. Not bad for a bunch of Kappa wearing, Buckie drinking ner'do wells.

It is not as though the rise of Mogwai has been continual and smooth but in recent times, the band has evolved into a massively regarded act, easily at the forefront of Scotish music and culture. They may not be an act that would draw a main stage sized crowd at T in the Park, but they have an audience that is large and sustained. Their headlining role for the East End Social event at Richmond Park in August 2014 is indicative of their size and stature.

In 2014, one of the most important years for Scotland, it is only right that Mogwai have been at the heart of so much that has been going on. January saw the release of 8th album Rave Tapes and an appearance at the Royal Concert Hall for a show during the Celtic Connections festival. As, or perhaps even more impressively depending on your outlook on life, the band also released a whisky in this month!

A headline show in Edinburgh in March was also undertaken before the band hauled themselves onto the summer touring cycle before returning to play during the biggest musical celebrations in the East End of Glasgow since Frankie Vaughn turned up to stop street gangs from fighting.

In the summer of 2013, Mogwai played an outdoor set, which saw the band perform their soundtrack to the Zidane film. The film doesn't live up to its reputation, it's a bit too dull and Zidane manages to get himself sent off, although that wasn't a rare occurrence from a player who sometimes struggled to balance his genius and wizardry with the seemingly simple act of behaving himself. This show had been well received and an indicator that the band's star was on the rise but the tented show in the summer of 2014 was a true indicator of the band's popularity.

The fact that the Zidane show by the Broomielaw took place on a Sunday evening was also very apt for the band in 2013. This was because the band was placed into millions of homes across the United Kingdom thanks to their soundtrack work for French show, The Returned, which featured on Channel 4. The fact that two notable pieces of soundtrack work were responsible for bringing the act to a wider audience shouldn't be treated as a coincidence. Mogwai have always been an act that has carried a cinematic touch and flair to their music.

This may be a lazy consideration; after all, any band that rarely utilises vocals, preferring to focus on the sonic landscapes of their music will often be placed into the soundtrack area. To do so would be to overlook the musical nature, style and indeed quality of Mogwai. There may not be a lot of lyrics in the band's back catalogue, but the songs can still take you on emotional journeys.

One Dove / Dot Allison

One Dove were in the right place at the right time with respect to their early singles (if we step aside a slight issue with a sample) but this good fortune didn't flow into their albums. Launching a debut single on Soma in 1991, being brought to the attention of Junior Boys Own and then working with Andy Weatherall on the second single was pretty much the way to go at this time, tapping perfectly into the Summer of Love dance ethos that was around.

Perhaps worrying that this was a fad that wouldn't be around for long, or looking to branch out themselves, before they even started thinking about an album, a different tact was made with the group's music, taking them down a more commercial path. In the end, the band was caught in the middle of the two styles, not really satisfying anyone. However, at least the group managed to release their debut album, they supposedly have a second album in the can, but record label politics ensures it will never see the light of day.

No matter the style of music served up by One Dove, the vocals of Dot Allison were at the fore and a solo career was always in the offing for Dot. Dot has been a vocalist gun-slinger for hire, working with a huge range of artists, gaining critical acclaim for work with Massive Attack but it was her work with Death In Vegas that was possibly best received.

After Dot's debut album Afterglow was well received without achieving great sales, her work and relationship with Richard Fearless from DIV, were factors in We Are Science, a masterpiece of electro-pop. This album had the commercial potential while showcasing the song writing talent and vocal skills of Alison to push her into a higher platform. This time, Andy Weatherall's Two Lone Swordsmen partner Keith Tenniswood, or Radioactive Man to his fans was behind the controls for some of the record and all of the building blocks that were needed were definitely in place. Dot even supplied vocals and co-wrote Visions with Slam in '01 while also supplying vocals for Diving Horses with Death In Vegas in '02, so she certainly had a lot of exposure in the build-up to the release of the album. Whether it wasn't the right time for this sort of album (unlikely) or there wasn't enough of a push (from various parties, including Dot) to make it happen, who knows, but We Are Science never took off and before too long, Dot was back working as a hired hand and there would be five years before a new album, the nice but a bit uninspiring Exaltation of Larks.

Sadly, too many music fans will recognise Dot because of the time she spent with Pete Doherty as opposed to knowing her for her own immense talent, but that's just how things pan out at times.

Optimo
You wouldn't like it sugar. Not really an artist in the conventional form for this book, more of a way of life for some people and one of the best taste-makers Scotland has ever seen. Whether you fell in love with the music in their club night, on their mix CDs or both, there is no doubt that JD Twitch and JG Wilkes were responsible for more missed Monday, more brilliant nights, more money spent on records and more sore throats from shouting "one more tune" than virtually anyone else you will find in this book.

Even with the regular Sunday night Optimo night consigned to the past, Optimo continues to play, promote events and release mixes. If you are ever feeling a bit bored of music and want to find something new to fall in love with, turn to Optimo and they won't let you down.

The Pastels

Taking over thirty years to release your fifth album (or six if you include a soundtrack album) may be a sign that a band isn't the most productive but a band like The Pastels can't be judged by sales or even albums alone. This isn't a band you would measure by the volume of releases; it's a band you judge by the quality of songs and their legacy of influence. With a star studded line up of collaborators over the years and a claim to inspiring a raft of indie guitar kids across four decades (so far), The Pastels are a major Scottish act who have been hugely inspirational for generations of bands and musuc lovers.

For me, I had read a lot about The Pastels before I had heard them or at least knew it was them. Given the reporting of the band, I was expecting lightweight and limp guitar pop that was pleasant, but lacking any bit or edge. It just goes to show you should never believe everything you read or hear. Tracks like Baby Honey from the debut album *(okay, an early single from a few years before the album)* and Nothing To Be Done from the second album are as jagged and as spiky as you could hope for. Perhaps the production never let the songs rip loose in the way that they would these days, but if there is a belief nowadays that the music of The Pastels is lightweight or foppish, its more based on their identity and image, as opposed to the music. In fact, listen out to the second half of the Baby Honey 12" and you can see the lineage tracing its way down from the Velvets and which would flow into the shape of all of the future Scottish indie kids that would follow.

A brief flurry of activity in the mid-90s would see another 2 albums added to the fore and then there was a lengthy gap before Summer Rain in 2013. You need to have a bit of patience to be a fan of The Pastels, but they aren't a band that let you down, when they get around to taking care of business.

The Primary 5

They weren't young and they were still(s) waiting on the cash....crap, David Crosby really ruins the possible jokes from that band doesn't he? Yes, a quick look through the back pages of Paul Quinn will leave you in no doubt that Crosby, Stills, Nash & Young, The Byrds and of course, the bands that he actually played with, were all evident on the recorded output of The Primary 5.

This isn't a criticism, not when the sunshine pop was served up in such a satisfactory manner. It may not have been anything groundbreaking but when you think of how good the songs were, it's a bit puzzling that The Primary 5 were never a bit bigger. Okay, Brendan realised that no one in the world was anxiously waiting for the off-shoot project from a Teenage Fanclub drummer but anyone that enjoyed the music of the Fannies would have enjoyed The Primary 5, it's as simple as that. This is a band it is well worth going back and checking out if you haven't' already done so, second album Go is an album you'll be more than happy to let run from start to finish, so check that out.

The Shamen

Say what you want about the Opening Ceremony of the Commonwealth Games (and the less said about the opening section the better), how fantastic was the Scottish team's entrance to the sound of Move Any Mountain by The Shamen?

Depending on what age you are, you may be flummoxed by the mention of The Shamen or you may dismiss them as the band behind the novelty-esque Ebeneezer Goode. For a band of people in between that age though, The Shamen were far better than that, pushing the music on and scaling some massive highs with their tunes and live performances. They rightly belong in the Scottish commercial successes, although, for many, the period between 1987 and 1991 was the most evocative of the band's lifetime.

Starting off being influenced by Love and the 13th Floor Elevators, the group made the switch from being influenced by 60s boundary pushers and psychedelic to being inspired by the latest in house music. Second album In Gorbachev We Trust, featuring Jesus Loves Amerika and the ecstasy praising Synergy was perfectly in tune and in time with the Acid House craze that was peppering the undercurrent in

Britain. The band, like many Scottish acts before them, moved to London, not to be closer to any record label, but to be closer to the rave scene. The act not only jumped on the bandwagon, they actually pushed things forward a great deal with their Synergy tour, combining dance music and rock in a way that seem commonplace now but was fairly innovative in the late 80s.

The band's En-Tact album, released in late 1990, continued mixing rock and dance in a strong fashion, with this period showcasing songs like Make It Mine, Hyperreal and of course, Move Any Mountain. This track reached number 4 in the charts and was a perfect embodiment of the times, in that the track received over 15 remixes at the time.

Sadly, this was to be a dark time for the group, with Will Sinnott passing away after drowning in Tenerife, when the band was filming a video for the track. In 1992, the group released Boss Drum album with Mr C now considered to be front and centre of the group, and commercial success rocketed the band to a whole new level of fame. This alone would have been enough to derail any group but coming so hard on the heels of the loss of a band-mate must have made the year even harder to deal with. Tracks like Ebeneezer Goode, LSI, Phorever People and Boss Drum ensured that The Shamen were a household name. For a band that had been at the cutting edge of an underground scene, this was a situation that wasn't completely palatable for long term fans or even the band.

Their next album Axis Mutatis wasn't as well received or as successful as Boss Drum, but even then Destination Eschaton was a decent single with a fantastically catchy chorus. The group's last album, UV, fused techno and drum n bass, ensuring the group would go out on their own terms.

Slam
Whether you know Slam through their mixes, their albums, the Slam Tent at T in the Park, Soma Records, their Arches or Sub Club residencies or some other place, their impact on Scottish music and culture for over 25 years cannot be overlooked. Positive Education remains one of the

most vibrant and popular techno tracks and even though it is coming up for 20 years old, it can still stop you in your tracks as much as it did the first time you ever heard it.

With a number of albums and mix collections to delve into, the back catalogue of Slam is well worth looking into, even if you don't have any inclination to go clubbing. With the focus of the book falling on the more traditional rock variants, there hasn't been much focus on the dance culture in Scotland but any book that does feature on this style would have Slam written throughout it.

Sons And Daughters

If you ever went to see Smog and came away raving about the support act almost as much as Bill Callahan, you know you've come across as a band that you're going to take a big interest in. It turns out that their performance supporting Smog at the Cottiers Theatre was one of the first Sons and Daughters gig, but you wouldn't have known from their performance. They were almost perfectly formed, and to be honest, the band's greatest moment was Love The Cup, their debut EP/mini album.

This isn't to say that they didn't have other notable moments throughout their career, they did, but the quality of the songs on that release showed such a consistently high level. Tracks like Fight, Broken Bones, Johnny Cash, Blood, Start To End, La Lune and Awkward Duet were angry, aggressive and had a sense of menace more commonly associated with Glasgow of the 60s and the 70s. The band's live performance would see Scott and Adele prowling and lunging, attacking the stage while David and Ailidh were the opposite, remaining in place, retaining the beat, providing the platform for the musical assault being carried out up front.

If anything, the EP and the initial buzz was too good and even though The Repulsion Box was decent, it didn't match the intensity of the debut EP. Medicine, Dance Me In, Rama Lama and Taste The Last Girl were of a high standard, but it possibly showed the merits of releasing an EP as opposed to an album.

To be honest, even though I bought the next two albums after The Repulsion Box, it was a case of diminishing returns. When the band eventually announced their split, it was met with a shrug, which was a massive shame considering the excitement and energy that the band had around them between 2003 and 2005.

Soup Dragons

Baggy chancers or badly misjudged over time? The Soup Dragons were far from the only band to move from a traditional rock sound into one that incorporates indie and dance, but they were one of the few that did it in such a bold and brash manner. I'm Free may be the millstone around their neck with respect to a career but it no doubt gave the band a pretty wild ride for a few years.

Spirea X

One of the things that sometimes stops Scottish bands and artists from making full use of their talents is confidence and belief. This was not the issue for Spirea X, if anything, there was a bit much confidence in Jim Beattie. Bailing out of Primal Scream before they became successful, Beattie regularly made comments comparing himself to God and Jesus, while having pop shots at other bands of the time, accusing them of being egotistical. In Jim's mind, his egotistical nature was okay because he thought he had the music to back it up. The band made a big splash on the back of a demo tape but they quickly burned up and out. Their album Fireblade Skies was released in July of 1991, they were dropped by 4AD in 1992 and the band had split in 1993. Beattie and partner Judith Boyle found more longevity in Adventures In Stereo, an act that stuck around for 6 years.

St Judes Infirmary

Are St Judes Infirmary the biggest Scottish band beginning with S? Absolutely not. Are they the best Scottish band starting with an S? Absolutely.

If your viewpoint of what makes a band is about more than just the music, that there needs to be a mentality and identity to a group as well, this band had it all. On top of their Velvet Underground influenced intellectual squalor, there was a genuine sense of "the last gang in town" about them, even if they did manage to get through drummers with the careless nature of Spinal Tap.

A band that consisted of family members and a childhood friendship was always going to be one simmering with energy and intrigue, but it was the song-writing that lifted the band to a much higher level, even if they never managed to make a public breakthrough. The brother and sibling duo of Ashley and Grant Campbell provided the songwriting tension but there was a lot more to the group than that. Oddly enough for a band whose strength came in their collective unit and style, each main member of the group brought something unique and important to the band.

Bassist Grant held the beating heart of rock and roll in his four strings, combining a tight playing style with a loose attitude to stage space and spatial awareness which always left you worried about a fractured skull being two steps away. Grant also delivered the majority of the lyrics, combining the Scottish swagger with the tell-tale signs of a heart and mind that wandered the world. If the band were a Scottish band, it was in balancing the love of home with the realisation that being anywhere else but here was probably the best way to survive in life. Still, if you have to be here, make the most of it, and in this lyrical style, the band captured the sense of life in Scotland for so many of their fans, and for millions more who have yet to hear what they have to offer.

Ashley's guitar work and underpinning vocals provided much of the joy and light to a band who could threaten to overwhelm you with a sense of darkness and intensity. Further light was provided by Emma Jane, not only in her vocals (although she could deliver a snarled and sniping line if the track required it), but in the liberal use of her melodica. Yeah, as if you needed another reason to love the band, they used a melodica, that's worth at least 100 points in the Band Top Trumps stakes.

All of that alone would have made St Judes Infirmary a force to be reckoned with but on top of it was the vocals of

Mark Francis, no, not the silver-tongued charmer from Made In Chelsea fame, an even more illustrious character than that! Mark probably won't be too happy at that reference being brought together in public again, but a good few other folk will get a cheap laugh from it, which should always be the main reason for doing anything. Forget all of that though; Mark's vocals had the ability to stop you dead in your tracks, every single time. Scotland has a lengthy list of stunning vocalists that deserve to be placed in the music hall of fame and it's no exaggeration to say Mark Francis deserves his place alongside luminaries like Billy McKenzie, Liz Fraser and of course, the shouty man from The Corries. For proof of Mark's vocal talent, check out songs like Tacoma Radar, Goodbye Jack Vettriano and the latter half of The Church of John Coltrane

Debut album Happy Healthy Lucky Month received a great deal of critical acclaim, but it just never caught a light. It wasn't the fault of the songs and it is probably fair to say that the band was hampered, like many up and coming bands, with a record put out by a modest label. It's one thing saying that you have to want success and you should continually push through whatever comes your way to be a success in the music world, but when you are juggling a "traditional" life with work and relationships and the band life, it isn't always easy to keep coming back for more refreshed and invigorated.

The group's second album was aptly named, This Has Been The Death of Us, and this was to be the final act of the group (although Deserters Deserve Death / Edinburgh School For The Death / Naked has ensured that anyone doing an Edinburgh Rock Family Tree will be spilling a considerable amount of ink for this group. Don't forget there was even Sacred Heart Losers in the first place, who were also a vital stepping stone into St Judes Infirmary).

Even the inclusion of Jack Vettriano and Ian Rankin on the album couldn't push the band over the top with respect to awareness and attention.

All that and they genuinely got through more drummers than Spinal Tap! Seriously, there was a spell where it wasn't even funny what they were doing with them...probably passing them on to Burke & Hare to keep the band in industrial strength vodka and eye-liner (all for Grant to be honest!) With the group now split by the passing of the years and the rolling of the seas, it's unlikely that St Judes Infirmary will ever get that day in the sun (with appropriate clothing and sunscreen applied) that their music deserved, but it was a hell of a ride for a few years. They're still a band I enjoy listening to and when I think back of the crazy years when I was reviewing and gigging to a stupid extent, they're one of the bands that stand out as making as it all worthwhile.

This is a review I wrote about the band back in May of 2005 after they played a set in the old Stereo (currently the 78 in Kelvinhaugh Street), and I still stand by it today!

Playing at 'Dolly Mixture,' a night that gives away free sweets and heralds the success of females in music, St. Jude's Infirmary rolled into Glasgow to win over a crowd buoyed by alcohol and e-numbers.

Opening track Montreal has been re-worked, becoming a more introspective, reflective song as opposed to its previous pop incarnation. The new version works well as an introduction to the set. The song also contains fantastic lyrics, conjuring up images of your favourite place and the feeling of endless exploration and awe. This is not a band to be confused with your standard run-of-the-mill indie breakthrough act.

Musically, the band carries many influences from 60s pop, 70s-swagger and 80s fuzz but rarely seem constrained by any expectations of what they should be. The bass almost strolls through the songs, at times underpinning the tracks at others sounding as though it came in from a different song. Either way, there is always an air of confidence that it knows exactly what it should be doing. If that wasn't enough, the lilting contrasting vocals of Emma and Ashley combine to lift the songs beyond the realms of their peers and rivals.

For new bands, the tricky areas in gigs are often the middle with the crowds' initial interest or enthusiasm sometimes ebbing away unless maintained. To their credit, the band kept a fairly consistent pace and quality throughout the set with St Jean and A Million Days in Fife containing enough confidence to belie the bands status and send customers to the merchandise stall to buy the home-made eps on sale.

On nights like this, it can be hard to judge who in the crowd is present for the band and who is out just for the event. Given that St Jude's carry with them a sense of menace, the dark clothing (Ashley's summer attire excepted) the skull and crossbones and the intelligence of the lyrics, it may appear that St Jude's have no interest in winning friends but that would be wrong. Sometimes bands can come across as too desperate for public affection but when you've got melodies and riffs as plentiful as this band has, there is no need to go cap in hand to the audience looking for approval. That said, as the gig wore on, the crowd grew more appreciative and the last song of the night featured some impromptu dancing at the front of the stage.

The night's final track, 'Little Sparta' is a bewitching upbeat track that gallops to the end with a jaggy, insistent rhythm and a melody that sounds instantly recognisable, but just unique enough to avoid comparison. Given their style and the music industries continual habit of overlooking quality non-mainstream acts it may be that St Jude's Infirmary will forever be a critic's band and one that got away. There are many worse fates that could befall a band but on current showing, they definitely deserve a chance to go as far as their ambitions and dreams will take them.

State Broadcasters

I can still recall the first time I saw The State Broadcasters play live. Well, they were actually sound checking but they were playing and it was live, so I think that counts. It was in The Mixing Rooms on West Regent Street. I can't quite remember where I first heard them, possibly in is this music? Magazine or somewhere online, but wherever it was, I liked what I heard and when I heard they were playing live, I made my way along.

I was due to cover a band in King Tuts later that evening,

The Mode from Govan, so I went along a bit early, went to the bar and was delighted to see the band already on stage. They were great, folky but poppy and a refreshing alternative to most of the other Glasgow acts at the time. I was saddened to see them walk off stage at the end of that one song but then felt rather stupid at the fact that this was their sound check and they wouldn't be playing for an hour or two. So I introduced myself to a few of the members, told them I that I thought they were great and we all laughed at my over-eagerness. I didn't get to see the band play that night, The Mode delivered a well-received crowd to friends, family members and the local following they had developed, but I've managed to catch The State Broadcasters many times since that night. As headliners, as a support act, as part of a full day show, in proper venues, in church halls and even in a living room.

They're a bunch of people who deserve all of the praise and success that they get because they really all are a brilliant group of folkie folksters. The fact that they accept my occasional attempts at humour and misjudged heckles from time to time indicates that they tolerate fools gladly, but they've always managed to come across as clever and warm people. I'm not one for saying that most bands are badly behaved, I'd say most of the groups I've had contact with come across a lot better than many of the "normal" folk I meet, but even with that mind, the Broadies really do strike you as decent folk.

That isn't the real reason why they deserve all of the praise and success that they get though. It's part of the reason, of course it is, but the real reason is that their music deserves it. Even from very early on, it was obvious that they had a broad range of songs at their disposal. The jaunty pop of My Binoculars, a track that brought the sunshine of Teenage Fanclub to mind, and the striding power of Our Favourite Park was matched by the slower haunting beauty of songs like Tenderness of Wolves or the wistfulness of Grass Stains.

Debut album The Ship And The Iceberg had great instrumentation, terrific melodies and classic vocals shared between Graeme Black and Gill Fleetwood. There was a lot going on with the record, not, in a way, that it was confusing or too much to take in, but there were layers to enjoy and a lot to work through. It's an album that works really well as a collective piece, an album that is the sound of a band that had honed their craft over a number of years. It also contains Our Favourite Park which manages to cram in an almighty range of styles and emotions in less than 4 and a half minutes. On the whole it is a song in a hurry to get somewhere, it has a real punch the air enthusiasm but as the song extends to a close, the repeated refrain of "Tonight" is really emotive and then bam, the follow-up line of "our love has died" hits you right in the stomach and heart.

It also contains the fantastic couplet, "I've been an arsehole, this fact is unarguable" which sounds so much better sung than written down and it is a sentiment we can all agree with. (I mean agree with respect to our own lives, not that we should agree with Graham singing it about himself!)

Given that the release of the record came around three years after the first time I managed to see them, that was certainly the case but given how many bands struggle to pull off the sound or style they are known for in the live arena, it is still an outcome that is worth highlighting.

It may have taken a few years for second-album Ghosts We Must Carry to be released and if you take the overall theme of the album, you may be worried that life had been tough for the band in the intervening years. There are still plenty of poppy and bright moments but on the whole, the second album seemed a bit darker and bleaker. With the album being released by Olive Grove Records, there was a better level of promotion and an improved sense of belonging for the album. With folky and intelligent pop going over the top and into the mainstream, there is no reason at all why the State Broadcasters couldn't have a huge crossover hit. They may not put themselves in the position often enough where this sort of situation will unfold but with a third album hopefully on its way before too long, the group will give themselves another excellent chance of being recognised and respected. You get the feeling that they are the sort of group that a select few will take to their heart and be really passionate about as opposed to being the sort of band that a lot of people like but few love. It's hardly the worst fate that can befall an artist.

If you're looking for a song to listen to in order to get into the band, I'll always suggest My Binoculars. However, songs like Let's Make T-Shirts, Takeshi and Kittiwake are all worth checking out and the band also have a rather stylish video for their single Trespassers, which is readily available on YouTube and other online video channels. The band also covered Billy Bragg's The Only One on their second album, which may provide some people with an easy way to get into the group.

Strawberry Switchblade

When it comes to music, I'm definitely not a child of the 80s. In fact, apart from some football games and the occasional band or song, the 80s is the one decade that I would choose to jettison from the list of decades. Yes, with the benefit of hindsight, the musical legacy of the 80s will be far stronger than the legacy of the 90s, but given that the 90s was the first decade where I was out going to gigs and started really falling in love with music, it's had a bigger impact on me, so that's the one I'm keeping.

The 80s were mainly rubbish though, especially the fashion. You have to say that the Strawberry Switchblade girls were pretty brave, cutting about Glasgow in this fashion. Yes, they may have been moving in the right circles when it came to the arty crowd and the music-set, but given that they would have to get from home to bar or venue, it was still a neat look to have in Glasgow in the 80s, which is far removed from the cultural bohemia it is today.

So you'd forgive me for quickly glossing over the band but then that would mean glossing over Since Yesterday, a fantastic track with a melody that takes up permanent residency in your ears and, by the way, it isn't paying the rent for its stay. Forget everything else about the band as this one song is more than enough to warrant their place in any Scottish music rundown. It got to number 5 in the charts and while they never matched this success, albeit they were understandably big in Japan for a spell, the duo managed to bewitch Britain for a brief spell, appearing on TV as often as the test-card for a few weeks. It wasn't to last though, and even the dresses and hairstyles would be usurped by even bigger and louder outfits. Never mind though, anyone that came after didn't have Since Yesterday up their stylish sleeves...

Superstar

Calling your band Superstar is one thing but titling your debut record as Greatest Hits Vol 1 is another altogether. It could have been misguided confidence, that world famous Scottish sense of humour or as Joe McAlinden put it, the Buckie talking! Yet another artist hailing from the same place as what seemed live at least half of all Scottish bands in the early 90s, you got the impression that McAlinden would have loved to have a big gap between himself and his Bellshill compatriots.

Not that he disliked them, far from it, but he seemed to be one that really carried the weight of being held and placed in this sort of company. Plenty of Scottish acts can claim to have been nearly-men and so close to victory but it seemed to be very much the case for Superstar. Hopefully, the Rod Stewart cover gave Joe plenty of money, allowing him a bit more freedom.

The Supernaturals

Perhaps the huge popularity and success of Smile painted the band in a certain light but The Supernaturals genuinely came across as being a band that were too happy and positive for their own good. This isn't something that Scotland does too well and clearly there was an air of suspicion around the band for many folk. This song has hopefully kept the band in royalties over the years, appearing on jingles, adverts and even on Phoenix Nights.

The lyrics of Everest remain as ridiculous, overblown and enjoyable as they did on first listening. Another band that did rather well for themselves at the time but perhaps haven't created a legacy that sees them being wheeled out over the years. There is far too much focus on nostalgia with below average bands from the mid-90s coming out of the woodwork to play sold out tours but The Supernaturals would be more deserving of this outcome than many of the other acts in this position.

Telstar Ponies

There was nothing new about them, but there was certainly something Neu! about them. The band deserves a bit of recognition for throwing in a different influence compared to most of the Scottish bands that were kicking around at this time. Again, like 18 Wheeler who frontman David Keenan left to start up Telstar Ponies, they may feel as though they were a little bit out of time with their style of music.

Sure they may have been around 15 years too late, but they were probably about 15-20 years too early as well. There has been a resurgence in the popularity of the driving style of music that originated in Germany in the 70s of late and anyone that looks for something in this field would be happy enough with the Ponies. Titles like Lugengeschicite and Innerhalb Weniger Minuten were hardly shying away from their influences.

The group's second album featured a bigger expanse of influences with the vocals of Rachel Devine to the fore, but it wasn't as immediate as the group's debut album. Repeated plays brought out a lot of enjoyable moments and passages from it, and a hell of a lot of positive reviews (then and over the years) but that was it from the band, even though they supposedly had a third album in the can.

Even without the 18 Wheeler link, Telstar Ponies were a band who were in the middle of the music scene at the time and if anyone attempted to do a Glasgow Rock Family Tree, the connections coming from this group would send you crazy trying to follow them.

You had Brendan O'Hare in the band for a while, although it may be easier to name the bands that Brendan wasn't in while Sushil K Dade from The Soup Dragons, BMX Bandits and of course, Future Pilot AKA was an early member. John Hogarty was also a BMX Bandits member while Devine went on to form Porch Songs Anthology with Gavin Laird from the band. Clearly the Glasgow music scene can seem small at times but when you think that this sort of narrative has been repeated time and time again, it can be difficult to keep track of everyone.

David Keenan also went on to achieve further success, both as a writer and as the owner of Volcanic Tongue, a Glasgow record store which in the summer of 2104 sadly reverted to being a mail order company.

Thrum / Monica Queen

There is clearly something in the water in Bellshill, or maybe it's just that so many people growing up there have a desire to get out and see the world. Thrum are just one of the many indie guitar bands that hail from this small, yet important, part of the world.

It's not really something that completely fits in the section under Thrum or Monica Queen, but the verse where Monica's vocals kick in during Lazy Line Painter Jane by Belle & Sebastian is easily one of the greatest moments in Scottish musical history. The track, combining the Glasgow style with that half-inched Velvet Underground style intro simmers along nicely and then this glorious vocal comes in from nowhere, taking the song to a much higher level.

For that section alone, Monica Queen is a name that should be noted by music lovers all around the world but there was more to the band and her than that. Thrum played the first ever T in the Park and while they were a well talked of band during this era, the volume of bands playing a similar style of indie guitar pop meant that it was going to take something special to break through.

The band split up in 95 and Monica has added her considerable vocal prowess to a range of songs and artists, while also releasing a couple of albums. Thrum were back in 2011, playing at T in the Park once again and a combination of Thrum or Monica Queen shows are regularly listed on Scottish and British festival line-ups.

You should also follow Monica on Twitter, she usually has some good tales about Glasgow life and you're never too far away from a Neil Young video or audio clip.

Twin Atlantic

When Twin Atlantic first burst on to the scene, they whipped up a decent following in next to no time. Inspired by Biffy Clyro and having the requisite amount of tattoos and long hair to appeal to a broad range of fans, they were a Glasgow band whose name was plastered everywhere and you were never really more than 2 days and 500 yards from a Twin Atlantic gig in the city. It wasn't quite my thing but there was a good sense of energy about their early releases and you could see why they were connecting with a fan base. Any band that had a decent set of tunes, a good look and were willing to work as hard as the band did, while getting support from magazines like Kerrang and support slots with major acts, was always going to have a chance to achieve more than their peers.

There has never been any big step on from this initial burst though and on their latest release though, they sound like Def Leppard with a Scottish accent. And that's not in a cool or ironic way that tries to suggest that Def Leppard are hip and commercial ground breakers. It's that they sound like Def Leppard and let's be honest, that isn't a compliment.

Uncle John & Whitelock

Noisy and chaotic buggers from a noisy and chaotic time in the Glasgow music scene. They should probably sue The Amazing Snakeheads for nicking their act!

Urusei Yatsura

The band released three albums in their lifetime; their last was called Everybody Loves Urusei Yatsura. This was a lie.

Wake The President

The amount of work and effort that the Sandberg twins have put into the Glasgow music scene over the years can sometimes detract from the fact that they are also in an excellent band that captures the off-kilter style of Glasgow life that is commonly overlooked by those wishing to chronicle life in the city. It's not as if they boys are going out of their way to find something different to sing about, they're just doing their own thing in a city that is pretty much about doing your own thing. Their Say Dirty record label may bring back memories of the time when MySpace was crucial in tracking down new bands and keeping in touch with new acts, but the label has a fantastic legacy.

As well as releasing their own material, the label featured acts like Endor, Zoey can Goey, The Sexual Objects and Peter Parker amongst others. This label was followed up with We Can Still Picnic which is also a club night but as a label, it currently plays host to Casual Sex, so it is as relevant to the 2014 music scene as any other local label. The lads vow to keep producing vinyl and creating artefacts that can be treasured and kept for years to come.

Wake The President provide all the juxtapositions that make music so much fun, in that they are dark yet intelligent, gritty yet poppy and fun. Both of their albums, to this date, are worth checking out, with the second album building and progressing from the post-punk and Orange Juice influenced nature of the debut album.

Yummy Fur / 1990s

There will be more than enough people to tell you about the greatness of Yummy Fur, Stuart Braithwaite even taking to twitter to declare the band as his favourite Scottish act, after he created a playlist for the Guardian, but they were never really a band that I got into or caught live. So with that in mind (and not wanting to open up the Glasgow Rock Family Trees that made up the groups' line-up over the years,) I'll focus on Jackie McKeown's next act, the 1990s.

Why didn't more people buy the music of the 1990s? Now that the band is seemingly on permanent hiatus, and the fact if you stick their name into Google, you've no chance of anything relevant coming back unless you add something else like a songs or album title, it's looking unlikely that they'll ever get their reward. The 1990s have the kudos and the street cred but with the pop songs they had, they should have had the album units and ticket sales that would make Calvin Harris blush.

The second album was bigger and rounder, but perhaps it didn't have the same sense of fun and cheekiness that was all over the first album. A set in the ABC2 on a Bank Holiday Sunday back in 2009 reinforced how fantastic the band were as a live act, the tightness of the set matching the pop sensibilities of the tunes, and this was a review I submitted at the time.

The Sunday night of a Bank Holiday weekend in Glasgow is always pretty special and the first May Day holiday always raises a cheer, what with it being the start of summer. Okay, the weather is still far too changeable to rush out in shorts and short sleeved tops but there's a change in mentality, heck, some Glaswegians even took a drink on the Sunday evening, such was the upbeat mood in the city. Part of the reason for this was city sons The 1990s arriving home to play to a small, yet excited crowd in the ABC2 venue.

Opener I Don't Even Know What That Is set the tone and if you appreciate the New York New Wave sound, you will be quids in with this band. Whether it's the Modern Lovers or Blondie influence, the mix of cool guitar with outrageously poppy melodies sees the band going down a storm with songs from debut album Cookies and new album, Kick.

The band then launched into Cult Status, which brought about a strong dose of interaction from the crowd. There's a fantastic line about one of the benefits that cult status can bring and it was sung with gusto by the crowd as opposed to the band, helping bringing the two closer together. All I can say is, if you have doubts about your wife, don't let her near the 1990 boys or there could be trouble ahead.

One of the strange things about the 1990s, especially in these modern times, is the fact that they choose to play three up front, with all band members pushed up at the edge of the stage. On home territory, such attacking prowess is probably expected but the fact that the band deploys the same line-up away from home is indicative of their nature and spirit. This also meant that the band used a drummer that can sing and as Michael McGaughrin was resplendent in a very stripey shirt, comparisons with Dennis Wilson were unavoidable.

Again, the hometown show was probably adding to the bonhomie of the night and certainly the band was playing in front of many friends and family but there is so much to enjoy with the act. As stated, the music does owe a debt to musical trends of the past but they manage to combine it with such a local feel that it feels really fresh. There is something extremely pleasant about hearing a band sing about the number 59 bus and knowing exactly where it runs and having a few stories to tell about it. That said, if a New York band sang about their subway trips in the same manner, they would be lauded for their storytelling so why shouldn't a local band be given the same praise?

The encore featured a cover of Radioactivity from Kraftwerk with the band making it sound more like a Neu song than a number made famous by the Robots. Taking the fun fun fun from the autobahn was a great way to prolong the evening but the evening was brought to a close by Pollokshields, the bands tribute to the South side of Glasgow location where something is always going on.

With new material blending effortlessly with the old and the sense of joy and fun positively dripping from every song, the 1990s deserve to be playing on a far bigger stage than the ABC2 and one can only hope that they'll experience a spike in popularity over the summer. Whether it is through getting one of their tunes on an advert or wowing a few festival crowds, you need to hear more of this band and when you do, you'll know you're supposed to be their friend.

The Zephyrs

It is not as if you have to look hard to find Scottish bands who have a hard luck story to tell but The Zephyrs certainly never got the rub of the green along the way. The band released their second album, When the Sky Comes Down It Comes Down on Your Head, the exact same week their record label folded. This meant that there was no budget or support to promote the album, the band were unable to tour in support of the record and even the group's publishing deal was lost. The album was well received and the limited live performances they played after the release of the record suggested that there was an audience for the music, but the lack of financial support meant that the band members had to return to their day jobs.

Thankfully the Zephyrs have continued, mining a sound that blends alt.rock with alt.country, which of course is likely to be too alternative for some, but appeals considerably to an audience that has supported the group with passion over the years. The Zephyrs are another group with more than 15 years in the industry to fall back on and they reconvened in 2014 to start pulling together recording plans and future tour schedules.

7: Every Picture Tells A Story

A picture may paint a thousand words but when you are a writer working to a strict word-count, they are no use at all! Thankfully that isn't the case here, or with most music writing, so I'm more than happy to offer up some excellent pictures taken over the years. All apart from one image can be attributed to Chris Reilly or Craig Mathison so you should thank them for the chapter you will probably return to the most!

Jackie McKeown of the 1990s at Connect Festival – 2007
– Chris Reilly

The Fire Engines at Connect Festival – 2007 – Chris Reilly

Shit Disco – Sauchiehall Street- 2006 – Chris Reilly

The Kills – King Tuts – 2003 – Chris Reilly

Snow Patrol – T in the Park – Chris Reilly

The Twilight Sad – Sauchiehall Crawl – 2008 – Chris Reilly

Saint Judes Infirmary – The Buff Club – 2006 – Chris Reilly

The State Broadcasters – Chris Reilly

Static – Unattributed

Honeyblood – Stag & Dagger – 2014 – Craig Mathison

Campfires In Winter – Tenement Trail – 2014 – Craig Mathison

Tijuana Bibles Tenement Trail – 2014 – Craig Mathison

Vladimir - Tenement Trail – 2014 – Craig Mathison

Vukovi - Tenement Trail – 2014 – Craig Mathison

8: After The Fight

And in one morning, it was over. It had been a long time in coming with a seemingly never ending build-up but in the end, the Independence Referendum turned out to be so like so many Scottish sporting and musical moments. A lot of hopes, dreams and effort had been used up only to look back on it a day later and realise that it had taken you no further forward, in fact, it may even have left you a bit further behind because knowing that you have to carry out that climb once again can take a little bit of your heart and soul away.

The population had their say, with a 55% saying No to the 45% who voted for independence, it was a close run thing but clearly the will of the overall nation was to say No to independence and to agree to remain part of the United Kingdom. Within hours, the promised additional powers promised as a last minute sweetener to facilitate the No vote looked to be removed from the table and a show of triumphalism in George Square that evening wiped out so much of the hope and optimism that had been held by both sides in the build-up to the vote. By the time the weekend rolled around, it didn't even seem as though we were back to where we started the process from, it seemed as though we had moved back a good few steps. Give it a week and we were being dragged into another war and you'd forgive folk for thinking that the entire year building up to this point had been in vain.

As always though, once the hangover and sense of doom started to fade away, there was a chance to pick out the positives. The referendum had produced a level of interest and engagement with politics that Scotland had never seen before. Virtually everyone was waking up to the fact that this was their chance to have their say and no matter what they believed in, there was a platform to get involved. You may not have agreed with the final outcome but it was democracy at its finest.

In the build-up to the campaign, it was notable to see where the support for the Yes vote lay. Social media seemed to be the catalyst for so much of the excitement and building interest in the battle for independence. Perhaps this relates to the fact that in the final analysis, the youngsters were more likely to vote for independence while the grey demographic was more likely to vote no. Perhaps this was just an indicator that social media was the preserve of the young while traditional media, pouring out scare stories and piling up fear, was the factor that won out in the end.

There was also a lot to be said for the way that the creative industries and areas galvanised the Yes vote. While not every artist was willing to declare their voting intentions or even get behind the Yes vote, there was no doubt that the overwhelming level of declared support from musicians was behind Scottish independence. Well, Scottish musicians anyway. You had David Bowie, who has hailed from England, New York and Mars in his time using a supermodel as his conduit at The Brit Awards to support the Union and you also had Japan's biggest drug-runner Paul McCartney saying No...well, John and Yoko were the couple that built a relationship on saying Yes. Irishman Bob Geldof also thought he had a say in the matter but that may have just been because Bob realised that there was an opportunity to get some publicity for himself. In fact, when it comes to Scottish artists saying No, you had Subo and King Creosote backing the status quo. No one thought to ask Status Quo what their opinion was, but given that the hairy denim clad rockers haven't been relevant since...well, I liked the psychedelic one about the matchstick folk...that probably wasn't too much of an issue. Billy Bragg got involved and he was quite supportive of a Yes vote but at least Billy gave some justification, hoping that Scotland breaking away could revitalise England and encourage a more devolved nation down south. Good old Billy, the decades have rolled by but he is still looking for a new England (even if Kirsty McColl did sing it better!) It is important to say that I'm still a huge Paul McCartney fan and he is as entitled to his opinion on the referendum as much as anyone and it certainly doesn't make a difference to what I feel about his music, same for Bowie. Mind you, I can guarantee that I'll never buy a Susan Boyle album from this point forward...or at any point in the past either.

Of course, when it comes to the output of musicians, what they do on stage is much more important and relevant, so it probably wasn't a shock to find a number of music events taking place in the run-up to the independence referendum.

The National Collective took to the road in July with the Yestival pitching up in all parts of the country, showcasing music alongside the cultural movement for independence. This was joined by the Festival of Common Weal, a day providing music, comedy shows, discussions and talks all based on the movement that is focused on a collective idealism for the country. Live acts that performed in the Arches include Shambles Miller, Zara Gladman, Gav Prentice and Randolph's Leap, creating a connection between music and the move for independence.

There was also the Songs for Scotland event which took place in Oran Mor weeks before the referendum vote. This was an event listed as being "a national concert of Scottish singers singing their support social justice and for Scottish independence." If you backed the idea, you probably felt that the Oran More and its stunning Alasdair Gray ceiling was the ideal setting for such a prestigious and optimistic event. If you didn't back the idea, you'd probably think that the pretentious West End venue was the perfect setting. Most people probably fell in between both of these opinions and while there was a lot of praise for the event, it never really seemed to capture the imagination.

This couldn't be said for the Yes event that was hosted at the Usher Hall in Edinburgh on the weekend before the referendum vote. Unlike the events blending music and a pro-independence stance to this point, this event featured big names as the battle to win people over reached its peak.

The line-up included Mogwai, Franz Ferdinand, Frightened Rabbit, Amy Macdonald, Eddi Reader, Stanley Odd and the paired down Deacon Blue outfit, McIntosh Ross. This was a rebel rousing evening, each short set bookended by reasons to vote yes and of the importance to ensure that the energy and momentum was maintained in the final few days of the referendum battle. It is unlikely that many people in the audience at the Usher Hall would have been undecided with respect to their vote, but this sort of event isn't solely about enthusing the individual in attendance. It was as much about encouraging the people in attendance to then go and spread the word about the positivity of the event, with social media updates of the event filling timelines on the Sunday and Monday.

While there was no real shortage of artists promoting their preference for a Yes vote, there wasn't much in the way of creativity with respect to songs advocating a Yes vote. Facebook timelines may have been filled with bedroom enthusiasts uploading their songs, poems and writings showcasing their thoughts of the referendum but when it came to artists properly recording songs and putting them out the general public, there was not much going on at all.

Which is why Stanley Odd's Son, I Voted Yes stood out from the crowd. They may have slightly bent the truth with respect to the (lack of) respect shown to Margaret Thatcher upon her passing but the rest of the song chimed with the hope that many people had in the vote and what it could offer to Scotland. The band is just one example of the Sound of Young Scotland in 2014 and there is a very strong chance that the band will have picked up many new fans and followers in the wake of this song. Musically it had a good flow but the lyrics encapsulated the hopes and aspirations of the vote, and of the possible changes it could bring about. There may not have been too many artists putting their thoughts and hopes for the referendum into a track but in this one song, Stanley Odd probably nailed it.

Another song that deserves a mention was Wolves by Helen Marnie, one quarter of Ladytron and Glaswegian, who also has a solo career. Helen has her second solo album scheduled for release in 2015 but a week before the referendum she released a song that while not solely about the referendum, did manage to capture the optimism and possibilities that were in reach. This was drummed home in the video, which started off by focusing on a Yes sticker on her keyboard.

When thinking about the campaign, there is no getting

away from the fact that the Yes campaign was the much more positive. You may think that this was always going to be the case, the Yes campaign was the one advocating change as opposed to keeping the status quo or avoiding the unknown.

Given that the No campaign was supposedly promoting the fact that the status quo was better for everyone, you would think that they would have been able to promote positivity about life on the island and why it should have been the natural choice. However, when it comes to getting people to take action, it is often easier to do so by promoting fear and the negative, which is the approach that the No campaign took. After the referendum was settled, many high profile people on the No side freely admitted that they would never have won without the fear campaign or the smear tactics that they utilised, particularly in the run-in to the vote. It was a disappointing end for everyone on the Yes side, but it was surely a bit disappointing for everyone in the country that the No campaign didn't think that the merits of the country had been worth trumpeting.

While there was no shortage of Scottish musicians and artists stepping forward to say that choosing independence made said sense, the No campaign could have argued that all of the great music was created in a situation that came about because of the Union. Okay, this may have been answered by the fact that great music and art is created in opposition to authority and ruling parties as opposed to being nurtured by it, but the fact remains that if there was any ounce of positivity in the No campaign, they would have had more than enough great musical moments to draw from. However, given that the no side was victorious, it's not like they actually care about how they achieved their win – independence referendums are very much a results business and it's all about getting the win.

In 2014, it was easy to see why so many people in Scotland fixated on the independence referendum but the Scottish people were not the only people who had a lot to weigh up with respect to the future of their area and country.

In Spain, Catalonia has had a lengthy battle for recognition and independence and while the call for

Catalonia to break out on its own has been long and continuous for many years, it had fallen behind Scotland in the race to be recognised as independent (until the 19th of September when of course Scotland fell to the bottom of the pile once again.)

In 1931, Spain became a Republic and the Generalitat, an autonomous Catalan regional Government, was created. However, the region was to experience power for less than 10 years in this state before the reign of Franco took over in Spain.

Between 1939 and 1975, the dictatorship of Franco worked to suppress the Catalan language, autonomy and culture while also severely opposing any form of political opposition to the ruling power in Spain. With many concentration camps, executions and forced labour being imposed on enemies of the State, it is believed that Franco's reign was responsible for between 200,000 and 400,000 deaths in just over 40 years. Before Franco died, he bestowed the title of Prince of Spain onto Juan Carlos de Borbon. Juan Carlos acted as Head of State during times of illness in the latter years of the dictator and when Franco died, he was pronounced the King of Spain, taking the title of King Juan Carlos I. Juan Carlos set out to usher in democracy in Spain and introduced the Spanish Constitution of 1978 (the Constitución Española). There is debate as to when Spain fully transcended to a democracy with various dates in 1978, 1981 and 1982 offered up but there is no doubt that the passing of Franco brought about great change in Spain, and it was welcomed in Catalonia.

In 1979, Catalonia was recognised as being a nationality and it was provided with a statute of autonomy. Catalan was also officially recognised as an official language of Catalonia alongside Spanish. Over the years there has been a building of interest and backing for Catalonia to gain independence from Spain and in 2012, more than 1 million people marched in a pro-independence rally.

There are many strong arguments and opinions on both sides of the Catalonian independence debate, as you would expect. The Catalans can point to the large cultural differences that exist between their region and Spain. They can point to the fact that Catalonia pays close to €20m in taxes to Madrid while being denied many promised grants and payments in return. There is also a growing will of the people for Catalonia to be provided with independence. A range of opinion polls has come back stating that there is more than 55% support and backing for Catalonia to be granted independence from Spain. This is an opinion that is likely to continue to grow and there is confidence on behalf of those fighting for Catalonian independence that if it doesn't happen now, it will have to happen soon.

Of course, even if these polls are correct, this means that 40% of the population is against gaining independence from Spain, still a high figure and one that may grow before a referendum. There is also the fact that the politicians in Spain rejected a Catalan authority request for a referendum on independence to be held on the 9th of November 2014. 299 MPs voted against allowing the referendum, one MP abstained and 47 votes were cast in favour. The Spanish Prime minister stated that allowing a referendum, and independence, would be a disaster for Catalonia and Spain.

The referendum itself was scuppered in advance of the vote with the constitutional court being pushed to declare the referendum illegal. They didn't quite bow down to the demands of the Spanish Government but in postponing the referendum until it could be ruled on meant that the hopes for independence being pushed through quickly were dashed. Dashed but not defeated and at the time of going to print, the Catalan President Artur Mas was pressing ahead with plans to hold a "consultation of citizens", which would be deemed to being lawful. It is clear that this isn't an issue that is going to disappear and there will be continued calls for more debate on this topic.

People leading the fight for Catalonian independence state that they provide far much more to Madrid than what they receive back from the State. Spain is a country that doesn't have its troubles to seek with respect to finances and the loss of income derived from Catalonia could have disastrous consequences on the entire nation. It is easy to say that

Catalonia would be better off holding on to the money that they earn but would this then harm the rest of Spain? You could argue that the prosperity of Catalonia is currently bankrolling some of the more disadvantaged areas of Spain, and if this income is removed from the country, the pain wouldn't initially be felt in Madrid, it would be felt in the smaller towns and villages as much needed State funding in these areas dries up. There will clearly be people in Catalonia who consider themselves to be Spanish and who wouldn't want to impose such a situation on their fellow natives but you can see why the rest of Spain is as desperate to cling on to Catalonia as the Catalonians appear to be to break free. Depending on what side of the story you believed in the run up to the Scottish referendum, the oil of Scotland may have been as important for the UK as the income derived in Catalonia was for Spain.

A slight difference between Catalonia and Scotland can be found in the fact that there is a greater level of confidence in Catalonia achieving success if they break free. With a population of 7.5 million, the region would automatically become one the 100 most populated nations in the world and they have a GDP of $314billion, which would see them rank in the low 30s with respect to economy. To place it into context, Catalonia would have a GDP that exceeds that of Egypt, Hong Kong and Portugal, sitting on the other side of the Spanish border from Catalonia. With a GDP per capita figure that is just as impressive, there is no real doubt that Catalonia would more than hold its own on a global scale, but as found in Scotland, numbers get nowhere near to revealing the full story as to why people hold a certain opinion about independence.

Catalonia is clearly a region that has independence, referendums and the fight for freedom on the tip of its tongue and in the beat of its heart. At this heart of the region is Barcelona, the city that so many people automatically associate with Catalonia and the city that would be the capital and shining light of any new Catalan nation.

There is a lot in common between Catalonia and Scotland and this is why there was particular interest in the presence of a number of Scottish acts at Catalonia's premier music festival (of course some people will fight the argument of Sonar, which is fine its own right but Primavera is something else entirely), Primavera Sound in Barcelona.

The festival has been going for 14 years and it provides a strong blend of indie and dance that appeals to Catalans. It also appeals to many people in Scotland as the regular crowds that depart from Scotland to the festival indicates. I am fortunate enough to say that the 2014 Primavera Sound festival was my fifth in total, making it the festival I have attended the most outside of T in the Park. I attended four years in a row in 2009, 2010, 2011 and 2012 and then gave 2013 a miss before returning for 2014.

The amount of familiar faces you find at the festival is truly heart-warming and as I remarked to my brother in Prestwick Airport in 2011 as we prepared to board the flight, "If this plane crashes, Nice N Sleazy's will go out of business." That's clearly the sort of upbeat talk you want to have as you get ready to board a plane, but it summed up the clientele who were also queuing up for the mass charge that Ryanair like to encourage when boarding their flight.

It's a festival where you can be sitting on a bench having some food and within five minutes find yourself chatting to a stranger about Cardonald and the Argosy pub. It's a festival where you attend and then three months later find yourself speaking to someone in Mono who you spoke to on the Metro line at the end of the day's (or nights to be more accurate) activities. Yes, all of these things can happen at and in the aftermath of T in the Park but the sun makes a massive difference as does the more relaxed attitude to everything.

To put Primavera Sound into context, in 2011, the festival tried a new payment system where people loaded up electronic cards with funds and then used these cards to buy alcohol. The system crashed and it took a couple of hours for a replacement system to be put in place, which meant that not many people were able to enjoy a drink for a couple of hours. It also meant that festival goers that had put a great deal of their money into plastic were left a bit short until the issue was resolved. There were some folk resorting to underhand tactics or nipping in and out of the festival site to find alcohol but on the whole, the festival shrugged its shoulders and got on with enjoying the music, the layout, the atmosphere and each other. This is not an outcome that would have happened at T in the Park. So, before we get too caught up on the fact that Catalonia and Scotland are similar, there are key differences. However, there is a certain kinship and 3 major Scottish bands were on the line-up for the 2014 Primavera Sound festival.

Mogwai
Chvrches
The Twilight Sad

When you have three options, all of a different level of importance to you, there is a tendency to trot out "The Good, The Bad & The Ugly" to provide a brief overview of the options but wouldn't be sufficient in this case. For starters, good isn't a strong enough word to do justice to Mogwai and you wouldn't rush to state Chvrches or The Twilight Sad in the other terms.

However, there was an element of great, good and indifferent to the three acts for me. Mogwai were a must-see act and it was actually at the band's Royal Concert Hall gig in January that plans for the Primavera trip were put in place. The official line-up for the festival was unveiled that evening and it was highly appealing.

Chvrches have definitely been one of the most talked about Scottish bands of the past year or two and I'm a big fan of their album. I wasn't the biggest fan of their live show but perhaps this was because the night I saw them in the ABC their lighting system didn't work. For a band with an electronic soul, that can be a fatal flaw and I came away liking the album a lot more than their live show. However, seeing the band play a focused festival set was certainly something that appealed to me so they were definitely on the list of bands to check out.

As for The Twilight Sad, they're just a band that I have never taken to. I caught them back in 2008 in the ABC2, it was at the end of a long Sunday of bar-hopping and band-watching but there was nothing from their set that night that stuck in my end. Equally, the band's recorded output always struck me as being all right but never really being something that grabbed me. I get the fact that there are plenty of people who have the band firmly in their heart who are currently turning away from this book in disgust but I think when you have a band that operates with such a high level of intensity, you either buy into what they do or you don't. I don't, but I get why there are folk that are head over heels about them. I was never likely to see them in the main festival site, there was always going to be a more attractive band on the bill for me but with the band playing a free show on Saturday afternoon away from the main festival site, there'd be an opportunity to catch them as well. I wouldn't bother going to see the band in Scotland but in this sort of environment, there's no harm in giving a band another chance to win you over.

With Chvrches and Twilight Sad playing on smaller stages, the Pitchfork and Vice stage respectively, this brought some benefits. The layouts of both areas created a limited area for the audience to watch the band play. This created a good atmosphere and a sense of excitement in playing to a packed crowd. Playing at an earlier time on a larger stage may have helped the bands to reach more people but whether these are the crowds of people that can be won over is an entirely different matter. It is often better for a band to play in a tightly packed area with a number of devoted fans and seriously interested onlookers as opposed to people wandering, chatting and killing time before their favourite act appears.

Chvrches were the first of the 3 Scottish acts to perform and it was certainly a victory for the group. There was a sizable crowd, the sound quality was good and the band came across well. I still didn't think there were enough strong moments consistently throughout their set, but they had more than enough good songs and positive moments to carry them through. After the festival, I noticed that a few reviews had said that the band were a bit cold when this certainly wasn't the case. Lauren was quite chatty, even going so far to talk about the 2 times she had attended Primavera as a punter. Given the travelling parties from Glasgow over the years, this wasn't a surprise but it surely suggested the band had bought into what the festival offered. Lauren's politeness was also shown in the fact that she chided the crowd for watching the band when Queens of the Stone Age were playing at the same time. A good few years back it would have taken a hell of an act to drag me away from the Queens at their prime but they are far from their best days. I managed to catch the final songs of QOTSA and while the power is still in place, the nuances and subtleties were no longer at the forefront of their show. There was also the fact that the end of their set made it all too apparent that Mark Lanegan was no longer hanging around. In that regard, those who had hung about for the Chvrches set were well rewarded. It could have been slightly darker, which is one of the perils of an outdoor festival in Barcelona, but the sound was spot on and the crowd definitely enjoyed what was on offer.

Twilight Sad got a very good crowd for their set, which was pitted against a variety of acts including Kim Gordon's new band and the start of Slowdive's set. Going by the band's reaction the following day, they loved it as much as their audience did. The group had the chance to please their fans again or play to another audience in a free gig in a park in central Barcelona. Park Cituadella was the setting for gigs on Friday, Saturday and Sunday. There were plenty of festival goers attending these sets, but it was also an opportunity for families with kids to come along and see live music. It stands in contrast to the festival circuit in the UK where it seems as though festival organisers are intent on squeezing every single penny out of people. There was a laid-back and relaxed atmosphere when Twilight Sad took to the stage, but anyone expecting the group to alter their performance levels should have known better.

The previous day saw the weather standing in contrast to the sets that were playing on the free stage. The sunshine LA pop set of La Sera (featuring Katy Goodman, or Kickball Katy to her friends, formerly of the Vivian Girls) was played out in the rain with the group holding a fear of being electrocuted. By the time the next band took to the stage, glorious sunshine had dried the wet seats and paving with the temperature now baking the crowd. This was the sort of changeable weather that felt like home, but Majical Cloudz found themselves playing in weather The Beach Boys may have found it a bit warm. The duo played one of the most intense sets I've witnessed in a long time and you can't help but think the weather gods or fate had gotten things badly wrong on Friday. Things were far better pitched on the Saturday for Twilight Sad though. There was no rain and while it was warm, the weather was mainly overcast with the occasional flurry of sunshine. It would be a lazy writer that would suggest this was a perfect metaphor for the set, which means I'm more than happy to suggest it!

As always, James was emotionally engaged and involved throughout the gig but there were moments of typical Scottish humour. When asking if there was anyone from Scotland present at the show, a cheer went up to which the frontman playfully responded "fuck off." Hopefully any Catalan youngster present wasn't up to speed with Scottish swear words but of course, it was meant in a friendly manner.

While Twilight Sad played a strong set, my personal highlight of the half-hour came when a girl, clearly on her hen weekend, stumbled by us to take pictures of the band. This was all the invitation some of our group needed to engage the girl with some terrible chat. She responded, in perfect English, "I'm sorry, I don't speak English." Her strong and swift reply was all I needed to laugh for the next few minutes. I also think it was the sort of humour that the band would have enjoyed, so it was fitting that it came as part of their set.

Neither of the sets of the first 2 Scottish acts had changed my opinion on the bands, but I was glad I had seen them. Saturday night though was all about building up to the Godspeed Ye! Black Emperor / Mogwai double bill. With the 'Gwai coming on at 1 in the morning, it was a dark backdrop for the band, perfect for the group's menacing sound and Rave Tape lighting accompaniment. The band played a major outdoor show in Glasgow last summer (the Zidane soundtrack show in Finnieston), but that was a show which had the start of the set played in daylight, which was certainly not the case in Barcelona. With Stuart adding a Catalan greeting to the standard "cheers, thanks a lot" phrase at the end of songs and a Catalan flag proudly displayed on stage, any local neutrals in the crowd were won over with a minimum of fuss.

It is not as though Mogwai are a band that curries favour in such a shameless way. They are a band that travels well, they are respectful to their hosts and of course, the band is well versed with the plight of the Catalan people and their own fight for independence. With an album released in January and some massive shows in Glasgow, Edinburgh and around the world, 2014 was a big year for the band. However, as supporters of the Yes campaign, you get the feeling that the outcome of Scotland's big political moment was equally important to the group. The band has made their feelings clear on the topic and they've applied logic and reason to their arguments. Whether you agree with Mogwai's stance or not, they've at least been consistent and able to back their beliefs up. I don't mind anyone voicing their opinion, but I do much prefer the opinion to have been thought about before being aired. That may be something which splits opinion for some fans but if the band continues in the same vein as their Royal Concert Hall and Primavera Sound gigs of 2014, there will be no complaints about the music.

Mogwai have come a long way since they were the kids better known for drinking Buckfast and wearing Kappa than their music. They were always an intense and strong band but over the years, they've added a few more strings to their musical bow. New songs like Remurdered bristle with energy, making me think of old school Japanese console games, possibly the best Final Fantasy song there never was.

With close to 4 hours of music with barely a vocal sung in anger, it says a lot for Mogwai and GY!BE's musicianship and variety of songs that the two sets flew by in a hurry. The feedback cacophony that signalled the end of Mogwai's set was the perfect way to bring the stage to a close and to build towards the end of the night and the festival.

There were a few more acts to see and Sunday afternoon offered more free bands in the Park Cituadella, but there was a feeling that Mogwai were the last big event of the festival, a fitting position for a band experiencing a big year.

With late evening Sunday flights heading from El Prat to Edinburgh and Glasgow, there were plenty of Scottish festival goers beating a retreat from Primavera before the conclusion of the weekend (a great benefit of a festival that runs from Thursday to Saturday). Others would extend their stay, taking the opportunity to feel as though they actually got a holiday in Barcelona but once again, Primavera Sound proved itself to be a top class festival and the 2015 festival, the 15th edition, is one that will welcome back plenty of Scottish music lovers. Apart from the weather (usually), there are clearly plenty of similarities between Scotland and Barcelona with the desire to party, drink and enjoy live music being prominent in both locations.

By the time of going to print, the results of the Catalan referendum were unknown, and of course the remains uncertainty over what outcome, if any, will arise from the vote. However, there were crossover strands between Scotland and Catalonia in 2014, and it was great to see some of Scotland's leading acts of the year take centre stage in the region, even for a short while.

9: Pull The Wires From The Wall

While having more mainstream media coverage would be good for up and coming Scottish bands, it would be completely remiss to overlook the work undertaken by BBC Radio Scotland and BBC Alba. The music played on these channels may not to be everyone's taste but they are doing a lot more than most operators when it comes to providing a blend of music that would not be found elsewhere.

Rapal

The premise for Rapal may be simple, get musicians on stage and record them, but it is a premise that works. The programme returned for a new series in August of 2014, hosted by Emma MacInnes and Vic Galloway, but it first aired on radio back in 2001 and has been on television since 2007. Like an increasing number of shows on BBC Alba, the programme and musicians involved didn't solely focus on Gaelic output. Yes, there were some folky acts singing in their native tongue which may have hit all the cultural points you expected from the show, but there was plenty of up and coming Scottish talent to look out for.

On the first episode of the 2014 series, Casual Sex were Vic Galloway's recommended act, delivering two songs in their standard sharp-shock style. In the second episode, Glasgow duo Honeyblood were the lead act, being welcomed into homes across the country days before they wowed audiences at the Last Big Weekend in Glasgow and at the Electric Fields festival in Dumfries.

The emergence of the iPlayer means that fans of the group can speed through the show and focus only on their chosen act, but Rapal has shown itself to be a show that's worth watching. It's a compact show, offering up 4-5 bands in its half an hour, and while it's unlikely you aren't going to like every band or artist, there is a decent chance you will find something that catches your interest.

It's great that Rapal is available and you have to say well done to BBC Alba in creating the show but this is generally the sort of show that BBC Scotland should be considering, at least on BBC2. A Scottish Jools Holland style show, without the boogie-woogie piano and the dull chat, lasting 30 to 40 minutes on Friday nights would be a great addition to the schedules. Timing the start of the show at the point when BBC4 starts to repeat its music output from the evening and when scores of folk are pouring themselves back into their homes after a night out would be a welcome addition to the TV listings. You wouldn't think it would be that expensive to put a show of this nature on, and you'd have a lengthy list of Scottish acts that would be keen to appear on the show. You'd also have a lengthy list of suitable presenters to choose from, allowing for squad rotation up front for the show.

Perhaps there are reasons why music shows are not the draw for TV anymore, and the internet has completely changed the way we discover and consume music, but sometimes being bold brings a great deal of benefits.

BBC Alba has also been prominent in bringing footage from a number of Scottish festivals. The BBC takes Glastonbury seriously *(for the summer of 2014, the organisation sent more people to the festival than the World Cup)*, BBC3 covers the Reading festival in great detail and of course, BBC Scotland takes a great pride in their coverage of T in the Park. If you love watching live music but can't make a festival, the BBC coverage is as good a substitute as you are going to get. This is something that BBC Alba has taken on, with the channel featuring Rockness, Belladrum, Hebridean Celt and many other events. The channel was even on hand to cover the Ceilidh event that took place at the BBC Studios in Glasgow during the Commonwealth Games. Scottish life has always had a focus on dancing and celebrations, which means that music and performers should be at the heart of their output.

STV Glasgow / Tenement TV

One good thing about the emergence of STV Glasgow is that it should provide an opportunity to shine a spotlight on emerging local talent. The core show on the channel, The Wan Show, sorry, The Riverside Show has provided an opportunity for acts to appear live and present their music to a local audience. The nature of the show means that the majority of acts you get on the show are going to appeal to a studio audience, but even with this in mind, there has been a diverse group of performers. From the zany to the po-faced, from the casual artist to the serious performer, anything which provides acts the chance to play live to a wider audience had to be a good thing. It is not as if an appearance on the Riverside Show is going to lead to overnight success and huge sales but it is good experience and it may help an act to pick up a couple of new followers.

It's not like The Riverside Show is the first programme to try this. When Newsnight Review was on the air, they aimed to close the show with a musical performance. More often than not this was a well-known act but with the show being recorded in Glasgow, there was the occasional performance from a local act. This may have been more due to a major name not bothering with the trip to Glasgow, or perhaps a need to fill a quota of local acts but whatever the reason, this was a good feature.

Another added bonus of the emergence of The Riverside a Show has been the occasional interview with a major act appearing in Glasgow. It is always good to see an interview with acts like Jurassic 5 on TV and no doubt it will have jogged a few memories and perhaps even shifted some last minute tickets for their gig.

STV have had a number of tea-time shows in the past which attempted to provide a magazine style show and it is inevitable that bands will feature, if not as prominently as I would have liked.

However, STV Glasgow decided to go all in with respect to a TV show and thankfully, the channel decided to get music fans on board to produce the show as opposed to letting TV makers run wild with their idea of what a music TV show should be like.

Long before STV Glasgow took to the air, the team behind TenementTV was gaining a great deal of publicity and praise for their site and music footage. The concept was simple. Bands were invited along to play in a West End tenement flat bad the footage was uploaded. The setting was excellent, the bay windows providing a stylish backdrop and you could tell that they have put time, money and effort into improving the sound and production levels.

The fact that there was a ready-made media option for music probably helped sway STV Glasgow towards the team, well that and the benefit of friends in high places, but there was a strong reason for choosing this team. Some music sites or media channels only look to focus on music they are passionate about or which fits into a niche of genre. One of the things that the Tenement TV team has focused on is covering a wide range of music. This offers a much palatable offering for a TV channel, making them the obvious choice for the new station.

Shows we have lost

There have been attempts to provide music television with a Scottish twist, and while shows like BBC Scotland's The Music Show or STV'S Chart Bite provided a much needed fix for music lovers, they never really got a settled position in the time slot, limiting their opportunity to grow an audience.

Chart Bite was very much of its time and it went for the old fashioned duo combination with Ewan MacLeod and Mari Steven conforming to a little and large format. The show did try to represent the chart, so there was a lot of mainstream music offered up to viewers but with everything else, there was a little too much effort put into being a bit weird. Perhaps the producers felt there was a need to be alternative to reach a younger audience but when you try to replicate the look and feel of The Word, but with none of the shock element so you can be placed into pre-watershed time slots, it becomes a difficult task.

The Music Show was a much more formal affair, but it worked a lot harder in showcasing Scottish bands and devoting time to major events taking place in the country. There were special programmes about Indian Summer, Chemikal Underground and the Belladrum festival while a lot of up and coming acts received a great deal of exposure. They also managed to obtain live footage from gigs taking place in Scotland, such as showing live footage from Teenage Fanclub,Belle and Sebastian and The View. With acts like Sons & Daughters, Aberfeldy, Popup, 1990s, King Creosote, Dananananaykroyd, Ballboy, Sluts of Trust, El Presidente, James Yorkston and St Judes Infirmary all getting air time, this was a music show that set out to help bands develop an audience and it should be commended for that.

Initially presented by Shantha Roberts, who was later joined by Vic Galloway, it was an interesting show taking bands outside of their more traditional locations, and there was also animation from David Shrigley and Kev Harper. Even written down now, it sounds like the ideal music show but perhaps there just isn't the sort of audience for a show like this.

When it comes to music on TV, it is probably fair to say that it is cyclical process. There will be a period of time without a music show and it becomes apparent that there needs to be something for music lovers. Then before too long, whether the sustained interest isn't there or the format isn't quite right to keep viewers interested, the viewing figures will drop off and music shows start disappearing from the air. And the cycle begins again.

Radio and Magazines

We may not have much in the way of TV but with radio and magazines, there are still some traditional ways to find out about new music. Vic Galloway is a name that crops up throughout this book, and with good cause. Vic is one of the most prominent champions of new music in the country and it is clear that it isn't just a job for him. The amount of times you see Vic at gigs enjoying bands indicates that he is clearly still driven by music, and when you consider his workload, the fact that he still makes time to get out as a punter should be an inspiration.

His show is pretty much essential listening if you are looking to keep in touch with new music in Scotland, and even if Vic is busy and unable to present, Nicola Meighan has provided an able deputy, ensuring the show goes on. The Vic Galloway show on Radio Scotland remains the number one option, especially in these iPlayer days, but Janie Forsyth usually manages to get a decent blend of music on her show, including live performances from good Scottish bands. In the first half of September 2014, she managed to get Honeyblood and The Twilight Sad in, which is not bad going for any show.

Ally McRae also flew the flag for Scotland on BBC Radio 1, taking over from Vic Galloway for the Scottish Introducing show, and then hosting a show with Jen Long. Sadly, this show came to a halt at the start of September 2014, limiting the opportunities for up and coming Scottish acts to receive some national exposure.

Aside from BBC Radio Scotland, there has been a boost for radio listeners this year with the fact that XFM Scotland returned to the airwaves. It is a commercial radio station but it is a commercial radio station that stands apart from stations like Radio Clyde or Heart, which means that you will get a different style of playlist than what you would get from the other commercial stations.

The strongest point about XFM Scotland in 2014 comes with the fact that they brought Jim Gellatly and Fraser Thomson back to a wider audience. Both were stalwarts of the previous XFM Scotland regime but more importantly, they are known champions of independent and up-and-coming Scottish musical talent, regular fixtures at festivals and gigs around the country. You're not going to miss a character like Jim at gigs and anything which can help to create a platform for alternative music has to be encouraged.

You also still have Billy Sloan kicking about on Clyde 2, serving up live sessions and keeping you up to date with all the music news from his good mates in the world of rock and pop. It's easy to see Billy as a bit of figure of fun but again, he is someone who has given countless bands a break over the years and there will be plenty of Scottish music fans who developed a love for a band through Billy's championing of them.

As you would expect in the online and digital era, there aren't too many magazines showcasing the importance of music in Scotland but we do have indicates that there is quality, if not quantity. If you still prefer to hold a physical entity in your hands while you find out about bands and gigs, you cannot go wrong with The List or The Skinny. The fact that The Skinny is available for free is a tremendous feat in this day and age, especially when you consider the depth of coverage on offer. You aren't going to like everything that the magazines cover, but there will definitely be plenty of interest and if you are open minded enough, there is likely to be something new that takes your fancy.

Online
The internet has obviously helped to bring views and news to people, as well as the all-important gig listings, so it is easier than ever before to know what is going on and who to listen out for.

Some of the best Scottish music sites include:

The Pop Cop
When it comes to Scottish music sites being held in high regard, you won't find too many that are more strongly regarded than The Pop Cop. It's a very good all-round site and when it comes to hearing news about bands and gigs of all levels, it is well worth following the Pop Cop on social media.

I don't always agree with Popcop and sometimes struggle to get the points that are being put across but, for all the minor quibbles about some of the editorials and opinions *(which people are more than entitled to have),* it's a great site that is often first with a lot of breaking news and they have played a tremendous role in bringing a lot of Glasgow acts to the attention of new music lovers. They've also got tons of playlists that will help you hear bands before anywhere else plays them.

There has been an evolution of the running of the site and with the editorial team of Popcop in recent times, but it remains a site that has its finger firmly on the Scottish music pulse and if you are keen to stay in touch with the latest news and tunes, follow the site on social media or bookmark it into your favourites.

Ravechild

I sometimes forget that Ravechild is a site that offers features, news and reviews, not in a bad way, but just because their gig listings are tremendous. If you are looking for the most comprehensive list of upcoming Glasgow gigs, this is another site that you definitely need in your favourites. Whether you are looking to plan ahead or you are bored that night, load up Ravechild and you'll be booking tickets, phoning friends and putting your shoes on in no time at all.

If there is a link to more information about a gig, they'll give you that as well and it's probably the best place to see all of the best posters and flyers for Glasgow music events. If you are serious about going to gigs and you fancy trying things that aren't always listed in the mainstream places, Ravechild will more than keep you up to date.

isthismusic?/Jockrock

I'll admit to being a bit biased with this one as it was isthismusic? that gave me my first break in writing about music and no matter what happens after that sort of thing, you're always going to have a soft spot in your heart for it. It may not be as flashy as some other sites and at times it isn't always as fast with the news but there is still a lot to like.

You great a really broad range of reviews and opinions on the site and if you feel that some of the sites are a little bit Glasgow centric, isthismusic? and Jockrock definitely give more attention and focus to the rest of the country. You can tell that the original magazine format is the main influence on the sites but again, snappy reviews and live appraisals is a large part of what music fans are looking for when they land on a music site. The Jockrock site is the one that is better suited to keeping up to date with news but both will provide you with plenty of opinions and ideas about what is taking place in the Scottish music scene.

Aye Tunes

It may not be as prolific as it used to be but Aye Tunes was an excellent site run by a guy who was getting his hands dirty and involved as much as it could. There were times when you felt things weren't going too well in the life of Jim but while this may not have been good for him, it made for good reading and there was usually an amusing anecdote wrapped up with the latest review of a band playing to him, the sound guy and the bar staff.

The site *(well, the one guy to be fair)* also put on a number of gigs over the years, so if you ever read a reviewer moaning about a night and think "aye, but could you do better?" Aye Tunes did. This is another site that has been around for a while but is being updated less frequently, which is part and parcel of getting on if it's just one person running the site. If you have some time to kill, feel free to dig through the archives and see when Aye Tunes saw your current favourite band play first!

Rokbun

Like Aye Tunes, Rockbun is a site that isn't updated as much as it used to be but when you consider how much time the main man from the site spends on Tinder and then meeting said girls from Tinder, I'm amazed he has enough time to brush his teeth, let alone run a music site! He's a great lad though, a very nice chap and one of the best elements about Rokbun was that it managed to straddle the East Coast / West Coast thing with Willie having a foot in both camps.

I suppose this means that there is a need for new blood to come to the fore with their own music blogs and websites, but there maybe isn't the same need for music blogs that there was a few years ago. The emergence of social media *(adding in options like Tumblr and Instagram)* to the main options and you have all the platforms you need to reach out to people and spout off about the music that you love. The more adventurous can add their own YouTube videos and recommendations as well so it may be that individually run music sites and blogs are not going to be as prevalent as they were in the past decade.

Manic Pop Thrills

This is a personal site that is updated on a more regular basis that the two that have just been mentioned, and the person behind it hails from Fife, so again, if you are keen to keep in touch with things happening outside of the big two cities, this is a good place to start and stay in touch with.

Everything Flows

Clearly nicking the title of one of the greatest songs ever is a tremendous starting point but this is another site that has kept going even with the blogger moving growing up and moving on. Like so many of the sites where it is an individual behind it as opposed to a collective, you can feel the passion and enthusiasm coming from every review and article. It's obvious that the person is only writing about the bands, music and gigs that he loves and checks out but when you've got a wide taste in music and a good knack for talking about music, you can get away with this approach. For what looks like a simple blog, there are always tons of video clips and images to keep things interesting as well. Again, another great blog where you can kill hours going through the back pages.

TenementTV

The TenementTV site is at the opposite end of the spectrum from isthismusic? and Jockrock. You could be forgiven for thinking that this site was just about the media content and the great performances that they record from their West End abode but the site has been expanding over the past year. This means that there is news, reviews, gig listings and plenty of other up to the minute stuff taking place on the site.

The team was very active at T in the Park, which coming on the back of their STV Glasgow slot, should mean that they have picked up a lot of new followers in recent times. The site is also behind the Tenement Trail event, the 2014 version took place in early October, so this is a site that firmly has its sights on world domination. There is an interview with two of the main guys behind the site in the interview section, they came across as decent people but you got the feeling that there was a great sense of ambition in their aims for the site. It'll be interesting to keep an eye on the site and see where they go from here.

With these sites, and plenty more sites, twitter accounts and Facebook pages, you can argue that there is no real need for the mainstream media to delve into the undercurrent and the soon-to-be acts of modern music. It would be nice to have something though, even if some of the tabloids tried to devote space to local gigs. The problem with that idea was that the writers seemed to have links with venues or promoters. It wasn't always the case that they would promote their own gigs or the gigs they were linked to, but it would happen enough times to be noticeable.

The problem is that there is no middle ground and if people are unaware of sites like Jockrock and Popcop, it can be quite difficult to find out more about the Scottish music scene and what acts are bubbling underneath the surface. This means if you are looking to get into a new style of music, you are going to have to stumble upon sites and social media pages to start getting a feel for what is around you.

While there have been numerous incidents which sum up the state of Scottish music in the mainstream press, one day springs to mind. I had a busy day with two interviews, a gig and a photoshoot/continuation of an interview lined up but that's part of the fun of writing about music. First of all, I met Shitdisco, another band that formed in Glasgow with the art school looming over them and it was clearly far too early for them to be up for an interview (we were meeting at the un-musician-ly hour of 4pm). Perhaps their management felt it was best for the boys to be roused at a reasonable hour but not even a mid-afternoon pint in the sunshine outside of Mono was working for them. They were an act that found themselves hitched onto the Nu-Rave bandwagon, a move that got them a lot of publicity but possibly lost them many potential fans as well. They maybe weren't the luckiest band in the world but I quite liked their music and they were pretty decent in any dealings I had them. We got a good bit of the interview done but the band weren't quite feeling it and asked could we meet again later on. I outlined my itinerary for the evening and we arranged a late night rendezvous at the top of Sauchiehall Street, a setting that was more familiar for the band.

From Mono, I took the leisurely walk over to the Academy where I was to interview We Are Scientists. I was never really sure about this act or how they made it so big. It was almost as if their personality and charm in interviews was as much of a factor in them getting to a certain level as their music was. The fact that they were considered to be at a reasonable level with respect to record sales and publicity was indicated by the fact that as I was making my way into their dressing room for the interview, Bev Lyons was making her way out.

Beverley Lyons eh? At least with Billy Sloane and his great mates in the world of music, you knew that at one point in his life he actually liked music and had some interest in the activity. Perhaps the puzzled look on my face at seeing Lyons exit the room was noticed by the band as before I started interviewing them, they had a question for me. "So uh...do you know that girl?"

"Yeah, she's a gossip columnist for one of the tabloid newpapers." It then turned out that Bev had spent a good deal of her interview trying to get the band to attend a fashion show or award ceremony later that evening or the next night. Maybe it never clicked with Bev that the band were in Glasgow to perform a show and then were heading off around the country to play other gigs. Anyway, the group found it all a little bit bizarre and if they got around to reading the Razz exclusive interview a few days later, they probably wished they had never bothered. Daily Record readers got to learn what We Are Scientists thought about The Killers and the Arctic Monkeys but not a lot about the group themselves.

As for the show itself, it was good to see The Blood Arm, a band I had caught in King Tuts not long before, playing in a much bigger arena, and they just about pulled it off. We Are Scientists delivered a well-polished and poppy set with the crowd going home delighted with themselves. I headed off to the top end of Sauchiehall Street with a phone full of recorded interviews and a notepad full of illegible writing. A noisy interview in Nice N Sleazy's was abandoned as a fun yet ultimately pointless endeavour and we felt the chaos of Sauchiehall Street by night was the perfect place for a photo-shoot and rounding off the interview. With the glaring lights of Mr Chips and the noodle bar providing the backdrop for the shots, the band gladly indulged in Buckfast...err Irn Bru and mean 'n' moody shots while drunken revellers made their way in, out and around the shot. I had been working my "proper job" during the day and then spent a couple of hours interviewing and watching bands (with easily the same time again in hanging about) but it never once felt like a job or work, it was all a good laugh. It was luckily enough that the photographer on the shoot was my brother, so it was much more of a social hangout (albeit with a professional outcome) as opposed to work.

I'm not trying to mock Bev Lyons, she has clearly carved out a great career for herself and I'm sure she won't lose any sleep over a no-mark like me having a pop at her but I'd be feeling pretty annoyed with myself if I had the chance to promote bands and reach out to folk but never took that opportunity. Again, editorial policy will no doubt dictate your approach to interviews and engaging with bands but I had a brilliant time all evening and managed to come out with a lot of worthwhile stuff at the end of it all. At the Big Weekend event in Glasgow and at the final T in Balado this year, Bev was present, still reporting for the Record and filling Twitter timelines with inane drivel and photobombed pictures of the artists.

You can see that the newspapers in Scotland have embraced social media culture with respect to football, bringing in a wider scope of views, and giving fans the chance to speak up for themselves. This helps to create even more debate and controversy, so of course it works for the papers. Occasionally you get one of the tabloids getting worked up about live music and providing a column for writers, but a lot of the time this was handed over to someone with a vested interested, say a promoter or someone with connections to a management team. It was a lot better than nothing, but it was falling far short from what should be on offer. The broadsheets offer a lot of good pieces, often from people already mentioned like Vic Galloway and Nicola Meighan, but there are sporadic and often lost amongst the tat and other cultural elements that papers try to squeeze in.

With the internet, you could argue that all of these traditional mediums are no longer important, but if you are just developing an interest or a love of music, these mediums could provide more of a helping hand or a point in the right direction. Then again, newspapers are commercial entities, not public service broadcasters, so it is not as if they are duty bound to provide anything which they don't feel will help them make sales.

The good thing is that we are no longer reliant on these mediums, and this is true for anyone who is looking to write about music. If you've read the book, you'll get that I don't think you need to have a perfect or strong grasp on the English language to write about music. It's far more important to get across what the music means to you or what your take on it is. For some writers, that will be delivered in immaculate prose whereas for other writers, it will be delivered in a short and snappy medium, and all points in between. There's no right or wrong way to go about music writing and if you have something to say, there's a chance that there will be people that want to hear it.

The options for a traditional career in mainstream music journalism may be falling, but there are still options and even if you don't get to carve out a living in the traditional way, there are still plenty of ways you can have fun and make living writing about music. While I always took music and writing seriously, I never really took the idea of writing about music (as a career) seriously, it was what I did for fun or what I used as a safety valve away from work and other elements.

I had a brilliant time, I got a lot of music for nothing (legitimately), I got to see a lot of bands play live for free and even my mates got benefits from it at times. I'm also delighted to say that I met some great folk along the way and a few of these people are still friends of mine, which is never a bad outcome of doing something.

10: I Know Where The Summer Goes

While 2014 offered a chance for a fresh start and so many innovative and new musical events, there was also a big finale in the Scottish music scene in this year. The 2014 T in the Park was announced as being the last one to be held at Balado. This led to an outpouring of emotion on social media and when it came to providing a hashtag to define the event #ByeByeBalado was pretty good, as far as hashtags go.

Not everyone likes change and for many people, Balado was the only festival home they had ever known so there was obviously going to be some concerns and complaints about the switch. On paper, the only people who have been made worse off with the switch to Strathallan will be revellers from Edinburgh, now facing a longer journey to and from the festival. Well, the locals in Strathallan who now have party goers descending on their area may not be too delighted about the switch but on the whole, there shouldn't be too much of a difference. Of course, the miles and distance don't always tell the full story, the quality and nature of roads can have a big impact on the amount of time a person spends travelling.

The thing is, festival organisers want to place their event in a rural setting, providing them with a greater degree of freedom for camping or having the ability to turn up the volume to a later hour. There is a need to find a balance between finding a convenient location and finding a location that is removed from civilisation to make sure that everyone can enjoy themselves without impacting on other people.

Clearly the venue is an important element of any successful event and the location of T in the Park has helped in developing the success of the festival. However, surely the most important memories of the festival are about the bands and the time spent with friends or the time spent watching others do daft things. These are all elements that will be just as valid and enjoyable at Strathallan Castle as they were in Balado. This is much the same as the move from Strathclyde Park to Balado. There will be plenty of kids bemoaning the move from Balado who weren't around for the Strathclyde Park days or who didn't think it was that big a deal. For a Weegie who had been to the first three T's, the move to Balado was a bit annoying, but it wasn't anything to get worked up about.

The element of annoyance wasn't because I felt that Strathclyde Park had any magical input into the quality to the event, it was just because the festival would now be held a lot further away from my home! In fact, my biggest annoyance about the switch in 97 and an increase in capacity size is that the nature of the line-up changed considerably. This wasn't solely down to the decision to bring in more punters; there had been a shift in what was the popular music of the day.

94, 95 and 96 were clearly the years when Britpop was at its peak although, in Pulp and Radiohead, the 96 T headliners were major acts at the height of their powers. In 97, things just seemed a bit duller and the switch in venue played a part in deciding we would take to the road and check out the Reading Festival instead. I was back at T, and at Balado for the first time in 98, and apart from the fact that the site was bigger, I wouldn't have been able to tell you any real difference about the festival itself. This may say a bit more about me than the festival layout but as long as there are stages, bands, booze and your mates, there isn't too much to worry about.

No matter where T in the Park is held, there will be music, madness and a bunch of things that delight and appall you, perhaps even in equal measure. There will likely be some teething problems in 2015 at Strathallan Castle and there will be a queue of folk lining up to say that it's not as good as it used to be but in the end, just like every T and probably every other festival, it'll be what you make it.

As a side note, at the start of July 2014, I was heading down to London to see Jack White and catch up with friends while some people around me were heading to the Sonisphere festival. The thought of going to a music festival which featured Limp Bizkit was quite a chilling one and this may have necessitated the need for them to get fired into the wine from 9am. Over the course of the journey, the topic of T in the Park and its move in 2015 came up. The words "Here, did you know that T in the Park used to be in Strathclyde Park" was a great line to make me feel old!

Who knows, with Glastonbury now looking towards its 50th anniversary celebrations, perhaps there will come a time when people have to strain their memory to recall the time that T was held in Balado.

I know it can be all too easy to mock T in the Park, but it deserves a lot of praise for staying the course, and there has to be a lot said for the fact that it will have gotten some people into live music. Even with many people's focus falling on having a good time, there is an inevitability that some people will stumble into a tent or in front of a performance that excites them. From there, there will be people who get the bug for live music and going to gigs.

Since T in the Park has become the feel good hit of the summer for many Scottish youngsters, there has been an increase in demand for live performances and gigs. It may be that the demand for live music has been driven by other outliers, with T being a beneficiary of it, but there is a case to be argued that many people want to replicate the feeling that they get at T, at other times of the year.

Heading out to a gig with friends is the best way to capture that feeling and when you start going to live gigs, you can get accustomed to it, and get a taste for it. There will be some people that only ever get remotely close to a live performance when they attend T in the Park, but you get the feeling that the festival has acted as a gateway to other live shows and events.

T in the Park will have its critics but when a festival runs for over 20 years with the attendance figures and ticket sales still remaining really high, it is easy to see that there is a hell of a lot of good associated with T in the Park.

There were also so many great non-music moments over the years and there is a lot to be said for someone making a definitive T in the Park book with punter, worker and musicians stories. It's not like Geoff Ellis to miss out on a money making trick, in fact, Geoff if you want a writer for the official one, get in touch…and I'll overlook the fact that you killed off Indian Summer and then the Connect Festival.

For me, moments like my sister in laws friend referring to Asian Dub Foundation as the Adrian Dove Foundation was the equal to some of the band's I managed to catch. There was the time we were having a drink outside one of the smaller tents when a van drove off from the side of the tent. Unfortunately, one young lady was behind the van taking a call of nature, leaving her exposed to the people milling around. It may not have been one of her better moments but it was certainly a talking point of the evening. The time one of our group was going on holiday a day or two after T in the Park so he decided to buy some band t-shirts as part of his holiday wear. He bought two black t-shirts, at least of different bands. There was also the follow on story later on when he thought he had lost the t-shirts but his more sensible better half had actually put them away for safe keeping. There was even the time I had been ill all week and wasn't going to go but a very late addition of The Strokes saw me haul myself out of bed and into town for the shuttle bus from Buchanan Street. It wasn't the best idea I ever had and even before we collected our tickets at T, my face was chalk white while my lips had turned a notable hue of blue. Thankfully The Strokes were on early and I held it together superbly for their short but sweet set. Mind you, that took it all out of me and before too long; I was heading back to Glasgow where I would fall asleep until late on Sunday!

The jokes, the sights, the number of times we found beer tokens and after a look around to see if anyone had dropped beer tokens and were looking for them (there wasn't, at least not that we could see), using said beer tokens. When you think that I never camped I could have probably spent double the time (if not more) at T than I did, which would have meant loads more stories on top.

Even the journeys have held some great memories. For me, the journey up to T in the Park was often about having mix tapes/CDs/MP3 playlists blaring and every one of them somehow contained King Tubby and Augustus Pablo's Borderline Dub, their take on the classic Ali Baba. Even to this day I cannot hear the line "my dream last night was about Ali Baba and the 40 thieves" without thinking of the journey to T in the Park. Yeah, you'd be surprised at how often that line comes up in everyday life for me. That and randomly shouting T in the Park at any point in the journey after the Kincardine Bridge are probably two of the most consistent elements of my life; such was the regularity with which they occurred

There was also one time on the Shuttle bus when we were about to jump off in Balado when someone in a hi-viz jacket marched onto the bus and loudly announced that everyone would be searched for drugs before they got off the bus. The colour drained from about three quarters of the passengers before the guy burst out laughing and said, "only joking, enjoy your day folks" and walked off the bus again!

However, while there is a growing feeling that for many folk, T in the Park wasn't really about the music, that wasn't the case with me. If the main aim was to get blitzed with my mates, we'd have done that in a pub or a house that weekend, making things a lot easier and convenient. It is not as though I've been to every T and even when you try and see a lot of bands, you know that you are destined to miss plenty more. With that in mind, I think I've got enough musical memories of T to last a lifetime.

There was the time Mercury Rev played and every song was met with an ovation so long that their mean and moody mystique was shattered into a million pieces due to their smiles at it all. There was the time Sonic Youth gave a master class in noise and energy. There was that three gig run which included The Polyphonic Spree, Super Furry Animals and The Flaming Lips. There was the time Kings of Leon played in the week their debut album was released and there was a bigger crowd for them than most bands' received all weekend. There was the time Snow Patrol were good yet unloved and Gary Lightbody quoted Bo Selecta lines during every break in the set. There was the time Shirley Manson played and the Beastie Boys made you forget about the freezing mud. There was the sunny afternoon when Spiritualized were just magical, with their (slightly curtailed) version of 200 Bars still ringing in my ears. There was the time Black Grape stole the show (and maybe other stuff) and The Verve made you believe they were teetering on the brink of stardom before they started acting like silly buggers and split up in '95.

Oasis were legendary in '94 and the Pulp and Radiohead shows in '96 gave Strathclyde Park the send-off it deserved. Countless moments and beats in the Slam Tent and for me, seeing New Order for the first time (when they eventually arrived on stage and overlooking Brandon Flowers popping up) very special. I know that the current version of Kraftwerk isn't the "real" Kraftwerk, but the rebooted mode, Kraftwerk 4.0 or whatever they should be dubbed were still excellent in a massive tent. Looking around and seeing virtually everyone wearing 3D glasses watching 4 mature German men standing behind laptops is a scene that doesn't come around too often, certainly in Perth & Kinross. There was also the sight of The Raveonettes bringing that great love sound to a sunny afternoon, offering a modern take on The Wall of Sound that didn't have mad Phil's fingerprints all over it. There was Cornelius and his multi-media show and the time DJ Shadow came with Cut Chemist to the Slam Tent and played a set that a lot of people weren't happy with.

T in the Park is now an essential part of Scottish life and it is a rite of passage for most people. I was lucky enough that the first T took place in 1994 and I had just turned 16, the perfect time to start going to festivals. I've grown older, without necessarily growing up, over the years at T and while it may not be something that I go out of my way for these days, it is something that I'll always look back on with a lot of fondness. I think a large part of that is because it has always maintained the approach of having something for everyone. Whether you are the sort of person who likes wearing fancy dress and insisting that attention is placed on you at various points over the weekend or you just want to keep your head down and see some bands, T in the Park is pretty much what you make of it, and if you don't enjoy it, its maybe more down to you than the festival itself.

There is even the fact that if you love music but don't like bands that have become successful (yet), there is even a stage for you!

T-Break

While there has been a growing feeling that T in the Park is more about the big names and radio friendly artists, there remains a desire to provide a platform for new bands and emerging talent to play at the festival. These acts may not be headline makers or musicians that will play in front of a massive crowd at the festival but it can provide many bands with an important step in their development.

From the very first T in the Park, there was a stage for emerging acts and if you are looking for a success story, the appearance of Glass Onion on the Caledonia Stage provides you with the perfect starting point. Okay, Glass Onion were to change their name to Travis before hitting the big time and the Caledonia Stage would evolve into the T Break stage, but even way back in 1994 at Strathclyde Park, TITP offered an opportunity for new bands to play in front of audience and experience a festival vibe. The renaming of the Caledonia Stage to the T Break stage occurred in 1996, the final year the event was held at Strathclyde Park before moving to Balado.

The fact that Biffy Clyro were one of the Main Stage headliners at the 2014 festival is one of the biggest endorsements you are likely to find for the T Break Stage. The band first appeared at T in 1999 and their 2014 appearance was their 10th appearance at TITP. Given the band has only been around for 15 years (and the festival itself is only on its 21st outing), this is an almighty achievement. There are fewer and fewer bands sticking around for this length of time so there are not going to be too many acts in a position to challenge Biffy Clyro as a band that should be synonymous with T in the Park.

Some may criticise the familiar pattern and feel to the T in the Park (any festival that continues to give space to The Stereophonics should be questioned) but if this is what the punters want, then so be it and hell mend them! There is also the fact that Biffy Clyro had been away from T for a couple of years, so at least there was a certain freshness to their appearance on the Main Stage, even if the 2014 festival saw the band take to the Main Stage for a fifth time.

While T Break provides the chance for 16 unsigned Scottish acts to play at T in the Park, the stage is not solely for these acts. In recent years, the number of artists appearing on this stage over the 3 days of the festival is in the 30s. Some of the bands that miss out on being included may feel aggrieved at the fact that bands not part of the judging process are selected to play but it adds an additional element to the stage, perhaps drawing in a crowd for one act that will hang around and stay for other acts.

In fact, when it comes to entertainment, the best part of T Break comes in the complaints and criticisms made by people regarding the bands that missed out. These complaints are usually made by unsuccessful bands or their friends, family members but you know what the internet is like, sometimes complaints are made by nutters that like feeling part of something. Whether it is Facebook, Twitter or individual music blogs or sites, as soon as the T Break announcements are made, it will be seconds before cries of "fix", "conspiracy" and "that band are bloody rubbish" are sent across the world wide web. I quite enjoy a good online meltdown and so far, the consistency surrounding the T Break complaints have been very enjoyable and I recommend checking them out.

(For the record, I clearly had played no part in any of the judging panels for the T Break. If you have read this far, you will have ascertained that no one would suggest that my opinion on bands should be relied upon!)

Other acts that appeared on the T Break Stage and made their way up the festival include The Cinematics and the 1990s.

One of the headliners for the 2006 T Break stage was The Cinematics, the third year in a row that the band had played in the T Break stage. The group managed to force their way on to the King Tut's stage in 2007, giving them four years in a row at the festival. As for the 1990s, they moved beyond T Break, playing the Pet Sounds Stage in 2008 and they headlined the Futures Stage in 2009.

In recent years there have been some eyebrow raising acts appearing on the T Break stage, including Thrum. Thrum played at the very first T in the Park back in '94 so it is fair to say that their appearance on the T Break stage in 2011 was a surprise, over 15 years since the band's first appearance at the festival. Admittedly, the band had split up in 1995, reforming in 2011 so they were starting all over again, but it maybe wasn't the sort of act that people were expecting to see on the stage.

There has also been the appearance of artists such as Lucy Spraggan and Diana Vickers. These artists were X Factor non-winners (let's face it, the only real winner from the X Factor is Cowell and it's probably best for me to not bother pointing out who the real losers are!)

It is not as if the T Break Stage is the most eagerly anticipated hot spot of the weekend, far from it, there will be probably bigger crowds lining up to get their phones charged up, but that isn't the point. It provides bands with something to aim for, it allows people who enjoy watching up and coming bands a place to seek something new out and it's been good for T too. The T Break Stage brings a lot of kudos to the festival and apart from bands who were rejected by the panel who decides what bands get to play at the T Break Stage, it's well received by enough people to make a difference.

When talking to Lloyd from Olive Grove Records, it was clear that appearing on the stage was more than worthwhile for the PRS money, which can provide an up and coming band with more funding than they would likely get from other sources. There isn't much of a fee for playing T Break, but you get a fee, you get the kudos of playing T in the Park, you get a couple of free passes for your family or pals and you get a VIP pass for the festival. If you then manage to win over a few fans at the festival or from the publicity surrounding the event, all the better. T Break is obviously an achievement for any band that is selected to play there, but equally, it probably isn't something that is worth losing too much sleep about either way.

One of the best things about the T Break stage is that it has probably influenced and encouraged many other acts to dedicate a stage to up and coming acts, providing many more opportunities for emerging talent to expand their horizons and gain the experience of playing at a major festival. In this regard, the T Break stage at T should be classed as a good influence on plenty of the other Scottish festivals, much in keeping with the festival itself.

T in the Park, love or loathe (or feeling indifference to) it has set a benchmark, be it or high or low, for other festivals in the country to be compared with.

Other festivals

When it comes to festivals in Scotland, there is a growing split between major outdoor festivals in the central belt and away from the central belt. One of the major drawbacks about hosting a major event in cities like Glasgow or Edinburgh is that there is no great desire to provide camping facilities. Events like Indian Summer, the Gig on the Green events and even the Summer Sessions at Bellahouston Park have welcomed bigger audiences than the boutique festivals that provide camping facilities, but they haven't found a long-term audience.

There are obviously a number of reasons for this. Firstly, the allure of sleeping in your own bed and getting a shower in your own home is a far more appealing factor than camping for many people. If it is possible to reach your festival or major music event from the comfort of your own home, it would be better to do so. There is also the fact that there is a lack of suitable space to provide camping facilities in Glasgow. If you think about the fuss that arose from the Summer Sessions in Bellahouston Park in 2013, could you imagine if they provided camping space in the other half of the park? That would have caused a considerable amount of problems and if you thought the local residents were in uproar after the gigs, just think what it would have been like if people camped!

However, for many people, the camping experience is an integral part of the festival experience. I'm more than happy to say that I have never camped at T in the Park, even after going so many times over the years. Being able to head back to my bed for a few hours' sleep and then enjoy a proper shower was far more appealing than trying to sleep in a camp site. It's not that I'm entirely against camping, I have camped at Connect and Reading but T in the Park is too close to my home to bother with the thought of camping. It's not something I'd choose for T, but I've found accommodation (be it hotels or friends' homes) for Rockness, Leeds, Summercase, Primavera Sound, Benicassim and even the Bangkok Rocks festival.

The fact that there are a large number of festivals in the north and south of Scotland can be seen for a number of reasons. There is a large amount of space for festival sites and camping facilities can be set up. The facility for camping ensures that locals can enjoy the festival while opening up the possibility for people to come a good distance for the festival. There is also a lot to be said for the fact that there are much fewer gigs taking part in this part of the world.

This isn't the case in the central belt where there are so many gigs to choose from. If you are able to see a steady stream of bands in venues that are close to home, you may feel as though the festival experience isn't as necessary or important. People in the outer areas of the country are far more likely to be receptive about major events that are taking place close to them. There is no doubt that the festival experience is now a rite of passage event for many youngsters in the country, as important as underage drinking and realising that Jimmy Krankie isn't a wee boy. You may combine the festival experience with some underage drinking but hopefully you'll never find out the truth about the Krankies at your big event.

The Boutique And The Beautiful

If you were to gauge general opinion about T in the Park, it would be fair to say that you would experience a wide range of answers. For some people, it is the highlight of the year, something to save up for and look forward to all summer. For other people, it is something to avoid with all of your might and energy. There are also tons of folk in between who aren't too fussed either way but when you consider the opinions and reactions, it is always the extreme elements that get the most attention.

Just because someone doesn't like the idea of T in the Park, it would be wrong to say that they don't like the idea of live music or festivals. There is a demand for a different type of festival and to be fair, this is an area that Scotland does okay with. There have been attempts at creating other major festivals in major cities, none of which have really stuck around, but there have also been plenty of great festivals around the country, providing something a little bit different.

In 2014, the Scottish festival circuit may have missed out on Rockness and the Insider Festival, but there were still plenty of other options to help people make the most of their summertime.

Some of the festivals that played a key role in creating a great summer atmosphere for folk included Eden Festival, Solas Festival, the HebCelt Festival, Wickerman, Belladrum, Electric Fields and Loopallu. Festivals like Wickerman, Belladrum and Loopallu have become well-known names on the festival circuit while Electric Fields was making its debut. All of these festivals offered something different to T, perhaps a cosier and more comfortable environment where families and kids would be tolerated, or perhaps musicians whom you may not find played on Radio 1, but which are none the poorer for it.

There is also the fact that having as many festivals to choose from provides choice, it allows people to find a festival that fits in with other summer plans that may have, and it ensures that Hector Bizerk are kept busy every week. Fair play to that outfit, they put the miles and hours in over the summer, and that was outside of playing their own gigs and holding their own Hectember Weekend in Edinburgh and Glasgow.

The Retro and the Stately Homes
Sometimes there is a need for a festival which caters to a more mature audience (or an audience with a more mature

taste). There is also the fact that festivals don't need to be a battle, feeling like you are putting yourself through hell to enjoy bands. There is a growing awareness that people are looking for comfort as well as music and alcohol from these events, which is something that is becoming increasingly popular.

The Rewind Festival has cornered the market in nostalgia while festivals like Party At The Palace in Linlithgow or The Kelburn Garden Party allow you to feel that you are at a much classier event. It's not as if the Rewind festival provides class, it's hard to look elegant when you are rocking headbands, leg warmers and an awful lot of neon (please insert standard "and that was just the guys" comment) but enjoying bands in the grounds of an old castle or palace is clearly a great way to enjoy live music. If you like the idea of live music but find the normal notion of a festival to be a bit too much to bear, you can still enjoy a great weekend with a little bit more refinery!

There was a broad range of artists at these events with The Party At The Palace straddling the old and the new in the best possible manner. The lads from The View or Edinburgh musician Carrie Mac may not have born when Deacon Blue or Simple Minds tasted their peak of commercial success, but this can only be a good thing when it comes to bringing in an audience for a festival. Whether it is mums and dads coming with their kids or social groups coming along in packs, these festivals need to be a bit smarter when it comes to creating awareness and creating a different sort of atmosphere has to be a good thing.

The Audio Soup festival, set in the hills of Dunbar, went a different route, putting on cover bands with up and coming acts to create a unique festival in a unique setting. The problem was, the festival organisers arranged for a band called Bohemian Wraps (Today) to play, which is quite possibly the worst band name of all time, and this would have cast a large and unattractive shadow over the event.

Alcoholidays

Given the success of T in the Park, it is no surprise that

other Scottish alcohol companies would think that a music festival would be the ideal way to promote their brand. You aren't going to start off and create a festival to rival T in the Park, but then again, there aren't any beer firms at the level of Tennents.

Brew At The Bog

The 2014 festival was the third Brew At The Bog festival, with Brewdog at the thick of it. The company likes to market itself as being the punk rock craft beer company but when it comes to the musical acts on offer, they would be better-described as a folk rock beer firm.

This is just one of the many festivals taking place around Inverness and coming at the start of May, Brew At The Bog is now being viewed by many as the opening point of the summer festival season.

The 2014 festival was a one-day event with 12 hours of music featuring acts like King Creosote, Roddy Woomble, Casual Sex, The Pictish Trail and many more acts.

Fynefest

While there were twenty or so bands playing over the course of the weekend at the 2014 Fynefest, it would be fair to say it is a festival that is as focused on craft beer and food as it is the music. Still, there is a chance to camp with friends and enjoy great drink and food while acts like The Hazey Janes, Bombskare, Natalie Clark and The Shiverin' Sheiks played.

Jocktoberfest

Billing itself as offering beer, bands and bratwurst, Jocktoberfest, held on the first weekend of September and supported by the Black Isle Brewing Company, offered up a similar sort of festival to Brew At The Bog and Fynefest. With the brewers conjuring up a special brew (but not technically Special Brew) for the event, craft beer fans would have been in their elements as much as music lovers.

Acts like Chris Devotion & The Expectations, Michael Cassidy and many more took to the stage over the course of the weekend. This is clearly a smaller event than some of the other similar festivals, but again, it is growing year on year, with plenty of rave write-ups from fans and performers.

The small nature of these events and the focus on quality food and drink helps these events to stand out for family audiences and people who have little interest in what the major festivals have to offer. Given recent trends, it is no surprise that craft beer companies are getting involved with this style of event. Craft beer is one of the latest elements to be dubbed the "new rock and roll" and the industry is growing its reputation and awareness by engaging its audience and creating an atmosphere that people buy into. These events will go down well on social media, creating a great buzz for the firms, allowing them to grow their audience and develop a reputation as being fun and hip choices. It also means plenty of bands get a chance to play in front of audiences who are likely to become followers (at least on a social media level) as well.

Dance Festivals

It would be fair to say that the majority of festivals in Scotland focus on guitar bands and acts of this ilk and nature. Yes, T in the Park has the Slam Tent and most reasonably sized festivals will have some form of nod to dance music, but on the whole, it is guitar music and the more traditional sounds that are found at festivals.

That is not to say that dance music fans cannot find festivals that are of interest, but the problem is, most dance events are held in the small hours of the morning which means that the standard Scottish festival times are out of sync with what people are used to. When you are used to clubbing in the Sub Club or the Arches on a weekly or monthly basis, bouncing out of the venue around at 2 or 3 in the morning, the idea of enjoying dance music from the afternoon or the evening may not be the most enticing idea. There is also the fact that these dance festivals seem to take place in big soulless sheds, not entirely conducive to the sort of atmosphere which provides the platform for a good night out. If you were to take the elements that make up for a magic evening in the Berkeley Suite or The Brunswick, you'll struggle to recognise them in the venues where you find these events. However, there are still opportunities to get together with your pals and have a great time that you won' remember.

The Riverside Festival

Taking place around the Riverside Museum in Glasgow, the Electric Frog weekend of 2014 had a retro feel to it. When I first saw the Saturday line-up, I had to double check I was not looking at a flyer for an event of 10 or so years ago. Not that there was anything wrong with that, it was a cracking line up of acts including Andrew Weatherall, Vitalic, 2ManyDJs, Matthew Dear, Felix Da Housecat, Slam and many more. Perhaps the organisers were mindful that there is a big market of dance fans that are more than happy to take a walk down memory lane, and perhaps these events are better suited to these fans.

If your clubbing heydays were a decade ago, you may be happier enjoying an event from 4pm to 11pm and then deciding if you head home or to the after-party. As you would expect, the event organisers worked with a number of local venues to ensure that there were plenty of plans to choose from to keep you occupied until 3 in the morning, and there were probably plenty of folk who headed to these events without bothering with the actual clubbing element.

Sunday brought in the Sunday Circus and Melting Pot element while it also had artists like Laurent Garnier, SJ Sneak, Francois K and plenty more. Given it was a Bank Holiday weekend, there was no excuse for not enjoying the Sunday to its fullest and it continues to be an event that people love. The moans and grumbles about beer queues and lack of facilities become smaller every year, and this may be an event that has some staying power about it.

Coloursfest

Of course, if you are talking about a dance event with staying power, you need to include Coloursfest, which was once again back for more in 2014. The first Coloursfest took place back in 2002 and you can bet that there will be plenty of people who have been to every one of them. To paraphrase Mogwai, "Hardcore will never die...but some of the fans will start to grow quite old."

The Braehead Arena is an arena that leaves me cold but with 6 arenas, including an outdoor stage, there is a lot to see and do at the event which started at 5 and had a licence until well into the following morning. Coloursfest is a festival that manages to live in its own bubble, gaining little exposure in the mainstream media, but still bringing in huge crowds year after year. This is an indicator that music scenes in Scotland can live and stand for themselves and that sometimes the role of media support is over-rated. Sure, the odd advert or piece in the Record or the Sun won't hurt sales but it's the word of mouth and online chat that ensures Coloursfest keeps going.

EH1 Music Festival

The EH1 festival billed as being the event that brings the summer to a close is a close relation to Coloursfest, taking place on the eastern side of the country. The Royal Highland Centre has hosted a massive amount of dance music events over the years, handily located for the motorway and not being too far from Edinburgh city centre. With 9 different venues separated by different genres and areas for the 2014 event, major names like Duke Dumont and Paul van Dyke ensured that there was a high level of interest in the festival.

The event was a midday to 3am affair, which is clearly a long haul for anyone looking to maximise their value for money, but there would have been more than one after party lined up for some folk. The fact that Coloursfest and EH1 attract around 7,000 fans for a single day of dance music is an indicator of their popularity. They aren't festivals in the traditional sense with there being no camping, but they are perfect examples of the large scale music events that are on offer these days.

Like many other festivals, there is a great deal to be said for the value for money of these major events. The prices for the EH1 event was around £40 + booking fee, which when you think you can enjoy up to 15 hours of music and a lot of big names, is tremendous value for money.

When festival prices are mentioned, there is often an instinctive reaction about the high cost of a ticket, but I genuinely don't think that is the case, if anything, festivals represent a good return for your money.

At the Mogwai event at Richmond Park, I was speaking to one of the bar staff (this was early on when it was possible to get a drink without missing a full set) who asked what the price of the ticket was. Having replied £40 or so all in, she replied that's a bit dear. I mumbled in agreement while lifting drinks but in reality, I'd have been happy to pay almost that entire fee for Mogwai alone and the list of other bands on the bill more than made up for the money.

I've paid a tenner to see Honeyblood before, Holy Mountain were excellent and would have been worth a similar amount of money and then Swervedriver were up next, and they were great. So that was three bands in a row offering up great sets, and knowing that you had Mogwai headlining, it was fair to say that there was plenty of value...even without thinking that in between you had acts like Young Fathers, The Twilight Sad, Fuck Buttons, The Wedding Present and James Holden!

£40 split between 9 bands means value for money and it would be the exact same when it comes to EH1 and Coloursfest, especially when compared to the cost of a night out to see one act or artist. There will be people that can no longer attend club nights on a regular basis, so the major dance events provide an opportunity to socialise with friends, keep in touch with music and have a great night out. Clearly, value for money is a personal thing with everyone having his or her own preferences and level of disposable income, but I think these events offer an excellent return for money.

Festivals we have lost

One of the bones of contention about festivals in Scotland has been the current lack of festivals for a more mature crowd in Scotland. There are plenty of boutique festivals that offer family friendly camping facilities but there should be something for the crowd that feel as though they have moved beyond the T vibe but are still capable of having fun out with the family environment.

Indian Summer was a perfect example of the sort of festival that could fit the bill. As the name suggested, the festival was lined up at the end of summer, the proper summer, not the end of the Scottish summer that takes place in mid-May in some years. It's location in Victoria Park was ideal for West End residents but it was easy enough to reach for everyone in Glasgow.

The line-up was interesting, far quirkier than the T in the Park line-ups for the corresponding years. Some will argue that the line-up was not as good, but it would be wrong to associate commercial success and crowd numbers with quality music.

The weather, as you would expect for Glasgow at the start of September was pretty rubbish with the rain only halting at times to give you a sense of optimism that things would get better. Once you had a hope that things would improve, the rain would return, pushing your spirits down further.

Despite this, there was a great atmosphere at the festival and with a music scene like Glasgow's, you rarely went twenty yards without seeing someone you knew. It wasn't a perfect festival, there was an underestimation of toilet facilities on the first day (the passion for drinking amongst Glaswegians, even the indie kids, should never be underestimated) but this was improved on the second day. Antony & The Johnsons may not have provided the most uplifting of finale to the festival, but it was certainly a quality set that wouldn't have been found at too many festivals.

One thing about the first Indian Summer event was that even though it was a big music festival in the city, it wasn't even the biggest music event taking place in Glasgow that weekend. Over on the south side of the city, Robbie Williams was carrying out the sort of atrocities in a sports stadium that would be more commonly associated with a South American dictatorship. Much like a dictatorship, there was undying obedience to a strange man and there was a notable uniform, drawing everyone together and indicating that this was the right way to behave. Jumping off the 44 in the South Side, a few of us had to make our way through a slow moving mass of people, swimming against the tide of pink cowboy hats and the lingering scent of Lambrini in the air.

Having these two events taking place in the city on the same day, with Scotland also thumping the Faroe Island 6-0 at Celtic Park, indicated the scope of demand for live music and events in the city. It was unlikely that too many people would have needed to make a decision between which of the music events to attend.

I really enjoyed the first Indian Summer festival, the people I met at the festival said they enjoyed it as well and there seemed to be a high level of positivity around the festival. There was a really good mix of artists with some acts having a lot of hype and praise about them. Shoving CSS into a tent when they were one of the most talked about acts at the time was a bold move. The fact that it was raining heavily at the time meant that even more people were desperate to cram into the tent and the security staff were fighting a losing battle in keeping the numbers to a moderately dangerous level. Tapes N Tapes were another act experiencing a lot of buzz and hype about them while Tilly And The Wall brought a strong novelty element. Hot Chip were at the peak of their powers, the Fall are always worth a watch, especially at a festival and Gang of Four were excellent. The only thing that slightly lessened the impact of the festival was the fact that I felt both headliners were a bit subdued (Yeah Yeah Yeahs and Antony & The Johnsons) but even with that, if you wanted to end the night on a high, the Optimo tent was absolutely buzzing.

The enjoyment of the festival was noticed by a lot of people and it was clearly big enough to pique the interest of Geoff Ellis. The next year, DF Concerts muscled in on the act, introducing the Connect Festival on the corresponding weekend of the following year. The festival took place in Inverary, creating the need for camping for most festival goers.

Indian Summer bravely battled on the following year,

moving to the middle of summer. This meant the festival name was no longer relevant and it also meant that it was coming very close to the T in the Park time. While the demographics talk surrounding Indian Summer or Connect may suggest that it was an older and different crowd from the people that attended T in the Park, clearly there is some form of crossover when it comes to the people that will attend these events.

The second coming of Indian Summer was bigger, the weather was better and the atmosphere was excellent once again. However, there did seem to be a certain stalling of the festival's momentum from the switch. There was hope that the festival would be able to continue, but there was also an incident with a generator and a swan pond that may have impacted on the festivals ability to maintain its licence.

With acts like Wilco, The Rapture, Daniel Johnson and Spiritualized, it was a tremendous line-up that stood apart from the other festival options in a Scotland but sadly it was not a festival that was to stick around. Much like the Gig on the Green events, a promising Glasgow music festival stalled before it got the chance to develop its brand.

So to Connect, a slightly more mature festival, perhaps for those who had outgrown T or who were looking for different ways to enjoy themselves. The fact that some of the promotional focus for the event highlighted elements like improved food and the ability to find places to relax would suggest that they know the food at T was shite and there were very few places to relax or take it easy. Okay, if you needed some chill out time at T you were advised to lay flat out close to the Slam Tent along with all of the other folk that had pushed themselves a bit too hard but there wasn't a proper chill out zone at the time.

These elements were a nice addition, but the real element that was going to make or break Connect came with the bands. The first year had a good selection of acts with old heroes like the Jesus And Mary Chain and The Fire Engines lining up alongside the current wave of guitar heroes like the 1990s while the Beastie Boys and Bjork were genuine bona fide headliners.

One of the things that I really took from the Connect Festival was that there were a lot of brilliant moments without it seeming to come together as a complete festival. The Fire Engines and Jesus & Mary Chain were both excellent, playing open air sets that seemed to have a blanket of grey surrounding the stage area. The utterly delightful Tilly & The Wall once again showed that you can have a novelty act that manages to deliver some good tunes and reasons to hang around. The Polyphonic Spree was at their best too, serving up their usual brand of infectious joy and happiness. At a festival, you're best avoiding anything which may have been described as infectious but with The Spree, you were on safe ground. In fact, such was the cheeriness of The Polyphonic Spree, they may have nudged Teenage Fanclub into second place for being the nicest and most pleasant at the festival.

The Fannies, as always, were great, but the same couldn't be said for the Primal Scream set, which attempted to appease everyone and probably did more to aggravate some folk. When a few songs into the set you've got Mani standing at the lip of the stage inviting people up on stage for a fight, you know that the Scream Team are not exactly firing on all cylinders. One of the problems was that when the band got a head of steam behind them with a few electro numbers, they would switch style and serve some rock n roll moments. When you've got a back catalogue as varied as Primal Scream, it's a difficult task to pull a festival set together that pleases everyone but perhaps the band would have better picking an era or genre and then mainly sticking with it. Aerogramme bowed out, Mogwai turned up the volume and acts like the Super Furry Animals, King Creosote, MIA and LCD Soundsystem ensured that this was a festival that always had something worth checking out, no matter the time of day.

With Bjork one of the biggest reasons many people bought tickets for Connect, it was always going to be difficult for acts that were scheduled up against her.

Still, it was wet, it was cold and it was dark, but I wouldn't have swapped watching Big Star on the second stage for anything. Upon grabbing a couple of drinks, one of the bar staff (which at some points were outnumbering the audience) kindly informed me that Bjork was playing on the main stage and seemed rather shocked when I responded that I was aware of this fact and that I was choosing to watch Big Star. There would be people back in Glasgow getting shivers down their spine at such a blatant disregard of Alex Chilton and the tunes that influenced so many Scottish artists! (I eventually saw Bjork play live in 2013 at the Berlin Festival. It was a performance that looked wonderful and was extremely engaging, but given that I probably hadn't heard a new Bjork song in around 15 years, it was never going to be a set for me!)

The Beastie Boys were tremendous, so much more enjoyable than their T in the Park set a few years previously (the day of the mud and the rain). The stage banter had the crowd wrapped around their fingers, in particular Mike D's calling out of the Duke of Argyll and informing the crowd that Inverary Castle, which was on the festival site was, in fact, his house. During the day, there were fears at the small size of the crowd at the festival but by the time the B-Boys were rocking the place, the crowd seemed to stretch back pretty far and they were in a great mood. The weather may have been wet and damp, but the band transcended that. One track that manages to pull everyone together though is Sabotage. Probably as well known for its video as the song itself, it remained a musical tour-de-force where every element plays a strong part in the track's success. The drums were hit ferociously and they drove the track and the sliding bass-run that features intermittently builds the tension nicely. After that, there was a pause before the repeating shouts of "Listen of y'all it's a sabotage" brought the song, and the night, to a messy, yet glorious climax and gave the Connect Festival its first ever legendary set.

The rain made the camping slightly uncomfortable but not as uncomfortable as the fact that my mate turned up thinking I had a 2 man tent with me. Technically he was right as it did end up sleeping two men for the weekend but it probably wasn't designed for that purpose! That was a source of mild hilarity over the course of the weekend but no harm done. The trek from the car to the campsite wasn't much fun, but this is the rarely the case. No doubt it's character building for the rest of the weekend.

As my brother and his wife set about manhandling their tent to life, I decided to take things a bit easier and took in the view with a beer. Before too long, my sister in law was getting slightly peeved by the fact that she was working hard while I was hardly working. I let her stew for few minutes more before unzipping my bag and letting the magic of a pop-up tent put me well ahead of them and their efforts. Pop-up tents are an absolute dream to put up but, for me at least, they were a nightmare to put down. I was all for abandoning the tent behind me but showing that it was just me that was a bit useless, my sister in law had it bagged and good to go within a few minutes. When you head to a festival, try and make sure that your group has a range of skills between you!

The Connect Festival returned the following year but much like Indian Summer, there didn't seem to be the same level of momentum behind it. Perhaps these festivals are great for the novelty value and are sure to draw an interested crowd in the first year then struggle to cement itself in the mainstream.

A lack of momentum also seemed to impact on the various events that Glasgow Green has attempted to host over the years. For me, the event back in 2000, was a fantastic weekend and while there may not have been an official tie-up with the Reading and Leeds English bank holiday festivals, it was organised by Mean Fiddler, the same company behind the big English shows, alongside Regular Music. This meant there was an opportunity to bring many of the bands up for Friday and Saturday shows. Acts like The Delgados, Super Furry Animals, Foo Fighters, Beck, Oasis, Primal Scream and Teenage Fanclub played and while there were acts like the Stereophonics on the bill, it was a massive line-up and only a reasonable walk from all of the main transport hubs in the city centre.

The following year the first day saw Eminem and Marilyn Manson as your main acts while on the second day, Travis and Green Day topped the bill. Queens of the Stone Age, The Strokes and Mercury Rev added some reasons to head along but it wasn't for me, even though it did seem to do quite well. There was to be another year for Gig On The Green, and although a combination of football, work and having no desire to be anywhere near Slipknot meant I sat out the Saturday, the Sunday was a lot of fun on a day of glorious sunshine. The Polyphonic Spree, The White Stripes and Pulp were excellent and The Strokes were all right as headliners, but it was a fantastic day out. The issue with The Strokes was that they were handed a headlining act amount of time, but they had little else on top of their immaculate yet short debut album. The decision to play a lot of their songs at a slower tempo filled some time, but it killed some of their joy and energy.

A change in branding occurred the following year, the event being primarily a Red Hot Chilli Peppers gig with added support, which meant that Gig On The Green only managed to make it to three years, but there seems to be less memory of it being a cohesive festival, especially when compared to Indian Summer or Connect. The middle year was definitely the best selling of the three years, with the 2002 event actually seeing the promoters requesting a drop in their capacity limit. Clearly if you are going to have a crowd of less than 25,000, providing facilities for a crowd of 35,000 can be a financial drain, so it made sense to officially downsize but it did suggest that there wasn't a level of demand to sustain the festival, at least to the extent of the Reading and Leeds events.

In 2004, Download, a metal festival took the position of the big festival on the Green that summer and even moved the event away from the weekend, two gigs taking place on a Wednesday and Thursday. For whatever reason, Glasgow Green has never managed to develop a festival brand or following, which makes the success of T in the Park even more impressive.

You wonder if the element of sponsorship plays a role in

the push behind a festival. Tennents were clearly the driving force behind T in the Park, getting tangible benefits and sales from their involvement with the event. When you think about other festivals, clearly there were drink companies involved (I think the first year of Connect was the first time I tried Kopperberg while the second year of Indian Summer was the first time I tried Tuborg) but the main sponsor that sticks in your mind from these events was Scottish Hydro, from the second Connect. This is primarily down to the fact that they dished out an awful lot of branded ponchos.

Clearly the firm believes that there is a market for associating themselves with music, their association with The Hydro is testimony to this, but it isn't really something that manages to create a genuine connection. Nor does it provide the firm with the opportunity to make sales all weekend long. A drinks company has the ability to shift considerable units over the course of a music festival but an energy company? That is going to be a much more challenging prospect.

It is not as though the fall in major music events or tie-ins is only associated with Glasgow, because Edinburgh has suffered as well. The Fringe in Edinburgh every August is most commonly associated with comedy, but there is an opportunity for venues and promoters to put on gigs and clubs. The regular music venues that work hard all year round in Edinburgh, such as Henry's Cellar Bar or the Electric Circus, realise the importance of offering music events during the Fringe but a casual flick through the Festival brochure suggests a limited number of interesting musical acts.

This wasn't always the case, with T on the Fringe being an excellent addition to the month's activities. Sadly, the change in the law regarding alcohol companies sponsoring major events saw Tennents pulling out of their musical sponsorship at the Fringe, and of the 3 day, 3 city Triptych events. These were both major losses to the Scottish music scene, limiting the opportunities of acts and bands of a certain level to appear in the country.

T on The Fringe came to a close in 2007 as well, although

it did experience a rebranding as The Edge festival in 2008 and it stumbled on for a few years. As stated above, I never really considered the T on The Fringe festival as a festival, I didn't even see it as being part of the Edinburgh Festival, it was just a number of one-off gigs that took place around the same time.

In saying that, there were some excellent shows over the years. 2004 saw the 5.6.7.8s, Sons and Daughters and Fiery Furnaces all play explosive shows in the heart of the city, in Liquids Rooms and The Venue while the big 2ManyDJs night, also featuring LCD Soundsystem, Soulwax and BRMC was a fantastic evening.

2005 saw the Pixies play Meadowbank (with support from Idlewild and Teenage Fanclub), Franz Ferdinand play Princes Street Gardens (with support from Arcade Fire) while Dot Allison and Sons and Daughters played on separate nights in the Liquid Rooms. 2006 saw Radiohead and Beck (who I missed due to the time constraint of coming through from Glasgow for a midweek outdoor gig) play at Meadowbank, so to be honest, I'd say 2007 wasn't as much fun as the previous years had been but it was a lot more fun than the remaining Fringe years were for gigs.

The idea of placing a lot of fantastic gigs and big bands on during the Edinburgh Fringe Festival is an interesting one. You could say that this is the perfect time of year because of the influx of tourists but sometimes there is just too much going on. If you're coming to the Fringe as a tourist, it's likely that you're doing so with an itinerary packed full of shows and if you're coming to the Fringe as a performer or crew member, you're likely to be busy. Anything which promotes music in Edinburgh is worth pursuing, but I'm just not sure if this was ever the solution. However, I managed to catch a lot of great shows over the years, and you won't hear me complaining too much about it.

The Triptych events, found in Glasgow, Edinburgh and Aberdeen took place around April and May just as the changing of the season brought about a new sense of optimism. This may not have been the biggest festival or music event but it had a very strong niche and there was always a considerable level of interest in the event.

Rockness was a big loss for 2014 and it was a festival I attended twice, in 2007 and then again in 2009. The setting was beautiful, overlooking the Loch and surrounded by hills and green scenery, when the sun shone down on the Saturday back in '07, it was impossible not to be uttering the word wow when looking around. As with T in the Park, there always seems enough people willing to party to make for a great environment and the atmosphere over the weekend was spot on as well.

With a line-up combining strong elements of dance and indie, there was every encouragement for people to get on with having a good time but for all that was brilliant about it, there were some aspects that were lacking on the first visit.

The size of the tents was deplorable. Even aside from the Daft Punk fiasco, a ten thousand capacity tent, for one of the most highly anticipated sets of the summer was bad but throughout the weekend, all the tents were filled to capacity or were being poorly managed by stewards who never seemed to know their job.

It can seem churlish to criticise this but when standing outside of Erol Alkan's set, seeing more than enough space within the tent to move freely but being prevented from entering the tent by stewards, who were probably working to orders, well it was just frustrating. There was a sense that the stewards and the police presence on site were there for their own entertainment as much as keeping the fee-paying punters safe and secure. If both of these achievements can be obtained, then great but if not, it's a concern. Likewise, the amount of mis-information being delivered by stewards at the bus and taxi rank was just wrong and could have made a bad situation much worse.

Rockness was always the festival that seemed to be a bit more mental and saw folk pushing it to greater extremes than some other festivals. Well, at least on a head count of attendees, it's not as if T in the Park is packed out with shrinking violets, but at Rockness, the desire to party seemed stronger.

Not that I can absolve myself or my collective group from

that. Smuggling in Cola-Cube vodka gave the Saturday in 2007 an unnecessary kick and then we found an organic cider tent that enabled you to pay cash up front as opposed to having to pick up tokens. Saving a few seconds in one round may not seem like a big deal but when you do that over a few rounds, it all adds up! There was also the incident during the Manics headlining set, which will see no names being mentioned.

Such is the nature of a friendly Scottish festival crowd, there will be times when people decide to share what they have with their fellow festival goers. This led to one of my friends being passed a bottle of poppers and being unsure of what to do next; he proceeded to drink the bottle! We stopped him quickly but obviously not quick enough. A considerable part of the remainder of the evening and the following day were spent discussing the potentially fatal consequences of drinking poppers.

The 2009 trip didn't involve anything as daft as that, but it certainly wasn't any better behaved. This is some going when you think that we only travelled up for a day session!

However, one of my most enduring memories from the trips to Rockness came on the Monday after the 2007 event. Preparing ourselves for the drive back to Glasgow on Monday afternoon, we stopped for supplies and noted that the local newspaper was running with the headline; "ROCKNESS A SUCCESS DESPITE DEATH." This of course meant that a good proportion of the journey South was spent discussing how many deaths would have been required before the festival was deemed to not have been a success.

Hopefully Rockness will return but if not, it will live on the memories and many more forgotten moments from people who ventured to the festival.

Multi-venue festivals are on the rise

While the number of major festivals in the central belt may have diminished, there has been a rise in the number of multi-venue events spread out over a day or two. Events like the Camden Crawl or the Great Escape from Brighton may be the big names when it comes to this style of event but in

Glasgow, the Stag & Dagger has been the most consistent. There was the Sauchiehall Crawl in 2008 and the Hinterland festival placed the focus on the bottom end of the city centre but by and large, the Stag &Dagger, primarily at the top end of town, is the one with the momentum and awareness behind it.

The number of venues at the top end of Sauchiehall Street provides an opportunity to have lots of bands playing over a short distance. Stag & Dagger didn't always get it right, one year they utilised The Captains Rest on Great Western Road and Stereo, which was slightly too much of a spread but on the whole, it's been an excellent addition to the Glasgow music scene. In fact, there was a slight issue with the 2014 festival which was down to the fact that it was such an excellent line-up. It is one thing packing your line-up with a great range of bands but when there are too many clashes, it is only natural that people will feel slightly aggrieved at spying money but not getting the chance to see a lot of bands.

The fact that there is an appetite for this sort of event can be seen with the fact that the team behind the TenementTV site (and TV programme) provides a multi-venue event in the city as well. The second Tenement Trail took place in October 2014, across a number of venues. Like most festivals, the festival has promoted itself in advance of the event with early bird tickets and a drip-feeding of the acts that are on the bill. With the STVGlasgow programme sure to have brought a great more deal of attention to the site, tand a line-up of great quality, it can only be hoped that this event continues for many years to come.

There was also one year in the mid 00's when there was a day festival spread out across venues close to some of the stops on the Glasgow Underground. It wasn't a strict subcrawl, but it was an interesting concept and something which turned into an extremely long day for people that were determined to see it all. There was a chance to catch acts in Govan, in the centre of town and in the west end. The culmination of the night came in the Oran Mor. It wasn't an event with the biggest bands, nor did it seem a well-organised event, the variety of venues meant that the stage times were not as tight as they could have been. However, it was ambitious and it showed the passion for live music. One area where it possibly failed in was with the lack of freedom with respect to bands you could see. Certain venues were only used at certain times; it wasn't as if every venue had a full-line up of bands that you could switch between.

Perhaps in different hands this sort of event could be a success but the amount of travelling around is possibly too much for a music event. Walking between venues located over a short distance is no problem but when you are travelling by public transport, even one as simple as the Glasgow Underground, there can be too many distractions or places to get waylaid.

There are other ways to create a music festival in the city though, and sometimes spreading out across a number of days, as opposed to a number of venues, is the solution.

Single venue festivals

King Tuts takes a slightly different approach to presenting a series of gigs. Clearly the more nights that the venue is open, the more chance of making money the venue has. This has led the venue to provide a series of gigs featuring local bands and up and coming acts in January and in the summer.

January is always a slow month, not everyone has money and too many people convince themselves to undertake a month of sobriety and healthier living. If the audience isn't there and the supply of touring bands isn't available, it is easy to see how a month like January could be written off by a venue like King Tuts. However, knowing that there always local (and local-ish) bands with devoted followers to tap into, King Tuts opens its doors to a series of local bands.

The summer period may not have the same feeling of people kidding themselves in about maintaining a healthy lifestyle, but again, there are plenty of other distractions and options for people and bands. So again, there is a potential level of downtime for the venue but this is negated by the Summer Sessions on offer. These include free acoustic sets at midnight and a lot of bands packed onto an individual bill, offering a better return for your money. For both of these events, King Tuts offers a season pass, allowing attendees to see a lot of bands for a lot less money.

It is also important to note that this style of event is not just found in Glasgow, there have been a number of similarly styled events taking place in Edinburgh. The Electric Circus has developed an excellent reputation in recent years for being an Edinburgh venue that has worked hard to bring great acts and decent events to the capital. In June of 2014, the venue hosted Electric Nights, a festival of music and art taking place over five evenings.

There was a good mix of events, with a line-up including a showcase event for up and coming musicians and artists, an experimental folk evening, a showcase for the Scottish Album of the Year awards featuring RM Hubbert and Meursault. There was also a night showcasing women in the art featuring music from Skinny Dipper, artwork from Rachel Sermanni and a DJ set from the TYCI collective. There was also a night curated by Will Anderson, a BAFTA award winner, featuring local acts such as Lipsync For A Lullaby and Beam.

It's not as though there is an overlying theme to the events, apart from being held in the same week and venue, but that alone can make a big difference in the promoting of an event, which helps the venue and the acts. It also helps the fans in the long run because there is more of a chance that they will find out about the event in good time, and they may feel more motivated to head along if they think that it is an event with a bit of excitement alongside it.

Edinburgh definitely has a poor reputation for gigs in comparison to Glasgow, but it would be wrong to completely dismiss the area. As said, the Electric Circus has worked hard, Sneaky Pete's has put on some great nights and I've never really had a bad night in there while I'm a big fan of Henry's Cellar Bar. Okay, it was quite close to where I stayed in Edinburgh during a brief sabbatical in the East but it's a proper venue with gigs and club nights. The Wed Red Bar at the College of Art was also an excellent place to hang out and if you are looking for music fun in the capital, these are venues you should be looking towards.

While the lack of a cohesive music festival during the Fringe is slightly annoying, Henry's Cellar Bar turned out to be one of the places to be during August 2014 thanks to the Pale Imitation Festival curated by Songs, By Toad.

The festival was running every Thursday and Saturday in August (priced at a fiver a night) with a season ticket on offer for £25. There was also an additional event held at the Queen's Hall, which was billed as being the final ever Meursault gig, well, at least the final gig using the Meursault name. Acts like Le Thug, The Leg, The Yawns, Deathcats, Jonnie Common, Jesus H. Foxx, Rick Redbeard, Ella The Bird (Siobhan Wilson's new performance name), LAW, Wozniak, eagleowl, Et Tu Brute, Naked and PAWS all performed over the course of the month. That's a cracking line-up of bands and at a fiver for three bands on each individual performance, there was excellent value for money to be found, which is not something you always find during the Edinburgh Festival. That is a month when there is a desire to gouge money out of people's wallets and hands faster than you can say "Err no, I'll have salt and vinegar please" but the Pale Imitation Festival set was a great antidote to that sort of feeling.

If you were busy in August or just like to give the Fringe a big swerve, there was another multi-day music event lined up for October 2014.

The Pleasance Sessions ran for just over a week in October and they managed to pack in a great deal of quality and diversity across its run. As with many of these events, it may not be a festival where punters are willing to head out every night, but there were a couple of events that brought a great deal of focus to the gig seris, making it feel more like a communal event.

At the very least, it will seem as though there is a fantastic run of gigs taking place in the capital, which is surely all that matters. Opening the event were The Twilight Sad, who unveiled their new album in an intimate setting. In a year when the band has already played some massive shows, this had the hallmarks of being another landmark gig, which the band's fanbase snapped up in no time at all.

That evening was followed by an event curated by Vic Galloway, featuring Casual Sex as the headline act. It says a lot about the quality of acts coming through this year in Scotland that Casual Sex are just considered to be one of the decent acts at the moment. In a number of other years, they would have been a stand-out band, delivering their art-rock sensibilities and sexy pop in their knowing style. Also on the bill was LAW, who has received a considerable amount of press and praise in 2014. Having worked alongside Young Fathers, the fact that the band picked up the Scottish Album of the Year award did her no harm at all.

Up next was the Olive Grove label, showcasing a number of their artists. With four acts on the bill, there was value for money and there is an expectation of quality when you see the label's name. Woodenbox, Skinny Dipper, The Moth and The Mirror and Call To Mind, who were fresh from T in The Park and Belladrum (if anyone can ever be considered fresh coming from those festivals) by the time of the Edinburgh set.

On the Sunday night, Neu Reekie! stepped to their fore with their usual blend of music and film with regulars Teen Canteen lining up alongside Fini Tribe, Dave Hook, Liz Lochead and Richard Jobson.

The dreaded Monday night slot was taken by Beerjacket, who was joined by Ross Elighton and Fake Major. Tuesday saw Roddy Hart and the Lonesome Fire headlining the Middle of Nowhere Label showcase.

Wednesday saw the Folk Club serving up Ben Sands and Paul Foot delivering the Hovercraft Symphony in Gammon # Major while Thursday night allowed The List Magazine to get their hands on the controls. Friday was handed over to The Insider Festival to take the lead and then on Saturday night, The Skinny Magazine brought together what was considered by many to be the set of the festival. The Phantom Band and Remember Remember have both delivered excellent albums in 2014, so putting them both on the same bill has to be classed as an excellent decision.

The Pleasance Sessions may not fit the notion of a festival that people first think of when they hear the word, but this is part and parcel of the way that musical events are being staged. The fact that there is a different entity, label or organization taking responsibility to curate their own night provides a wide range of music, but each night and gig is strengthened by the unity that the whole event offers.

One-off events for 2014

On the one hand, music is for everyone but, on the other hand, and this is the most important hand, music is definitely not for everyone. This isn't a problem and one thing that has been notable in 2014 is the fact that some pretty big concerts have been put on for folk that don't particularly like music or get excited by what the rest of us would deem to be of interest.

The BBC excelled themselves with their Live At The Edinburgh Castle gig, supposedly held to commemorate the opening of the Commonwealth Games. Now, the only opening in Glasgow that Edinburgh folk would celebrate would be the opening of a wormhole to drain the city out of Scotland. However, even with this in mind, the BBC decided that putting on a show, screened live on TV, would be the best thing to get people in the mood for the Games.

To ensure that Saturday night BBC viewers would feel at ease, Jessie J and the Kaiser Chiefs were placed high on the bill, although whether viewers would recognise them without a swivel chair would remain to be seen. Smokey Robinson was wheeled out as the classic artist while the reformed Culture Club were brought in as the Class-A group. Rizzle Kicks ensured the night was down with the kids and the trumpets while Paloma Faith gave people the chance to enjoy their Saturday night in the company of an annoying and over-bearing woman, which certainly saved the hassle of going to a pub that night. Katherine Jenkins was something for the dads, Il Divo were for the mums, and God only knows why Alfie Boe, One Republic and Ella Henderson were being wheeled out. At this point, someone probably realised that only the multi-national contingent from Il Divo and the

American offerings of Smokey and One Republic were dragging this away from being an English line up (yes, Katherine is Welsh but she is one of those Welsh people that sides with the English to boost sales, so she can't be classed as adding anything to the cosmopolitan mixture). Some diversity was assured with the inclusion of Pumeza but Pumeza's appearance ensured that South Africa provided more representation on stage than Scotland did with respect to the main acts. Not all was lost though; the BBC Scottish Symphony Orchestra and non-funnyman Fred MacAulay were lined up to provide a token Scottish element to the watching audience.

It's not as though Edinburgh had the stranglehold of strange gigs and events in 2014 though, with a concert being held at The Hydro to commemorate the start of the Ryder Cup. I suppose if you are having a range of gigs to commemorate the Commonwealth Games, it isn't so strange to hold a gig to commemorate one of the biggest golf and sporting events of the calendar. The event promised to be a lavish affair with Scottish Ballet, RSNO, NTS and Scottish Opera all being involved in the event. The golfers were introduced on stage and Scottish acts like Eddi Reader, Texas and Midge Ure were all lined up to perform. Perhaps the organisers of the event determined that people who like golf are of an age which meant that they listened to music in the 1980s and if this is the case, fair play to them for finding the acts that will appeal to the audience. In an attempt to make sure that some people under the age of 30 recognises the artists on the bill, Nina Nesbitt and Twin Atlantic were added while Jake Bugg was also on the bill, perhaps to ensure that at least one non-Scottish act is performing. In this regard, the Live At Edinburgh Castle gig and The Ryder Cup Gala Concert have created a perfect balance.

11: Your Town

It is important to not get too bogged down in focusing on Glasgow when you think about what Scotland has to offer with respect to music. While there are many parts of the country, certainly away from the central belt which hold a strong tradition of folk and Celtic music, there are other places where there are mini music scenes with bands and promoters working hard to create something that can sustain itself.

Probably the biggest shock when it comes to Scottish cities and music is how limited Edinburgh is, especially with the inevitable comparison with Glasgow. This isn't to criticise the hard work and effort that is put in by music lovers in Edinburgh, which will be discussed, but the differences between the two cities are vast with respect to opportunities and promotion.

Edinburgh may be the capital city, with a large student population, but its failure to rival Glasgow is about a lot more than just the fact that the capital's population is around 100,000 smaller than its West Coast rival. When trying to look at Scotland as a whole, and determine if there is a characteristic trait that runs through the nation that provides the platform for our musical endeavours, a quick look at Glasgow and Edinburgh shows that this isn't the case.

Located less than 50 miles apart, these are two very distinct cities, each with their own nature and overriding personalities. It is no exaggeration to say that Glasgow has a lot more in common with other industrialised towns like Manchester or Liverpool, while Edinburgh would be closer to educational areas in the south of England. This isn't to say that the Edinburgh experience is any more or any less Scottish than the Glasgow experience, but for people looking in, it is likely that one or other of the cities will represent what Scotland is like for them.

Edinburgh may be the more transient city, with students coming in to study but not looking to lay down roots in the area. Similarly, the presence of major finance firms in the city may ensure that young professionals have enough to focus on without having the time or energy to plough into sustaining a musical scene.

There have been great Edinburgh acts like The Fire Engines, The Scars, The Proclaimers (although Leith will argue over the ownership), St Judes Infirmary (although the bands remained a Fife act at heart) and Young Fathers but the number of Edinburgh acts that grab your attention is probably smaller than the number of notable bands that have emerged from Dundee. Perhaps there is a lot to be said for music, much like football or boxing for previous generations, being a form of escape and an escape route for the working classes.

Edinburgh is also badly served by the range of venues open to them. The Corn Exchange resembles a school hall and any good gig I have witnessed in there has always been in spite of the venue rather than because of the venue. The loss of the Picture House was a cruel blow because this was exactly the size of venue that Edinburgh needs. Its location was perfect in the heart of town and being relatively close to one of the train stations but it never really seemed to cement itself with a local audience. As someone who regularly travelled through to gigs at the venue, I certainly wasn't alone with Scotrail trains or 900 buses ferrying through a decent proportion of gig attendees on any occasion I was there. Looking at the way the Academy and the ABC have cemented their place in Glasgow, when there was already local venues of a similar nature, drove home the fact that Edinburgh was really lacking in somewhere that people could recognise as being a home for live music.

The Usher Hall and the Queens Hall have played home to many great gigs and acts but music is jostling with other entertainment options in these venues, limiting gigs and perhaps putting a dampener on the atmosphere at times. Small venues like Sneaky Petes, The Electric Circus and Henry's Cellar Bar are all excellent for their size and probably over-achieve in the level of bands that they bring to the city. Numerically, Edinburgh isn't that badly off for venues, not when you think about venues such as the Liquid

Rooms, the Bongo Rooms, The Caves, The Hive, the Forest Café or even the Voodoo Rooms. Anyone that is serious about live music in Edinburgh needs to check these venues out on a regular basis and ensure that they have the ability to keep operating. The return of La Belle Angele in late October was a boost to the city, as was the fact that a couple of familiar faces are behind the venue which will have a capacity in the 500s. Anything which provides another option into the mix has to be seen as a good thing and it is not as if Edinburgh acts can honestly say that there are no venues available for them to play in. Everyone has their part to play in creating a scene and bands have to play their part as well. This isn't to say that the lack of an Edinburgh scene is the fault of bands, but from the outside looking in, it does feel as though everyone needs to pull together because much smaller towns and cities than Edinburgh seem capable of achieving much more.

One problem for acts in the city is that even though the venues aren't that far away from each other, Edinburgh isn't that big a city, they all seem isolated in their own location.

This means that there is no real sense of community. I enjoy The City Café and the Southern Bar in Edinburgh nearly as much as I do Nice N Sleazys but with Sleazys, you get the impression it is a musicians bar, a place to congregate and form plans or be part of something. Add in the fact that you have places like the 13th Note, Mono or the Glad Café where you get the feeling that musicians frequent them regularly, you have the semblance of a scene before you even start looking. Even if you hate the idea of a scene, and it can cause as much bad as good at times, anything which fosters creativity has to be taken as a positive thing when looking to make music.

The two Edinburgh bars I mentioned are (or at least were, sometimes if you blink in an Edinburgh bar you open your eyes to see it has been given a trendy makeover) great bars where it is clear that plenty of musicians hang out and socialise, but it never seems as though that is the driving force of these bars.

All of which means that it can be too much trouble and

effort to create a scene in Edinburgh. Fair play to everyone that tries but when you keep on pushing and realise you are making little headway, it is easy to see why it is easier to move on to something else.

This is why you find other areas in Scotland with a much more exciting music scene, even when the population is smaller. You could argue that having a smaller population size and area is helpful, because there is more chance of likeminded people bumping into each other. Edinburgh is a small city, but it is still big enough to have many separate areas and elements that limit the potential of stumbling onto likeminded folk. The emergence of the internet should help to make areas smaller but there is still a great deal to be said for being able to see and hear scenes yourself.

The success of Young Fathers throughout 2014 and in particular at the Mercury Awards should have presented an opportunity to paint the Edinburgh music scene in a better light. However, if there was any thought of the local authority seeing this as an opportunity to raise their profile and try to connect with this success, it was immediately shot down in an interview The Guardian conducted with the band just after they received their award.

"Edinburgh Council are really fucking bad"

That was the exact quote from Graham Hastings before he detailed how the council has been known to try and limit anything creative or noisy in the city, before describing it as a city "for tourists and rich, middle-class people."

This isn't just a view held by Young Fathers, you will hear the same accusations and complaints being made by countless Edinburgh musicians and music lovers. For a city that has a worldwide reputation for arts and culture, it manages to do a great job of minimizing the amount of culture its residents have access to throughout the year. Even the Fringe is far better set up for outsiders coming in as opposed to local residents and promoters doing their own thing, which is why the gigs and music events that were put on in 2014 were very worthy of note.

It may be that Edinburgh has the people and drive to create a music scene on a par with many of the other parts of

Scotland, but when you are continually being rebutted and harassed, you eventually stop trying. It would be wrong to put all of the blame on to the local council but when it comes to Edinburgh lagging behind smaller towns and cities in Scotland with respect to music, it has to be a factor.

When you look at Dundee, the fourth largest city in the country and a population close to 150,000 people, there has always been a musical history and there has always been bands breaking through. Even in the current climate, there is an exciting wave of Dundee bands coming through and it is no more linked to The View than the wave of current Glasgow bands are linked to Belle & Sebastian or Franz Ferdinand.

With venues such as Beat Generator, Fat Sams, Reading Rooms, Buskers and Caird Hall, there is a variety of venues, with varying capacities and different atmospheres. There is also a good supply of satellite towns and villages around Dundee, some of which have their own music venues and offerings feeding into the demand for music in the area, or which host people who know that there is a local platform for live music in this part of the country.

When you take an interest in Scottish bands, you will inevitably start to pick up a feel for the venues that are trying something different or which are working hard to provide a platform for music. When you speak to musicians and bands about shows and tours around the country, it is the same names and places that get mentioned for certain cities. For Dundee, the work of Daisy Dundee and Andy Wood has played a massive role in creating the current platform that bands have. Acts like Vladimir and Model Aeroplanes clearly have the talent, the fact they are in demand across the country shows that there is more than a local nepotism behind their success, but the fact that the city and certain people have provided the platform to play regularly and work with other bands is a crucial component on their success.

This was the case in Paisley back in the latter half of the 2000s when there was quite a decent scene going on, and venues were more than happy to allow bands and artists to play. On the one hand, Paisley is only a 10 minute train journey from Glasgow, so you could argue that anyone looking to see a band didn't have far to go to reach Glasgow. However, looking at it from the other side, if there was a night when there wasn't anything of great note on in the city, there were nights packing in 3 or 4 local bands or songwriters taking place in Paisley. If you timed the train from Central correctly, you were in the middle of Paisley in about the same time you could have walked from Central to the ABC, so there wasn't that much of a hindrance in getting around. At that time, a lot of work in promoting local bands was being carried out by Cheryl Galbraith, and all of the local bands spoke highly of her. As time moves on, and scenes ebb and flow, you lose track of things and it's been a while since I have been at a gig in Paisley. However, in the run up to the Commonwealth Games, it was great to see media coverage of Cheryl playing a significant role in organising many of the events and ceremonies. Local scenes are not just a case of providing a platform for bands and artists to develop skills and an audience; they can provide a platform for all forms of jobs in the music industry.

If you can't play a note to save yourself, write about music, look to work on the promotional side or get involved with light or sound engineering for venues. Without bands and artists, a scene is never going to take off but similarly, bands and artists will never really take off unless there is a good supporting role of people helping them along the way. This is why there is a notable music scene in Dundee in 2014, it was why the music industry was looking towards Fife for a number of years, it was why there was a notable music scene in Paisley between 2005 and 2007 and wherever the next big non-Glasgow music scene takes place, it will be a factor in the success of those areas as well.

While every other town and city in Scotland will try and disassociate themselves from Glasgow as much as they can, there is no doubt that the areas which have developed a music scene will have similarities. The love and passion for music has to be there but after that, it is the fact that there are so many people willing to get involved that makes the difference.

If you are looking for Scottish traits, there are tons of the stereotypical ones you can mention with respect to why scenes take place. It definitely takes a bit of confidence and gallus attitude to start doing things in the public eye. The easy approach in life is to do nothing but if you want to achieve something, you need to take a risk or two. There is also the fact we often hear the word no so often that eventually, you have enough and decide to take some form of action.

If there is no music scene taking place or nothing that excites you, you can let it bring you down or you can look to change it yourself. Our rubbish weather may ensure we look for activities that can be carried out indoors, which means playing an instrument and making music is a sensible option, but it's unlikely that you'll be the only person in your local area that feels the same way about live music and acts.

One encouraging thing about this year has been the number of localized festivals taking place around the country. This follows on from the multi-venue festivals that were discussed in the Festivals chapter but if there isn't enough of a focus to sustain an emerging musical scene over the year, there should at least be enough of an impetus to sustain it over a weekend.

The Killie Dirty Weekender (leaving all jokes aside) celebrated its third year in 2014 and the people behind the event were comfortable and confident enough to venture into Glasgow with a separate event. If promoters can arrange a good line-up, there will be people looking to buy tickets and venues or bars are always going to be interested in anything which gets a good number of folk through the door. The 2012 event took place across two venues, Dirty Martini's and Bakers Nite Club. In 2013, these two venues were utilized again with The Granary being added to the mix. In 2014, the number of venues in use jumped to 5, with Bakers Nite Club and The Granary being joined by the Grand Hall, Liquor Lounge and The Hunting Lodge. In a town, if something is happening, people will take notice, including other venues, and it is likely that they will want to become involved or they will want their own slice of the action.

Dunfermline Live, which took place in October, was another great example of a multi-venue single day festival that was able to attract big names to the town. Sure Embrace have seen bigger and better days but as a headline act for a town like Dunfermline, they are still going to put on a show and bring in the punters. The festival was staged across 6 venues spanning the full day and there were plenty of great up and coming Scottish acts on the bill as well. You know it was a 2014 Scottish festival because Hector Bizerk were playing but other stalwarts of the year's festival circuit such as Vladimir, Tijuana Bibles, Neon Waltz and The Velveteen Saints were on the bill too. Add in plenty more bands and top Fifer King Creosote and it all added up to a great day. The organisers were also keen to point out that over the course of the weekend, there were also 12 venues hosting free shows that were in keeping with the spirit of the festival, which meant that other venues, other bands and other people all got the chance to enjoy some live music. Getting the buy-in and support from the local community can make a massive difference to these events, and it will be interesting to see if the Dunfermline Live event returns in 2015.

There's always going to be an audience for music across Scotland and while Glasgow hogs the headlines and the major touring acts, there is no way you should think that the city is the be all and end all when it comes to music.

12: Some Andy Talking

After listening to music, one of the best things about music comes with being able to talk about it. I took the opportunity to speak to a number of people involved with the Scottish music scene in 2014 to get their opinion on where we are and what they really think of the music, bands, venues and audiences in the country.

Tenement TV

This has been a massive year for the team behind Tenement TV. The website has been growing in size and stature, venturing out from the bay window and capturing a great deal of live performances at festivals and events across the country. The company has also found its way onto STV Glasgow with a weekly TV show while the latest instalment of their Tenement Trail event took place on the 4th of October.

I chatted with Chae Houston (Founder/CEO) and Jamie Logie (Creative Director).

Where, when and why did you get started?

[CH:] It launched in October 2011. I had the initial idea and I worked on it with my other flatmate at the time Paul McJimpsey (a promoter for PMCJ Events) and we got in touch with Jamie with the intention of filming some new bands around Glasgow. Paul had a good knowledge of the scene so we started there. We had the idea back in January of 2011 but it took quite a while to get it up and running. Originally in our practice sessions it was one camera and we didn't get the best of sounds. So I got a sound engineer in, we got a few more folk involved and we were able to launch in October of that year.

What was the inspiration in starting Tenement TV?

[CH:] When I was in a band I loved sessions, I had watched plenty of great sessions online and I was fortunate enough to play a session for Balcony TV, in Dublin. I liked that idea and it felt right to do it in the flat. We've got such a great location with big bay windows, it was always going to look great. From there, we knew we wanted to do something with great sound quality and make it as professional as possible.

It was originally just going to be local bands but we got a break with bands like Bastille and Kodaline, and then it really took off. From those two bands, we've been to feature a lot of big acts.

The sessions have clocked up more than 2 million views on YouTube, has there been a moment when you thought you've made it to the big time or there was a turning point?

[JL:] At one point we had Kassidy in, which was a big moment and we also got Steve Craddock *(Ocean Colour Scene, guitarist with Paul Weller)*, which brought a whole new crowd to what we were doing. That really helped widen our audience because people wouldn't like or know some of the acts we used up to this point but then they would really like someone we filmed. After this, the views started piling up and then we started to work on other projects such as curating our own festival *(The Tenement Trail)*, and everything we were doing just added to the attention we were getting.

The earlier bands were great, the first band we had were The Imagineers and they had a really good pull for us, but you could see it building.

[CH:] I think getting acts like Bastille and Gabrielle Aplin were big breaks as well.

You're on STV Glasgow, how did that come about?

[CH:] We have a friend that works at STV and we think he was dropping a few hints to Paul Hughes, the producer at the new channel who was overseeing the new content. He gave us a call and got us into STV for a meeting. They seemed to love the sessions and very quickly we got confirmation for an 8 episode series. It moved fast, before too long we were editing with Jamie working hard pulling that side together.

[JL:] It was a bit stressful at first but we're at the stage now where we are joined at the hip. This means they can take some of the edits and do some work. We're at the stage where we're all working together but it's been good to have strong backing and something to lean on there. We're not a broadcast channel so it's been good to get help when we need it. It's great that as well as the internet stuff we do, we've now did production work for a TV channel.

Would this be a possible career path?
[JL:] Of course, aye. I've really enjoyed it. What we do, we see it as our career but we're lucky that we don't see it as a job or work.

Have there been any music TV shows that have influenced you?
[CH:] For me, Jools Holland as it features a great mix of bands and there is something for everyone. I don't want Tenement TV to be just about underground bands or cool acts. We want to get some mainstream acts involved as well.
[JL:] I was a massive fan of the Old Grey Whistle Test. I've gone back and watched that from start to finish. It's good because it features so many different bands and covered so many different time periods, there's a lot to like.

What internet sessions or TV shows have inspired you?
[CH:] The Black Cab sessions in London are excellent and I've mentioned Balcony TV. With respect to production quality, All Saints did some brilliant work in the All Saints Basement Sessions. That looked great and it was really well done with great sound. There is also La Blogotheque in Paris. They're getting nominated for a film prize because their work is so arty and cool. They run through the streets of Paris and their work looks so good.

With the internet, is TV still relevant for music?
[JL:] Of course. There will always be groups of people who don't get the chance to watch the internet at certain times.

There'll be times when people are over at their pals house and they'll not want to sit in front of a computer screen all night and that's where music on TV is important. It's a bit different that we get the chance to jump between the internet and TV and I like that there's a choice for people.

[CH:] It's easier to get mainstream music on to TV. Across our episodes you'll see Gabrielle Aplin who has appeared on E4 and Channel 4. You'll also get to see The Temperance Movement who are doing a lot of TV work and big shows at the moment, they're supporting The Rolling Stones for 4 gigs in Europe!

These are the acts that you'll get on TV and while it can be harder to get new bands noticed, because STV Glasgow is a local channel and it's a community feel, there's scope for new local bands. I think there'll be people who are really up for seeing local bands on TV, especially when they're playing in a Glasgow tenement.

Do you feel there's enough music coverage in mainstream media *(TV, radio, newspapers?)*

[JL:] It depends on what you're looking for and with so many people liking different things right now, you can't please everyone. The thing is with music though, you'll get a lot of stuff on and you may think that's not my cup of tea but you'll probably watch it anyway to see what is out there.

[CH:] There's an unlimited chance to get your band seen and heard online so there is always that but maybe newspapers could do more for new acts and with music. At the moment you get one page or columns here and there. I really hope that Tenement TV getting on TV is great for music in general because it's not always easy getting music on to TV.

[JL:] Radio is still a really good way of introducing a band to an audience. That's still really strong.

[CH:] Yeah, that's how bands still make it these days. Get radio play and then bloggers and websites like ourselves take notice and pick up on things.

What are your ambitions for Tenement TV?

[CH:] We've got some cool things coming up. We have a big

campaign that we can't mention just yet but we're going to have a large sponsor on board for it and that's going to be really good. This will launch before the end of the year. I also want to build the Tenement Trail up, our second one will be taking place this year and it's a multi-venue music festival. I want to get that to the level, at least, where Stag & Dagger is now. We're also maybe going to do a quarterly magazine, maybe even in December of this year if that goes well. In October that will be us up and running for three years and that will coincide with our second Tenement Trail. Maybe after 5 years we can look to really cement what we are doing.

Apart from that, just grow everything we do, reach more people on twitter and improve the website.

As the session is such a big part of what you can do, your website can be sometimes overlooked but there's a lot on it. You provide news, reviews and features so there is more to Tenement TV than just the sessions. Are there any websites that have inspired you or you aspire to reach the level of?
[CH:] There are a few but I should say that Nadine Walker got on board about a year ago as our online editor and she's been great. She's helped to pull all the track reviews, live reviews, news stories and features together. We've now got a few editors around the world doing reviews and creating content, so we have content coming in from New York and London as well. We've just put a review of Eagulls live at the Mercury Lounge in New York so that's something different. Nadine has really helped us to take the website forward and it's more than just the sessions on site.

I really like Pitchfork and that's professional although maybe at times it's a bit up itself. There is also Pigeons & Planes and Consequences of Sound. Some of the quirky ones are good to keep up to date with. You have La Blogotheque who do stunning sessions and you have Pitchfork that are mainly media and this is where I think there is space for Tenement TV. I want us to get more editors involved, produce more quality content and give people media content and great sessions. I do think our sessions match any sessions website around the world.

Who are your favourite new Scottish acts?
[CH:] Model Aeroplanes are doing really well and I think they'll go far. Honeyblood have just announced their UK tour and a new album coming soon and they seemed to go down well in America.

[JL:] The Amazing Snakeheads, their albums doing great.

[CH:] I really like Paws.

[JL:] Baby Strange

[CH:] So yeah, Model Aeroplanes, the Amazing Snakeheads, Baby Strange and Honeyblood are 4 new bands and Paws who even though they have a few albums are doing really well. There's 5 Scottish acts that are really doing great things at the moment. They're flying the flag and doing great things overseas. You have Prides as well, another band who are doing well. These are the bands that are doing things like SXSW and being well received.

What's the thing that excites you most in 2014 in Glasgow or Scotland?
[JL:] I'm really excited about the Kelvingrove Bandstand opening, that'll be amazing. That's been one of the things since my childhood and I think it'll be a fun place to go and see a gig.

[CH:] Absolutely. I used to say to my mum when I was a kid "when are they going to do that up, it'll be amazing."

[JL:] I'm looking forward to the buzz from the Commonwealth Games. I think it'll be diverse and the energy will take Glasgow off a bit more. Glasgow is a really nice city so I don't see why it shouldn't be even better at a time like this.

[CH:] It's not in Glasgow but I'm definitely looking forward to the World Cup this summer.

The State Broadcasters Interview

As stated in The Bands section of the book, The State Broadcasters are one of my favourite groups and have been for a number of years. Over two albums, the group provides a wide range of songs, from the whimsical and uplifting to the reflective and downbeat. With a range of instruments you won't find in too many acts in Glasgow, and a vocal one-two that never fails to delight, the music on offer more than matches the clever and inquisitive lyrics.

The interview with Graeme Black and Pete MacDonald from the group was carried out in April 2014.

For anyone who hasn't heard, or heard of, the group, what would you say about the band?
[GB]: We've made two albums, both of which we are all quite proud of. One is quite poppy and reasonably cheerful, while one is not.

The poppy one was the debut album, and the not so poppy one was the second album?
[GB]: Yes. I think we're better now than what we were when we started.

Do you have any idea of the tone or mood of the third album?
[GB]: To preface all of this, I think one thing we both really like is bands that do something a bit different with every album, but still sound like the same band. I think that's difficult to do well, and I think there are only a handful of bands that manage to pull it off but it is something I really like and it's something that I aspire to for us.

With that in mind, it will be a bit different again but it will still sound like us. Our second album, Ghosts We Must Carry had a very strong theme running through it and that was deliberate. It was almost...not one dimensional, but it was designed to follow a path and I think we achieved that. With this one, lyrically at least, I've not set any parameters to it and we are touching on a lot of different themes. The songs we have completed so far have different styles and there is some poppy stuff and we've tried to use some different instruments, like synths. We're trying to fit in a more choruses and sing-alongs!

What would be your proudest moment or moments with the band?

[PM]: The two album launches, both of those nights, for me, were quite emotional. Those two nights were the most fun I have ever had while playing music and in some ways, as much fun as I have had doing many things. It's a unique feeling.

[GB]: It's quite scary because if you are making music and releasing it, you want people to like it. I don't quite buy into this idea of not caring whether people like it or not when you make music. If that was really the case, why would you bother releasing it? Surely the point of making an album or carrying out any creative process is you want other people to enjoy it. There is an argument that you just feel the need to create and you do it, which is fine, but music is so much about the communal experience and connecting with people. It is scary but if you believe in it, you like it and you're proud of it, you maybe don't worry about what other people think but I would be devastated if no one else thought our work was good as well.

I think the fact that we've touched a number of people in Glasgow, and that people value our music and say they enjoy coming to see us, it makes you feel good.

[PM]: Yeah, I've received a couple of letters or emails here and there, there are little things that people say or send to you that hits home. When you make music, and perhaps not a lot of people come along to the gig or buy your music, it is nice to be reminded that you are connecting. I can say that someone letting me know that they've spent a tenner on an album or that they've enjoyed our show is great. Even just a tweet, something that shows you've connected is great.

[GB]: Making an album or writing a song is not an easy thing to do if you want to produce something that you are proud of. The process can be simple, you can sit down and write a song in 10 to 15 minutes, it can seem easy and effortless when it flows out of you but pulling it all together is a process. You also have the fact that you've created something and it's going to be put out there for people to judge and that makes it a difficult thing to do. This is definitely the case if you are a fragile person anyway. The process of the second album, for me personally, was quite traumatic (at which point Graeme laughed), I wasn't necessarily in the best of places when I wrote that album. However, I'm really glad that we did it because I really like the album and I think this new album is going to be more fun.

[PM]: Going back to what Graeme said about music being a communal experience and about music being difficult, I agree with that and if you go back to the two album launches, that was true. It was a difficult process. You're sharing with people things that you've agonised over for a long time and you get an instant response and you see people smiling. That and seeing people really listening and absorbing it is great but it brings those two elements together. That and it's live music which is really important. Doing your own gigs is important and it's a big thing at times.

[GB]: It can be a wee bit conflicting at times. If you're in a rock band and it's just about being out there and blasting it, then that's what it's about but we're doing something, without resorting to a cliché, that features a lot of you or everything of you in that song, it's quite an internal conflict you have to deal with. I'm not saying I'm or we're on a different level but we have to make the decision to open ourselves up and put it out there. If you had any sense about it, you probably wouldn't want to write about certain things or put it out there that you've thought about certain things but somehow, that's what comes out. If you believe in it and you're creating, you have to go with it. It can be a love hate thing, for me, and there have been times when I thought I can't do this anymore but I always get myself back into it.

[PM]: *(In his best Michael Corleone voice)* Just when I thought I was out, they pull me back in.

[GB]: This one though, while I don't have many themes, I am embracing how great music can be and I'm trying to write about that and I'm hoping there'll be a couple of songs about that.

[PM]: It'll get on the radio, they like that. Songs about music being good and being played on the radio is what the radio wants to play. A chorus about a song being played on the radio, that's the plan!

It's all mapped out then, 2015, The Year of the Broadcasters!

[GB]: It would be very nice if more people liked us, and I suppose there are other things we could do about that, but...

[PM]: I think anyone who says otherwise would be lying. Anyone who makes anything, you want more people to see it and then like it.

Do you think there is anything unique about the Scottish music scene that has influenced acts and artists?

[GB]: I would imagine that most small countries or towns and cities in larger countries will think that. So yes, I do think there is a trait or belief of a trait in Scotland but I'm not sure if that's unique to us. However, when you start to think like that or it becomes an identity, especially in music terms, it starts to happen anyway. It can then become contrived like any music scene. At the beginning of a scene, it can be magical but fairly quickly, it can become dull and unimaginative.

[PM]: Maybe the fact that we're a smaller country plays a part in this. There are many people who are seen as having a great English identity; guys like Billy Bragg or Morrissey but this may not be the case in really large countries. There are probably American singers who would be appalled at the idea of being billed as being the archetypal American singer, so it maybe comes from being a smaller country where is a greater leaning towards having your own identity. There's often a danger of thinking that there is a distinctive Scottish voice. I'm always wary of too many self-aggrandising statements like that because like Graeme said, I think most artists feel that about themselves and where they come from. Sometimes people say these things, from the point of view that we're better because of that.

[GB]: There must be something in it when you think of

musical scenes like Seattle, Nashville, Memphis, Manchester. All these different things and musical moments happened and they can't all be media constructs. I think what happens is that these scenes are very organic at the beginning but as they become more popular and the mainstream media catches onto them, they tend to become a bit of a joke by the end of the scene. To be honest though, that hasn't really happened in Glasgow. I don't think we've had a scene that's ever been as big as something like Madchester, and it's always been quite entrenched in indie.

Is the media element more important than other factors?

[GB]: Britpop had the advantage of being London centric, so they had the media behind it, which made it easier to take off. Not all of the bands were from London but it was ultimately a media construct. I don't think it had its heart in a geographical identity; it was more of a sound.

There were a lot of good bands but it became damaged quite quickly and you were almost embarrassed to say you liked the music or certain bands because there was so much crap. It was very good fun, and although I'm probably going off point here, it was good because it helped to rejuvenate live music. We're still reaping the benefit and we owe a debt of gratitude with respect to live music. For all Oasis had their faults, they were a band that went out and killed it live, so even that scene had its moments.

Do you have a national pride in music, would you look out for a Scottish band more than a similar band from another country?

[PM]: That's really difficult. I'd say some of my favourite bands are Scottish but I don't think their identities are Scottish. For instance, one of my favourite bands is the Blue Nile. They don't make music that I would say is Scottish but at the same time, Paul Buchanan writes a lot and sings a lot about Glasgow and living in a rainy city. Of course, this could be about any rainy city and I think the music of the Blue Nile resonates with people from other rainy cities, and of course, in non-rainy cities, but they are huge in Manchester.

To catch on to that point, Elbow played the Hydro recently and Guy Garvey dedicated a song to the Blue Nile, saying that Manchester is a rainy city and is similar to Glasgow and perhaps there's a link there. Of course, I said at the time, "Wet Wet Wet are from Glasgow and they're rubbish, you don't draw a link to them!"

[PM]: Elbow seem to be held in great affection in Glasgow, and maybe that doesn't fall into nationality but an outlook. Maybe a band from Manchester will say more to people from Glasgow as opposed to a band from Dundee.

Does this mean the idea of Scottishness is too broad?

[GB]: It depends on how you connect with music. Sometimes you connect through lyrics, or if it's a good tune. If it's through lyrics, there is more chance I'll connect with it if I can understand the environment it is coming from. Having lived in Scotland all my life, it's easier to see why I've connected with more Scottish bands.

I quite like listening to African music, especially from the rhythmic point of view but I don't think I'm ever going to really fall in love with it but I think that's just me. For me to really fall for a song or band, I have to an emotional attachment to the lyric somewhere or at some point. It is complicated though and from a personal point of view, I'd be more inclined to fall in love with a Scottish band than anyone else, but I suppose that hasn't happened too often.

Is there a lot to be said for the fact that there is a greater opportunity to see local bands, especially when they are on the up?

[GB]: That's true. I really like The National and they're now huge but I caught them at the Barfly and there were 20 people there and I feel the way about them in the same way that I've fallen for Scottish or British bands who have come through the ranks. I think there is a lot to be said for when you see a band and if you see them early and they go on to be big, you'll have a stronger affection for them. Again, I think lyrically, I think the lyrics of The National are written about dysfunctional people and locations and places. There's a lot of character studies and I think a lot of the best Scottish music does that. Okay, a lot of the best music from anywhere does that.

The notion of Scottishness is a very difficult one to define. Say you take the Proclaimers, they're got a huge following and you would instantly say that they are a Scottish band. They're big around the world; some of it may be due to the ex-pat following. However, you've also got Arab Strap. They've both got big followings outside of the UK, Arab Strap did very well in Europe

[PM]: Is that down to their distinctiveness and their voice, their Scottishness, or is it just down to people liking the songs? I've spent time in the States and they see British and Scottish music as somehow better, or maybe more intelligent, because it's something different. I think the fact people have to seek out Scottish bands a bit more, makes it more interesting.

[GB]: The fact that Scotland is relatively small means that there are connections between bands. People who are fans of bands are drawn to that and like the fact that there are other bands to enjoy or jump onto from there. You know, that Belle & Sebastian album had the name Arab Strap in it and the fact that half the bands have played in other bands, people like that and they like to immerse themselves in something they can identify with or feel part of.

[PM]: It's like SXSW and they do a Scottish showcase. It's a fairly disparate bunch of bands but as a band, you'd kill to get on that. Lots of people will come along to it on the back of one big band and this means as a band you want to be involved it. If you were putting on your own show, there's no guarantee of drawing any crowd so it's easy to see why it's a good for bands.

I think the whole Icelandic thing is interesting and worth thinking about. That's smaller than Scotland and they've got a crazy number of bands who have done exceedingly well. I can't quite get my head around that!

Is it the darker nights?

[PM]: It's probably a factor. Iceland is quite supportive of artists, there is generally more of a structure to be able to make a living or receive funding. How many times have you seen a Glasgow band, thought they were in line for something brilliant and then they break up. It's usually for practical reasons, like a member moves away or gets a job. In Iceland, I think there is more of an opportunity to be creative. Obviously people in bands will work and have jobs but I think there is less pressure and more support to be creative and focus on the band.

[GB]: I think that's true and it's the case in Sweden. I read that this was the case with The Cardigans and they were all on benefits but it was accepted that they didn't need to look for work because they were in a band. That's clearly not going to happen under this Government. Another thing about Iceland though, is for these bands or artists to have a sustainable career; they couldn't just stay in Iceland. I'm sure there is a folk scene in Iceland and some artists will make a living playing there but acts like Sigur Ros and Bjork had to get away to make a career. Interestingly, they had to look outwards and I don't think that is the case with Scottish bands. Maybe logistically, the support isn't in place in Scotland.

There's a lot to be said about Scotland having wilder audiences, would you say that this is the case?

[PM]: From playing gigs, it's hard for us to say as we're not after a wild audience. The more respectful the audience, the better it is for us. I hate going to gigs and there are folk talking loudly but that happens everywhere. From our own playing perspective, it's hard to tell but I have been to some gigs and all it takes is for one person to shout something and its then open season. I'm not sure if that's a Glasgow thing or a Scottish thing.

[GB]: I think it may have started in the variety hall stuff where the Glasgow audience made comedians cower in terror and it's gone on from that. If a band embraces it, it can be a joyous experience. I've not been to many gigs in too many places but I can compare Glasgow and Edinburgh and there is a difference. I've seen the same acts in both cities and the Edinburgh crowd is more reserved. I've enjoyed gigs in Edinburgh but at times, the difference in crowd is really different. Is it maybe the venue? If you go and see a band in the Barrowlands then it's going to be a rowdy crowd but if you see them the next time in the Queens Hall, it will be quieter or more subdued.

[PM]: I think some people see it as a badge of honour that we have this reputation. I think some people think it's expected and we need to live up to the reputation. If a band mentions the Glasgow crowd in advance or on stage, the crowd feels as though they have to live up to the hype.

[GB:] I think when this happens, it's almost self-fulfilling. Bands hear about it or read about it, they talk about it, the crowd reacts to it and it all goes in a cycle.

[PM]: I had a conversation with a friend who was down in England visiting friends and she was talking to band who were over from the US. The band was saying they were in Glasgow a few nights before, they had never been in the city before, they had no idea if they had an audience and they were expecting to play in front of a few folk. However, the band said there was an amazing atmosphere and it was a wild night, unlike any other show of the tour. I'm not sure what to take from that, maybe it was the night of the week.

[GB:] There was a gig Wilco played in the concert hall in Glasgow a few years back and the next night they played in Manchester. There's video footage of the Manchester gig where Jeff Tweedy is slating the Glasgow crowd as being quiet and terrible the night before. This sounds unimaginable but the gig was on a Monday night, it was the concert hall, so maybe that plays a part.

Really, Wilco were great that night?

[GB:]Yeah, I really enjoyed it. I wonder how much of a say a band would have in the venue. I know some bands have a say and take an interest in the venues they play but the venue can really have an impact on

[PM:] You'd also imagine the reason why many bands play the Academy or the O2 is because if you are booking a UK tour, it's much easier to book them all.

What are your favourite venues?

[PM]: Barrowlands is the obvious one, as a place to go, given that we've never played the Barrowlands. I think I get more excited for a gig if it's at the Barrowlands. That is partly to do with the fact that there are fewer gigs there these days, so it's more of an anticipation thing when you do get to go.

[GB]: There is something magical about and I think with most things you love, you can't explain why.

[PM]: It seems like everyone feels the same way about it. Maybe there is a mythology about it and you hear about the Barrowlands before you first go and that makes you more excited and then it goes from there.

[GB]: When I was first going to gigs, pretty much every act of a certain size who came through Scotland tended to play the Barrowlands. So it was a place where some of your fondest memories of going to gigs were all at the Barrowlands. I don't tend to see as many gigs at the Barrowlands these days and I'm not sure if the venue puts on as many gigs these days or if its bands I don't know of. I feel a bit sorry for people who don't get the chance to experience the Barrowlands.

I think there's something special when a Scottish band plays there. I remember seeing The Delgados play there and they seemed so chuffed to be playing in the Barrowlands. It was one of those nights when everyone was smiling, it was an event gig.

It's a benchmark isn't it? Maybe in the way the older generation talk of the Apollo or the Playhouse.

[PM]: I saw Dylan in 2004 play the Barrowlands. I don't know how it came about that he was playing at it. He played the SECC the night before and it was announced on the day of the gig that he was playing at the Barrowlands. Whether he had a free day and he knew the mythology..I don't know. I've seen Dylan play in larger rooms, but in the Barrowlands, he was smiling, the band was smiling. Maybe he's not used to playing venues where he is that close and he did say at the end it was one of the best gigs he had played in years. At time I thought he was bullshitting but Bob Dylan doesn't need to say that for anyone's benefit. The atmosphere was amazing and Bob may not be used to that sort of atmosphere these days. He plays in the big sheds where the heritage acts go, it's the one gig of the year for some people in the audience and it's all a bit flatter. I just found it really interesting he played there when he didn't usually play that sort of venue.

It was £40 for a ticket and at the time I thought ******* hell, that's expensive, and it was at the time, but now, that's the going rate. Apparently, you can blame The Eagles for this! When they announced their comeback tour, they were charging around £80 and £90 for the shows and some promoters were saying "good luck with that" but the tour pretty much sold out. I think from there a lot of people realised they were underestimating how much money people would pay to go and see a band. Tickets have gone up a lot in the past 10 years.

[GB]: I also really like, both having played and as a fan, is the 13th Note. The one on King Street and the old one on Glassford Street. It's not going to be the best sound in the world but there's something unquantifiable about it, there's such a nice feel. There's no stage but it has that institution feel about it.

[PM]: I think most musicians from Glasgow have played a formative gig there and generally, I think it goes well. Maybe there's something about audiences in the venue, it's not just folk who have wandered in off the street or you are playing in front of a pub audience. I also really like the Glad Café as a place to play and see bands. I like everything about it. Also, growing up in Aberdeen I really enjoyed the Lemon Tree. It's a lovely space and I saw some very early gigs there. We played there years ago, it was a great gig, but it's a great venue.

I also really like the Insider Festival, I know it's not a venue, but I really enjoyed playing there and being there.

What's your take on festivals in Scotland?
[GB]: I've got a strange relationship with festivals in general, not just in Scotland. I think festivals have slightly damaged the live music experience. I think now you get people going to one or a couple of festivals a year and that's where they see

all the bands that they would have otherwise seen throughout the year.

It's not the same as going to see a band in a venue or on their tour. I think its slightly sullied live music *(said while laughing)*. If a festival is good or has something about it, it works but too many are corporate and similar. There are some bands that say okay, we're playing festivals and that counts as our shows in this area or part of the world. The way it should work is that an album comes out, a band tours and then they do festivals.

[PM]: No one releases an album in summer anymore because of the festival circuit. Even if you release an album that is perfect for release in June, no one does it. You get albums that are so in tune with summer and people love them and it's the soundtrack of the season but nowadays, these albums aren't released in the summer. It's maybe because I care about the album. The live experience is an amazing thing but I really care about the album and I think the importance on festivals is because of where the money is now in the music industry.

The money isn't in albums, it's in live shows and festivals and the album loses its importance. Now it's like festivals and live shows are reason enough whereas they used to be to support albums.

[GB]: I think there's a danger in that it makes sense for bands. If you're an American band and you are coming to Europe, it makes economic sense to hit the festival circuit and there's a danger that becomes the norm and people stop doing the tours. I think this is a worry because it means you stop seeing bands doing what they should be able to do properly in a proper environment. Even in the best festival, you're never going to get the best performance. It's a different environment and the sound is never going to be that good.

[PM:] Bands also have their festival set which isn't the same as their standard set.

[GB]: I think there is a place for some festivals though and even though they are going away or dropping down a bit, a good one can be great. Ones like the Cambridge Folk Festival look amazing and a small one like The Insider, which we've done a few times, has a really good feel to it because it feels special and an event. You don't play that festival to make a lot of money.

[PM]: I'm conflicted about them because there are some you look at them and think that'd be a great way to see so many bands. However, T in the Park, the line-up seems underwhelming and easy of late. I know Glastonbury is much bigger but they try to pull rabbits out of the hat every so often and T in the Park seems safe. You can almost predict the headliners before a line-up is announced

[GB]: Of course, they have the T Break which is a good thing. It's not something to be totally dismissed

[PM]: T in the Park clearly caters to a certain market. It sells out, people are happy to book well in advance and pay a lot of money for it. The line-up, especially as years go by, reflects that. Ultimately, it's probably bands that I don't like but even at T in the Park, there's probably still enough bands for me to have a good day out.

[PM]: Kraftwerk, they, or he now as it's just the one guy and that goes back to what Graeme was saying because that might be your best chance of seeing them. Someone like Kraftwerk could say that they/he could sell out a tour across the country but it's easier to announce a number of festival sets and that's them done. That is the same for bands and promoters, it's easier and they're still reaching to an audience. However, as someone who plays music, I'd always prefer to play my own gig.

[GB]: The one festival I was always intrigued by was Connect. It was obvious that it was going to fail and it was unlikely to make money but it was different. I went both years and it got a lot of things right. It's a shame it fell by the wayside quickly.

[PM]: I think festivals can be damaging. It's maybe down to my taste but some are good and some aren't. T in the Park is obviously successful but not for me but then again, Insider was great and that has become my benchmark for comparing festivals to. I don't really like festivals but I do like Insider and I look forward to it for a good few months building up to it.

I think they've got it right as there's good music but it's in a beautiful location, it's the right size and if you've got a young family, everyone can have a great time and kids can run about. It's got a great atmosphere and they have plenty of things right. Maybe with a smaller festival size, you can take greater control of elements like that. I prefer the smaller ones but again, I prefer going to gigs than festivals.

Another thing has occurred to me, because as long as it gets people out to see live music, that's great but in Scotland, the majority of locations are not in the central belt. If you're a teenager getting into music and you live in the Highlands, you won't get the chance to come down to Glasgow or Edinburgh to see bands. For kids like that, these festivals are a great thing and that's another good reason to have them.
You have/had Rockness, Belladrum, Ullapool, Brew at the Bog, and Insider, all within 100 miles from Inverness.
[GB:] Wickerman as well at the other end of the country

The central belt is seeing a rise in the number of city centre gigs over a day or two, what is your take on them?

[GB]: I wonder what the aim was for these gigs. If I was going to see a band at Stag & Dagger, I'd likely have gone to see them do at their own gig. It reminds me a bit of the In The City stuff, I'm not sure if that's the vibe but that's the way it seems. It seems a decent idea for a punter but if there were 5 bands you'd see at the festival, you'd likely go see them at their own gig. I'm not sure if that's great for a promoter. Then again, there may be some bands you think are alright but maybe wouldn't pay money to see them in their own right, so that could be a reason.

It may be that it attracts bands as well; some acts may feel they don't have an audience and would struggle in a certain city but this sort of event helps them to develop an audience. Even if you're a band playing a new city, it can help to get a similar sounding local act to support you. It may be the promoter is thinking long term and placing a band on this sort of bill will help to develop an audience for the next tour or next year.

[PM]: We're not very well suited to most festivals...

[GB]: To be honest, we don't get asked. If we were asked, we would do them.

[PM]: That's true, when I think about it; we've never turned down a festival.

Who are your favourite Scottish acts?

[PM]: I've already mentioned The Blue Nile and Hats is one of my favourite albums ever. I'd also add Orange Juice but even people like Bert Jansch. Does Ivor Cutler count? I went to see the National theatre of Scotland thing and that's fantastic. He is one of my favourite musicians.

With respect to acts like Franz Ferdinand, Big Country or Rod Stewart who may not all be technically Scottish but are classed as Scottish, what do you feel about those acts?

[PM]: Well, you've got Withered Hand. Dan Wilson is English but has lived in Scotland for years. He became a musician due to his experience of working with Scottish acts so would you say he was a Scottish act, even though he sings with an English accent? I'd say he is Scottish.

Actually, that ties in slightly with the referendum as well. There's the debate about who gets to vote, should Scots expats get to vote? I think if you choose to live here, you have a right and to that extent, I'd say someone like Franz Ferdinand should be classed as a Scottish act.

[GB]: Also, if Rod Stewart says he Scottish, he's Scottish and we should all accept that!

For best Scottish acts, I find it really hard as there are some bands that I used to really like and they meant a lot to me but they don't really anymore, so my favourite Scottish acts change over time. I have to mention Karine Polwart though, who is one of my favourite songwriters of all time. I think she manages to combine songs about issues and small p politics with great arrangements and beautiful sounds. Also, Pete will hate me for this but I like The Proclaimers.

[PM]: I won't hate you for that at all, they've written brilliant songs.

[GB]: I like them up to a certain point; they're a bit of a cabaret act now. They had a run of form, first 4 albums that were really strong. I don't think you can underestimate how odd it was for them to sing in a Scottish accent. It's now de rigeur for Scottish bands to do that and some do it to a level where it's annoying but that was unheard of until they came along. Those first 3 or 4 albums are really great albums and they were a fun live experience. You'd look around and there would be grannies and the trendy people, I like that. They've got songs that aren't party tunes but you have people singing them at the top of their voice.

[PM]: Like Cap In Hand, it's very political it's got a great chorus to sing along to and people are happy to sing along, maybe even regardless of how they feel about the political element.

[GB]: One of my favourite albums of all time is Edwyn Collins with Georgeous George, which is a really good pop album. I'm not totally convinced by all of Orange Juice, I like some of it but I really love Gorgeous George. I saw him a few times around then.

On stage or just walking about?

[GB]: Sorry yeah, live, on tour. Obviously they had to release Never Met A Girl Like You about 5 times for it to be a hit but the shows were bonkers.

[PM]: The title track is brilliant as well.

[GB]: I'm not overly enamoured with an awful lot else but one guy that I really like, and he started around the same time as us, is Beerjacket. He's just been consistently very good and strong, so I'd place him up there. Randolph's Leap are excellent and I think you can see how they could go bigger.

Any Scottish bands that you think should have made it big but missed out?

[GB]: I really like Endor and they should have been doing as well as We Were Promised Jetpacks or Frightened Rabbit. They were a superb live band.

[PM]: I personally thought their songs were great and they

were better than those acts.

[GB:] You knew you were going to get a good show from them when they played, their songs were excellent but it just didn't go for them.

[PM]: Interestingly, I think this goes back to what we were saying earlier about bands getting support. I know for a fact that they had professions they wanted to go and do. If there was an alternative for them and a real chance for them to make money while making music, there's a good chance they'd have stuck around and would still be making music. I agree with Graeme, they were a band that should have been bigger. I was lucky enough to play some shows with the band but that was after I was a fan. For me, their songs were better than anyone else's of the time.

[GB]: Over the past 10 years, coming out of Glasgow, I'd say that's fair.

[PM]: I just hope they'll be properly remembered by people.

[GB]: They will be by me.

[PM]: They made one album and I think there's a few things they would have done differently and there was a few missed opportunities. I'm not sure if it was the way it was promoted or the way it came out. I think they'll feel they may have made a few compromises but that said, they are now making very good music and great things as a continuation of Endor I suppose.

[GB]: Another album I really like, without being the biggest fan of the band, was The Great Eastern by The Delgados. I seen them a few times and I liked them without being a massive fan but that album was just superb. With Scottish bands, it seems to be that I like specific albums or certain times. It's the same with Belle and Sebastian. I think they've became a brilliant live band and I'd go see them every time but I wouldn't necessarily buy their albums. He's a bit of a showman now as well and The Boy with the Arab Strap and Dear Catastrophe Waitress were excellent. They remind me a bit of Squeeze in that they make intelligent pop. Maybe there's a touch of Lloyd Cole and the Commotions in there as well, they're quite smart.

Anyone else?

[GB]: I like Eagleowl.

[PM]: I think Over The Wall should have been bigger. If they had been given the opportunity to make a living they'd have had a better chance. Bands would love to spend more time doing band stuff but when you have bills to pay, mortgages to pay and families to support, you can't always do it. The Over The Wall album is brilliant and there are songs on there that are brilliant.

Thurso is the theme tune of Burnistoun and it's a great pop song. I've seen them play it at festivals and their own shows and there is a lot of love for them and its exuberant pop. There is a lot of love for them in some places, and they have been on certain radio shows but they never made it as big as they should have done.

A month or so after the interview took place, The State Broadcasters were given the chance to support Over The Wall at their final Glasgow show, in Oran Mor in May

[PM]: One of the best albums I've heard in years is Good News by Withered Hand and its one of my favourite albums in years, I love it. I'm not such a big fan of the new one but that doesn't matter, he made a great album that deserves wider recognition. Mind you, it's a scratchy independent record and he'll never play stadiums but he writes the hook of a chorus better than anyone else.

What do you think of the level of media coverage and support in Scotland?

[GB]: I think radio is still really important for emerging bands and I think Radio Scotland tries hard. The problem is that, stuff like Vic Galloways show is that most people that listen to it are other bands and then genuine music fans. Scotland can't support its own version of 6Music, there's not the audience for it. I think Radio Scotland does its best, they have a culture/arts show during the day and they try to get emerging acts on.

Do you think more could be achieved through TV?

[GB]: That is an area where there can be criticism for BBC Scotland. They tried The Music Show but why they don't they just do a Rapal on a larger scale? I don't think it's expensive to make and the bands would be up for it. Things like Jools Holland haven't changed the format and that probably helps people to find new bands. Folk that no longer buy magazines or listen to the radio but if they know one band, they will watch and hopefully find something else.

[PM]: When I was growing up, I used to watch it and this was a time when very few bands came to Aberdeen. As a 14/15 year old, I'd watch Jools Holland and Id usually like at least one band an episode. I'd find out about bands that weren't alternative that I'd grow to like or there would be a band I love on it, like Eels. They wouldn't really get exposure on British TV so that was great.

[GB]: I can imagine Rapal may suffer, like the Vic Galloway show, in that the audience would be the bands and the hardcore fans. There is a need to bring in established bands and new bands, like the Music Show tried to do. I know it's not easy to do but you have to try. 6Music does it, you're never more than three songs away from a song you know but in the gap, you've a chance of hearing new songs and new bands.

Clearly the referendum vote is placing a large focus on Scotland this year. Are you intending to vote and do you know which way will you vote?

[PM]: Yes to both questions! I actually go canvassing for Yes Scotland, which shows how strongly I feel about it. It's maybe an easier decision for me to take a leap of faith. I started out as a no voter but as time has gone on; I have swung completely in the other direction. I just think it's really important.

[GB]: Since it's become a minor possibility, I've believed it would be certainty to get to this point after we had devolution. I don't think many people felt like this but after devolution, I was certain we would reach this stage. I felt from there, if the opportunity came up, I would be keen for an independence vote, so it's been in my mind for what seems like forever. I say this as someone who has never voted SNP. If you vote for them, you have always felt that but for me, I always had a feeling it would happen.

My politics are not represented by any of the main parties in Britain or Scotland and actually splitting up a Union is not how I would prefer it to be. However, in reality, it's the only way we will get closer to the sort of politics I would like to see. Briefly, there is more chance of us getting the type of government I would like us to have in an independent Scotland. The opportunity to have fewer politicians on the payroll is enough for me. We don't need MSPs and MPs. The ones we are getting rid of are the ones that fiddle expenses and whatever. If you don't like politicians and you aren't a political person, vote Yes for that reason alone. I think if you're left leaning in any way, it's the only way of getting the type of Government you may like. If you aren't left leaning...well...

[PM]: For me, on top of what Graeme says, I'd add that the people best positioned to make decisions for this country should be here. Each country in the UK has their own unique problems and issues and I think there will be a greater ability to address these issues if we take control. Let's face it, Trident is not an issue in places like Cornwall or even Newcastle but it is a real issue for us and I would like a say on that. As Graeme says, having fewer politicians makes a difference and being able to hold them to account is important. Knowing that we can vote them out if we don't like what they are doing is a big thing, for me, and I think most people.

As a band, do you worry about being open about your political stance or beliefs?

[PM]: I don't think we have enough fans to worry about alienating people! I do worry about it slightly. We run our own twitter and Facebook accounts and we have made the odd political statement from time to time on it. You know you are accountable but we don't worry too much.

[GB:]We haven't really written political songs but I think if you know our stuff, you will gather where we are roughly coming from. There are some bands over the years who haven't written anything overtly political but you can tell where they are coming from and what their views are.

[PM]: We're a six piece but as far as I'm aware, I think all of us are voting Yes.

[GB]: Thinking of myself as a fan of bands and artists, I'd like to think I could differentiate enough to still buy music that I liked even if a band held different political views.

David Bowie received a lot of coverage for his Brit Award comments, what did you feel about that?

[GB]: I'm not personally a big fan of Bowie. I felt it was a bit cool and if you are going to make a statement, for someone who is an enigma like Bowie, I thought it was a great way to do so. I don't have a problem with people expressing an opinion about the referendum. To be frank, it's not going to make a difference. People should not be allowing David Bowie, via Kate Moss, to influence their vote and if it does, well...It's the media exploding it all. It resonated at a pun level on twitter.

[PM]: I really like Bowie and Gill from the band is an even bigger Bowie fan than me. You have to be careful but everyone is entitled to an opinion. For example, in conversation I'll talk about Crimea and other world events, so why shouldn't other people?

[GB]: Bowie has represented a certain type of Britain, in an iconic way, so it is understandable he will represent Britain in that way. Of course, he is also very detached from the UK. It's weird how people get upset. Could you imagine if Quebec had a referendum, and Justin Currie toured over there and said they should stay part of Canada? An artist doesn't mean any more or less than anyone else.

[PM]: I was more disappointed in Eddie Izzard than Bowie. This is because he became more of a face for that viewpoint and I think that is down to his own political ambitions. He is talking from an emotional viewpoint as opposed to understanding the political elements. I was a fan of his growing up. He's different from Bowie in that he is more active, still raising funds but I think a lot of it is down to him gaining experience and developing a political side. He is a Labour party supporter; I think he wants to be the Labour candidate for London Mayor. Given the Labour party line on Independence is no, it makes sense for him to take this stance to pick up brownie points.

[GB]: Comedy and music are a bit different. Comedy shows can have a political edge. You can go and listen to Billy Bragg for the songs, music and tunes without worrying about the politics. However, could you go and see Mark Thomas if you don't like his politics? Music is different, there are more levels. Comedy is a different ball game, and Eddie Izzard is a different ball game as well. Izzard is a comedian, so he's probably perfect for being a politician!

[PM]: People will care more about what David Bowie says as opposed to what Alasdair Darling says or what Gordon Brown says, and in some ways, that isn't a bad thing!

Do you think the views of celebrities or musicians will help people to take more notice of the situation or the choices they have?

[GB]: I think in Scotland we're politically mature enough that we won't be swayed by what a celebrity says. In the main, we recognise that for what it is. We've voted in enough elections and this campaign has helped more people to engage with politics. There will always be people who aren't really interested who will be swayed by the media but I think politically, we are mature and see through things like this. I think a problem in the mainstream is that we don't have enough balance in the media with respect to the referendum. It's only really the Sunday Herald that has nailed their colours to the Yes side.

This was before the paper took the bold move of backing the Yes campaign on their front page in early May, but the paper was heading in that direction at the point of the interview.

[PM]: I think it's a demographic thing and people of a certain age remain more likely to be influenced by what the papers say. I find the Daily Record interesting. They're traditionally a Labour paper but there have been an increasing number of Yes articles. I think they're aware that there is a perception of change for this vote and I think they're trying to keep readers on board.

[GB]: The Record realises that Scottish Labour is a basket case. I'm not a SNP voter but you have to be mature enough to say they have governed very well, certainly better than what the current Scottish Labour would do. They've brought through many things are things that Scottish Labour should be doing. For whatever reason, perhaps due to the party machine in London, Scottish Labour is not what they were. Perhaps the Record is stating that we've been abandoned in these ideals and beliefs.

[PM]: Labour for independence is growing.

[GB]: What I like in America is that bands do things like Rock The Vote and get people voting, regardless of what they are voting for. This doesn't really happen in this country.

[PM]: The National Collective does a small thing like that but it could be something they do more of.

[GB]: I worry a wee bit, especially with the different groups online, is that you can feel outside of it all. I'm not involved with the Yes campaign, I observe it but I'm not part of it and I think some of the online stuff comes across as being sanctimonious, which really doesn't help. You need to get out there and charm the grannies as it were; you can't just play to your intended audience.

[PM]: It seems like a lot of people are talking about the political issues and that's good. Regardless of how they vote, people are thinking about "how my country should be run" and that's good. Topics of conversation like land ownership are coming up now, people are engaging in social justice more and in general, people are just paying more attention. I feel positive about the whole thing. Some of the political debate hasn't been up to standard but it had got people engaged in these issues and I take this as a good thing. I think that even if the vote is no, there has been enough dialogue that people will demand more and more. I think it's important it happens now but I don't think it's the last shot at it. Once you are aware of political issues, you can't stop caring about them so people will continue to care. If a No vote is returned, I'll be gutted but people will definitely continue to engage and care.

[GB]: I am inclined to agree that a No result doesn't mean the final shot. Things like the Common Weal has arisen and there is a drive to look at how we behave as a society, how we look after each other. Even things like the 4 day week. These things were not on the agenda for discussion for the media but they are front and centre now. I think when people are affected by economics; there is a need for people to get political. We are living in age of foodbanks and offensive policies from the Coalition government and when these things affect people, people become political. I think engagement was inevitable. The same thing happened under Thatcher so perhaps it's not all about the independence vote, but there is an air of political debate and discussion that hasn't been present for years.

I think as a generation we are living through something seismic. This is stuff they'll teach kids in school forever and that should be cherished. I can't imagine how I'll feel on the 19th of September.

[PM]: I'll be hungover either way!

[GB]: Nothing will have changed and everything will have changed on that day. In 1997, when we had a Labour government and I was still a Labour voter, it felt massive. I had only lived under the Tories and you felt at times the Tory rule would never end, maybe it didn't! No, we got devolution from it, and in general, it was a slightly giddy and optimistic feeling and I'd be happy to have that sort of feeling again.

Olive Grove Records

Founded in 2010, Olive Grove Records is an independent label formed by two well-known names from the Glasgow music scene of recent years. Halina Rifai, who founded the Glasgow PodcART and Lloyd Meredith, the man behind the Peenko blog, set out to create a label that ensured all profits went to the artist, while providing a platform for artists to release music and progress in the industry.

I caught up with Lloyd on the day Belle & Sebastien opened the Commonwealth Games, and a few days before Olive Grove teamed up with the East End Social for an event in the Bowlers Bar, just off Glasgow Green.

Acts from your label playing at The Bowlers Bar as part of the East End Social this weekend. first of all, are you excited about the event?

Yes, very much so. This has been planned for quite a few months; essentially it came about because I manage Randolph's Leap and we've been looking to put on our own event for quite a while. We've wanted to do something a bit different from what is taking place, not just a normal gig, so we've been working with Johnny from Lost Map to see what we could come up with.

We compiled a wish list of bands that we wanted to play at this event, and given that The State Broadcasters and Randolph's Leap are pretty much intertwined these days, they were one of the first bands we thought to ask. Yeah, I'm really excited for the weekend; it should be a lot of fun.

Of course, it's not just about The State Broadcasters and Randolph's Leap, it's a fantastic line-up spread out over the course of the day.

Yes, we have our latest addition to the Olive Grove family, Skinny Dipper and they are a 9 piece band. 8 of them are girls and God only knows how we are going to squeeze everyone in because the venue only holds about 80 folk. The stage probably has space for 4 people and we're looking to squeeze 9 folk on stage at one point! I don't know its' going to work.

We've also got Duglas from BMX Bandits who is coming along to do a set, we have Neil from Meursault coming along from Edinburgh as well as David and Scott from Kid Canaveral playing a stripped back set. On top of all that, we have Uncle Vic Galloway spinning some tunes and compering so hopefully there's something for everyone.

Given that there are plenty of people involved with Randolph's Leap anyway, are you just drawn to the biggest bands that you can find?
When we first started with working with Randolph's Leap, there were 6 of them...now they're up to 8. I love the noise and I think its brilliant watching a band with so much going on. However, in practical terms, it's a pain in the backside because trying to get an 8 piece band to tour is pretty damned hard. Of course, now we've got a 9 piece band, but we'll try to get them on the road. We try to get our bands playing as much as we can, including outside of Glasgow as much as we can but you can probably imagine the practicalities are quite difficult at times.

Is there any scope for buying an Olive Grove minibus?
I've thought about this! Looking at the finances for the band I occasionally think we can buy a van, and then I think bands can rent it off us, and then I think we can get a coach. Eventually I catch on to myself and say Lloyd this is stupid...but yeah, it has been thought about!

You do realise you are two or three steps away from having your very own Olive Grove commune?
Ha, I think my wife would leave me if I did that but my daughter would be quite happy, she likes our bands.
Swings and roundabouts...no, let's not promote divorce, don't go down that route.
No, that's not going to happen.

As said, you manage Randolph's Leap, and they've

developed in size and in stature in recent years. How do you feel about the progress made by the band?

For the past 4 years, my life has been pretty much intertwined with Randolph's Leap. My daughter was born 4 years ago and two months after that, we released Randolph's Leap EP and since then, they've been intertwined.

When will your daughter become a full blown member of the band?

We'll train her up, see what she can do and then see who we can sack *(Lloyd laughed throughout this entire answer).*

No, it's been amazing because I've always wanted to be involved with the music industry in some way or another. I originally started with the Peenko blog and then progressed onto the label with Halina, who does the Glasgow Podcart, so it is something that I've always wanted to be involved with. Therefore, to see the rise and development of the band is just amazing. It's down to a lot of hard work from so many people. For me, Adam is one of the best songwriters in Scotland, he makes me laugh and he can bring a tear to my eye, he's fantastic.

It's been great seeing them win people over and get bigger. When they started off, they were being written off as being a bit twee but through constant work and great songs, we've overcome that to a certain degree. We're getting more people involved and interested now. We have Johnny from Lost Maps who has provided great support, Duglas from BMX Bandits has always been there as well. I've noticed we're starting to get more and more radio folk involved as well now.

We've always had Vic Galloway, who is brilliant, but now we're getting Marc Riley, we're getting Huw Stephens playing them on Radio 1 and it is all the little things that are coming together to make things seem as though it's getting bigger.

I feel, and it's something I've been guilty of in the past, is that twee is used in a lazy and not always

correct manner to describe Glasgow bands.

I agree.

The thing is, we're recording this on the opening day of the Commonwealth Games and at Kelvingrove you've got Belle & Sebastian playing. They're probably the band that defines twee for many people but a more robust and entertaining live act you couldn't wish to see these days.

It's laziness. If you've come across the Randolph Leap song Indie King, that is Adam's way of trying to address that twee identity people place on the band or other acts. You can't pigeonhole acts as easily as you would like at times.

Okay, what are you general feelings about the Commonwealth Games and all of the music events that are coming to the city in the next few weeks?

I'm really excited and I think it's fantastic for the city. It was a few months back that Stuart from Chemikal and East End Social asked us if the label wanted us to do something. At the point we were thinking of doing something similar to what we did at Celtic Connections and Randolph's Leap were looking to do a quirky gig so that has all come together.

I mean c'mon, tonight I'm off to see Belle & Sebastian at the Kelvingrove Bandstand and that's a venue I've wanted to see used properly for years and it's the band I've always wanted to see there. There are also so many free gigs that it has hard to keep up with, and there's stuff at Glasgow Green and at the BBC.

One of your acts, Call To Mind, performed at T in the Park. How did they find that occasion?

Oh it was great fun, I was up with them and we all had a great time.

I take it this is one of the big perks and reasons why you run the label?

Absolutely, you've got to have some reasons for doing it! We were up on the Sunday and it was the first T I've been to in 2 or 3 years. That time, I was up with Randolph's Leap, and I drove the van, so I was sober and it rained and it was one of the most miserable days of my life! Going up this time was fantastic as I didn't have to drive, it was sunny and the whole vibe was amazing. It wasn't overly busy for them but the people that were in the tent really seemed to like it and the sound was probably the best that they ever had. They got some amazing videos out of it as well and I think it has done a lot of good for the band, which will probably come to light in the next few weeks. *(This was the news that Call To Mind were added to the daytime Radio 1 Playlist as part of the BBC Introducing format, with the band's A Family Sketch track being played for a week from Monday the 4th of August.)*

T was great and this weekend it's Wickerman so that's something else to look forward to. The album has done really well too. We've been talking to the band for a few years about doing an album and it was only when Creative Scotland funding became available that it was possible to press on with the album. The album was recorded out at The Old Mill in Strathaven and that went well. It just took time to get it mixed and mastered but it sounds great and we're all very happy with it. It's probably one of the best albums you've ever released.

Mind you, I probably say that about every album we've released. It's been more of a slow burner that some people take time to get into it but when they do, they really get into it, maybe in the same way that people take to The State Broadcasters. Not everyone is into it or loves it but when they do get into it, they really love it and fall for the band and the music in a big way.

After Wickerman, there will be Belladrum, so that will be a hometown show for them and that is on the Saturday. On the Friday, Randolph's Leap are performing and that is the equivalent slot that Wooden box played three years ago. That was the most amazing gig I have ever seen Woodenbox do and a year later we had their album out. They packed the tent out and people were going crazy for it. So now, with two of our acts going up there to perform, I can only hope they'll receive a similar response but again, I'm really looking forward to it and it should be amazing.

Following that, we are doing a headline show in Eden

Court in Inverness in October. We'll have the Cairn String quartet playing with them and it's a really big theatre so that should be great. There are not too many indie-pop shows in that neck of the woods so I'm hoping that a lot of people are excited for it, it should be special.

Call To Mind will also be playing at the Wickerman Festival, *(the same weekend as the East End Social gig.)* How important is the summer festival circuit for up and coming bands?
For us it is vital and it is the best way to go out and get exposure for our bands. Not everyone wants to come and see bands in a dingy pub and at these festivals; we get families coming along with kids, who wouldn't have the chance to see us. It's the exposure of playing in front of so many other people that is the important thing.

The fees that you get for playing these festivals isn't the biggest thing about them but the bands can get a decent amount of PRS for playing. For instance, for the Randolph's Leap slot at T in the Park, that helped to fund the album they released. It was the financial starting point to build upon, so PRS and exposure to a bigger market make these festivals essential for us as a label and our bands.

What are your favourite Scottish festivals?
I love the smaller festivals. I feel too old to go to T in the Park these days. I enjoyed the recent one but I felt about 100 years old as it was just wee kids that were there. It was also too big for my liking. For me, Wickerman and Belladrum are two that I really like. There is also Insider, and we had our own showcase up there, with Jo Mango, Woodenbox, The State Broadcasters and Randolph's Leap, so that was great.

The State Broadcasters really speak highly of the Insider festival.
Yes, probably because I was driving and took my wife and daughter and I spent my time running about daft organising everything! If I was there as a punter, it would have been outstanding. I'd also really like to go to Brew At The Bog but I haven't been yet. It looks amazing but I can't vouch for it

yet because I haven't been.

When it comes to fun, a trip to Wickerman a few years' back with Randolph's Leap was brilliant because it was just carnage, okay, mostly on my part. However, Belladrum is equally as much fun because it's a nice vibe and people get into it, really liking the bands and just jumping about to whatever is on.

People might say the same about T in the Park but it's just channelled in a different way?
Exactly...but they're more likely to come and see an unsigned band in a tent at one of the smaller festivals than they are at T. As a comparison, I think around 2-4,000 people came to see Woodenbox at Belladrum and yet at T, there were probably the same, if not less, people watching Twilight Sad in their tent. You'd never get that for small bands at a big festival because there is so much going on.

Any thoughts on the fact that most Scottish music festivals are occurring away from the central belt?
I think it is getting away from the culture of the promoters running everything. There is a sense of free reign to promote these things when you move away from the central belt. There is clearly a great deal of control in the central region but when you move away, that isn't there. There's also a sense of adventure about setting off somewhere you haven't been so you appeal to the locals while drawing people from further distances.

What were your influences and inspirations in starting up a record label?
We looked at what Fence were doing and what Chemikal Underground were doing and of course, we looked at Song, By Toad, because that was more of a comparable level to what we were aiming for. We just wanted to release music, we both had our own sites and we both had a good understanding of what was happening in the Scottish music scene but we were frustrated that there weren't people out there releasing it or promoting it. We felt there was a gap in

the market for what we wanted to do.

So Halina and myself met up and we agreed on the ethos that we don't take any money from it, all profits go back to the artist to help them. We initially said we would like to be a stepping stone to help bands move on but that hasn't quite happened too much but in a sense, I'm happy with that because we have created a good community. Obviously Randolph's Leap have moved on to Lost Map but even with that, we're still very heavily linked with them, and always will be. If they ever come up with weird little releases or there was something that Lost Map didn't want to release, we'll step in, no problem!

We wanted to be part of the music scene but we wanted to put our own stamp on it. We've never set out to have a folk sound on the label, perhaps I've led the way a wee bit on that but we're always open to new ideas and bands. It's not to say we'll never release a record by a heavy metal band or a dance act, there have been people we've talked to and things haven't worked out, so yeah, we're open to different things.

What have been the biggest challenges and problems in running a label?
The hardest part is finding the time. We do this on top of everything else. I do it on top of a full-time job, I'm married, we've got a wee girl and its finding time. I spend my free time dealing with the label and music stuff. A lot of it is just admin and keeping on top of things. When you have so many bands, that you are essentially managing in a way, there is so much to keep on top of and make sure that things are getting done. Also, all of our bands are quite large and this adds new challenges in arranging events and admin. There is a lot of undue stress and there are highs and lows but of course, there are many great moments involved with it.

What moments have given you the most joy?
For me, the Celtic Connections show at Oran Mor this year was the pinnacle. I had worked on it for about 6 or 7 months, we had to pitch it to the Oran More and Celtic Connections. I also got Moth & the Mirror back for the event, they hadn't

played for around 3 years, and just the feeling I got at the end of the day when it was all over. I don't think I'll ever top that but I'll aim and try to.

Even the picture of all the performers on the label really drove home how many people you work with and the talent involved with the label.

That is another thing, getting that organised was a lot of work. The photographer was the girlfriend of one of the band members, I had known her for years as well, but it was so stressful. It wasn't like you could go around some dressing rooms and order people upstairs, that had about 2 weeks of planning just for the photograph. Co-ordination was vital for the whole event.

What ambitions do you still have with the label and music?

I genuinely haven't thought about it. It's not one of these things I worry about because a lot of the time I didn't get the chance to think because things just keep on going. We haven't released a second album by a band yet and that is one I want to tick off, and we will do soon.

We'll be releasing a Jo Mango remix album in September, we'll have Woodenbox with their third album, albeit second for us, and we should have The Son(s) second album. As for they two, it just depends on who comes to us first with a finished product. That'll definitely be a great box to tick off; getting a second album out from a band is a big ambition we'll achieve soon.

We're doing another showcase set, this time in Edinburgh as part of The Pleasance Sessions, and I'd like to do another showcase at some point, but not for a while. I don't want to have an overkill of these showcases, even at festivals, so we'll space them out.

To be honest though, I just want our bands to be happy. I don't care if they sell 10 records, as long as they're happy. I think some of our bands have done well on other labels but they weren't too happy, and I think they're happier with us. I emphasise that we are a family and we have a lot of cross-collaboration going on, which is nice. For example, we've just had some of the Skinny Dippers girls working with Woodenbox. As it comes to making progress and achieving ambitions, as long as everyone is happy, we'll be doing alright.

Grant Campbell

As the bassist and co-songwriter from St Judes Infirmary, Grant Campbell played his part in one of the most thrilling Scottish tales of the underdog dishing out a few burst lips and bloody noses before eventually succumbing to a fate that was probably determined before they first played a note. A well-travelled lover of European football, Grant would be able to draw you more than enough comparisons between the band's performances and those gut-wrenching, kick-in-the-teeth moments of loss when a win looked on the cards. Even for all that, or maybe because of all that, St Judes remain one of my favourite Scottish bands of all time.

After the demise of St Judes Infirmary, Grant moved on to Deserters Deserve Death, quickly renamed as Edinburgh School For The Death, where a debut album hinted at promise but once again, fortune and favour worked against the band. In 2014, Grant was part of Naked, a departure from the sound, if not outlook, from his previous bands. I caught up with Grant in early August.

Do you think that there is a collective Scottish trait or psyche that runs through the population...and the bands?

I think there was a post-war socialist psyche which when married with the geography of Scotland, as a cold, northern country; engendered a certain stoic, tolerant, benevolent attitude. I think that this has been eroded, not only by the decline of socialism and heavy industry but through other positive factors, the opening up of the world through the internet and cheap air travel.

I am a bit ambivalent, on the face of it, to the concept of thinking that we are somehow different, and by inference better than other people because of an accident of birth we fell on one side of line drawn by the bloody hand of a king or dictator is a reductive one; yet at the same time, there is a pride that we have arrived a tolerant, decent society. We are on the whole good people.

I think the psyche of the bands match that of any group

of young people on the geographic periphery of Europe originating from a distinct cultural conglomeration that is border by a bigger, and in terms of musical impact, more successful neighbour. Scottish bands do tend to support each other more and likewise our home crowds do support their bands with a fervour that is almost sporting.

Are there elements that separate us from other nations and nationalities?

I don't think we are all that different from wider secular Northern Europe. Not much different from the rest of Europe, and not in essence not that different from the rest of the world. To me Scottishness, is a happy accident of history, culture and community, wherein we've arrived at a secular concept of tolerant society and decent modes of behaviour, then dressed it up in Tartan and doused it in whisky!

The phrase "Wha's Like Us" (and follow on lines) are battered out regularly, do you believe in this saying? If so, why?

No. I don't really know what we are like in order to make a comparison with the rest of humanity. Are we any different from the Welsh? Are they not a small left-leaning, decent nation?

I mean there is no clear founding doctrine or belief in the Scottish nation. There a stress on Freedom, which is great but I would suspect that almost everyone in the world believes in freedom and finds it preferential to servitude or slavery. There is a vague were all `Jock Tamsons` bairns which isn't really a founding ideology, but is a grand and noble sentiment. Scotland has ended up as a very secure, democratic and tolerant state.

There is a wider belief that we are in essence good lads which is fair enough but so are most Geordies, Mancunians and Liverpudlians. What does it mean to be Scottish? It means as much or as less as it means to be Algerian or Spanish or Samoan. The older I get the more internationalist I get.

Do you think that there is this element of Scottishness in you and how you make music?

I think with St Judes there was a Scottishness in that we were fascinated with wider Scottish Culture, as we didn't want to sing about America and alternative / indie / whatever / music at that time was very based on traditional notions of Britishness, the Beatles, Britpop, Kinks all that dross. It was also to a certain degree a defensive mechanism, and in part a defiant gesture, as we were geographically on the periphery of the wider UK media / industry, which was much more of an issues in pre-Internet days, than it would be today.

Do you have a national pride in music? Would you look out for a Scottish band more than a similar band from another country?

No, but in truth yes.

You've travelled, toured and stayed over the world, in that time, what did you miss about Scotland?

Errr...my inebriation being socially acceptable. I also missed the Fife coastal rail journey, Irn Bru, Scottish football in the papers, and a dour, fatalist and obscene sense of humour.

Similar question, was there a general reaction to Scotland or a perceived idea of Scottishness?

I remember working abroad and a Palestinian woman coming up to me and taking my arm and telling me I should be proud and her sorrow at my peoples struggles against oppression. She had just seen Braveheart. The more I travel the more I realise that we've won a watch, everyone loves us.

Fife. The Fence Collective, James Yorkston, Vic Galloway – when you were growing up did you ever think Fife would be considered as a cool location?

We were from Kirkcaldy. They were geographically, aesthetically and emotionally completely estranged from what we were trying to achieve, and indeed what we were. I never personally made any link with them being from Fife. I mean it is great what they did and I salute them they exerted no emotional pull on us.

What are your favourite Scottish bands?
The Jesus and Mary Chain, Khaya. 55's, Lowlife, Claude Speed, Desc, The Leg, Belle & Sebastian and Mogwai are good too.

What are your favourite Scottish venues?
Wee Red Bar, ECA. Sneaky Petes, Upstairs at the Old Forest.

T in the Park – Scotland at its finest or bam central?
It's a large national festival, sponsored at birth by the country's biggest brewery. It is what it is and it isn't for me. I know lots of people, many of whom music tastes I respect, love it. The whole festival idea chills me, camping, the toilets, that many people - shudder.

If you were tasked with creating a new Scottish anthem – would you select an existing one *(and if so, what one)* or what overlying lyrical theme would you take for a new anthem?
I would make an instrumental drone which built up to include instrumentation from every ethnic group in the country ending on 1967 minutes of white noise.

In your career, what's the biggest thing you look back on? What's the poorest thing or biggest regret?
It sounds banal, but the best was the songs, when they came together and they levitated above the ground. Also when the Church of John Coltrane got in touch with us, was very humbling. The biggest regret was real life swallowing up the conviction to take our ideas to their natural conclusion.

What is it about drummers that made them so difficult for you to hold on to one for a decent period of time?
I have often pondered this. I think that the drummers

psyche is beyond the ken of a mere mortal such as I. In essence they occupy the lowest hierarchy in a band, stuck at the back, have to carry all the gear, sweat through a gig; but at the same time their scarcity gives them a strange currency. However, much like after your 5th divorce, one must ponder whether oneself is perhaps partly to blame?

You've worked with Vettriano and Rankin – heroes of yours?
Yes. They are both self-made men of their own invention. The fact that once outsiders they are now within the walls that they once gazed through doesn't detract from that.

Any other Scottish heroes?
Bill Shankly, Jimmy Reid, Hopey from Love & Rockets was half Scottish too I believe.

You're East Coast – is the over-riding sense of nationalism the biggest element for you or do you indulge in the East Coast/West Coast rivalry? Can you do both – be patriotic but love internal rivalries?
We love Glasgow but they were always our rivals in a healthy, fraternal way.
To put this to the test – Reid Brothers -The Proclaimers or JAMC?
Jesus and Mary Chain! The Proclaimers were always something that I feared I would fall into in middle to old age – like liver spots, gold and casual sexism.

Is there a Glasgow bias for music? If so, is it deserved? Is it because Glasgow drives for it more?
The essence of it is Glasgow cares, Edinburgh doesn't. It is incredibly hard to build up and audience in Edinburgh, which means that after a while it doesn't really matter. No matter how great or how dismal you are it isn't really reflected in audience size, so you have a greater freedom, you never have an unconscious urge to play to an audience because there simply isn't one. However, I'm sure everyone

has the same gripe about their home town.

You get acts like Big Country or Rod Stewart who aren't 100% Scottish but are instantly recognised as being Scottish. Is this right?
Yeah. Of course, my sense of Scottishness, is that anyone is welcome. If you wanna pull on the shirt, ye can play for the team

Any Scottish bands you think will come through in the near future?
I think Young Fathers could be one of the most important bands to come out of Scotland probably ever. Law too who will be massive and deservedly so. Golden Teacher will get bigger and bigger. Vladimir, DeathCats, Wozniak, it's actually the best time for Scottish based music in years.

Any great Scottish bands time and people have missed?
Khaya, 55's Candy Store Prophets, Desc, lowlife.

Any unsung people in the Scottish music biz you think are deserving of praise or acknowledgment?
Gary from Bubblegum Records in Glasgow. Andy Wood, Dundee promoter / musician. Both love music with a pure and true devotion that shames us all.

Chris Reilly

If you are looking for someone to blame for this book, this guy has to take a sizable chunk of the criticism. While music is fairly easy to get into, having someone on hand to give you a head start makes it so much easier. Chris is my big brother and since I was *(not legally old)* enough to get into gigs, we have been going to see bands, something we still do this day.

Chris was also the bass player in a number of Glasgow bands in the 1990s, with the best known of the groups being Static.

What was the first gig you went to?

My first gig was back in July 1986 and it was The Smiths at The Barrowlands. It was the Panic tour, they did a short Scottish tour when the single came out, and that was a pretty good first gig to go to. After that, I went to quite a lot of gigs in a short period of time, probably quite a lot of dodgy bands in there as well, so The Smiths were definitely an excellent one to start with. After The Smiths, I saw bands like Big Country, Spear of Destiny and a lot of gigs at The Barrowlands, but I suppose I was 15 at the time!

What was the music scene like back then?

Being 15, it was all new to me. The Smiths were my favourite band at the time and it was just a period of having to find the music that I liked. I didn't have any big brothers so I took a lot from the NME, Melody Maker, Sounds, even Smash Hits had a few decent bands at the time. The Smiths and the Jesus & Mary Chain appeared in Smash Hits regularly.

I worked in a place that had the radio on all day and it was hellish. They would have Radio 1 on and it was a bonus if you heard something you liked. You'd be lucky to get one or two good songs during the day. At that point, even hearing something like The Mission or The Cult was a highlight! It was mainly Stock, Aitken and Waterman dross and Bros and other things that rhymed with that.

I had no control over the music but luckily after a few months, I was moved into a smaller office where I could listen to my own music. I'd have my tapes ready for every day in the office. The first 6 months to a year though, it was the radio and it was awful.

For TV, you had a few things. You had The Chart Show on Saturday morning and there was a two minute indie bit and you would get a thrill of seeing a 10 second clip of a song you liked. I'm not too sure when it started but certainly mid to late 80s. *(The show appeared on Channel 4 between 1986 and 1988 before switching to ITV, where it ran between 1989 and 1998.)* There wasn't a great deal on TV at the time. You had Top of The Pops, and there weren't many bands that I liked on that. You had The Tube, although was coming to the end of its run when I started to get into music. The Old Grey Whistle Test had ended and we were a good few years away from Later with Jools Holland, so I was probably caught in the middle of things.

There were things like The Oxford Road Show, which you'd want to watch occasionally but not all the time. A couple of years later you'd have Snub TV.

What sort of gig venues were you going to at this time?

When I was 15, I was only really going to the Barrowlands. This was partly down to the fact that it was a venue I knew I could get into but it was also down to the fact that this was the level of the bands that I wanted to see. I progressed to Fury Murrays and Student Unions, although that was a bit difficult at first because you had to get signed in. It wasn't really until I was 17 that I started getting in a bit more regularly. When I was 18, a couple of friends had started Uni so that became a lot simpler. Between 15 and 18, mainly just the Barrowlands and I went to the Playhouse in Edinburgh a couple of times.

In 1988, I went to a Festival called Fife Aid. *(This event was billed as Fife Aid 2, with the original event taking place in '86.)* This was a bit of a disaster to be honest as we went through to see the Sugarcubes and never got to see them because they turned up late and we were told that they would be appearing much later on, so we headed into St Andrews for some food and beer. When we got back into the site, we arrived in time to see them saying goodbye. The only act I seen at Fife Aid was the claymore swinging Jessie Rae, and his all new sound. He was bizarre and he was on the U-Sound label, which was a pretty cool label with a lot of great acts from Bristol. I don't even know if he was Scottish, it was a bit strange, maybe he's Rod Stewart's mate?

So that didn't put you off of music, you even played in a few bands with Static being the best known of them. Tell us about them.
It was 1991 before we played any gigs but we had been messing about for a couple of years before then. We never knew anybody in bands.

Was there no thriving music scene in Pollok?
There were a lot of bands...all flute bands. We used to go to rehearsal rooms a lot, the one we went to was called Tower Studios, at Charing Cross. One of the guys that worked in there was called Richie Dempsey, most bands in Glasgow will know Richie one way or another. He's drummed for half of the bands and he has done the sound for the other half. A great guy and really helpful for us when we were starting out. He gave us a lot of advice, got us a few gigs, he helped us set up for gigs as well. We never had a clue; we would turn up with our guitars and amps and then wonder what do we do?

Our first gig was at King Tuts, which was a good place to play your first gig but the promoter knew that we had loads of mates who would turn up for the gig, always keeping one eye on the takings, so that's why we were on the bill, supporting The Real People. Tam Coyle was the guy that booked us; he's been DJing in Glasgow for probably close to 50 years. By that point, King Tuts was not long opened and we then played Strathclyde Uni, Glasgow Tech, Cotton Club and we played in Nice N Sleazy's in its first few weeks. We played Edinburgh a few times, Aberdeen, Cowdenbeath and we made it down to London as well. We were close to getting signed but it didn't happen. There weren't many Glasgow bands getting signed at the times.

Any reason for that? Had all the Scottish bands of the 80s ruined it for the next generation?
We were an indie guitar band; we were around at the start of shoegazing.
Given that the three of you came from Pollok, the fact that you all owned shoes was quite an achievement.
That's why were shoegazers, we wanted to keep an eye on them. We had a wee bit of interest and out of nowhere after a few gigs, our demo tape seemed to do quite well. We were never the greatest live band and we used a drum machine, which puts some people off right from the start. It was good fun at the time. It was all pre-internet days, so it was harder to promote things, and it was pretty much dependent on word of mouth. We didn't get into the NME or any of the weeklies but we did get into a few magazines. There was a London based magazine that sent someone up for a feature and interview, they were positive about us. There was also M8, a Scottish magazine at the time, who were supportive. They gave us a few features and would also list any upcoming gigs we had. We did a few things with The List as well. It was a small pool though, unless you were actually going to gigs and seeing posters of upcoming gigs, it has hard to get your name around.

We were on Radio Scotland a few times, Beat Patrol but I'm not sure how big their listenership was. The best thing for us was playing with a band we liked or who had a similar sound. We always felt we'd have a chance of winning over an audience if we played something similar to the bands they were there to see, so we tried to go out and win over 200 people at a time, or at least a small percentage.

That worked to an extent and we got some excellent supports. We played with Teenage Fanclub, The Real People, Fatima Mansions and Levitation. That was Terry Bickers band after he left House of Love and we really liked them, so we were delighted to get that support slot. They were great with us, we played with them a few times but they were friendly and passed our demo tapes on to a few people. When they came back to Glasgow on their next tour, they asked us to support them again so that was a thrill to have someone you liked looking out for you like that.

We played with Y Cruff, who would go onto become Catatonia when they added Cerys Matthews to the band. We also played with the Milltown Brothers. Some of the Glasgow acts of the time we played with include AC Acoustics, Fenn and Thrum. Aye, it was a good time.

Anything you would have done differently?
It might have been better if I learned how to play my instrument before we started playing gigs, that might have helped. No regrets but we did manage to snatch defeat from the jaws of victory a few times. We had a really big gig lined up in London in front of a lot of magazines and music business people. Of course, we missed the sound check because we got lost.

On the way to the venue or in the venue?
On the way, it wasn't a Spinal Tap moment. It was a tiny venue so we couldn't have got lost in there. That didn't do us any favours because when we played the sound was awful. We were feeling a bit down before we started playing and our singer Gerry was fairly pissed off. I'm sure he sat down for one of the songs. However, a few days later through in Edinburgh at Potterrow we played one of our best gigs. If it had been the other way around, who knows what might have happened.

Not that I have any regrets from it though, we had a couple of great days in London. We had no money, we thought we were going to get paid for the gig, but we didn't get the money straight away, we had to send down receipts later, so we didn't really eat for 2 -3 days. We managed to get a few free beers here and there and I got to dance with Courtney Love at a club but all in all, it was a good trip and being in a band was brilliant.

What are your highlights from seeing bands live

over the years?
Some of the early T in the Parks were brilliant and I think The Smiths gig is still one of the best gigs I've ever seen. The shock of the volume, the adulation and the way that Morrissey controlled the crowd was amazing. I haven't seen many frontmen that powerful, this was at the time when The Smiths were at their peak with The Queen Is Dead just being released. The crowd was manic. Happy Mondays at the Hacienda was another great one, My Bloody Valentine at the Building and Printing were excellent. Actually, some of the Shamen shows at the Building and Printing were real events; this was before they became a comic book band. The Shamen were really pushing good music at the time.

I'd also say about 80% of the gigs I've seen at the Barrowlands have been brilliant.

Do you think the Barrowlands still has the same reputation?
There is a lot more competition for the Barras now; obviously you have ABC and the Academy at the same crowd level. It's not as if the Barrowlands has had to up their game because they have done zilch over the years. It still smells the same and looks the same. I know that if they did try to make changes a lot of folk would complain but they certainly haven't upped their game to match their new rivals.

One thing that has changed and I'm sure it has to do with the health and safety, is that if you get a sold out gig at the Barrowlands now, there is a lot more space than sold out Barrowlands gigs from years ago. Stuff like The Smiths and The Pogues were absolutely mobbed, a lot more so than modern gigs. I also don't remember them opening up the back door at the Barrowlands when I first started going. Maybe I didn't know about it but that's changed I suppose. It was always a nightmare getting down the stairs. I don't think I would like a lot more gigs at the Barrowlands these days because pretty much all the ones I do see are special.

I've been to some empty gigs in the Barrowlands as well. That Petrol Emotion played and the place was half-empty. There was also a Radiohead and Blur gig, for BBC Radio I think, that wasn't well advertised and I think it was put on at short notice, that had a really small crowd.

That was a great gig, Blur were just coming back with Modern Life Is Rubbish and Radiohead were just starting to get going. Both of the bands were great and I'd say there was less than 500 people at the gig.

What other Glasgow venues do you love?

Once I reached 18, things got a lot better. The QMU had some excellent gigs, as did Strathclyde Uni. Sonic Youth and Mudhoney played a great set. Dinosaur Jnr were meant to be on the bill as well but they pulled out. They played two nights, the Saturday and Sunday night. I've probably not been to a gig in Strathclyde Uni in 20 years but they used to put a lot of great gigs on. *(Since this interview, Chris had been back at Strathclyde Uni to see Kasule and Public Service Broadcasting play during Freshers Week.)* There was also a House of Love gig at the Tech, which was probably the loudest gig I have ever been at.

I think Nice And Sleazys has really came into its own in the past 10 years but the early years were very good, I saw some brilliant bands in there. There were also some great shows in the early days of King Tuts - Blur, The Charlatans, Levitation and The Boo Radleys were all brilliant in there, all great shows from bands on the rise.

If we're talking about gigs with a low turnout, Martin Carr, touring as BraveCaptain, in King Tuts must be one of the most poorly attended gigs we've seen?

Yeah, it's a sad thing when you've got someone you really respect and admire playing to a virtually empty venue. Maybe at times you're one step ahead of everybody else, or a few steps behind. Martin Carr is someone who really knows how to snatch defeat from the jaws of victory though, it's like he has an inbuilt ability to fuck things up.

What do you make of the average Scottish gig crowd and its reputation?

Well, I think there is one common thing that makes the difference and that's alcohol. It makes people more open, susceptible and up for it. Sometimes it's a great thing but at times, it can be a right pain and of course, there are other issues surrounding alcohol in this country. Sometimes you see bands that have people going wild for them when they're just average but its more about the night itself and seeing other people react, so the crowd goes mad.

That's my take on it. People love music all the world over and there's nothing really in Glasgow that means people like music more. There are a lot of people in Glasgow that like rubbish music but if you look hard enough, there's a lot of really good music and good people working in the industry.

One good thing about the reputation is that it ensures bands keep coming through here, which helps to sustain the image of Glasgow as a music city. If you had to put your finger on the aspect that makes Glasgow such an amazing place for bands to play, it is the city's relationship with alcohol, sadly...but it does make for some amazing gigs. There are also some amazing venues, which is something that Edinburgh doesn't really have. They have some excellent wee places but when it comes to venues of a good size for touring bands, it's badly lacking.

Through here, we've got plenty of great small to medium sized venues, although we were struggling for a larger venue. I had stopped going to the SECC because it was so poor, it was really hit and miss. There's nothing worse than paying £40 to £50 when the sound can ruin your night. The Hydro seems a lot better sound wise, even if it does seem a bit too big for me and my tastes. It's difficult to get the same feeling of excitement in a place like The Hydro that you would get from Sleazys.

What have been the biggest changes for you over the years?

There weren't a lot of small venues to see bands coming up or coming through. There are places like Broadcast and Stereo which offer up something new. You've also got the 13th Note, which is brilliant for Glasgow acts. It's probably at a level below Nice And Sleazys and King Tuts, but it's an important stepping stone to get to that level. I also really liked the Barfly, the old 13th Note Club, and I saw a lot of good gigs in there.

One of the things about some of these places in Glasgow is that it is the same people who have been running events and venues for years. I was talking about Tower Studios and that was owned by the guys that own Stereo and Mono, so they've been about in different guises and venues for years. Tam Coyle is still DJing, Paul Cardow, who does gigs in Broadcast, has been putting gigs on for years too. A lot has changed though, and there are more corporate elements involved, with T in the Park with Dance Factory moving on and of course the ABC and Academy brands.

I think T in the Park has got a lot more people into music. Obviously a lot of people first head along for the craic but I think there'll be people who maybe weren't too bothered about live music beforehand who develop a taste for it from there. It's maybe pushed music into the mainstream and the thought of going to gigs is a lot more open to everyone these days.

It's a natural progression. Say you were at T in the Park and you really liked a band, you would go seem them the next time they tour, say at the ABC or the Academy. In there, you'll see all the posters for upcoming gigs, including the smaller venues and you'll stumble into new bands and places from there. When I was 16 and going to see bands, I was insatiable for live music and I wanted to see as many acts as I possibly could, out 4 or 5 nights a week at times.

Also, the weather in Glasgow and Scotland isn't great so having the chance to do things indoors and meet people is a big part of life. However, when it comes to changes over the years, it's definitely been the venues.

Any ambitions left with music?
I want to keep going to see lots of bands but it is expensive. I know there are a lot of free gigs taking place, especially this summer, but for standard shows, even with local bands you're looking at a minimum of a tenner.

Stuart McHugh

So as not to lumber Chris with all the blame, it is only right to point the finger at the person who gave me my first big break in writing about music. After having bored my mates with gig reviews sent by email, I was politely invited to try and get them published somewhere else.

Having been a regular reader of the is this music? magazine, I decided this was as good a place as any to start. The next thing you know, Stuart responded, I was on board and I've been boring the general public ever since.

So Stu, how long have you been involved with the Scottish music scene?

Been listening to music and going to gigs since I was a kid so over 40 years ago, but not around the specifically Scottish scene until comparatively recently... there wasn't that much Scottish punk around *(not compared to indie bands nowadays for sure)* even though I saw the Skids early on, but I didn't see much around the Postcard etc revolution, maybe just a bit young and out-of-town to be a regular in city centre pubs in Glasgow. Would have first got 'involved' nearer to the 90s - actually swapping reviews *(and Peel tapes!)* etc with grungers in Seattle and offering a take on Britpop, which I hated as a rule, and as you might expect tending to cover the more ignored Scottish acts around at the time in the form of reviews and tips. That lead to me doing some reviews with a couple of magazines *(bigwig and BFM)* as well as compiling reviews on my own website at vacant which quickly formed a Scottish arm in Jockrock.

What have been the biggest changes you've noticed in this time?

Over the space of 25 or so years... the internet I guess. Got me into writing and then obviously hosting my own content as well as making contacts with people around the world. And ultimately it's led to the death of the music press *(pretty much)* and thousands of replacements in the form of websites and blogs -- there's no one place to read about music, no one opinion you can trust *(and no, I'm not going to count the NME there!)*. Radio is on the way out too, or at least *(if you exclude 6music, where would we be? etc)*. Indie-ish programming has got absorbed into the mainstream to an extent and stuff that would have been considered radical 20 years ago has been cleaned up and packaged by what remains of the majors to the playlist committees.

There's other more incidental changes but mostly related to technological progress-- promoting bands via the web etc of course, but also recording - it's so cheap, you can do an entire album at home, sell it online, no need to the majors, no need for bands to fret about getting 'signed' *(and 'signed;' and 'major' are meaningless terms anyway)*. And the fact there are college courses - bands are more 'professional' now, which can hide a lack of talent I suppose, but at least the majority of bands will engage with the audience rather than mumbling song titles between tunes... and they can play their instruments, which to be honest isn't something that I always approve of!

Overall, do you think the progress and changes have been for the better?

Obviously, 90%, it has been for the good. There are some foibles like music being harder to sell, plus cheap recording and promotion means that bands can almost immediately record and release rather than working their way through the toilet circuit *(as a non-musician maybe I should leave whether that's good or bad to the bands!)* But there are an awful lot of bands to get through, some good, some not so. It's better now as it's not all Oasis wannabes or indie landfill any more, though some, myself excluded, would argue that Biffy and FR clones aren't any better... personally I prefer my landfill that way!

What inspired you to get into music journalism?

More that I fell into it really - as I say I'd been doing rough reviews of stuff in Scotland for mainly US types, one or 2 wanted to start their own zines and I tidied up stuff I'd written *(did a Peel piece for Hubcap)*, same happened *(not sure how now!)* for Robots and Electronic Brains... I eventually gathered together some stuff and did a Jockrock zine, in spare time at work... a few mags started up at different times in Scotland, in lieu of having my own it seemed logical that I help out by giving them some reviews. I actually was doing software reviews, Macformat etc for extra cash, I eventually moved to a better job where I wasn't so desperate for cash, so I did more and more music writing instead.

What inspired you to take responsibility for a magazine / website etc?

It started from the zine really which was a compilation of stuff that had previously been on the web, in a backward kind of way. Though the first website *(vacant, then jockrock)* was also a compilation of stuff. It was, sort of, a project around a bit of software called Pagemilll that Adobe had taken on and I got 'assigned', seemed that I could use it as a test site but have something useful to populate it.

It was then I got made redundant and after trying to go it alone freelance - there wasn't enough money - and doing Vitaminic, The Fly, Chemikal Underground etc, I thought might as well fill in the gaps waiting for freelance work with doing an actual magazine. Though it was rather more work than I'd anticipated and there wasn't much time left to take freelance stuff anyway!

In your time you've been a writer, editor, gig promoter, gig photographer, DJ(?), anything I've missed out? Any role you haven't undertaken but would have liked to?

Er... marketing person kinda *(with The Fly and Vitaminic)* and manager *(co-manager actually which is maybe where both went wrong - with post rockers Pariah, and then for Cruiser - Faustian pact more than partnership, with Marc Almond's manager Stevo)*. Both, the latter particularly, were a lot of hassle and heartache for no return for the band never mind myself so 'never again'.

Kind of wanted to start a label - which I did in a sense

(very loosely!) with the cover CDs - but it's maybe less exciting / easier now, bands can do it themselves anyway - I'd have started one to release bands that I thought should have had records out, but it's easily done now!

Any people you admire/respect/look up to on the Scottish music scene?

Bands I guess for doing what they do, the Chemikal lot, for keeping going and making a success out of it. Apart from that I could spend all day naming names, everyone that's doing it for the right reasons and persevering with making and promoting music - on the indie level that's quite a lot of people!

What have been your best moments?

You mean apart from being first person in Scotland to interview Coldplay? I suppose there's obvious stuff like getting out that Franz piece - though we didn't know for sure at the time how big they'd be - but wee things now were big at the time, getting the first mag off the press, etc. Can still remember the excitement of getting an ansafone message from Steven Pastel agreeing to go on my radio show at SubCity- I suppose I'm a bit blase about that kinda thing now - but bands tend to be pretty approachable, especially ones that are part of the 'scene' locally.

Do you have a favourite Scottish act or time of music?

Like 'favourite album of all time' for many people, it'd change dependent on mood, time of the year, whatever. Scottish music's heyday was maybe the early-ish Chemikal time *(Peloton era),* but there's always something good round the corner. Like trying to pick a favourite child or something.

Have any times made you feel as though it was time to give up?

Probably around halfway through this set of questions! Ach, I am unlikely to give up on music completely and I'd imagine I will still write about it when inspired. I have probably got into a kind of either rut or groove *(depending on how much fun it is at the time)* as I am constantly churning out the Jockrock news as well as putting up reviews, sorting out writer passes etc, and if I want to do something like actually go and see a show then I get way behind. I gave up the mag of course as it physically wasn't possible to (1) advance it further and (2) afford to eat. The day job is preventing me doing what I'd like to do with Jockrock in particular but of course it could never pay for itself anyway, so I'd imagine that it may peter out at some point - if I have to stop longer than, say, a fortnight's holiday, then it'd be fairly possible to get it going again.

Was there a band you felt were destined to make it to the big time and missed out?
Oh, just one or two! I suppose there is a difference between bands who I think should have been bigger and those who are actually a bafflement in their lack of success. A few were ahead of their time perhaps - the two I managed... Pariah I'm sure must have predated Sigur Ros, while Cruiser were... just amazing, uncategorisable *(maybe that was the problem!)*
Honourable mentions go to Odeon Beat Club, Josephine, Won Mississippi *(yeah, I know not even Scots!)* - I could go on...

Was there a band that made it to the big time and you are still left wondering why?
You can usually see reasons for bands making it big - whether they've jumped on a bandwagon and timed it well, or had good management or press backing, or there's a grudging acknowledgement that they have tunes or some sort of 'charisma' ,or just come to the forefront and filled some sort of gap in the market. Oasis then! Scottish bands... one or 2 that got signed and it was clear that they were just in the latter category i.e. someone with a bit of cash thought they could be the Scottish Oasis. A few of these had some minor success but never lasted.

How do you feel about the range of festivals on offer

in Scotland?

It's not bad now. T used to be ok when it was in Hamilton and for a few years at Balado but I'm now happy enough missing it as there are the likes of Wicker and Doune. T and fests like that are too large for me, I got sick of only seeing half a set as I had a 20 minute walk to the tent across the way, you don't get that at the smaller fests I mentioned, again, early T was fine as there was no real 'travel' time between stages). But I'm the wrong person to talk to, as I am very jaded with larger live shows in general - sound's often average to poor, sightlines for big stages are rubbish, wind, people chatting around you, short festival-sized sets... give me a show at the Note any day!

Oh and I miss the likes of Indian Summer. Still haven't forgiven DF for Connect! Get Off My Pavement was pretty good as well, if you can actually call it a festival in the Buckied-up neds fighting in the mud sense.

Do you feel TITP is more about the music or the excuse to party?

er... yup, party! It always was perhaps but surely more so now. Which is odd as they now have so many bands on - headliners are just same old same old of course but there must be a dozen stages with what looks like every indie band in the UK with a good agent. If I did decide to go I'd probably be able to strike off a lot from my must-see list as indie landfill *(in my eyes/ears)* but Zane Lowe listeners or whatever must be like me in the early days, completely spoiled for choice.

Scottish crowds have a reputation of being "more up for it". Is this a good thing or a bad thing?

Good in that the country has this great reputation from bands the world over, which means that they are perhaps more likely to tour etc. Bad for me *(again!)* in that there will be a lot of singing and chanting which at best will drown the band out. Not that you get that at the Note ;-)

Is the reputation more about alcohol as opposed to

love of entertainment?
I have seen pretty sober crowds just as up for it as those at T or Bellahouston or wherever. Though I'm sure a bit of lubrication does move things on a bit!

Glasgow gets most of the praise/acknowledgment for gigs, music scenes, crowds etc. Is this justified?
Aye *(said the Glaswegian)*. Just this week, end of May 2014, there's been a lot of chat about Embra and its lack of venues, I think there were hopes the council would step in and build a Hydro-style venue. Edinburgh is the only city big enough to challenge, and there are reasons why it hasn't - more non-natives living there, so a more transient population, especially students, more 'genteel' perhaps, a lack of tradition or continuity... this latter one is definitely the city's problem, I can't think of any venues that have remained consistent or steady for more than a few years *(Queen's Hall and Bannermans excepted)*. Bands form around venues of course and there's no Note or Sleazy's where musicians congregate. a few venues have been turned into yuppie flats of course, and there have been several mysterious fires which have seen to others - I can make you a list as long as my arm!

All this is very unfortunate for the musicians of Edinburgh of course. Though although the other towns and cities are too small to compare *(Dundee has always had a scene and I guess Aberdeen has at least promoter, shop and zine-wise)* they have had similar lack of consistency on venues *(again, can't think of many venues in either city that have been putting on shows as long as Sleazys etc)*.

Are there parts of Scotland you feel don't get the recognition they deserve for music?
I'm not sure what you need to do to get acknowledgement. Fife is recognised as being a real hub of fairly successful musicians, but Dundee and Aberdeen, less so recognised. I think that Dundee perhaps most of all, but unless you produce a world-sized band *(SnowPatrol aside)* people may not think of the city in those terms. Also, say Lanarkshire, is kind of recognised in a way but also as it's absorbed into

Glasgow *(the Mary Chain having a 'G' postcode)* it may be overlooked.

Is there enough support, encouragement or opportunities for bands and acts in Scotland?

Not speaking as a band member it's hard but also coming from a more objective angle... the Arts Council were always very encouraging to itm?, I have to say that first of all! Some will complain that some bands get funding to record while others don't and it can be as much about form-filing as talent, but I'd say that support is pretty good. It'll never be enough, of course!

Is there enough mainstream media support for Scottish acts? Does it matter as much with the internet?

Music in general is getting less and less coverage in the papers. I find that the internet is really disparate and papers act as a focal point and also a place where there's a captive audience -i.e. your dad might come across a mention of Fat Goth in a paper, he might not pay any attention but someone with a passing interest in music - Coldplay fan, say - would perhaps pick up on them. Whereas they are unlikely to see a Fat Goth piece on Facebook, unless a friend with unusually diverse taste in music pointed them to it or if they happen to read blogs - not even sure NME or NME.com act as a metafilter anymore.

Same may go for podcasts etc, there are just so many that can never hope to cover everything. 6music is the equivalent, I'm not keen on the idea that they are being our arbiters, and they are still governed by PR companies and pluggers, but they do gather together a good mix that will break some new stuff.

Are you a believer in national characteristics or elements? If so, do you think that there is a "Scottish trait" running through acts or genres?

Ginger hair is a proven fact. Which is odd as I can't think of many ginger musicians *(Lulu aside)*. Not sure it's in the genes but the alt.folk thing definitely is coming from tradition.

Are there any acts you would characterise as being typically Scottish?

Tricky one. I do like the fact that bands aren't afraid to use their own accents any more *(god knows what was going on in the 80s)* but there are now an awful lot of strongly-accented singers around, all much broader than their speaking voices. I am probably supposed to buck the trend here, but the Proclaimers and Aidan Moffat - well, a no-brainer really. And King Creosote and chums - any bands coming from that folk thing -See also Dumb Instrument, Mouse Eat Mouse, Runrig... We did have a spate of bands who we'd have been able to class as sounding Scottish a while back, but they were all post rock, so probably anyone form Chicago might have disagreed *(especially if they did a non-instrumental!)*.

Would you be more interested in a Scottish band as opposed to a similar style of band from a different country?

Only in that I will have a vested interest of sorts i.e. checking them out for review or airplay or whatever, even the fact that I'd be more likely to catch them live if I liked them. Actually, I suppose that answer is a resounding 'yes', though I'd not favour them, which is what crossed my mind. More likely to give them constructive criticism perhaps!

Do you think there are any genres or musical styles that Scotland does best?

The obvious ones I suppose, jangly art-pop, post-rock, alt.folk... there's not a massive punk or metal heritage, there's not bands in these kind of numbers that the first three genres have. Though plenty of rubbish metal bands at school etc, maybe they evolve into grunge or noise rock or whatever, you occasionally see 'cooler' musicians in GnR Ts.

What's your favourite venues in Scotland?

The Note's maybe my top venue *(just checking here I have namechecked it more than once...).* Sleazy's, Henry's, Stereo *(for various reasons).* The ABC (1) for bigger shows. Glad Cafe's good. Armadillo *(great sound)* and now the Hydro *(just for not being the SECC)* for *really* big shows!

Any venues no longer with us that you really miss?

Ach, loads. Mainly in Edinburgh! Cas Rock, The Venue, the Attic, I was living through there in their heyday. Picturehouse was ok - good for the scene there, so clearly it had to go! I can't prove that there's someone who either hates rock music or is from Glasgow behind the amazing string of closures, but the evidence is all there. Doghouse, Starka,.

Any venue that you just can't take to? (Mine is the Oran Mor)

Mine as well ! Well, that and the ABC2 -awful room shape, the Academy -just a big barn, SECC -bigger barn, Arches - bad sound so often... I'm very particular about seeing/hearing music in a good environment, but when it comes down to it, if it's not in a 3/4-filled Note with an attentive and enthusiastic audience - this applies as much to Nick Cave and Flaming Lips shows as it does Frightened Rabbit or Odeon Beat Club - then I'm going to find fault with it!

Turmoil and big events often inspire artists. Do you expect a lot of music/work to come from the referendum?

Not sure if you mean in the run-in or afterwards, I guess both really. I'm not expecting that many bands, even the ones that have nailed their colours to the mast, to produce anything that could be described as 'rabble rousing' or 'standard bearing' or whatever - should we expect 'Yes' bands to write an anthemic song, or heartfelt prose? I'm not sure why, I'm just not expecting any of those bands to go that far, though some of the acute old school folkies might, as their work is maybe more narrative. I suspect that if it's a 'No' then there could be a few wrought funereal pieces emerging though...

Should the opinion of musicians/artists matter in the run up to the referendum election?

It's a hard one - of course you shouldn't be paying attention to someone on the basis of their 'celebrity' or we'd all be taking advice from Joey Essex or Susan Boyle. But it is very tempting to listen to what's said and twist it to one's own ends!

As Billy Bragg said vote yes and David Bowie was perceived to say vote no, is one more relevant than the other?

Well, Billy has been involved with politics much more so... ah, no, that is the obvious path to take especially from the Yes' side. Though he is a lifelong socialist and Labour man, so that fact *(rather than his status as a 'pop star')* is of some interest I'm sure. Bowie... well, he's hardly the man on the street, but his view came across as that, someone who knows the Scots and cares about them. Doesn't matter that he's a megastar, or one who's had very dodgy political views in the past...

Do you think the outcome of the vote will have an impact on the Scottish music scene?

Again, many ways to interpret the question... if "will independence have an impact?" then of course, finances will change, Scotland will be more of a nation in the eyes of the world, markets will be different for musicians even if the web etc has meant changes will be more limited than they might have been in '78... I think for the nation, if it goes 'No' then that'll be that, independence will be dead, and any sense of national pride may evaporate. I'm not saying that bands will stop singing in their own accents, but it could kind of go that way. Very hard to trumpet about the Scottish nation, whether it's Scottish Week in NYC or a Saltire sticker on a Mogwai guitar, if a majority say that we're not actually a nation.

What are your hopes for the Scottish music scenes in the years to come?

Well, it's been pretty good these past 10, 20, years - if it was good at the grass roots in the 60s and early 70s with folk *(I'd not really know)* I think it must have had some kind of hiatus around punk time. Predictable answer - I'd like to see it going from strength to strength. And I'd like to see it focused on more - the reason I started itm? was that I felt so many bands were getting ignored by the London-based press - turning this towards the indie / indy debate again! Quite how the scene is 'marketed' or represented after a Yes vote I'm not sure, the world is becoming smaller and more connected, so it might be up to Scottish-based *(web-based)* publications gaining a worldwide presence - we can't rely on NME.com or drownedinsound or whatever as they will have their own favourites and, in the case of the UK, 10 times as many bands by population, which pales into insignificance when you look at the US. I'd love to run a website full-time that gathered *all* the news, reviewed all the music, and I'm surprised that no-one has found the time and money to give it a go - the likes of Bellacaledonia, wingsoverscotland are doing it for the arts, politics etc, but nothing related to music, perhaps because these are politically-driven there's more of a 'cause'. Maybe independence will act as the catalyst for something that can remain in place long-term and like the scenes themselves, continue to expand throughout the world.

Campfires In Winter

As there are so many up and coming bands in Scotland, it would be impossible to see or hear them all. The thing is though, once you see a band's name a few times but don't get around to checking them out, you may actually subconsciously feel as though you have checked them out but didn't really like them.

Somewhere in the first half of 2014 I think it dawned on me that this was the situation I was in with Campfires In Winter, and I decided to rectify that over the summer. I'm pretty glad I did because the band are excellent live and I'm hopeful that an album due for release in 2015 will bring the band to a wider audience.

I caught up with Boab from the band in the build-up to the group's Christmas gig in Glasgow.

How has 2014 been for Campfires In Winter?
It's been grand. We've played some great venues and festivals and we're just about to start recording our debut album.

Any particular highlights from the year, or any moments you would prefer to never live through again?
Headlining Tut's in January for the first time was pretty special, as was the reception to our festival slots and the We'll Exist single in July. As for moments I'd never want to live through again, Denny and Wullie's chat from the backseat on the way to Liverpool Sound City was a real low point. Another low point was sitting in an Aldi car park eating a pork pie for breakfast one morning after a heavy night in Inverness.

According to some online sources – which shouldn't always be trusted – it seems as though 2014 is the band's 10th year anniversary. Does it feel like 10 years since you started?
Nope, it genuinely feels like we just got together a couple of

years ago, like we're still wee boys. We've been together in one form or another since 2004, when we were at school. We became Campfires at the end of 2009, and Denny replaced our old drummer in 2011 but that's the only lineup change we've had. I suppose that's when we probably started taking the whole band thing seriously.

You've played a good few festivals over the years, any highlights or great moments?

I think we've had a great time at every festival we've played. Sound City in Liverpool was pretty special. It was our first time in England and we were expecting an empty venue but actually ended up really busy. I always love the Inverness gigs too, as we've got some good pals up there, and we always get a good crowd. So getting to play both Brew at the Bog and Belladrum this year was fantastic. Plus, we got to see Tom Jones.

You have a big Christmas special show to round the year off in style, would you say that you have all been good boys this year?

We're always very good boys. Always. ;-)

Tell me more about the Christmas special:

It's on 17th December in the pretty spectacular setting of Sloan's Ballroom, Glasgow's oldest bar. As well as ourselves, we'll have Deathcats and Friends in America playing, two of my favourite bands in Glasgow just now. There shall be Christmas songs, and a guest or two join us on-stage. We'll also have various other wee things going on around the hall It's going to a proper Christmassy affair, with jumpers and mince pies and stuff.

What's better – Christmas or New Year?

Christmas. I'm not really into New Year all that much. It's okay and I do normally do something to celebrate it but I just enjoy Christmas is just far more.

The video for the We'll Exist single featured Daniela

Nardini – how did that come about?

Just down to pure chance, really. We met with Richard, the director, and he was really interested in working with us. He liked the song and thought his friend who was an actor might be interested in playing the lead. Turned out his friend was Daniela and luckily she was into the song as well.

2015 looks set to be a big year for the band, tell us what you have planned?

We'll have load of shows, hopefully a tour (or two) and a few releases, including our debut album in the autumn. And hopefully some more festival appearances!

Any bands or songs that have come to your attention this year?

Well, two that stick out for me locally are the bands we have supporting at Sloan's, Friends in America and Deathcats. I've been into Deathcats for a long time now but hadn't really heard much by FIA until they released their new single in the summer. Have loved them since. Prehistoric Friends are another, their single Bermuda Triangle was one of my favourites of the year. And Call to Mind also released a phenomenal album. Then there's the new So Many Animal Calls EP out on the Bloc+ label. And the Cutty's Gym EP from the same label. That's only a handful, but local music has been fantastic this year. I've missed so much out here.

What do you want to achieve in the year(s) ahead?

I'd like to release numerous albums and tour Europe and hopefully even further afield. Ideally, I'd like to make a comfortable living doing this. If it doesn't work out like that, then we can always look back and go "well, we had a great time, didn't we?"

Richie Dempsey

One of the things about the Scottish music scene is that you can walk into any bar or venue and there is a good chance you will recognize a face. If you have spent any time in Glasgow venues or watching bands, there is a good chance you will recognize the face of Richie Dempsey.

Richie has spent a lifetime in the Scottish music scene and I caught up with him to hear about his work as a sound engineer and all of the activities he has enjoyed over the years. Of course, if you were to ask if Richie was the sound guy, the response would normally be "well, he's alright..." but given the amount of assistance he has provided to bands and artists over the years, Richie is clearly the sound guy in more ways than one.

Chris Reilly, just one of the Scottish artists who was helped by Richie over the years, also joined us for the interview and Chris' comments will be in italics.

You're a familiar face in the Glasgow music scene but how many roles have you had Richie?
Taking it right back with respect to jobs, I was working in a record store but even before then, I had been in a few bands like Stretchheads. The record store job was great as it helped me to develop a lot of contacts but then I got fired on the 20th of January 1990. It was the day Partick Thistle got beat 6-2 from Aberdeen in the Scottish Cup. I got sacked at half past four. I was annoyed because if they sacked me at half past two, I'd have made it in time for the game!
After that my next role was at Tower Studios where I was engineering, although it was studio engineering. I worked there and then the studio relocated to where The Flying Duck is now and it was renamed Shelter and then we changed it to the Apollo. It was a really good place, it had three rehearsal rooms, a bar/venue and we built a recording studio in it. So I ended up doing live sound in there. When I was doing recording sessions with bands a few of them asked me would I come and do live sound for them. The two things are totally different and it was horrible when I realised that doing live

sound was not what I wanted to do.

So I binned that...apart from doing it for most of my life!

You were also a caretaker.

Oh aye, I was a caretaker, the rock n roll jannie at the 13th Note. So I was still in bands, I was doing a lot of engineering, working in a venue and I did a fair bit of promotion. I worked with John Williamson where we ran a record label, Sano Music and events like the 10 Day Weekend.

The 10 Day weekend was great, it was Arab Strap's first gig and one of Mogwai's first gigs and a few things at King Tuts. I've also did a bit of tour managing when I've been on the road, so I have did a lot of roles, all while allegedly having a very good time. I've did everything in the music business apart from be successful.

You also did the lights for us at one point.

Oh aye, so I did. I did the lights for you guys (Static) and Napalm Death! I went to see Napalm Death at King Tuts one night and I knew the guy that was doing the sound as they didn't have their own sound guy with them. So there's me, four pints in, asking this guy if I can do the lights and he let me have a go. It really hurt my hands; I thought if I continue with this I'm going to end up with arthritis so my lighting career didn't last too long.

What sort of bands have you worked with and where has it taken you?
Kinda everywhere. It's been good. I've not been to Africa or Russia, but I'm not bothered about that. I've actually had a great time of late, in the past year I've been working with Of Monsters and Men, an Icelandic band and they were doing massive shows, so that was great fun. It was really educational as well.

About 15 – 16 years ago I was doing sound in the 13th Note with like 5 mics and 4 cables and a DI box. None of them worked that well but you had to make it work. I was then on the road with Idlewild and my first gig with them was at a festival in front of 40,000 people and my first thought was how the fuck do you make this work?! It was a fast learning curve but it was great and I got to see a lot more of the world. It was good playing in these big venues but you found you always kept doing small venues every so often so you had to keep in mind how you do they gigs. There were in-store shows, small tours and private parties, so even though I've worked with some big bands, you never totally move away from the small shows you first did. A small gig is harder than a big one, I find.

Idlewild gave me the opportunity to get on tour and I'll always be internally grateful to them. I've been doing sound for them for around 12 years and that's been great . I've worked with Teenage Fanclub and Oceanzise, who may be the best group I've worked for, it's like mixing Genesis, pure prog rock, well, it's like Genesis without that Phil Collins guy. Who else? The Delgados and Bis, I also got some managerial experience with Bis a long time ago, at the time of the Top of the Pops stuff. Paradise Lost as well, tons of bands.

Do different genres impact on your job?

You get people that stick to the same sound of music, there are some metal guys that only do metal and they are really good at it. I think it's good to do different bands. I'll go back to the word educational and seeing how people work in a live situation is really interesting. Of Monsters And Men are great on record and live. There are so many of them and they're all doing tons of stuff, but it's all there for a purpose and it's brilliant to mix. Them and Oceansize have been brilliant to work with.

There's a girl I do sound for called Emily Smith from the Borders and she's a bit folky and it's pretty much setting a balance for her. So that's really different but is enjoyable and brilliant in its own way. The better the band, the easier it is for a sound guy.

You play a big part in people having a great night; do you feel like it's a lot of pressure?

It is but it depends on a number of things. If I'm comfortable with the band and the music then aye, it can be okay but you do feel the pressure at times. The first couple of gigs with a new band you are trying to make sure you make the gig sound as much like the record as possible because that's what most people are there to hear.

I've probably given myself a hard time because I want it to be brilliant and I know when I go to gigs I want things to sound great. The thing is though, you hear people moaning about certain elements when it's not even three bars in to the gig and you think give the guy a break. When you sound check, you're in a big empty room and then when it fills up, it's a different environment.

I love my job, its good fun and it gets less nerve-racking when you get more confident. I'm only human, I do fuck up and there may be people saying this guy's shite I've heard him before! It's a thankless task because when you walk into a gig, everyone is a sound engineer because they all have an opinion on what they want to hear.

Has it affected how you go to gigs?
Very much so. The downside is, although its maybe my age as well, I used to go see bands all the time. I enjoy going to gigs but it has to be bands that I really want to see. I'm no longer into the idea of heading along to Nice N Sleazys and then saying; c'mon we'll go downstairs and see who is on. When I was younger, I'd do that but I've not got the patience for that anymore.

Also, I need to protect my hearing and you could walk into any gig like that and the sound is just like (Richie makes a gargled static noise and moves his hands to and from his ears), so it's like nah, I'm not doing this.

What are your best and worst venues?
Probably the worst I've done sound in is The Aragon Ballroom in Chicago. It's fucking horrible. It looks amazing, it's huge, it holds 5,000 people and the ceiling is full of stars. There are royal boxes and balconies around it but the sound is awful.

The guys that work in there know it and they tell you straight from the off that the sound is shite. Even from the start I asked for some tips and the guy just laughed. I said, so you think I'm fucked already and he replied, pal, I know you're fucked already!

I think the ABC in Glasgow is a great venue and The Barrowlands as well of course. I don't think there's any need for me to be negative about of the venues in Scotland because they are all pretty good or you can tell that they're trying to make sure there is as good a sound as possible.

The Lemon Tree in Aberdeen was painfully underused but it was very well spec'd. Great monitors, great PA, good sound on stage and it sounded really nice. I can't argue against King Tuts and that venue is one where even if I felt the sound was a bit shite, people will say that they loved it. And that is important for a sound engineer. It's not about you, it's about the band and it's about the people paying their money to come along and see the show. Even if you're having a bad day or you think the sound is shite, you need to make sure it works for the band and the audience.

What about Edinburgh venues?

Edinburgh has fuck all man, there are no venues. Haha, Edinburgh has fuck all, there's the title of the book. It's a real shame because I love Edinburgh and it's such a nice place but it doesn't have a lot going for it musically. Try to think of bands that come from Edinburgh – The Fire Engines, and all the bands that came from them, Josef K, Idlewild, The Scars – its not a lot.

Do you have any advice for aspiring sound engineers?

Yeah, don't start! Learn a trade, become a plumber or an electrician!

I didn't study to become a sound engineer and a large part of me wishes that I had and if you get the chance to study it, definitely think about it. However, a big part of the fun for me is that I'm learning every day, which means I'm always being challenged. It's not all about how loud it is, it should be about how clear the sound is but of course, it's all about the band as well.

If you want it enough, you have to work hard. Obviously with the music industry who you know makes a difference but if you are willing to put the work in, you can get on. Ask around at wee venues or form a band or work with a band and take it from there. Be prepared to get absolute pelters from people and websites/magazines will slate the sound. Even if it doesn't mention the sound, it doesn't mean it's bad, in fact, if they don't mention the sound, you're doing alright. You need to be prepared for some hard knocks. I don't want to sound wanky about it but it is an artistic thing, you're helping to create the sound and it's your impression of what the sound should sound like.

When you're doing it for a gig, if I'm trying to please 5,000 or 20,000 people, it's tough and you'll never please everyone but you need to work towards making it a good night for everyone.

I suppose you hold the power to shape the night?

There was one time I came off an Idlewild tour straight onto an Oceansize tour and I met them in Germany. They said, we're doing these new songs from the second album that I hadn't heard by the time and they were great, so I was having a great time mixing them. About four or five nights into the tour, they asked me if I wanted to hear the album, and I did, and I was relieved because I did get what they were going for. There was another one, Clap Your Hands And Say Yeah and I thought it sounded great but then I heard the record and thought I've been doing this all wrong. Mind you, they seemed to like it and no one seemed to moan but if I'd heard the record first, I'd have mixed it differently.

It's good to get a bit of background about what a band does but sometimes you don't get the opportunity and you just have to go for it. After the event, it's good to go back and check the point of reference and see how you did. Sometimes I've been spot on, at other times I've been way off. Sometimes, depending on the band and what they want, that can be alright.

Sound engineers are really important for bands. I'd say for new bands starting up, if you get on well with the sound guy, they'll look after you. When we were starting out we were playing with this well-known band, the guy used to be in Primal Scream – Spirea X – and we weren't getting on with him, but nobody was and the sound guy never liked him either. We were second on the bill and because the sound engineer liked us and not him, we were twice as loud as the headliner.

That's totally true. You've got to remember that the sound guy is working with bands all the time and if a band pisses him or her off, they're putting themselves in trouble that night. If you get on with the sound engineer, you're far more likely to get what you need, obviously within reason, but the sound engineer has this power.

When you go on tour or doing a show with a band, you need to look at yourself as not just a sound guy, you're another member of the band. You need to be as good as them. If a band is having the gig of their life and it sounds like it's underwater or like there's pillows in front of the speakers there's no point. So you feel part of the team on tour. I don't mind working on my own, but I like throwing ideas around and working together. Also, don't drink before a gig. Your hearing changes because the top end starts to drop down a bit. If you hear loads of high end, check the amount of drink on stage next to a band. It's not all the time but it's happened more than enough.

There was one gig in America when we weren't supposed to be playing because the singer wasn't well so we had a day off. We all had a few drinks and then decided to head along and see the support band play and when we got there, the promoter talked us into doing a mini set, so of course, I'm a good few drinks down the line and I thought, I'm not right to do this because I can't hear it properly. Some guys can do it, and I won't knock them but for me personally, I can't do it.

Has there been any cross-over between your band

work and engineering work?

The bands I've been in were a very big influence on what I've ended up doing. One night I was in the rehearsal rooms at Tower with a band and I thought, how brilliant would it be to work here. So I asked if they had any jobs going and the guy said no, but if I had spare time I could come in on my time off and see how it works.

So one Saturday I went along and did a session and thought it was brilliant and from there that would then impact back on my bands, thinking about how I could make the sound better? Turns out we couldn't and we split!

To be fair, when I was in Fenn, it had an impact because we were able to jump ahead of the queue and use the studio when no one else was using it. As I worked there, and had access to it, we didn't need to save up to £300 to record a demo or record so that allowed us to get ahead.

I did the DeSalvo album there as well but with that, I just did the drums and left the engineering to other people, so I acted like a drummer, hanging about and annoying people! I enjoyed that because I didn't have to do as much, compared to everything else where I was hands on, in fact, really hands on so it was great to let other people do that line of work.

I don't have a choice, I can't do anything else. I'm a drummer and a sound guy but I don't get to drum as much as I would like. I'd say I'm a better drummer than a sound guy but hey, I'm making a living out of it and having a great time. There was a spell about 15 years ago where I may have started a cleaning career. Can you imagine that? Cleaning houses dressed up as Hong Kong Phooey? Nah, this has been great for me over the years!

Do you have any major musical ambitions left?

Nah, I'm happy with what I've done. I get a wee twinge of regret at times when you see other people who are getting success and you think why did I not get that but then you think, nah, I did alright and don't be the bitter guy because the bitter guy is the bad guy of any story.

You had a record out, you played some brilliant venues,

played with some good bands, worked with some great musicians and millions would kill to do what you do...

Aye, I wake up some morning and think what the hell is going on. You know, I wake up thinking; I've got to go to Spain or Australia today, it's alright.

One time a few years back, I was working at the Camden Crawl and it was mental, I had four different gigs going on so it was hectic and you're thinking, this is a bit rubbish. Then, you give it a minute and you think, I'm currently standing outside the Dublin Castle in the sunshine having a drink and my phone goes, it was my girlfriend at the time, who is now my wife, and she was phoning to say she was having a shit day in the camera shop she was working in and this customer was this and this customer was that and then I think, wow. It's so much fun. You get good days and bad days, like any job, but really, I've no regrets and I've had so many amazing times.

When I did my first record, I thought, this was all I wanted to do. When you get your first piece of vinyl, it's a hell of a feeling. I remember our bass player phoned me saying he bought a brilliant record that I had to hear. So he came round and put it on and I was like, that's us. The test presses had arrived and I was like, I don't even need to hear it, I just want to see it! So that was a brilliant day itself, one of the best.

I, or we, maybe never took it far enough to reap the benefits but funnily enough, when I was in a band, I hated touring. Obviously my work as a sound engineer has taken me all over the world but when I was making music, the touring side never appealed to me. Obviously then I was younger and I liked being at home, going to the games and hanging out with my mates or my girlfriend. Now I'm older, it's what you have to do and nowadays, I'm away for a much longer stretch than what I would have been in a band. That makes it sounds as though I'm going to jail, I'm not, I definitely tour with bands. I'm going to rock Jail.

Rock n Roll Jail. The film the Ramones never made.
It's a shame about The Ramones. You get The Stones still

rolling on, apart from the guy that died lifetimes ago, but The Ramones are gone. I mean Tony Bennett is still alive and Joey Ramone isn't.

There is no God!

Haha, no, sorry, I didn't mean it like that, Tony Bennett's alright, I'd go see him these days.

What are the biggest changes in the Scottish industry since you've been working?

When we were in bands at the start, there was no money. When I joined Fenn, there was money kicking about. EastWest gave us money to make a demo and there were companies throwing money at bands in Scotland for a short while.

Even when I worked with Bis there was a bidding war with some stupid offers and I think that some bands, who I won't mention, did get a lot of money and shat it right up the wall. They went to fancy places to record their album with the attitude that the record company was paying for it, and of course, the band was paying for it eventually. It wasn't quite Duran Duran and Rio stuff, but some bands were going to places they didn't need to and they wasted the money they got. There was money on hotels and flights and it all added up to what the label had to recoup and if the record didn't sell, bands were fucked.

One thing I've changed, see when we used to go to the Barrowlands ages ago, it used to be a really big band. Nowadays, it's still a special venue but it seems to be a lot less special with respect to who plays there. I remember bands would have to be a level of say Ride or the Sugarcubes to get a gig at the Barras but nowadays it seems open to a lot of lower bands.

I think more people go to gigs, there is more exposure of live music, gigs and festivals, especially with the coverage of Glastonbury on TV and media coverage of big shows. It means you get some pretty average bands starting out at say the Garage level, which means that the bands who are capable of filling the Barras no longer have to be that special or brilliant. As a venue, it's still magical but I think more folk go to gigs and that means you get acts of a style or quality playing there that wouldn't have done years ago.

I go away for six months and the Glasgow music scene is completely different. I don't recognise any of the names of the bands that are playing.

It's the same guys; they're just playing a slightly different style with a new name.

And the same skinny ties! That's probably a really good point as there is a lot more music on TV but it's the sort of music I hate.

A few years back I was doing Roskilde and after the work I was doing, I went back to the hotel and was just channel surfing. They were showing a Slayer gig! I think it was part of the Big Four stuff, (Slayer, Megadeth, Anthrax and Metallica) It was live on TV in Denmark and the week before in Britain, we got Glastonbury and the BBC gave us all the shit of the day.

You need to go red button or online to get the decent stuff.

The only band I've seen on TV that made me sit up was Elbow. That guy is about the same age as me, ginger and portly and he was alright. Up until this point it was Nikki Minaj and Tinie Tempah, it was all nonsense and this just seemed quite different, that was alright.

The guy that runs Radio 1 should be a guy who was in a band or who worked in the industry, not some guy with a background that put him in with the right place. The sort of guy that has been to Glastonbury three times and is yet to take acid!

To be fair, BBC Alba is showing some interesting stuff.

That's true, I saw Holy Mountain on it once

They have a show called Rapal, which is a wee bit like the Alba version of Jools Holland.

Do they have a guy that gives you the boogie woogie. Can you imagine a guy playing boogie woogie piano in front of Holy Mountain? Brilliant.

Last week they showed Casual Sex (which led to the obligatory discussion of how better Alba's viewing figures would be if they did show casual sex regularly).

They're a fantastic band, one of the few good bands that I've heard of late, they sound very "then" but aye, they're magic.

I like the fact that in France, there is a regulation that French radio stations have to play a certain amount of French bands in their playlist. I know over here you have Janice Forsyth who really play a lot of new Scottish bands but if you come across any of the other channels, say Clyde, it's awful. I mean, I can't even think who these stations or DJs would play.

Clyde would play you Calvin Harris, Emile Sande and probably invoke the three foreigners rule and claim Snow Patrol.

When we started, there was Beat Patrol and John Peel. There was no outlet for indie bands in Glasgow, there was no internet and getting your name mentioned in a letters page of a music paper like NME or Sounds was about as good as it got outwith of playing gigs.

And you had to listen to it there and then, there was no replay function. I think Vic Galloway has a really good show and he is very enthusiastic. There will never be another John Peel on radio stations these days. I actually met Peter Easton (Beat Patrol presenter) recently and he's a brilliant guy. I remember he phoned me up, my mum answered and he was asking for Richie Stretchhead. That was to tell me he was going to play our demo that night. I thought it was one of my mates putting a voice on! So of course, from there, you call up your own mates and try and get as many people listening in as well.

We got the same call as well, Beat Patrol played us too, and it was the same feeling as you. You felt delighted and then it was about trying to contact as many people as possible.

I spoke to John Peel once. We convinced ourselves that the best way to get exposure was to get a Peel Session and I took responsibility for that. So I phone up the BBC at about ten to 10 and got through to him. I'm speaking to John Peel, and I've got my script in front of me but I'm struggling to get the words out. We talked for a while and I did eventually ask for a session and he said yes, although they had a backlog so we couldn't arrange it there.

That was great and it was so much more personal then. I actually spoke to John Peel, it's not like you get a tweet from someone, it was a proper conversation and a connection. It was hard back then but if you did get something, like a slot on the radio, it was a small victory. My life is a run of small victories!

Any bands you are proud of?
Biffy Clyro, I'm very proud of them. I worked for them for two weeks once, and they were brilliant guys and a really good band. I'm also very proud of Teenage Fanclub, they are a national treasure and if you don't like Teenage Fanclub there is probably something wrong with you. I don't think I've met anyone who doesn't like Teenage Fanclub.

They are brilliant guys as well.

They are fantastic guys, that's the thing about Teenage Fanclub. They are the nicest people and it's impossible to dislike them. I went to America with them a good few years ago, just before 9/11.
It wasn't them that did it was it?
No...well, off the record....No, obviously not. They were a perfect example of the better the band, the easier it is to work with them. I've also got a lot of time for Franz Ferdinand.

You obviously knew Alex from the 13th Note days so you'll know him from way back.

Oh aye, the thing is, you probably meet Alex most years at festivals and he hasn't changed a bit, neither has Paul, Paul is the exact same guy as he was in the Yummy Fur. Success hasn't changed them at all and that is a great thing. I think there was a spell for Glasgow or Scottish bands that charted well, I won't name names, but bands in the charts with money had an ego and once you get the ego, it's hard to get shot of it.

This then meant when these bands were no longer successful, they really struggled. When you are a good guy though, you're always a good guy.

What about bands that didn't make it that should have done?
Motor Life Co. A totally brilliant band, completely misunderstood by the masses because they were clever.
People don't like cleverness
They don't, they really don't.
I was a wee bit shocked that Franz made it so big.
Yeah, but Franz had a look as well and some really catchy bits and it worked. Motor Life Co. though were just a bunch of guys that got on with. They were a brilliant band, quite proggy but not self-indulgent proggy. They were a refreshing band. They did a residency at the old 13th Note and I did sound for it every week. It was on for a month and I was thinking why isn't this place packed, why isn't there a queue around the block?

They were probably too brilliant too early. They're a favourite band of mine. Or of course Dawson. And Static, what the fuck happened to those guys, where are they now?

The drum machine did quite well.

You've seen audiences all over the world, does the Scottish reputation stand up?
Oh aye, definitely, they don't fuck around. There are Brazilian audiences, its football and music over there, so it's the same thing as here, it's so passionate. You then get a gig in Germany and the audience is like...(Richie then stands motionless while staring at an imaginary stage – a fantastic example of the German audience but not the best answer for a written interview). Germany is a brilliant place to tour but the audience is different. They applaud and they enjoy music

but they really listen and I think it's different in Glasgow and Scotland. I think our audiences feel it and they really want to be part of the gig. They'll let you know if your shite because they'll leave. I've been in at gigs when it was busy at the start, and then by 30 minutes, there's 6 or 7 people left.

Was that because of the sound?

Haha, aye, probably! No, people will give you abuse or leave, and that's fair enough. It's tough but it can be a good gauge for bands.

It's a different world these days. John Williamson and me (John went on to manage Belle & Sebastien), worked together and we used to do the 10 Day Weekend. This was an October festival, we ran for two years. We even gave a tape away with bands like Mogwai, Arab Strap and the Delgados. We ran Sano Music, we released Jock Scot, My Personal Culloden, and a record by a band called Elevate from London. They were a bit like Girls Against Boys. We went through Vital, back in 1997 and at that time, the internet was just powering up, but it wasn't quite there yet.

Oddbox Records is a good label at the moment, but. You'd be daft to start a label and print any more than 500 copies. Ours wasn't a successful label but I'm really glad we did it. I mean, we weren't like Chemikal Underground.

Aye but what have they done of late?

Aye, exactly. I'm amazed they've stayed alive and stayed so strong, they're brilliant and they make sure they release on vinyl and vinyl has come back. That is brilliant. I also think one of the greatest things that has happened to Glasgow of late is the East End Social, which is obviously from Chemikal Underground.

I know people say it was great that we had some of the Olympics in 2012 and obviously we had the Commonwealth Games this summer. I think there was a lot of money spent that we didn't need to, no one needed to turn Hampden into Barlinnie. I stay close to Hampden Park and this has impacted on my morning jog! Also, there have been political elements to it but did we need to spend so much money in certain places?

So with all that, the East End Social has been brilliant.

They've all worked hard, but Stuart Henderson has done a fantastic thing and it's been brilliant and I hope that there is a legacy from it. The event they had at the end of May on Duke Street was amazing.

It was such a good day. Stuart and myself did a pub crawl the week before I mean drinking in the East End, I had never done that before, that was like taking your life in your hands, but it was really nice. We were telling pubs that next week was going to be a bit different, almost like the West End coming to the East End and we were a bit concerned about it but it turned out brilliantly.

So many folk from the East End got involved and went to see bands in local bars and shops, and it was a great day. See if we could make that happen two or three times a year, it would be amazing.

I think there was a spell when people forgot about Chemikal for a while but then the Aiden and Bill album, and Hubby being recognised at the SAY Awards has pushed them back into the spotlight. It's not as if they have are plugging themselves with the East End Social work and that's really admirable but I think people need to know what Chemikal Underground have pulled together.

It's not just the big events but there's been loads of local events and the tea dances.

I heard so many good stories about that tea dance. I was told that a couple were taken up the stairs and burst out crying when they got there. They hadn't been to the Barrowlands since the 1950s and it hadn't changed. The first couple to dance at the event had actually met at the Barrowlands so that was brilliant. There was no loaded agenda or musical reason by Chemikal in doing events like that and they should be acknowledged for that, because it was a really nice thing for the people, and you don't always get that in life. Stuart said to me it was probably the most rewarding thing he had done in his life and I can see it, can you imagine, taking a couple back to the place where they first met and it was done up and looking great?

As well as the East End Social, the Kelvingrove Bandstand

has been a great re-addition to Glasgow as well, have you seen anything there?

It looks brilliant doesn't it, that's a great addition but no, I never caught anything. I've not seen anything at the Kelvingrove Bandstand since 1985 when I met the drummer from Simple Minds, got his autograph, I was made up!

Honeyblood

You're never far away from a new band looking to steal your heart or your money in Scotland, and it is good to see a band you've seen in tiny places make it to a larger level.

Even with that, I probably came to Honeyblood a lot later than a lot of people, at T in the Park when 2013 when they and Kraftwerk were the only two bands I was bothered about seeing on the Friday night (the only day I went that year). There may only have been two of them, with Stina Tweeddale on guitar and vocals and Shona McVicar on drums and vocals (at this point), but they made such a noisy impression, I've been to see them many times since.

The interview with Stina took place in May, just prior to the band performing at the Stag & Dagger festival in Glasgow and 2 months before the release of the debut album.

You're on the brink of releasing your debut album; does it feel like it's been a long journey to get here?
I guess it has, we didn't rush into recording our first record which I'm glad about. We did only take 10 days to actually record it, but the planning was there for a long time before.

Do you think Choker and Killer Bangs are good entry tracks to get into the album?
Definitely. Both songs are pretty different sides of the album, and there are more than that on there too.

What's the darkest lyric on the new album?
The one where I sing 'fucking' a lot, I guess – Braidburn Valley.

Is there a general way you create songs or are you flexible with song writing?
Mostly, the songs start with an idea from me and my guitar. I know its clichéd but one of the songs on the album actually started off from me singing in the shower... I never thought that would ever happen, but it did! We do have jam sessions also that sometimes amount to a cool riff or to help get

structure sorted for songs.

Do you have a best memory from recording the album?

So many... finishing the album on the last night actually sprung up on us. Afterwards we shared a drink with Peter (Katis, a producer who has worked with Interpol, The National, Frightened Rabbit and The Twilight Sad) and a few other people who helped us out on the album. I guess that feeling of knowing its complete is like no other.

What are your plans and hopes for the rest of the year?

We're going to tour a lot! We are just heading out on a UK tour for May and then some festival slots and some shows abroad before the album is released July 14th.

Would you prefer to tour the hell out of this album or tour moderately then make the next record?

Touring is fun so I think we're pretty excited to be doing that. Although, once the album is out I'm sure we'll be itching to get back in the studio.

You played a couple of acoustic gigs pre-Christmas – any plans for more of these?

Yeah, we're doing a little acoustic set during Stag and Dagger Festival and I just got my acoustic back so if there is demand for it, I'm up for playing some sets.

Now that the dust has settled on SXSW and your US tour, what are your thoughts on it?

It was mental. The best fun and really amazing to tour with WWPJ (We Were Promised Jetpacks). I think we were incredibly lucky to get on with them so well. The venues were great and very crazy to meet American folks who know our songs.

You're touring with Courtney Barnett – do you approach support slots differently from your own

headlining gigs?
I guess there's less pressure when you are a support act. You don't need to be at the venue as early and you can relax and watch the main act after you've played. We don't differ much in our set except from it's usually shorter and we don't play as many slow songs.

You are playing Live At Leeds and/ Stag & Dagger this weekend– What's your take on these city festivals over different venues?
I think they're awesome fun. It's always a great day. We did Tramlines in Sheffield last year and The Great Escape in Brighton. You always bump into friends who are playing also which is nice when you haven't seen them since the last festival.

How was your TITP 2013 experience and what are your ambitions for future festivals?
As you can imagine, it's a bit of an honour to play the festival when you are a Scottish band. We had a surprisingly big crowd which we weren't really expecting seeing as we hadn't released anything by then. We'd love to play it again.

What's your general take on TITP and other big festivals?
I grew up saving all my money as a teenager to buy tickets for festival season. They're so much fun, especially when the sun stays out. It's something we are definitely looking forward to playing more of in the future.

Do you feel as though you are part of a scene in Scotland?
I think it's hard to tell. I think of the music 'scene' as people who play in bands in Scotland. So in the respect, I guess we are.

What are your favourite Scottish bands?
Some amazing bands that I love like Cocteau Twins, Camera Obscura and Belle & Sebastian are Scottish. New bands we

love are Poor Things, Secret Motorbikes, Siobhan Wilson and Laura St Jude. They're all babes.

What are your favourite Scottish venues?
Sneaky Pete's probably my favourite one.

Are there are any Scottish bands you love that people have overlooked?
I guess it's hard to say... I think within Scotland, most good Scottish acts are respected and well loved.

You've been to America, England and beyond, is the reputation of Scottish crowds being wilder a deserved reputation?
Some of the crowds in America gave them a run for their money, that's for sure. Especially the New York crowds and San Francisco. They know how to have a good time, just like Scottish crowds.

Bar Bloc

There is no shortage of great bars and venues to enjoy in Glasgow and over the past 10 years, Bar Bloc has been a mainstay for music fans, diners and folk looking for a late night drinking venue. The bar was closed for a short period at the end of August/start of September 2014 for refurbishment and I caught up with Chris from the bar in the days leading up to the re-opening of the venue.

Hi Chris, first of all, when is the re-opening date?
Hi. Well we have our full public re-opening weekend on Sept 5th and 6th. The 5th features Stuart Braithwaite of Mogwai performing a DJ set and the 6th sees electro act Roman Nose teaming up with Dirty Marc for our monthly Deathkill 4000 night.

Both of these are preceded by a "soft-launch" invitational event for staff, friends, associates, all of whom will be plied with free food from the new menu, complimentary drinks and live performances by three of our favourite Scottish solo acts. But unless you plan to kill someone and steal their skin, you will already know if you are going to that one.

Is there a big change in the venue?
Well, we made the toilets less of a HAZMAT issue and we filled in the bite marks on all the tables. Basically, we restructured the interior to be a little more practical for a busy bar. To try and avoid bottle-necks when the place is packed. We also improved the utilities and layout so it a more pleasing environment for diners and revellers.

Behind the scenes we also took the opportunity to improve the facilities for bands, DJs etc. The audio visual stuff is much better. The sound system is now a match for any comparatively sized venue. We have been gradually progressing in those avenues for the last 4 years. This was just a great chance to take a bigger leap forward.

Do you expect any grumbles from regulars about the new look?

Yeah, I expect the people who enjoyed broken toilet seats and mould to be furious.

Are you able to announce what events are lined up for the grand reopening?

There are lots of events. See above. September in general is very strong during the Fresher's period. It is up there with our December line-up. I am particularly happy that bands we have worked with via the label, such as Campfires In Winter, Felix Champion, So Many Animal Calls, will be making appearances.

The venue is well known for the amount of free gigs and clubs – will this continue after the refit?

Yeah, in fact we have now dropped the £2 post-midnight riff-raff-deterrent door charge at weekends too. We are now full-time free-time.

Do you think the free entry element is important to what you offer?

Absolutely. Sadly the culture of music has changed to the point where bands now have to persuade people to come and see them – practically beg in some cases. We allow a risk-free chance to see new music. We are adapting to the new musical economy.

It is an especially advantageous model for young touring acts out-with the mainstream who can't pay for thousands of pounds worth of advertising coaxing people to their shows. As long as we maintain a high standard, people will come to see what we offer because they trust us and, even if they hate it, they didn't waste any money. It's not ideal. It limits what we can give bands and I wish we could pay twice what we do but frankly we can sit about lamenting the state of the music industry, which is gradually devouring itself, or we can try find a way to exist and encourage/support bands in this scary new financial reality.

You're not just a gig venue and bar, you've a great reputation for meals and deals – will there be any

changes to the food side of the venue?

Yeah the food menu has been evolving at a Lamarckian rate for the last year and that shows no sign of slowing. The kitchen team is strong and the ideas are flowing. Having seen the new menu I can say it is full of some of the most innovative bar food in the city as well as continuing with the weekly offers that have made the place so busy.

One thing I've found about Bloc is that you seem to cater for lots of different music genres on your various nights – was this a conscious decision or was it stumbled upon?

In my opinion, it is short-sighted and self-indulgent to book a narrow spectrum of styles. We want to be an inclusive venue, not an exclusive one. Cliques are for assholes. The more people that visit us from across the board the better and the more artistic cross-pollenation that encourages the better. A lot of people have been turned onto bands and even genres in Bloc that they might never have touched otherwise. The free entry aspect plays a big part in that mind-expansion too.

The only thing that is important is that the standard, across styles, is maintained and that means I have to leave my own prejudices at the door when booking. Well... most of them....

If someone has never been to Bloc before, what club nights would you recommend coming along to and seeing what the place has to offer?

It's probably not wise to pick favourites. Clearly I hold all the nights to a high standard and all are doing well. Personally my favourite DJ is Dirty Marc, who runs Deathkill 4000 on the first Saturday of every month. He's got a lot of experience and his combination of styles (mixing Shellac with Ice Cube and Black Sabbath into Kavinsky) is at times simply inspired. His periodic live acts tend to be truly innovative too. REPEATER and TariboWest have proven to be consistent and ambitious live events since their arrival. For a pure mad rammy, Fantastic Man always leaves footprints on the ceiling. For something more traditional, the folks of Blas Collective, on Mondays, are stars of the Celtic Connections circuit and the entire vibe of that night is chilled and rather terrific.

Any highlights or moments the bar is particularly proud of over the years?

The big names that drop in usually leave a mark, such as Clutch, which was obscenely excellent. Scott from Frightened Rabbit once tanned 3 Balkans (88% vodka) as well as half a bottle of his favourite whisky before climbing around the tables of a capacity room for a December acoustic set few will forget. Likewise, We Are Scientists, Marmaduke Duke, Twin Atlantic, Twilight Sad, Admiral Fallow and more have all dropped in for wild secret shows.

For me though, my personal favourite shows tend to be the underground bands from Europe like Electric Electric, Marvin, Sheik Anorak, Adebisi Shank and so on. Also I don't think there has been a better performance at Bloc than those by The Cosmic Dead, Adam Stafford, Vcheka, Vasquez or United Fruit.

Given that you offer food/drink, live music and club nights – do you feel you are in competition with all the bars and pubs in the local area or do you feel you are a bit more specialist?

We are in competition with any chain restaurant, generic bar or cynical exploiter of the local music scene. By contrast, we are in cooperation with all of the other wonderful independent restaurants and bars, including Nice N Sleazy, Mono, Stereo, 13th Note, PivoPivo, The Roxy and Flying Duck to name but a few.

The PAWS and We Are Scientists show in July caused quite a stir – how did that come about?

It came about thanks in no small part to our friend and unemployed Elvis Costello impersonator Bryan McGarvey of the pop band Jackhammers. But it was only possible because the guys from PAWS are thoroughly decent folks to deal with and totally mindful of where they came from in the tradition of all of the best DIY acts. They played at BLOC on the way up and, now that they are doing well, they were more than happy to come back for an intimate night of screaming and musical bludgeoning.

We Are Scientists are friends of PAWS (and really very nice people too) and, when Phil and Co mentioned it to them, were delighted at the opportunity to play a frantic, feral, emotional show inches away from the people who love them most. Those fans will never forget that experience and it was our privilege to give them those memories.

Any major plans for the rest of the year?
Absolutely. The gig diary is looking epic. I know what shows are coming and it is our best close to a year since the bar began hosting music. December will be something special. We are also releasing a series of compilations through our record label around the time of the reopening and into late Autumn featuring some of the great acts we have worked with. That will be a real pleasure.

What are your hopes for the future?
Converge. I absolutely will get those noisy bastards to play in this bar if it kills me.

Rachel Hair

While there were plenty of mainstream or indie acts playing sets around the Commonwealth Games, there was an attempt to ensure that there were a lot of different musical styles represented.

The Kelvingrove Bandstand was brought back to life in the summer, and this was the setting for a tremendous range of free gigs during the height of the Games. I talked to harpist Rachel Hair, who performed as part of the Rachel Hair Trio, at the Bandstand on Tuesday the 29th of July.

Hi Rachel, you've been invited to play at the Kelvingrove Bandstand as part of the Culture element of 2014. How did that come about and how excited are you by the prospect?

We just got an email asking if we were able to play. We jumped at the chance to take part. The Commonwealth Games are massive for the city and we're hardly athletic and unlikely to be involved with the event in any other way, so yes, we jumped at it. It's good to be part of the buzz of it all and we are very excited by it.

For those people who may be unaware of you or the Rachel Hair Trio, can you give us some background on what to expect from your show?

For the trio, it's myself on harp, my friend Jen on guitar and we have a guy called Cammy on double bass. We play Scottish flavoured music but it's a lot of our own material. We try to fight against what people expect from the harp and we try to make it a bit more upbeat and groovy! We don't play the stereotypically angelic harp music and most people seem pleasantly surprised when we play. It's happy and upbeat, so it'll be perfect for a sunny evening, which we'll hopefully get.

Why should people come along and see your show on the 29th of July?

It's free for a start and it'll cheer people up. Also, it's looking like a great evening. Before we go on stage the film Local Hero is being shown so going from that to us will hopefully be good. A great film and then us playing upbeat stuff, so I think it's going to be a lot of fun.

Have you any plans to check out any of the other acts performing or any other bands this summer?

The first week of the Games I'm around and I'll be checking out some of the things going on at Kelvingrove Park because that is handy for me. There's also a lot going on in Glasgow Green, including the Struileag Stories which is a Gaelic project. I know the writer and some of my friends are in so I have heard so much about and I want to see as much as I can.

Celtic Connections is also running a number of things so I'll definitely catch a few of their events and gigs. And I've also managed to grab some tickets for the Games so it'll be a hectic week. I was hoping to go to the mountain bike event on the day of our gig but I've had to pass them on because there's just too much to do. I felt going to that and getting back for our sound check and then the gig and then probably having to pack because I'm heading off to America the morning after the gig may be a bit too much for one day. I felt it was best to have some chill out time. It's going to be a great week.

Okay, so after Kelvingrove you are heading off to America and Canada, how do you feel your music is appreciated over there?

In the past, I've always played with Irish shows and this is the first time I'm going out completely by myself. I'm performing at the biggest harp festival in the USA and I'll be playing in front of a really "harpy" audience, and they'll know what I do, so that'll be great and I'm really looking forward to that. I'm also heading to Canada for shows and I've never played there before so I'm really looking forward to that. There will be plenty of Scottish ex-pats over there so it'll be interesting to see how the songs go down.

The Trio will be heading over to America next summer

so that is something to look forward to as well but this tour is going to be great.

Are there any characteristics to a "harpy" audience we should know about?

They are quite scary to play because they know exactly what you are doing, or what you are trying to do. That is scary but in some ways, it makes you focus and concentrate even more. I'm also going to be teaching some workshops as well at the festival so it's going to be a great trip. I like the teaching element; it provides me with a way to pass on the music I love. It's a lot more interactive, which I like.

Is there a difference between a Scottish audience and a North American audience?

I find the American audience to being a bit more open to harp music whereas in Scotland the more traditional style of the harp player is probably the prevalent image. They both have their strong points though and I'm happy to play where I can.

After North America, you are heading to Norway and Denmark?

Yes, they are school tours. They have this amazing scheme that every child has to see at least 6 concerts every year in school. We do two to three concerts a day, around thirty minutes a set, and we finish at around half two in the afternoon. It's amazing! It's the complete opposite of the standard day of a musician – you're leaving at half seven in the morning and playing early but finishing up in the afternoon when back home you'd be heading to your soundcheck. You also get the weekends off.

They're amazing concerts because we play our songs but then we talk to them about our music and Scotland. I really enjoy doing them.

How good would this be in Scotland?

It's mad. I know the money thing is why it doesn't happen here but it's such a great programme. Kids get to see drama groups and all different forms of bands and music. I'd love for that to happen in Scotland.

You've spent a lot of the year travelling, has there been an added level of excitement or interest in your shows or you due to the fact that this is a big year for Scotland?

Everyone is talking about Scotland and there's more attention on the country, so I think it's good for us. Obviously the independence referendum is a major talking point but with the Commonwealth Games as well, Glasgow is on everyone's lips and people are happy to talk about these things. I love travelling and I like being able to see new places, even test-drive to see if I want to go back for my own holidays.

You play solo, as the Rachel Hair Trio and in other pairings or groups, is it hard to keep track of what you are doing next?

Sometimes, and I need to focus my practice and rehearsal on what I'm doing next. If I'm practising for a show where it's just me and the guitarist, I know I need to fill out the sound a bit more because the double bass isn't there. It'll be a bit tricky in the next week or so because I have to practice for the Trio stuff and for my solo stuff. I have to fill out my sound a bit more when I'm solo, so it's a case of being prepared and practising for what is coming next.

I like being a solo artist because I have the freedom to change what I'm doing on the spot but I love playing with the Trio because of the energy that comes with playing with others. I love travelling with The Trio as well because it is great to experience all of these things with other people. Playing solo is fun but it can be a bit lonely at times.

It's not just practising specific stuff, its writing as well. The summer is good for this because I have some free time but I'm creating music for an album as well so there is the song writing process to think of. As we're a Celtic band, I tend to concentrate on melodies and when we work as a trio, I work on melodies and have a few ideas for chords but it's when we come together as a trio that it falls into place. Jen knows what works for her and then we'll work with Cammy to get rhythms going. I may then go over the top of that so we work differently to most bands but we get there in the end.

How do ideas and melodies come to you?

I've woken up and had to write melodies into the voice memo recorded on my phone, which is a Godsend in being able to record melodies as they come. I'll often get ideas as I'm waiting to play or record so it's just a case of sitting down and finalising them all.

We usually work towards goals and at the moment we're writing for the album so do we work to rough deadlines. I'll maybe work for an hour on one element and then do something else. I like to leave things for a while and then come back to them but we have deadlines and that pushes me along at times.

You've performed at the Edinburgh Fringe, at Celtic Connections and even on TV for the Hogmanay celebrations – do you have any best moments that stand out from your years as an artist?

The gigs I remember the most are the ones where I've played with the Trio and it's just clicked. We played one recently on the isle of Mull and that was great because the energy we had was really exciting.

There have been some crazy moments though. I went all the way to Macau once and played for 2 and half minutes. I must have spent about 17 hours travelling, got put up in the Venetian Palace, one of the biggest casinos/hotels in the world and only had to play for 2 and a half minutes, that was bonkers.

We played one of the biggest Celtic festivals in the world, the Lorient Festival, and we had a ball so that was great as well. A good gig for us is really just about the energy and excitement on stage and having a good time, so it can happen anywhere.

You hail from Ullapool, what are your thoughts on the Loopallu festival and the range of music festivals

in the Highlands?

We love it, and I love being involved with festivals. If we can play once or twice we get to hang around and soak up the atmosphere and see other bands. One of the annoying things about being a musician is that you're always playing at weekend and you can miss people because of your own shows. When you play at a festival you get to see the other acts.

Loopallu is amazing; it's really helped to put the Ullapool on the map. It's a great village but this has helped to draw attention to the area and the other things going on in the city. The whole community gets involved.

There have already been moans from Strathallan with T in the Park heading there for 2015, how does the Ullapool community deal with the festival?

I think the community embraces it, you have to. It's like Glasgow and the Commonwealth Games. If you continually moan about the roads being busy, you'll miss out on it. You need to throw yourself into. It's a positive thing for the village, it brings in income and it puts us on the map, I like it.

Do you feel there is too much attention on the music scene in the central belt compared to elsewhere in Scotland?

I'm not sure. A lot of the gigs I go to see are the folky or Celtic style ones and that there are lots of festivals around the country. In my genre of music, its better spread around the country. Funnily enough, for my genre of music, in Glasgow we have the opposite problem to the rest of the country. Everyone comes to Glasgow in January for the Celtic Connections and this means they often miss Glasgow out on their year-round tours. Celtic Connections is a phenomenal festival and its great we have but sometimes for the rest of the year we miss out a wee bit but Scotland as a whole is doing okay.

Of course, you lived in Edinburgh for a while and studied music at Strathclyde University, do you feel

there is a different sort of vibe or interest in music around the country?

I find in the city the folk that come to see a gig are coming to see you specifically. However, in a village or in the highlands, people will come to an event because it's an event and there may not be a lot on at other times. This means people will come along to see what is happening without knowing much about you. It can be a bit harder to reach folk in the city because you are competing with so many other events.

Aside from your touring schedule for 2014, what is next for Rachel Hair and what musical ambitions do you have left to achieve?

We're recording an album at the end of the year, that's just been confirmed. I think it'll be officially released in May or June next year, so I'm not totally rushed to get it out. Next year we are touring USA and Canada in the summer, then it's a Scandinavian tour, then Belgium and then there'll be a Scottish tour in September.

It's a bit crazy as I tend to work a year in advance. I'm grateful for phone diaries that go more than a year in advance now. I have a few writing projects on the go as well, I'm looking to do a lot more composing, which is outside of the Trio. It's slightly scary but I really enjoy it.

Stephen Nicolson

The singer songwriter night is a major part of the Glasgow music scene, providing the setting for a great night out and the platform for emerging talent to develop their confidence.

The Carnarvon Bar has played host to a singer-songwriter night for a number of years and I managed to catch up with one of the main men behind the night, Stephen Nicolson.

How long have you been involved with open mic nights?

I've been involved for about 7 or 8 years and that was when I first started going to the Liquid Ship, a pub on Great Western Road, which was close to my flat. I used to go on a Wednesday night, the Acousdeck night, and it was an intimate venue, quite dark and I thought the talent was generally pretty good.

It was run by a guy called by Graeme who I still keep in touch with and he comes to our open mic nights. It was a cracking venue, fantastic talent and it wouldn't take too much to pack it out. It was a great way to spend a Wednesday night. I had been playing in a few bands over the years and I was a bit disillusioned with it all. I'm not saying I was ever a great musician but I worked hard at it. I played in all sorts of bands, punk, metal and indie and I always felt that I was the guy running about organising everything.

When you feel that you're the one making all the calls, changing your shifts, driving folk around, you get fed up and I just wanted to play a bit more guitar as opposed to bass. It was a good way for me to practice guitar, find a wee bit of a voice to sing, I had only provided backing vocals by this point, and every week, I'd try and learn a new song.

It took a while to pluck up the courage to get involved with the open mic night but it was a great starting point for me and I learned loads really quickly. I also met a lot of people because there was a good hardcore crowd that was there and you saw the same faces. It was good to learn a lot of new styles and influences and it really opened me up to new ideas and different playing styles. There were a lot of covers thrown in and I got to hear about a lot more bands through it, which has influenced my listening of music.

I was doing this for about two to three years and then an old friend I had been at school with, Jimmy, started to come down and we would jam together. After this, I lost interest in a little bit, life was moving on, but I had met enough people to know that I wanted to keep doing it.

How did you get into running a night?

It came through Jimmy and we jammed really well and had a lot of fun, we clicked musically. He gave me a lot of encouragement to play and sing, and we have a similar taste in music. Jimmy is a far more talented guitarist and musician than I am but we got on great. He then started managing the Carnarvon pub, an old-fashioned pub which had become run down but Jimmy took over and started making positive changes.

He wanted to bring in an open mic night, bringing in more pointers, creating a vibe but also providing a platform for people to play. This was also after the Acousdeck night has stopped running, so we wanted to bring something back, give performers more chances to play their music to an audience. It's not as though we were the only open mic night in this area and stretching out to the West End. There are a lot of events like this, sometimes it seems like every second pub and it's the same for town, south side. The open mic scene in Glasgow is really alive at the moment.

What's behind the number of different open mic nights?

I think there's an element of a few different things. Pubs need to bring in money, especially when the economy dipped but I think there's an element of more people learning to play guitar and sing at home. When you now have YouTube, the X-Factor and online tablature, it is far more accessible for people to sit at home and learn chords and songs. There's a real opportunity for everyone to sit at home and learn how to do something, and this creates the platform for more performers.

I don't want to be an X-Factor artist or on Britain's Got Talent but I do like the idea of being in a pub playing songs in a great atmosphere to people that want to hear music. It's not about making money; it's a hobby or a form of artistic pursuit for me. However, there are people who use the open mic slot to develop their talent and showcase what they can do, with a view to making it somewhere in the music world.

Is there also the fact that some people will do anything for a free pint?
Haha, aye, perhaps!

I think most pubs that do an open mic night will provide a free drink for performers. One of the best nights we had last year was when Ray Manzarek passed away. I'm a big fan of The Doors and so is Jimmy, so we felt we had to make a big night of it and we decided to celebrate the life of Ray, we would offer a free whiskey for all performers. It turned out to be one of the busiest nights we have ever put on, there were performers queuing out of the door to play! I think word had spread around every busker on Sauchiehall Street and we have about 40 people looking to play. We went through about 2 bottles of whisky that night.

I remember the event after Lou Reed passed away, you had a bit of a tribute to him.
Yeah, we like to do things like that. Last year we were trying to generate a bit more interest in the night and rather than just hosting a standard open mic night, we decided to make it a bit of a theme. We had a birthday party, we had our Christmas special, Halloween and we had a Wimbledon night as well. Any nonsense we could think of to make our promotional texts and messages a bit more interesting, and the night itself.

Having a theme makes it less run of the mill and what we found was that while not everyone was hugely talented, we like the fact that we had a platform for everyone. A theme can help to bring people along and make it seem more fun, so it all helps.

Has anyone that played with your or at your nights gone on to bigger things?

Bob Dick has been a regular at our events and he plays in the band Verse Metrics, who have been touring around Scotland and developing a name for themselves. They class themselves as being a Maths Rock band. A few of the boys who play in wedding bands come in and play with us as well. I think most of the people who come along will play in an amateur band as well as playing with us.

Is there also the fact that an open mic night is the level that some people are aiming for?

Absolutely, especially for our open mic night. I think our night is as much a social scene as a platform for performers. I like playing but I also enjoy the night as a way of winding down after work and I know a lot of people feel the same. There are other open mic nights in Glasgow that are more focused on the performance levels.

There are some great open mic nights in places like Nice N Sleazys, where people are expected to focus entirely on the open mic element. There's no background chat or TV, there's no punters having a laugh while performers are playing, it's very much focused on the artist and the music. That puts pressure on performers but you'll find that the people who perform at these events are more serious about their music and have their skills honed to the pressure of this type of event. Our focus is more relaxed but that's not to say it's all a laugh or performers aren't respected, there's just less pressure. There's a level for everyone.

For you, what are the key components of a successful open mic night?

I think you need a welcoming host, someone who takes the time to speak to people and put them at ease. It can be a daunting thing to perform in front of people so you want to put people at ease. Often people come in alone and a bit shy for these events so I think if you make an effort to make people feel comfortable, it helps people to play better and to enjoy the night. I'd like to think that between Jimmy and myself, this is something we do; we both know what it's like and what it takes to get up and play in front of others, so we want to make people feel welcome. Our bar staff are great as well for creating a good atmosphere and making people feel welcome.

You also need a good sound system. When we started off, we didn't have a good sound system so Jimmy and myself invested in one from our own pocket. We had the opinion that if we were going to do it, we better do it properly and provide the best mics and a good sound system.

It's probably not loud enough for a full band set-up and it's on its last legs now, which we are replacing, but it has done us very well over the years. That was a great investment that helped us.

What sort of crowd do you get at your nights?
It varies. At our night, we find we get a mix of punters that are there to drink in their local. Some of them will enjoy it, some won't! At times, some of my friends will come down for the night out and the social aspect of the event and there will be others that come in solely to listen to the music.

It varies, some nights are really busy and then there are other nights that are quiet. Some nights we are busy with drinkers and not performers or vice versa. There really isn't any logic or pattern to it, and there's no correlation between the weather and the turnout. It seems like a random turnout but we've had some great times.

We had a guest artist one night, I set up a Facebook page, did a bit more promoting for it. There was an artist called Shantell Ogden, who somehow found our open mic and got in touch with us on Facebook. She said she was coming through Scotland and Ireland and she would love to play our open mic night as she had heard a lot about it! I think someone had written on Facebook that they had a great night at our open mic night and she has picked up on this. She has written songs for the TV show Hart of Dixie, she has been on Country Music Television and she was heading over and stumbled across.

We made an effort to promote it, printing off posters

saying there was a country music star coming to the Carnarvon Bar. It's not really Nashville...but I suppose there's a few cowboys in it.

It was a big night, plenty of regulars in, lots of friends and family came down, it was tremendous.

What do you make of the Scottish crowds, and their reputation, in general?

I think it's really deserved. I know some folk will say that it's just because they're all drunk, and that is an element to it, but I think people like to switch off from their day to day life. Historically, this is the case and music has always been a great relief. This isn't even at events or open mic nights, think about family parties where it's one singer one song and people having a party piece that they perform. You know what it's like, your uncle Johnny has a guitar out again!

Similarly, you've got gigs and people go out of their way, even in midweek, middle of winter and they'll make the most of it. I know that happens all over the world but I think in Scotland, gigs and socialising are really important to wind down and relax away from work, it's a way of switching off. This ties in with me and why I like to perform and get involved with an open mic night.

What Scottish acts do you like?

Teenage Fanclub, I like what they've done. Primal Scream are definitely up there as well.

What is your favourite Scottish venue?

Barrowlands without a doubt but to be fair, The Hydro is superb. I went to see Prince when he played and it was an excellent night in an excellent venue. One of the best gigs I've been to but I've liked a good few gigs at Glasgow Green. If you get the weather its excellent. I also don't mind the Academy but I suppose it's about the right band and where you are. If it's a chilled out gig, being upstairs is decent but if it's a heavier one, you want to be down the front, making the most of it. Also, I'm a shortarse and I can't always see so being close to the stage helps.

I'm also really excited about the Kelvingrove Bandstand opening up, and we got tickets for The Waterboys. Mike Scott was born in Edinburgh, so that's a Scottish act I like, in fact, if we're counting them, that's my favourite Scottish act.

We all count Rod so you can claim The Waterboys if you want!

Oh aye, The Waterboys are my favourite then.

Any musical ambitions you want to achieve?

I want to learn a bit more jazz, well, I don't know much at the moment, so I want to learn how to play jazz music.

Isn't jazz just making it up as you go along?

It's actually really tricky, it's a lot more difficult than I thought, it's like learning a new language. The chord structures and rhythms are different, there's more logic and theory to it than I thought so I'm getting pointers and tips from a mate who is highly skilled at it.

TYCI

Looking through the amount of current artists, and well known acts who have made their name for Scotland, I think we can be proud of the number of female artists who have made it to the fore and shared their talent with the world. However, it is still easy to see why many women can feel as though they are marginalised or at a disadvantage trying to make it in the music industry, much as they would feel this way about trying to be a success in any other industry.

I was lucky enough to catch up with TYCI, a female collective that do a far better job of explaining what they offer than what I could, so I'll leave it to them to explain what they provide.

You'll be aware of Lauren Mayberry as the lead singer from Chvrches but Lauren is also a highly regarded journalist and a co-founder of TYCI. Anna Hodgart is an actress and key component of the TYCI team while Lis Ferla is a music journalist and renowned blogger, who also plays a strong role in the variety of activities TYCI undertakes.

TYCI is a collective run by women – what are the mains and ambitions of the collective?

[LM]: To encourage discussion of women's issues in open-minded way, hopefully bringing the conversation to people who haven't thought that feminism was 'for' them before, and also to showcase talented women in different industries.

[AH]: A secondary ambition is to create networks for and of women locally, through our online and live event platforms – we create spaces digitally and in real life for women to talk to each other about things that concern – and celebrate all the awesome work women are doing!

The term feminism means many different things to different people, is this something you try to embrace at TYCI?

[LM]: Absolutely. We want people to talk about issues and try to see things from different perspectives whilst always being respectful of each other. Feminism can sometimes feel very academic and unapproachable but the best way to combat this is to find different ways of engaging people with the issues.

[LF]: That's why our approach has been to use gigs, club nights and zines as our primary platforms, along with more traditional methods of activism. If we can challenge people to think about why they're less likely to see female acts and DJs while they are having a good time at one of our nights, or provoke and inspire through a zine left lying in a pub or coffee shop, that's exactly what we want to achieve.

What do you think your role is in the current climate?

[LM]: For me, TYCI is about community and learning. And as far as I can tell, there aren't really any other groups in Scotland who do what we do on so many different platforms. We have a website, a zine, a radio show, a podcast and a live event series in Glasgow, all geared towards promoting female talent and challenging the status quo.

[AH]: It really feels like our conversations are taking place in a pretty empowering, local, grassroots way but what's exciting is that due to our online presence we have the ability to reach people anywhere and everywhere and engages with issues that are global.

On the one hand, we supposedly live in more enlightened times but everyone can probably think of daily instances of "isms" - how do you think society compares to what it did a decade or two ago?

[LF]: I think that society benefits from a general awareness that sexist, racist, homophobic, cissexist, ableist etc attitudes and actions are unacceptable, but as those notions become increasingly ingrained in the workplace, media and popular culture we're increasingly seeing a backlash against what is often written off as "political correctness" - and those of us who recognise these behaviours as damaging are told to "lighten up" or that it's "only a bit of banter". You only have to look at new research published by the NUS this week which found more than a third of female students had experienced unwanted sexual comments to see how serious the problem still is: the difference between now and 20 years ago is that we now have places where we can talk about it.

What have been the highlights of your time so far?
[LF]: Standing onstage with the women of the collective handing out raffle prizes at our massive Christmas 2013 show and seeing how huge the thing we had created had grown. I already knew that there was a role for a collective that put female achievement front and centre, but I'm a big angry feminist - seeing the sheer scale of the hunger for what we do made me a wee bit emotional!
[AH]: A highlight for me was our International Women's Day Pop-up Festival. We programmed a range of performance artists and musicians in all of Stereo's nooks and crannies. All of the proceeds went to legendary Glasgow Women's Library which felt really special.

Chvrches, Honeyblood, LAW, Teen Canteen, Siobhan Wilson, Skinny Dipper and Bdy Prts. We've had a great run of Scottish female acts/ female fronted acts come through of late. Do you feel as though this is a scene worthy of highlighting or should we just be looking to celebrate artists in their own right?
[LM]: All of those acts have actually played TYCI events which is very cool. I think there are, and have always been, talented women playing in the Scottish music scene. It isn't about their existence or lack thereof – it is about the fact that these talents are not promoted on an equal level, and that they are still viewed by a large section of society as 'niche'. If you look at any festival bill, Scottish or otherwise, bands with female performers in them are still completely underrepresented. And without highlighting the fact that this discrepancy exists, how can we ever hope to change the situation?

Following on from the great acts of late, any tips or suggestions who will be next to make it from the Glasgow scene?

[LF]: Guitar-pop trio Tuff Love and eight-piece "almost a girl band" Skinny Dipper are two of my current gangs of hometown heroines. Yes, they're both played TYCI nights too - but that just shows how much we love them!

[AH]: I think LAW (Lauren Holt) is another a big favourite of TYCI – she's already making pretty big waves though.

While you promote up and coming artists, you've had some great established artists like Helen Marnie and Adele Bethel do DJ sets. Are you consciously trying to blend the established and the new or do you just like what you like?

[LM]: In terms of booking, we try to cover broad and diverse a range of things. It's always great to have well known women supporting the cause and also to showcase new talent where we can too. A good mixture I think is the key.

[AH]: We also like to 'match' band and DJs whether that's by purposely contrasting or by programming artists that have a similar vibe – it all depends on the event!

Any established artist you would love to have DJ for you?

[LF]: I think I can speak for all of TYCI and say Kathleen Hanna, of Bikini Kill/Le Tigre/Julie Ruin notoriety. Her role in the riot grrrrl movement has made her something of a godmother for us - plus, her picks would be amazing.

[AH]: YES. Kathleen Hanna, please come DJ at TYCI.

You're recognised as one of the leading club nights in the city at the moment – how did that all come together?

[LM]: I started the website in October 2012 and the live events began in November 2012. Initially, the idea was that the blog would help provide an identity for the live events, making them more than your standard gig and hopefully providing a kind of community feel, but as more and more people got involved in the collective, we were able to expand into radio, broader online content and bespoke events outwith our regular Bloc gigs too which has been great.

[AH]: I think there's definitely been a public appetite for these events – showcasing awesome music from female artists and creating spaces to have fun and dance in that are 'femm-centric', welcoming and open.

You have a club night on the 20th of September in Bloc, can you tell us about that?

[LM]: Bloc has just been renovated so this will be our first event in there since it had its wee facelift. We've booked a Welsh pop band called Cut Ribbons as the live act and for DJs we have Future Fight (one half of the Glasgow Roller Derby DJ duo Summer Slams) and Kid Canaveral. Kid Canaveral have been really supportive of TYCI so it's great to finally have them on an event. And, as ever, if you write 'TYCI' on your knuckles, you will get into the venue for free all night.

[AH]: We'll also be raising money for an awesome charity – Anxiety UK – with some great prizes up for grabs. It's going to be great!

You've used your live events to support a number of charities and great causes – is this important to you?

[LM]: Definitely. We run a monthly raffle and the proceeds from each goes to a different charity, including organisations like Rape Crisis, Refuge, Women For Refuge Women, The Orchid Project and Prostate Cancer UK. The venues we work with and the people who come to the events have been really generous, and I think it's great that we can bring something even more positive out of the live events. Whilst the gigs are about creativity and entertainment, it's also nice to be able to promote and support the work of such great charities at the same time.

Is it difficult to find the balance between making sure people have a great night while also looking to positively impact on people with respect to awareness and what you do?

[LM]: I think it's all about the tone of it. Since we've tried to create an inclusive, community vibe at TYCI events, most people are happy to get involved when the raffle bucket comes round because it's all very good natured. Plus, people tend to be a bit more free with the cash once they've had a couple...

You've held nights in a number of different Glasgow venues. Do you ever find the nature of the venue impacts on the type of night you have?
[AH]: Different spaces offer different challenges and opportunities – for instance Stereo allowed us to programme live performance for the first time at our International Women's Day Event which was just brilliant. It's really great to be able to look at a space and think what fun could we fill this with.

It's easy to think that you only focus on music but you focus on all of the creative arts – is there any artform you've covered that you've been surprised at how much you enjoyed?
[LF]: Of all the events we've hosted so far, our International Women's Day special this year was my favourite. Away from TYCI I'm a music journalist, so it's definitely my area of expertise - but the combination of theatre, dance and music our live events leading lady Anna pulled together on the day was incredible, more like an old-fashioned variety show than a gig. And the atmosphere was electric!

You issue a monthly fanzine – how much work does that take and how do you decide on the content?
[LM]: The monthly zine is made by our amazing design gal Cecilia Stamp. We take a selection of features that have been on the site the past month and collect them in the zine which is then distributed around Glasgow and also published on our ISSUU profile for TYCI followers based elsewhere. The covers are designed by a different artist each month.

You also host a monthly radio show –again, how do you decide the content and focus for the show?

[LM]: We have a few people who help out with the radio programming, mainly Halina Rifai (Podcart) and Amanda Aitken (Lost and Found). The presenters of our monthly Subcity radio show put together playlists of new and classic lady tunes, and we also play homemade / TYCI follower-made jingles and audio interviews. For the podcast, we choose six new songs a month and make each episode streamable on our Soundcloud.

Haight Ashbury Questions

It's one thing punters showing some longevity when it comes to going to gigs and shows but when a band continues to stick it, long after their peers have given up or succumbed to what would be classed as normal life, you really need to doff your cap. Over the years, I've stumbled across a number of great bands and one Glasgow act that has shown quality and consistency over the years has been Haigh Ashbury.

A very early review of mine was based on a group that Haight Ashbury evolved from and while the quality of my work probably hasn't improved since then, the band reaped the rewards for a lot of hard work in 2014 and all being well; there will be more good fortune to follow in 2015 and beyond.

I caught up with Scott from the band to talk about gigs, tours, records, prestigious support slots and how the band should be classed as Glasgow trendsetters.

For people who may not be aware of you just yet, could you tell us a bit about the band?
We're a Glasgow 3 piece that have been going for about 5 years, our set up is a guitar bass and vocal harmonies, the band is myself (Scott), my sister Kirsty and our friend Jen.

The next chance people will get to see you perform in Glasgow is on the 20th of October in Stereo supporting Young Marble Giants. Are you looking forward to the gig and how did it come about?
We're mainly looking forward to gigging again since it's been a few months since our last lot of touring finished, as a band you get used to busy summer! YMG are on the same European booker as us 'Julie Tippex' so when they booked a UK tour we got asked to support cause it should be a good fit!, they're a very cool band and have been influential to people we're big fans of such as Kurt Cobain so it should be great!

Some of the best Glasgow (and near to Glasgow)

bands have been influenced by similar influences to yourself – do you think there is something about the Glasgow psyche or personality that means this style of music is particularly appealing?

I'm not really sure, there's all sorts of different music coming out of Scotland just now, I'm not really sure what the style or main influences are but it's just great to see Scottish and local bands do well, and from a selfish point of view it's great to draw attention to the area for all the right reasons!

Your 4th album has just been completed – can you tell us a bit about that?

We were planning on spending the spring this year taking our time with it and enjoying recording again but the way things worked out with tours that came out of nowhere it essentially became two sessions of 4 songs, after that it felt wrong to force more cause you're in a different place, so we decided to leave it at that which felt right, having a shorter album is a nice change up from the last 3 which we have fully loaded.

Do you have any plans in place to promote and tour the record just yet?

We'll definitely be gigging again as much as possible early 2015, until then we have gigs scattered about to end this year and start getting the singles out and about!

A lot of people got the chance to see you supporting Paolo Nutini on his recent tour. How was that experience for you?

It was excellent, it ended up spanning 3 tours and a couple of months so it was great for us, mainly because of how unexpected it was. When we started out we were lucky enough to do a few high profile tours with the Vaselines and the Waterboys very early on but since then we have really done our own things and concentrated on our own gigs in Europe, so this was a really fresh change.

Paolo picked us personally for it all so that was a huge compliment and most importantly Paolo and his whole team were extremely generous with us. At some point or another all of his team helped us with something or another, from fixing Kirsty's bass 5 minutes before the Barrowlands, to his guitar tech rebuilding my wee cigar box guitar, to Paolo letting us crash on his tour bus, really good people!

If anyone has gone to gigs in Glasgow over the years, they would likely have seen you perform or be in the crowd, do you have any favourite memories of your time gigging so far?

I have great memories from the days when we played 3 or 4 times a week at all the Glasgow bars, its became the start of any night out, we would be playing a few songs somewhere or other, like Bar Brel, or Rio Cafe in the west end. I think our proudest gigs have been being able to turn up in Berlin or Vienna and pull a great crowd, that's always blown us away because it's so far from home!

What would be your favourite Glasgow venue and do you think there are any differences between the Glasgow scene now compared to when you started out?

It's an obvious answer but the Barrowlands and King Tuts are our favourites, although there are places like ABC that I love to see bands at that we haven't gigged. We haven't gigged in Scotland as much as other places over the last few years so we're not in the best place to answer, but from living in Glasgow I don't think its hugely different. Trends change but as long as people can play and have people watch them for free as much as possible that's all that matters. Big ticket prices can kill gigs for new bands; as long as the band get a beer and get to play that's the most important thing at the start!

You've also developed a strong following across Europe, how do you feel that came about?

Initially we were very lucky to have our first single picked up by BBC6 Music and it got a lot of air time and they followed that up with album of the day for our first album. That level of play led to opportunities at festivals designed for introducing up and coming bands in Europe, in France and Austria, similar to Brighton's Great Escape. From then on we made great connections with bookers and had lots of help along the way from radio stations continually playing our new tracks. That let us continue to build in France, Germany, Austria and Switzerland, even as far as Hungary, Slovakia, Slovenia and Czech Republic. The amount of countries has been great because it's led to loads of touring constantly back and forth.

Do you notice any differences between Scottish and European audiences?
Everywhere has their own advantages and plus points. Our French gigs have all been at a level of a cool bohemian underground scene, always in cool smaller places then crashing at someone's apartment , Austria and Switzerland were more 'professional gigs' but all of these places have always had cool young crowds for us, but that all down to great bookers and reps that we've been lucky enough to work with. We've never played a bad Scottish gig so it's no different here but you judge your own country differently because you know it so well.

Do you have any tips for anyone thinking about releasing their own material or working with a small independent label?
I think at this level it's just about continuing regardless and releasing as much as you can. We don't get attached to our albums and songs, we just want them to be there for anyone to find, recorded and set in stone then we move on with what's new. If it's been a success or got some play then great, if not hopefully next time.

Amongst the band's press photos are snaps taken in the Kelvingrove Bandstand area a few years ago. Clearly you were trendsetters in ensuring the venue was renovated, how do you feel about its reintroduction to the Glasgow music scene?

Those pics at the band stand were supposed to be a Brian Jonestown rip off, with all our friends joining us and wearing black instead of white, then it poured all day and it became an umbrella shoot! The band stand was just a cool setting really close by. We're delighted its back up and running. We got asked to play supporting the Waterboys at the summer nights sessions just after the games but sadly I was in Croatia so we missed the chance! Hopefully next time, that would have been a great experience as we as a band all stay within 5 minutes of the venue.

The Bandstand was an integral part of the Commonwealth Games celebration in the city, were you swept up in the Commonwealth excitement?

Yeah it was great, the girls got really involved and all around my flat was surrounded by activities, brilliant atmosphere for the city.

Do you have any musical ambitions you would still like to achieve?

As long as we get to keep doing this as often as possible we're happy!

Wozniak

The music of Wozniak means that they are more than worth listening to, and deserving of a place in any review of Scottish music in 2014. They have created a strongly atmospheric sound and are one of the leading lights of the scene in Edinburgh at the moment.

However, the band also undertook a Kickstarter campaign this year to fund the recording and release of their EP, which is something of interest to many people. Kickstarter is becoming an increasingly common and important option for artists looking to make an impact or generate the funds to release something.

I managed to catch up with Sarah from the band in early October 2014 to talk about the Kickstarter experience, and life for the band in general.

To get started, can you give a brief introduction to the band?

Wozniak are James, John, Sarah and Simon – we formed in Edinburgh in 2012. A few of us had played some covers together for fun but we quickly decided to do our own thing, without really knowing what that might be. It's evolved into a huge post-rock, shoegazey noise with reverb, delay, driving bass and tumbling drums.

Did you have all the songs written before you started the campaign?

All except the mysterious Gesamtkunstwerk which just kind of materialised out of the reverby ether in the studio! The others were all written, rehearsed and gigged beforehand, honest.

Why did you decide that Kickstarter was the platform to use to raise funds?

Crowdfunding seemed like a good way to go. We thought we could offer supporters some good rewards and it was more of an exchange, rather than just about raising cash. It genuinely felt like when people pledged, they were offering their support for the band and the music as well as making a financial contribution. Kickstarter was quite well-known and some cool projects had been funded that way, so we just went for it.

Was there any particular Kickstarter project that inspired you?

Looking at other projects to see what was going down well was interesting. I really liked the rewards offered by an Australian Band called Royal Chant which were really funny – things like getting dressed up as a dinosaur to act out their own version of Jurassic Park. They seemed like good guys, so I donated to them.

Was Kickstarter easy to use and setup?

Yes! The hardest and most time consuming bit was coming up with a video concept and creating that. Fortunately, there are two professional film-makers in the band...

How did you decide upon what bonuses to provide to backers?

We put lots of effort into this, thinking about what our fans might like and what special gifts we could give, or talents we could share. In the end, there were probably too many options! Most popular were mentions in the CD booklet and tshirts. Strangely no-one went for 'dinner with Wozniak'. We offered the chance to name the EP which was quite bold – a total stranger from Colorado snapped that one up and that's how it came to be called Pikes Peak.

Do you think need a social media presence to make this sort of project work?

Most of the success of our campaign was down to social media. We spread the word on Wozniak's Facebook and Twitter pages, as well as on our personal profiles and friends shared, commented and supported from the start. As the deadline approached, we twigged that there was 140 hours to raise our remaining £141, so we got on Twitter and when we woke up the next day, we'd reached our target!

What was your reaction to the support you received?

The response was fantastic. When we started the campaign, we'd no idea if we could reach the target. The generosity and positivity of people really blew us away. We were so surprised when we got the £150 pledge from the USA, especially since we didn't know this person at all. And of course, our fans, family, friends and co-workers all got involved, donating, sharing, harassing on our behalf.

Did the nature of funding create any additional pressure in recording the EP?

Creatively, we didn't feel any extra pressure I don't think. It was just about making the best record possible and I hope we've achieved that. There have certainly been some good reviews. We were very aware of budget and time though – it was important that it didn't go all Kevin Shields and take forever.

Would you utilise Kickstarter again in the future?

Not in the near future – we were so grateful for all the support we got through the EP campaign and wouldn't want people to feel we were taking advantage.

Any tips or suggestions you would provide to bands maybe thinking of using the same strategy?

Fulfilling reward commitments can take time (and a little bit of cash) too, so factor that in. I knitted a hat which was great fun but quite time consuming – it was lucky only one person went for that reward.

Do you think Kickstarter projects will become more common in the years ahead?

I think so. Not many bands make enough cash to sustain themselves, even when they're signed. Crowdfunding gives a platform to raise the upfront funds that are essential to make recording, tours and other projects happen. It gives bands a bit more control over the finances as well as the creativity. I know that there are critics out there – some say it's too easy for bog standard music to get out there and some independent record shops are not keen as they see it as another way for bands to sell directly to fans.

What are the bands upcoming plans?

There are a few gigs lined up in Edinburgh – we're at Oxjam on 24/10, Limbo on 9/11 and our Christmas show is on 12/12 with Gigantic Leaves and Book Group at Opium. We're also about to start work on our debut album and there will be a taster track from that ready to go in November, although the full release won't be until well into 2015.

Anything you'd really like to achieve with the band?

Make and release a tremendous album, play some shows a bit further afield and continue to inflict tinnitus wherever we go.

Any music or bands you have been impressed with this year?

Well, it's been all about the return of Slowdive this year. That's been a big deal for 50 per cent of Wozniak! In terms of bands we know and love, we've played some great gigs with Edinburgh's Gigantic Leaves and We Came From the North this year and it's great to see Deathcats (from Glasgow) and Vladimir (from Dundee) playing to bigger and bigger crowds.

Holy Mountain

You expect record labels to hype the latest releases but when Chemikal Underground unveiled Holy Mountains Ancient Astronauts this year, they did so by proclaiming it the rock album of the year. This was spot on or not far from the mark, showing that Glasgow still had the ability to get a little bit dirty and sweaty when it was called for.

I caught up with Holy Mountain after the band had enjoyed a busy summer schedule but just before they headed out on a weeklong UK tour which culminated with a headline set in Stereo.

How would you describe your music to someone who hasn't yet heard you?

Andy just bought these pants from Primark. They've got a picture of the universe printed on them, pretty psychedelic. If you hold them up to your ear after the 7th day of tour and have a good listen whilst sticking your fingers inside a plug socket you get a pretty good representation of what we sound like.

How good did it feel releasing your album this year?

It's like a pub cleaning shift on a Sunday morning after a really horrendous Saturday night. Vomit everywhere and you're hungover. It's really brutal. But then you finish your shift and it's still only 11am on a Sunday and you can go and party party party.

How does Ancient Astronauts differ from Earth Measures?

Earth Measures was really hot and we had a lot of fun but it wasn't really working out. I think we were both looking for different things. Then we met Ancient Astronauts and just hit it off straight away. We just *get* each other, ya know? The keys, the vocals, Earth Measures just wasn't capable of that kind of commitment.

Do you feel as if you're flying a flag for rock music or

do you just do what you do?

We prefer bunting to actual flags. Tie dye bunting with little pictures of piece symbols and hash leafs. I think you can get them in Urban Outfitters.

How did it feel coming on at Glasgow Green after Sidney Devine?

It turns out he isn't actually a steak and kidney pie but a real life man. By the time we landed on stage most of his crowd had left. I can only assume they were also expecting a pastry delight and were too disappointed to stick around for us. He had fantastic white cowboy boots that he wouldn't let us try on.

You played two big summer shows in August, how did you find them?

Andy suffered from a rare case of Short Guitar Lead syndrome at Glasgow Green and the not so rare Getting Pished Before Playing syndrome at Richmond Park. Both shows were highly enjoyable and we will one day return to Richmond Park to walk our dogs and sail model yachts in the boating pond.

What did you make of everything that was taking place in Glasgow this summer?

Gregg's July addition of the Mexican Lattice was particularly satisfying. Allan and Andy summered in Aspen but Pete says that he broke into the Glasgow Green complex at night and actually ran faster than the Usain Bolt machine whilst performing paradiddles on his travel snare.

Do you approach support/festival slots differently from your own gigs?

It's easier to channel cosmic energy at festivals as there are no ceilings to stem the patter flow. We book our own shows around the lunar calendar for maximum tidal influence. There is less pressure to perform wizardry at other people's shows.

You are undertaking a 7 day tour in October. Do you feel that now you have an album out that there is a different level of expectation placed on your live shows?

There's always been a big level of expectation from HM live shows but there are only so many keyboard players you can explode/have abducted/sacrifice before people get suspicious. We don't need any more trouble with the law. We will continue to try and budget for pyrotechnics as long as we have a label to bill.

You play 18th October in Stereo, what are you feelings going into a hometown gig on the last night of the tour?

See the bit at the end of Bill and Ted's Bogus Journey where they realise the still can't play then time travel to get lessons then come back and they are fleein' and the crowd all explodes? Stereo will be that times a million

Does the band have any plans for 2015?

We live 100 years every day. Hopefully we will have time to find a new album.

Any ambitions beyond this point?

To live 1000 years every day. And to tour more than two weeks a year.

Any bands or music you have enjoyed this year?

GOAT and Windhand.

Appendix A: Alternative Titles

I like puns and it was obvious I was going to come up with a lot of puns for the potential book title. Here are some of the best and worst, you can make up your mind about which is which:

2014:
The Year of Indie-Pop-Dance

Scotland The Rave and Other Musical Forms

Genetically Engineered To Make Music

Loch 'N' Roll

Take The High Notes

Well Plaid

The Groups and Songs from Northern Britain

Rip It Up And Start Again?

Watt's Like Us

The Amp Din Roar

Caledonia Calling

All Jock Tamsons Bands

I'd Rather Jock Than Fleetwood Mac

Been A Long Time Since I Jock N Rolled

The Sad Eyed Story of the Barrowlands

Set The Controls For The Land Of No Sun

Top of the Scots

It's A Long List Of Scots If You Want to Rock n Roll

Never Mind The British, Here's The Scots

Scotland The Braw

From Just Like Honey to Honeyblood

One More Tome! One More Tome!

ABOUT THE AUTHOR

What can you say about Andy Reilly? Well for one, he casts no shadow...no wait, that's vampires. Andy casts a big shadow and to be honest, it's about time he did something about that. If only he spent more time in the gym than he spent in bars, gig venues and clubs. Still, you can't have it all can you?

There's nothing overly special about Andy, not like the talented musicians and enthusiasts he has written but he hopes you enjoy reading about them as much as he enjoyed writing about them.

OTHER BOOKS BY THE AUTHOR

The Glasgow Underground & Nicotine:
A short story collection, entirely set in Glasgow, but taking the debut album of The Velvet Underground as a jump-off point:
http://www.amazon.co.uk/Glasgow-Underground-Nicotine-Andy-Reilly/dp/1494343401/

Definitely Maybe:
A look back at the Oasis debut album, its impact at the time and its influence on music and culture in Britain over the years:
http://www.amazon.co.uk/Oasis-Definitely-Maybe-Here-There/dp/1499332246/

Made in the USA
Charleston, SC
16 November 2014